Trajectories of Neoliberal Transformation

This book has both empirical and theoretical goals. The primary empirical goal is to examine the evolution of industrial relations in Western Europe from the end of the 1970s to the present. Its purpose is to evaluate the extent to which liberalization has taken hold of European industrial relations institutions through five detailed, chapter-length studies, each focusing on a different country and including a quantitative analysis. It offers a comprehensive description and analysis of what has happened to the institutions that regulate the labor market, as well as the relations between employers, unions and states in Western Europe since the collapse of the long postwar boom. The primary theoretical goal of this book is to provide a critical examination of some of the central claims of comparative political economy, particularly those involving the role and resilience of national institutions in regulating and managing capitalist political economies.

Lucio Baccaro is Professor of Sociology at the University of Geneva. He received his Ph.D. in industrial relations and political science from MIT. He has authored numerous articles on the comparative political economy of industrial relations and labor markets, as well as on participatory and deliberative governance.

Chris Howell is the James Monroe Professor of Politics at Oberlin College. He received his Ph.D. in political science from Yale. He is the author of two books, *Regulating Labor: The State and Industrial Relations Reform in France* and *Trade Unions and the State: Constructing Industrial Relations Institutions in Britain, 1890–2000*. The latter won the 2006 *Labor History* prize for best book in labor studies.

Trajectories of Neoliberal Transformation

European Industrial Relations Since the 1970s

LUCIO BACCARO
University of Geneva

CHRIS HOWELL
Oberlin College

CAMBRIDGE
UNIVERSITY PRESS

CAMBRIDGE
UNIVERSITY PRESS

University Printing House, Cambridge CB2 8BS, United Kingdom

One Liberty Plaza, 20th Floor, New York, NY 10006, USA

477 Williamstown Road, Port Melbourne, VIC 3207, Australia

4843/24, 2nd Floor, Ansari Road, Daryaganj, Delhi – 110002, India

79 Anson Road, #06-04/06, Singapore 079906

Cambridge University Press is part of the University of Cambridge.

It furthers the University's mission by disseminating knowledge in the pursuit of education, learning, and research at the highest international levels of excellence.

www.cambridge.org
Information on this title: www.cambridge.org/9781107018723
DOI: 10.1017/9781139088381

First published 2017

Printed in the United States of America by Sheridan Books, Inc.

A catalogue record for this publication is available from the British Library.

ISBN 978-1-107-01872-3 Hardback
ISBN 978-1-107-60369-1 Paperback

Lucio: A Cosetta
Chris: For those I love and who, miraculously, love me back

The simple reaction of ingenuous emotion is to adhere with trusting conviction to the publicly recognized truth and to base one's conduct and fixed position in life on this firm foundation. But this simple reaction may well encounter the supposed difficulty of how to distinguish and discover, among the infinite *variety of opinions*, what is universally acknowledged and valid in them; and this perplexity may easily be taken for a just and genuine concern for the matter itself. But in fact, those who pride themselves on this perplexity are in the position of *not being able to see the wood for the trees.*

– Hegel, *Elements of the Philosophy of Right.* 1991[1821]:
preface, pp. 11–12, author's emphasis

Contents

I

Introduction

Trajectories of European Industrial Relations

As with most academic monographs, ours has both empirical and theoretical goals. The primary empirical goal is straightforward enough: to examine the evolution of industrial relations in Western Europe from the end of the 1970s up to the present. The time period is designed to capture the break in postwar political economy that began with the crisis of Fordist economic growth experienced by most advanced capitalist societies in the 1970s and to trace how national industrial relations systems have fared since. Our purpose is to evaluate the extent to which liberalization has taken hold of European industrial relations institutions. We undertake our examination through five detailed chapter-length country studies – of Britain, France, Germany, Italy and Sweden – and quantitative analysis of these five countries plus an additional seven Western European countries and three non-European ones. The book offers a comprehensive description and analysis of what has happened to the institutions that regulate the labor market and relations between employers, unions and states in Western Europe since the collapse of the long postwar boom.

We argue that liberalization in the realm of industrial relations is best understood as involving an expansion of employer discretion: greater influence and control on the part of individual employers over wage determination, hiring and firing and the organization of the workplace. Thus, liberalization should be evident in the reconstruction of industrial relations institutions to expand employer discretion. This is likely to include, but not be limited to, decentralization and individualization of bargaining, deregulation of the labor market and decollectivization, involving a decline in the strength, size, centralization and coverage of class organizations, primarily trade unions. We also argue that institutions are often quite plastic, in that the same institution can, under different circumstances, come to function in a quite different manner than in the past. Understood in this way, liberalization may also take place through the "conversion" (Streeck and Thelen 2005) of existing institutions from discretion-limiting to discretion-enhancing. As such, evidence of liberalization can be found in changes in the form of institutions (the dismantling of existing institutions and the creation of new ones), in a greater ability on the part of employers to bypass or ignore institutions that limit their discretion and in changes to the manner in which existing institutions function.

Our country case studies, encompassing a wide range of types of political economy and including the largest economies in Western Europe, show a clear liberalizing trajectory from the end of the 1970s to the present. In all cases, employers had greater discretion over their firms and their workforces at the end of the period than at the start. While liberalization has taken place in different ways and at different speeds, and European political economies currently rest at different locations along a liberalizing trajectory, they all appear to be heading in the same direction. The most striking feature of our survey of industrial relations developments across Western Europe is not the range of national variation at either the start or the end of the roughly thirty-five-year period under investigation, but rather the transformation in industrial relations institutions that has taken place everywhere across that period. The landscape of industrial relations has changed in fundamental ways since the end of the 1970s, and everywhere in the same direction, involving an expansion of employer discretion.

Given our empirical findings, our theoretical concerns should come as no surprise. The primary theoretical goal of this book is to provide a critical examination of some of the central claims of comparative political economy (CPE), particularly those involving the role and resilience of national institutions in regulating and managing capitalist political economies. The field of CPE is one of the most intellectually vibrant within political science and comparative macrosociology, focusing upon the origins, trajectories and performance of national economic institutions in a comparative framework. CPE has long been dominated by theoretical approaches that emphasize three linked arguments. The first is the central, independent role of institutions themselves in mediating between structural economic change and the choices available to political–economic actors; institutions play an important role in insulating national political economies from common economic pressures (Hall and Taylor 1996; Steinmo, Thelen and Longstreth 1992). By institutions, scholars mean everything from a financial system to organizations such as unions or employer associations and widely accepted practices such as collective bargaining. Thus, institutions have provided middle range explanations for national differences.

The implication of a CPE that relies heavily upon institutional analysis has been a theory of change that emphasizes the role of history and of path-dependent effects (Pierson 2004). Thus, a second and related argument within CPE is that institutions encourage incrementalism and path dependence. Institutions are argued to be highly resilient and resistant to change, encouraging economic and political actors to defend existing institutions or to make relatively minor changes along an existing path. This tendency was accentuated in the initial formulations of the Varieties of Capitalism approach (Hall and Soskice 2001b). Thus, institutions created in the quite distant past can continue to shape the behavior of actors in the present, and to make radical changes in the direction of a given political economy unlikely.

It follows, and this is a third linked argument, that the field of CPE has traditionally been hostile to the idea that the main institutions of advanced capitalist societies are undergoing similar transformations and becoming more alike. For at least the last thirty years, the field has been dominated by approaches and empirical studies that emphasize the enduring diversity and range of distinct national capitalisms. The resilience of institutions has been used to argue for continuing institutional heterogeneity in capitalist political economies, even in the face of heightened international economic constraints. Even when institutions have clearly undergone substantial change, the expectation of those working within the CPE field has tended to be that change will be shaped by local interests and nationally specific factors, so that there is no reason to anticipate common trajectories of change or common cross-national patterns; rather, the institutional landscape of advanced capitalist societies is likely to remain characterized by national diversity even in the face of powerful liberalizing pressures (Thelen 2014).

There are good and legitimate reasons for all this. Any common trajectory of capitalist political economies is likely to be hidden by the long periods of time involved, by the incremental nature of most institutional change, by differences in the timing of change over the last three decades or more, by a privileging of form over function in the analysis of institutions and by habits of mind and the sociology of knowledge production; most of us have made deep intellectual investments in understanding comparative (usually national) difference, and CPE has a laudable commitment to local knowledge. One can add that it derives also from the gradual displacement of capitalism – as opposed to markets – as an object of scholarly inquiry that has taken place within much of the social sciences, and with it the inability to make sense of transformational change across the advanced capitalist world. The simple reality is that contemporary analysis of political economy has been much better at explaining differences than identifying commonalities.

Our book builds upon recent work within the CPE field that has begun to contemplate the possibility of more radical, transformative institutional change (Campbell 2004; Hall and Thelen 2009; Streeck 2009; Streeck and Thelen 2005). The book takes issue with each of the core arguments of the field noted above, proposing instead (i) that institutions are heavily dependent upon the social, political and economic contexts within which they operate for the manner in which they function and the outcomes they generate: (ii) hence that institutions can change quite rapidly, both in form and in function; and (iii) that a careful examination of contemporary capitalist political economies reveals a common liberalizing tendency in the trajectory of industrial relations institutions, as everywhere employer discretion has expanded and the balance of class power has shifted against labor.

The plan for the book is as follows. Chapter 2 lays out the theoretical argument of the book, examining the literature on institutional change as a starting point for rethinking the sources and mechanisms of change and the relationship between the balance of class power, the transformation in capitalist growth models, and the role of political–economic institutions. The chapter proceeds to elaborate a meaning of liberalization in the sphere of industrial relations as fundamentally involving an expansion of employer discretion, before outlining an understanding of institutional convergence as movement along the same trajectory rather than institutional identity. Chapter 3 provides a quantitative analysis of institutional change in industrial relations for twelve Western European countries. We also include in the analysis three additional liberal market economies (of which there are very few in Western Europe). The quantitative analysis indicates important elements of a common liberalizing trajectory, particularly with regard to trade union organization, industrial conflict and collective bargaining decentralization. Nonetheless, this analysis also demonstrates important continuing differences in institutional form. We argue that due to the limitations of available cross-country measures, large-N analysis is at best able to capture liberalization as change in institutional form but not liberalization as institutional conversion, and we make the case for detailed case studies and process tracing of institutional change.

There then follow five chapters, Chapters 4–8, each containing a detailed country case study. These cases have been chosen to run the gamut of varieties of capitalism, to include centralized and decentralized cases and those that have seen a resurgence of social concertation. In short, we have chosen "hard" cases for an argument that claims to have identified a common trajectory of institutional change. Together, they provide remarkable variation in institutional setup. Each country case follows a common outline, beginning with a stylized portrait of the industrial relations system at the end of the 1970s and of the extent to which institutions enabled or constrained employer discretion in wage setting, work organization and labor market regulation. The chapters then trace the process of institutional change over the subsequent thirty years, concluding with a stylized portrait of the industrial relations system in 2015. We pay particular attention to moments of crisis in industrial relations, when reform efforts multiplied, and to the relative roles of employers, unions and governments in the process of institutional reconstruction.

Chapter 9 provides a comparative analysis of the case study evidence, examining mechanisms of institutional change and the extent and form of liberalization in industrial relations. The chapter then proceeds to a discussion of the role of trade unions, employer organizations and states in institutional change. The case studies indicate both that employer organizations in practically every country underwent radicalization in the course of the 1980s and 1990s and were thus more willing to contemplate quite dramatic change, and that states – often thought of as largely passive or ineffective actors in the current period – were crucial players in creating the conditions for wide-ranging liberalization. Chapter 10 steps back from the quantitative and case study evidence to locate the liberalization of industrial relations within the broader framework of the collapse of Fordism, explaining how the crisis of institutions enabling the transmission of productivity increases into real wages and aggregate demand has led to the emergence of different post-Fordist growth models, all characterized by inherent instability.

We have each incurred substantial intellectual debts in the process of researching and writing this book. We are extremely grateful to colleagues who have read different portions of the manuscript and offered precious advice. They include Kerstin Ahlberg, Conor Cradden, Colin Crouch, Frank Dobbin, Marc Blecher, Pepper Culpepper, Steve Crowley, Christian Dufour, Martin Höpner, Christian Ibsen, Anders Kjellberg, Michel Lallement, Marc Lenormand, Olivier Mériaux, Sofia Murhem, Tommy Öberg, Jan Ottosson, Markus Pettersson, Jonas Pontusson, Damian Raess, Veli-Pekka Säikkälä, Tobias Schulze-Cleven, Marco Simoni, Fritz Scharpf, Wolfgang Streeck, Kathy Thelen and Mark Vail.

Lucio Baccaro would like to thank in particular Chiara Benassi and Jonas Pontusson for joint work that has inspired (and in the case of Chiara contributed to) parts of the manuscript, and his wife Cosetta for putting up with him throughout the process. Chris Howell would like to thank the countless trade unionists and researchers who have read draft chapters, offered invaluable feedback and taken time to help with this research, and especially Rebecca Givan for collaborative work that helped develop some of the early ideas that inspired this book.

2

Arguing for Neoliberal Convergence

This chapter makes the theoretical case for institutional convergence, along a neoliberal trajectory, among the political economies of Western Europe. We will elaborate further below what we mean by neoliberal convergence, but it is worth emphasizing at the onset the degree to which the field of CPE has traditionally been hostile to the notion of convergence. For more than thirty years, for the great majority of those working in the field, the mission of CPE has been all but conterminous with identifying and explaining the enduring diversity and range of distinct national capitalisms. Many of the seminal works in the field have argued that broad economic changes – whether understood as the product of shifting regimes of accumulation, deindustrialization or the forces of globalization – are experienced differently and have very different effects in different countries. The result has been that the dominant theoretical approaches in CPE are dubious about the likelihood of common consequences, similar trajectories or institutional convergence (Berger and Dore 1996; Campbell 2004; Garrett 1998; Hall and Soskice 2001b).

The absence of expectations of convergence in these analyses is primarily a result of the centrality that has been accorded to institutions in the discipline of CPE and the characteristics attributed to political–economic institutions. Indeed, "the idea of persistence is virtually built into the definition of an institution" (Thelen 2009, 474) and contemporary theories of CPE have, to a large extent, been built on the back of institutionalist theorizing (Hall and Taylor 1996). Institutions have provided middle range explanations for national differences that mediate between broad structural explanations, which tend to anticipate convergence in industrial society, and narrowly political arguments about agency, which privilege partisan policy choices.

The remainder of this chapter is organized into three sections. The first surveys the literature on institutional change within CPE to demonstrate its persistent resistance to convergence arguments. The second section lays out our argument that institutions are inherently malleable, capable of functioning quite differently in different economic contexts, and that therefore there are strong reasons to anticipate convergent institutional change. We argue that in the current period of capitalist growth, the trajectory of institutional change is best characterized as neoliberal. The third section of this chapter sketches out an alternative approach to CPE and to emerging capitalist growth models – one heavily informed by the power resources approach, regulation theory and heterodox economics – which, we believe offers an explanation of the broad liberalizing character of institutional developments in the sphere of industrial relations over the last thirty five years. We will return to this alternative approach in the final chapter of the book to sketch out the implications of the universal tendency toward liberalization of industrial relations that we describe in the empirical core of the book for the stability and future of contemporary capitalist growth.

2.1 Theorizing Institutional Change

This is not the place for a comprehensive review of the evolution of institutionalist theorizing. Suffice it to say that, following on the heels of Shonfield's magisterial *Modern Capitalism* (Shonfield 1965) and the efforts of the contributors to the volume *Between Power and Plenty* (Katzenstein 1978) to explain divergent responses to the oil shock in the mid-1970s, academic attention shifted from an emphasis on one political–economic institution to another: corporatist institutions (Schmitter 1974), organized labor (Cameron 1984), financial institutions (Zysman 1983) and employer organization and institutions of employer coordination (Soskice 1990, Swenson 1991). But all the while, the structuring role of institutions has remained central.

The resilience of institutions has been used to explain the absence of widespread convergence in capitalist political economies and the persistence of distinct national institutional sets, even in the face of heightened international economic constraints. Institutions mediate common economic pressures, distribute power among actors and offer solutions to coordination problems facing market economies. As Steinmo, Thelen and Longstreth (1992) argued, institutions have independent power to structure the distribution of economic power and the behavior and even interests of economic actors.

The implications of a CPE that relies heavily upon institutional analysis has been a theory of change that emphasizes the role of history in politics and generates path-dependent effects (Pierson 2004). It illustrates, in Shonfield's marvelous phrase (Shonfield 1965, 88), "the way in which a living tentacle reaches out of past history, loops itself round, and holds fast to a solid block of the present." It is these characteristics of institutions that contribute to expectations of continuity, of minor incremental change along an established path and of a stickiness in which strong pressures exist for actors to use established institutions to respond to new economic conditions.

Institutionalist approaches within CPE received a new urgency in the 1990s, when wide-ranging political and economic developments raised once again the possibility of a broad convergence in the institutions of advanced capitalist political economies. It was in this context that the varieties of capitalism (VoC) literature associated with Hall and Soskice (2001b) emerged. This approach identified firms as the primary actors within capitalist economies, seeking to "bring firms back into the center of the analysis" (Hall and Soskice 2001b, 6) suggesting less prominent, less strategic roles for both state actors and organized labor. In this approach, institutions are important primarily for their ability to solve coordination problems for firms. Thus, the importance of institutions for VoC theorists is less that they distribute power or sanction behavior, and more that they facilitate information flows among actors, permit "decentralized cooperation" (Culpepper 2001), and solve familiar collective action problems, such as the underprovision of training. Among capitalist economies, this approach identified two broad ideal-typical types of political economy: liberal market economies (LMEs) and coordinated market economies (CMEs). The former rely primarily upon unregulated labor and capital markets to solve coordination problems, while the latter rely more heavily upon nonmarket forms of coordination.

The tendency within most CPE to an account of limited institutional change was accentuated in the initial formulations of the varieties of capitalism. The familiar mechanisms of path dependence and positive feedback were bolstered by the role of institutional complementarities and comparative institutional advantage. Institutions are rarely able to perform their roles in isolation; rather, there are likely to be interactions and complementarities among institutions. These complementarities imply that there is a tendency for institutions to reinforce each other, forming interlocking ensembles of institutions spanning the various spheres of a political economy with the result that a particular set of institutions is highly resistant to change. Furthermore, because countries enjoy a particular "comparative institutional advantage" for specific types of production, this in turn encourages actors, particularly employers, to reinforce and defend those institutions rather than to challenge and transform them. Thus, for example, in a central claim of the VoC approach, skills serve as the link between institutions and a production regime; the ability to emphasize either general or industry-specific skills is reinforced by an interlocking set of training, social welfare and industrial relations institutions, which in turn affords a comparative advantage in certain kinds of production (Estevez-Abe, Iversen and Soskice 2001).

It followed that this approach was deeply skeptical of the likelihood of convergence: "nations often prosper, not by becoming more similar, but by building on their institutional differences ... Thus, much of the adjustment process will be oriented to the institutional recreation of comparative advantage" (Hall and Soskice 2001b, 60, 63). If anything, institutional arbitrage is likely to consolidate difference, rather than erode it. As Thelen (2009, 474) notes of the resulting theoretical edifice, "as illuminating as this framework has been on the question of institutional reproduction, scholars working in this tradition have generally had much less to say about institutional change over time."

The VoC approach was, in many ways, the culmination of more than a generation of scholarship in CPE. It built upon the emphasis within that tradition on the resilience and diversity of national models of capitalism, with the resilience explained by the path-dependent qualities of institutions. To this tradition, it added theoretical rigor by embedding path dependence in arguments about institutional complementarities and comparative institutional advantage. And it further offered a micro-foundational argument to explain why actors should be expected to defend existing institutions.

It should be said that there has always been some dissent from this emphasis upon cross-national diversity and limited institutional change within the field of CPE (Coates 2005). Regulationist approaches to political economy, whether in their French (Boyer 1990), British (Jessop 1990a) or American (Kotz, McDonough and Reich 1994) versions, have been far more interested in institutional change by virtue of their assumptions about the inherent instability, conflictuality and dynamism of capitalism. This alternative view of the way capitalism functions, one we share, is something to which we shall return later in this chapter. For this tradition, and what gives it its name, the importance of institutions is that they are mechanisms for permitting *regulation*. Regulation was the "master-concept" developed to explain the period of largely stable growth for three decades after the Second World War" (Neilson 2012, 161). What resulted was essentially a punctuated equilibrium model that emphasized temporal discontinuity and a degree of synchronicity across the advanced capitalist world in the timing of structural economic change: the form of economic growth known as Fordism everywhere went into crisis at some point in the 1970s, to be replaced by post-Fordism, though one that went by almost as many names as there were regulation theorists.

But even here, in an ironic example of theoretical convergence, distinct national models of capitalism have come to dominate the landscape of regulationist theorizing, particularly that associated with Robert Boyer (Boyer and Saillard 2002, Part V). Delineating the core dynamics of the emerging growth model (or "regime of accumulation") gave way to identifying its institutional prerequisites, with the unsurprising result that the focus of much regulationist research has become the variety of national regulatory mechanisms: "Examining the extent of convergence in terms of the regulation of core capitalist forms is lost from the research agenda, and instead the theme of national diversity shifts attention to the contingent political struggles that endogenously generate specific path-dependent national trajectories" (Neilson 2012, 169). Nonetheless, the regulationist tradition of political economy remains distinct in its emphasis upon the changing physiognomy of capitalism itself and its inherent crisis tendencies. As such, it remains an important theoretical tool, to which we return in the last section of this chapter.

Quite recently, in part in response to the perception that the early formulations of the VoC approach were somewhat static and functionalist, theorizing and debate over the degree and form of institutional change have moved to the center of the field of CPE. This has taken place on the back of a less functionalist, more political reading of the dynamics of capitalist political economies, one that emphasizes contingency, power, contestation, the fragility of the political coalitions that undergird institutional construction (Streeck and Yamamura 2001, Streeck 2009) and the ideational preconditions for institutional embedding (Blyth 1997, Culpepper 2008).

It bears mentioning that there always were internal differences within the VoC literature. For example, while in Soskice's account (1999), employers in CME countries were conceptualized as having prestrategic preferences for coordinating institutions, employers' support was considered to be strategic as opposed to prestrategic in Thelen's account (2001), and contingent on labor's countervailing power. This second interpretation was from the very beginning much closer to that of power resource theorists such as Korpi (2006a) or Streeck (2009) than the first.

Over time, from this more political stream within the VoC approach have come a renewed emphasis upon institutional experimentation, a less functionalist interpretation of the process of institutional reproduction and greater space for actors to reassess their interests and contemplate institutional change (Hall and Thelen 2009). It is also important to note that even in its original formulation, this approach allowed for the possibility of convergence on the LME variety of capitalism, noting that it is easier to deregulate CMEs than for LMEs to develop coordinating mechanisms and musing that institutional reform in one sphere "could snowball into changes in other spheres as well" (Hall and Soskice 2001b, 63–64). We would argue, and our cases indicate, that the unraveling of CMEs and the further liberalization of LMEs in the sphere of industrial relations had been well under way for more than a decade when this statement was written.

The most fully formulated argument in favor of gradual or incremental transformation – in which an accumulation of small, barely perceptible changes becomes transformational over time – came from Streeck and Thelen (2005). They acknowledge that most institutional approaches understate the degree and significance of change, that intensified competition and a greater commitment to market liberalism have exerted real pressure on institutions and that one cannot assume that economic actors will always seek to defend existing institutions rather than modify them. They identify a series of mechanisms by which incremental changes can have transformative effects (Streeck and Thelen 2005, 31). For example, the same institutions can take on new functions, latent effects can be activated, existing institutions can atrophy and peripheral institutions can take center stage. In a similar fashion, Campbell (2004) has articulated a more "actor-centered institutionalism" (the term originates from Scharpf (1997b)) in which entrepreneurial actors, working within existing sets of institutions, engage in various forms of incremental change; change remains path-dependent but it can, over time, become transformational.

In these more recent formulations, the firm-centric focus of the original varieties of capitalism approach, in which the interests of employers largely drove institutional design and employers were expected to defend the resulting institutions on the basis of self-interest, has weakened, not least because of abundant evidence of widespread and systematic employer efforts to reshape existing institutions (much of which we will present in the empirical chapters of this book). What one scholar wryly noted with regard to Germany is equally true elsewhere in Europe: "the disjuncture between the *stated* interests of corporate actors in Germany and the deductive-functionalist interests *ascribed* to them by the 'Varieties of Capitalism' literature is striking" (Kinderman 2005, 435, emphasis in the original). In her most recent work, Thelen (2014) articulates a theory of institutional change in which employers and firms are largely dislodged from the center of analysis (for commentary see Howell 2015). In their place is an emphasis upon politics and political coalitions, in which how and to what degree labor is organized is at least as important as business organization to the resolution of battles over institutional change (Thelen 2014, 29–32).

The recent work on institutional change introduces an insistent dynamism and an important return to politics within CPE. A further benefit of this work is its contribution to a delineation of mechanisms of institutional change, a delineation upon which we lean heavily in our own work. But is worth noting that while these more recent theorizations do mark something of a break with the dominant approach to CPE, in that they are compatible with a high degree of institutional change, they nonetheless reject the likelihood of institutional *rupture*, instead anticipating an accumulation of gradual, incremental changes that may become transformational over time. Additionally, they continue to emphasize that the trajectory of change is divergent, driven by local factors rather than pressures that are common to all advanced capitalist political economies.[1] On both conclusions, we part company with these recent developments in institutional theorizing, as we discuss in the next section.

If national political–economic institutions are in a state of almost perpetual reconstruction, subject to fragile, shifting political coalitions, the obvious question facing CPE is whether there are common pressures and trajectories of institutional change. The recent developments within institutionalist theorizing surveyed above have opened up theoretical space to explore transformational change within the core institutions of capitalist societies. This in turn permits the revival of a central question in CPE: Are capitalist societies marked by tendencies toward convergence, and if so, to what degree? It is to this question that we now turn.

---

[1] For example, Martin and Swank (2008) have argued that a significant degree of institutional change is compatible with continued elements of policy divergence, and also emphasized the role of regime design and of the public sector in the trajectory of institutions.

2.2 Capitalism, Convergence and Neoliberalism

The sharpest break from the mainstream of CPE over the last thirty years has come from the recent work of Wolfgang Streeck (2009, 2011), and with it the most forceful argument for taking instability and change in national political economies seriously. This in turn has implications for our expectations about the diversity and range of trajectories of change. As he argues, "the time has come to think, again, about the *commonalities* of capitalism" (Streeck 2009, 1, emphasis in the original). Streeck urges scholars of political economy to shift focus from institutions and institutional logics to capitalism and the logic of capitalism, and to follow through on the implications of that shift by recognizing the inherently contradictory, conflictual, anarchic and fundamentally unruly nature of economic development. Thus, profound institutional change should be understood to be the norm, not the exception, in capitalist societies.

Taking capitalism seriously, not only capital as an interest or an actor, but capitalism as a distinct, historicized social formation involves reviving the insights of an earlier tradition of political economy, one that emphasized radical uncertainty, perpetual innovation, the capacity of markets to undermine themselves, a continuous boundary war between commodification and self-protection and the tension between legitimation and accumulation (Boyer 2011, Habermas 1975, Polanyi 1944). This involves a different conceptual approach, with quite different implications for institutional change than those that have dominated CPE in recent decades. As Pontusson noted (Pontusson 2005, 164), "the VoC literature has a great deal to say about 'varieties', but surprisingly little to say about 'capitalism'...[and] theoretically privileges considerations pertaining to efficiency and coordination at the expense of considerations pertaining to conflicts of interest and the exercise of power."

It is perhaps not a coincidence that as political economy has lost sight of capitalism as its object of analysis, so too has the field found itself deemphasizing power, conflict and asymmetric class interests. Yet, as a distinguished tradition from Marx to (most recently) Streeck has emphasized, capitalism's inherent dynamism, anarchism and unruliness are not well captured by the notions of stable equilibria, path dependence, coordination problems and neat institutional regulation that pervade contemporary political economy. Within a game-theoretical framework, equilibrium is a state of the world that no actors, given their utility functions and sets of beliefs, have an incentive to change. It can only be changed by an external shock. Approaching capitalism or capitalisms as if they were institutional equilibria in the game-theoretical sense means that we have to sweep under the rug endless empirical manifestations of drift, hollowing out and both incremental and radical institutional change. It also means that we have to ignore or reinterpret the actors' own words when they say, in no uncertain terms, that no, they do not want to reproduce a certain set of institutions but to fundamentally change them. A fair amount of modern political economy has been engaging in this business of sweeping and reinterpreting.

In our view, the only notion of equilibrium that is applicable to a capitalist economy is the old mechanical notion of equilibrium as *Gleichgewicht*. The word "equilibrium" means "equality on the balance (*libra*)." It is a temporary state of stasis in which the vectors of forces impinging on an object are on the same axis and counterbalance one another. As such, it is a rare occurrence. This old notion of equilibrium is much more dynamic and much more attuned to the reality of contemporary capitalism than the game-theoretical one: it does not assume that (given their utility functions and set of beliefs) actors agree on the same outcome, but only they are not yet sufficiently powerful to decisively shift the center of gravity in their favor. Those actors are nonetheless working to move the system in their preferred directions.

Adopting a "mechanical" notion of equilibrium puts "political" back into political economy. It also goes back to the 1950 and 1960 roots of political economy. In fact, this was the notion of equilibrium embraced by pluralists (Schattschneider 1960; Truman 1962). Equilibrium as *Gleichgewicht* sees the institutions of capitalism as the resultants of competing forces. These forces may balance themselves out for some time, but this view does not expect the resulting equilibrium to be more than a temporary situation.

This approach raises questions about the centrality accorded institutions by scholars in the field of CPE in explaining the functioning of capitalist political economies. A capitalism in which, in a well-known formulation, "all that is solid melts into air" (Marx and Engels 2002, 223) is not well suited to a political economy that emphasizes the relative autonomy of institutions from the societies and economies within which they are embedded. Institutions matter, certainly, but their causal primacy is less than scholars have suggested. More important is the *force field* within which institutions operate: the economic and class drivers that shape how institutions function (Korpi 1983; Korpi 2006b). This is of particular importance within industrial relations, where class cleavage remains predominant, and thus changes in the relative organizational and mobilizational capacity and in the perceived interests of class actors are likely to overwhelm the mediating ability of institutions and ensure either their reconstruction or their reengineering (Hyman 1989, Ch. 2).

We suggest that a large part of the reason that the institutionalist literature finds it difficult to acknowledge the presence of a common neoliberal trajectory in the evolution of national political economies is the expectation that if this common trajectory really existed it would manifest itself as "institutional isomorphism" (Di Maggio and Powell 1991), that is, as the emergence of a common institutional form across countries. In the case of industrial relations institutions, what would be expected is a flattening of the institutional landscape toward the topography of an archetypal liberal market economy characterized by weak unions, weak employer associations, and arm's-length enterprise-level bargaining or individualized bargaining. Because the quantitative evidence for this flattening has often been limited (Golden, Wallerstein and Lange 1999; Lange, Wallerstein and Golden 1995; Wallerstein, Golden and Lange 1997), one concludes that national industrial relations regimes are highly resilient to the forces of neoliberalism and globalization. In contrast with this view, our argument is that institutions may change in a neoliberal direction while remaining *allomorphic*.

Acemoglu and Robinson (2006)'s crucial distinction between *de jure* and *de facto* power inherent in institutions is helpful here. *De jure* power is congealed in institutional form; *de facto* power depends on the contingent force field in which institutions operate. While in the case of some institutions *de jure* power shapes outcomes pretty much directly, in the case of other institutions outcomes are contingent on the *de facto* power balance among the actors involved. Most industrial relations institutions rest on contract rather than law, with the result that these institutions shape interactions among actors but rarely directly dictate outcomes. For example, the outcomes of centralized bargaining may be very different depending on whether the actors settle on high wage increases commensurate with the ability to pay of the most dynamic sectors and on a rigid wage structure, as in the Sweden of the Rehn–Meidner model, or whether they settle on wage increases that match the productivity growth of the most sluggish companies, as in the Ireland of the "Celtic Tiger" (Baccaro and Simoni 2007). These institutional outcomes are independent of institutional form, which is approximately the same, and are shaped by the bargaining power of the actors involved. It is these characteristics of industrial relations institutions that contribute to explaining why they are endemically internally contested, why their functions depend crucially on the power games that are played in and around them, and why they are likely candidates for processes of institutional change.

In fact, many institutions, and certainly those in the sphere of industrial relations, are highly plastic: In a new context, subject to a new set of pressures and constraints, the same set of institutions can be reengineered to function in a manner very different from that of the context in which they were created: "formal institutions do not fully determine the uses to which they may be put. This is one important reason why major change in institutional practice may be observed together with strong continuity in institutional structures" (Streeck and Thelen 2005, 17–18). Institutional plasticity permits mutation in the function and meaning of existing institutions, producing different practices and consequences in new contexts.

We certainly do not want to close off the possibility of institutional rupture: the wholesale reconstruction of institutions as an existing set of institutions is replaced with a new set. There are cases of this in our book. But the mechanisms of institutional change can also be subtler (Streeck and Thelen 2005, 19–30). Earlier or submerged characteristics of an institution, long dormant, can emerge under new conditions. Parallel, once secondary institutions, which played only a peripheral regulatory role during an earlier period, may emerge to take on new importance in a different context. Thus, the hierarchical ordering in any bundle of interdependent institutions can change as competing sets of institutions have different valences for the actors concerned, which themselves shift over time. Mechanisms can also be created or given new significance that permit actors to bypass or escape from institutions altogether, creating pathways to new practices alongside the formal institutions. The key point about these alternative mechanisms is that they require no change in institutional form, in the institutional topography of a political economy, and so are difficult to capture in quantitative analysis. A focus upon form alone will understate the degree of institutional change.

The result is a range of characteristics of institutions that – like capitalism itself – point in the direction of permanent reinvention, change and discontinuity. Thus, resilience and continuity of institutional form is perfectly compatible with convergence in institutional functioning. And far from a picture of limited incremental change along an existing path, one can anticipate quite radical and transformative change.

We are arguing, in short, that a focus upon institutional forms is likely to miss the malleability of institutions – the degree to which a set of institutions can appear largely unchanged but in fact come to perform in quite different ways from before – and thus the extent of institutional convergence. As Kinderman notes with regard to the German case (Kinderman 2005, 433), scholars have tended to focus upon "continuity of structure, and having established this, have inferred continuity of content."

More than forty years ago, a Royal Commission investigating the state of British industrial relations argued, in a famous formulation, that there were "two systems of industrial relations. The one is the formal system embodied in the official institutions. The other is the informal system created by the actual behavior of trade unions, employer's associations, of managers, shop stewards and workers" (Royal Commission on Trade Unions and Employers' Associations 1968, paragraph 46). It is this disjuncture between form and function, structure and practice, that creates the empirical space for identifying institutional convergence and for understanding the underlying trajectory of European industrial relations over the last three decades and more.

It is important to be careful and clear in any discussion of convergence. We are not making a coarse argument for institutional convergence. There is limited and conflicting evidence of convergence as identity, a glacial flattening of the institutional landscape to an identical topography. We are not arguing, in other words, that industrial relations in Sweden or Germany today resemble in some clear-cut sense those in Britain, that the CME category has been emptied so that the advanced capitalist world is populated solely by varieties of LME.

Convergence does not require the same institutional form, and indeed, different starting points and different mobilizational capacities on the part of class actors make it unlikely that institutional forms will converge. Different institutional inheritances and actor identities from one country to the next will pose different obstacles and create distinctive flashpoints and sources of conflict over institutional reconstruction (Hyman 2001; Locke and Thelen 1995), even when the underlying source of institutional change – whether that be deindustrialization, internationalization, a change in the growth model, or some other broad economic shift – is the same. Thus, for example, "Economic internationalization...imposes new agendas on established national institutions, even where it leaves them on the surface unchanged" (Streeck 2007, 545). As with the concept of equifinality, the same end state can be reached by different paths; much cross-national research on the decentralization of collective bargaining, for example, indicates that the mechanism and form of decentralization can be very different from one country to another, even though the end state may be the same (Karlson and Lindberg 2010; Traxler 1995).

We argue that convergence is more likely to involve the adaptation and reengineering of existing institutional sets to perform in a similar fashion and to generate similar outcomes than to involve the appearance of the same institutions everywhere, with the result that the *trajectory* of institutional performance across countries is convergent, but not the *form* of institutions. Institutional convergence, as we use the term, refers to a common direction of change and a common functioning of institutions, rather than necessarily a common set of institutions, though widespread convergence of the form of institutions is also possible. And we argue in this book that, despite quite different starting points, different paces of change and different politics of change, there is clear evidence, at least in the sphere of industrial relations, of a common direction of institutional change.

We argue that the common direction is best characterized as neoliberal. A discussion of the meaning of neoliberalism and of its differences from classical liberalism is beyond the scope of this book (for an excellent extensive treatment of this issue we refer to Dardot and Laval 2009). It suffices it to say that, unlike classic liberalism, neoliberalism is not about limiting state intervention and returning to some form of laissez faire. It is instead about using state power to bring about (and institutionalize) a market order, that is, a society in which individuals conceive of themselves and relate to one another as providers of specialized services in all spheres, and coordinate their interactions through the principle of competition and the associated price system (for a path-breaking analysis see Foucault 2004). In line with this approach, the country cases in this book demonstrate that the state is far from passive in the process of liberalization. In fact, it is the most important agent of liberalization.

Neoliberalism is a general process of market liberalization (Harvey 2005), or the "disorganization" of once organized political economies, involving the trend "away from centralized authoritative coordination and control towards dispersed competition, individual instead of collective action, and spontaneous market-like aggregation of preferences and decisions" (Streeck 2009, 149). Neoliberalism is also an economic philosophy that inspires a set of economic policies. Thus it is associated with a particular strategy of macroeconomic reform (Williamson 1989), involving trade and financial liberalization, fiscal discipline (to be achieved through expenditure cuts rather than tax increases) (Alesina and Perotti 1997a, 1997b; Alesina and Ardagna 1998) and disinflation, to ensure which governments are willing to give up full employment. In addition, it involves a series of structural reforms across a range of markets and policy areas that are intended to be compatible with and to enable the maintenance of the macroeconomic framework summarized above. Höpner, Petring, Seikel and Werner (2014, 7) define liberalization policy as "the politically enacted and politically legitimated delegation of allocation and distribution decisions to markets." All these definitions – economic philosophy and associated economic policies, increasing relevance of markets – are related and certainly capture important elements of liberalization, but in our usage, liberalization is broader than what governments do; as we elaborate below in our discussion of liberalization in the sphere of industrial relations, it can include any policy or institutional change that has the effect of expanding *employer discretion*.

There is an important debate as to the usefulness of liberalization as a descriptor of institutional change in advanced capitalist political economies. For some scholars, it is "justified to characterize the prevailing trend in the advanced economies during the last two decades of the twentieth century and beyond as a broad process of *liberalization*" (Streeck and Thelen 2005, 2, emphasis in the original). Indeed, in this powerful formulation, liberalization may be the privileged direction of institutional change during periods when political mobilization – particularly on the part of labor movements – is absent because "liberalization within capitalism may face far fewer collective action problems than the organization of capitalism" (Streeck and Thelen 2005, 33).

For other scholars, liberalization is a crude, overly all-encompassing category that "obscures more than it illuminates" (Hall and Thelen 2009, 22). Liberalization is multidimensional, it may affect one sphere of the political economy and not others, and its impact is likely to vary depending upon particular sets of institutional arrangements.

Despite these remarks, there is no doubt that the distance between VoC and its critics has considerably shortened in recent years. For example, in Thelen's most recent reformulation of the Varieties of Capitalism argument (Thelen 2014), while the process and form of institutional change may vary, yielding multiple trajectories of change, the *direction* is everywhere the same, and is everywhere captured by some notion of liberalization, however crude (Howell 2015). Thelen (2014) has pointed to multiple "varieties of liberalization" at work across the advanced capitalist world, each having different distributive consequences. She argues that the type of liberalization has implications for the extent to which egalitarian capitalism remains viable. In this we wholeheartedly agree. It is a mistake to conceive of neoliberalism as compatible only with one particular institutional set: the archetypal deregulated LME. Rather, neoliberalism is a *protean project*, compatible with a wide range of institutional forms and achievable via a number of different causal paths.

While a significant amount of convergence seems to have taken place in the field of scholarly analysis as well, there are important remaining differences from our analysis. First, the shift from explaining "varieties of capitalism" to explaining "varieties of liberalization" seems to have been made without any critical analysis of what went wrong and which aspects of the previous theoretical apparatus needed to be reconsidered, which leaves the external observer with a feeling that the goalposts have been moved. Second, VoC scholars are not ready to concede that the manufacturing sectors in formerly coordinated market economies have undergone liberalization. They refer to renegotiated coordination instead (see also Hall 2007). According to this new argument, liberalization is essentially the result of a compositional shift in the economy. While the manufacturing sector remains coordinated, it is shrinking in dimensional terms due to deindustrialization. It is argued that the production regime prevailing in the service sectors does not require the same institutional ecosystem and institutional complementaries as manufacturing, but relies much more heavily on the logic of market coordination. Thus, liberalization is the result of the decline of manufacturing and the rise of services in capitalist economies. As we argue in the German and Swedish chapters, our view is instead that liberalization has taken place first and foremost in the manufacturing sector itself, and that the liberalization of manufacturing has had important consequences for the growth models of countries, unleashing further reforms.

Recognizing the danger that "liberalization" can be used imprecisely, we elaborate below how we are using the concept, and what it means in the specific sphere of industrial relations. At its core, arguing for a common trajectory of liberalization of industrial relations for us means demonstrating that there has been a steady expansion across the advanced capitalist world in *employer discretion*, as constraints on employers – in the form of labor law and collective regulation – diminish. This is a more precise formulation of the oft-cited demand on the part of employers for greater flexibility: that employers should have greater discretion vis-à-vis labor and state actors.

It follows from the distinction between institutional form and institutional functioning that liberalization should be visible in two movements, one having to do with institutional processes and the other with institutional outcomes. The former movement involves, first and foremost, deregulation: the elimination or relaxation of institutional barriers. Referring specifically to industrial relations, deregulation eliminates constraints upon capital's discretion through the removal of legal or contractual restrictions at the workplace level, in the broader labor market and in society.[2] In many cases, the removal of institutional constraints is a return to an earlier deregulated era. Institutional deregulation involves one or more of the following: a shift from higher levels of collective bargaining to lower ones, closer to the firm or workplace; greater recourse to individual bargaining between employee and employer or unilateral employer decision-making; a shrinking in the collective organization capacity of class

---

[2] Traxler (1995, 3) employs the term "disorganization" in place of "liberalization" in his discussion of change in industrial relations, but his dimensions of change are similar to those used here: decentralization, deregulation and disorganization of the collective capacity of class actors.

actors; and a restructuring of labor market institutions to reduce the level and duration of unemployment benefits, make benefit payment contingent on active search and willingness to accept available jobs, lower employment protection and in general eliminate all mechanisms interfering with the free meeting of demand and supply (Blanchard and Wolfers 2000; Blanchard 2006; Layard, Nickell and Jackman 2005; Nickell 1997; Nickell, Luca and Wolfgang 2005; OECD 1994; Saint-Paul 2002; Siebert 1997; Traxler 1995).

Institutional deregulation may also operate through mechanisms that permit class actors to bypass or ignore formal institutions and institutional rules, one of the forms of institutional change noted above; this process, sometimes labelled "derogation," can be seen when unions and employers are given exemptions from labor law or higher-level collective agreements under certain circumstances. For this reason, derogation tends to require a more active role on the part of the state. An industrial relations system in which actors are allowed to ignore institutional rules with impunity is subject *de facto* to deregulation.

The second form of institutional liberalization involves a transformation in the role played by formally unchanged institutions from discretion-limiting to discretion-enhancing. In contrast to a process of institutional deregulation, it involves what Thelen has described as "institutional conversion," as institutions come to take on different functions and generate different outcomes (Thelen 2004, 36). Institutional conversion is made possible by the plasticity – the mutability of function subject to context – that, as we noted above, is a characteristic of institutions in the political–economic realm. An example would be centralized bargaining, once the linchpin of an alternative system to liberal capitalism based upon a large and interventionist public sector and the political correction of market inequalities. However, with institutional conversion, centralized bargaining can become an institutional device to produce outcomes, such as real wage growth systematically trailing productivity increases, that the market itself would be unable to produce. Another example of institutional conversion might be a change in the functioning of works councils so that under new conditions they come to encourage cooperation with an employer and identification with the firm rather than serving as workplace agents of industrial unions. In both cases, the formal institution remains unchanged, but under different conditions, its very plasticity permits a conversion in function and behavior and is likely to generate different outcomes.

Thus, to the extent that we see decollectivization and decentralization in the form of institutions themselves, or a continuity in their form but a transformation in their content such that they contribute to the liberalizing outcomes noted above, we can say that the trajectory of institutional change is in a neoliberal direction.[3] Liberalization as institutional deregulation can be captured empirically by looking at the form of institutions, whereas liberalization as the result

---

[3] The starting point is also important. Decentralization of bargaining may be just as consequential when national bargaining gives way to sectoral bargaining as when sectoral bargaining is replaced by firm-level bargaining.

of institutional conversion requires going beyond the form and looking at the internal functioning and outcomes of institutions. For this reason, our book provides both a quantitative analysis of trends in industrial relations indicators, well suited to examining changes in institutional forms, and qualitative case studies, better suited to capturing changes in the outcomes of institutions.

What liberalization as institutional deregulation and liberalization as institutional conversion have in common is that they both allow increased employer discretion in personnel and labor market strategies. Employer discretion has three interrelated dimensions: (1) discretion in wage determination, that is, the extent to which individual employers can adapt wage rates to the individual circumstances and ability to pay of their firms, and use wage differentials to recruit, motivate and retain key employees; (2) discretion in personnel management and work organization, for example, the ability to organize work time flexibly to accommodate peaks and lulls in demand and to deploy labor across functional specializations or job categories; (3) discretion in hiring and firing, that is, the degree to which the employment relation approximates the model of *employment at will*. The metric, therefore, of the liberalization of industrial relations institutions is the extent to which they expand employer discretion over time. We make no claim here as to how employers will use their greater discretion along each of these dimensions, only that they will prefer greater discretion to less.

We argue that, despite heterogeneous institutional sets and country-specific developmental trajectories, there is substantial evidence that industrial relations systems across Western Europe have been transformed in a common neoliberal direction, in other words, toward greater employer discretion in employment relations. Streeck (2009) has usefully distinguished between "Williamsonian" and "Durkheimian" institutions. Not all institutions are coordinating devices that allow economies of transaction costs and credible commitment by actors. Some institutions are obligatory and limit actors' discretion in accordance with collectively shared social values and goals. On the evidence presented in the remainder of this book, while the coordinating properties of institutions have managed to survive in some cases, their obligatory properties have been relaxed everywhere.

2.3 Industrial Relations Liberalization and Capitalist Growth

Making employer discretion the primary indicator of liberalization in industrial relations puts class actors and class power at the center of the political–economic story that we wish to tell. It suggests that a power resources approach to CPE and a focus upon the shifting physiognomy of contemporary capitalism are necessary to understanding the fate of European industrial relations systems over the last three decades and more (see also the discussion of power-based explanations in Emmenegger 2015, Thorn 2015). We have argued that CPE has been resistant to the possibility of a common liberalizing trajectory of industrial relations institutions because of longstanding theoretical assumptions in the field: a midrange emphasis upon institutions and their internal logics rather than upon the changing face of capitalism; the expectation that institutions can successfully refract economic pressures without themselves being transformed; and a focus upon the form rather than the function of institutions. As a result, the diversity of national varieties of capitalism has tended to overshadow the importance of broad changes in capitalism across time.

The primary goal of this book is to demonstrate that a common trajectory of liberalization has in fact occurred in industrial relations in Western Europe since the oil shocks of the 1970s. We will be happy if, by the end of the book, we have established this one simple fact, which, we would argue, is at odds with the received wisdom in the field of CPE. Analyzing the causal factors underlying the common liberalizing trajectory that we have identified is not the main focus on this book. However, if we argue, as we do, that scholars need to pay more attention to the social and economic force field within which institutions operate, and, as Streeck has compellingly argued, to bring the analysis of capitalism back to the center of political economy, it is incumbent upon us to offer some commentary – albeit schematic – on the broad constellation of phenomena that accompany the transformation of industrial relations across the advanced capitalist world, and thus to add further elements to how the common trajectory that we identify is neoliberal in character.

We argue that the liberalization of industrial relations is part and parcel of a general crisis of the Fordist wage-led growth regime in advanced countries and of the uncertain search for alternative growth models that has ensued (Boyer 2015; Lavoie and Stockhammer 2012; Stockhammer and Onaran 2013). Industrial relations institutions limiting employer discretion were a common feature of the Fordist model based on wage-led growth. Interestingly, while they reduced the room for maneuver for employers, these institutions also increased capitalist viability and stability: by indexing real wages to productivity increases, they simultaneously ensured that aggregate demand would expand sufficiently to enable the growth of productive potential.

The Fordist model began to unravel in the 1970s, and its decline was due both to shifts in the international economy (trade and capital liberalization) and to the accumulation of endogenously generated problems (e.g., wage-push inflation and deindustrialization). The crisis of the Fordist regime altered the balance of class power and facilitated shifts in state policy and the weakening of labor's organized power, which allowed employers to act on their preference for maximizing discretion and ultimately liberalized industrial relations institutions. The collapse of the Fordist model and the accompanying shift in class power against trade unions thus created the conditions for the developments we detail in the country chapters that follow. In turn, these developments closed off a return to the old model of wage-led growth. In a few countries, more competitive labor markets and the consistent application of policies aimed at strengthening the profit share of national product eventually generated the conditions for the emergence of post-Fordist growth, in which growth was sustained not by real wage increases, but by greater household indebtedness and by stronger reliance on foreign demand.

We will deal with the crisis of Fordist wage-led growth and the emergence of new growth models in the final chapter of this book. In this section we emphasize two changes. First, in line with power resource theory, the weakening of organized labor has meant that employers are more free to act on their own first-order preferences, irrespective of labor preferences and the need to work within shared collective institutions. Second, employers are less likely to have an interest in supporting collective industrial relations institutions, and this as a result of deep-seated changes in the growth model over the last three decades that have had the effect of reducing the importance of collective institutions inherited from the earlier Fordist era.

One of great strengths of theorizing within political economy in the last two decades has been renewed emphasis upon employers and the firm, whether through the focus upon employer coordination (Soskice 1990), historical research into the role played by business interests in the construction of Fordist-era labor and welfare institutions (Swenson 2002) or the attention paid to the coordination needs of firms (Hall and Soskice 2001b). A political economy of capitalism should never need to bring capital back in! Yet as the field has evolved, a particular set of assumptions about employer interests and preferences has become near-hegemonic. These emphasize the extent to which institutions are the product of the rational coordination needs of firms rather than the balance of power among economic actors, and thus employers will have little incentive to dismantle those institutions when that balance changes. Those same coordination needs are anticipated to produce cross-class alliances around shared interests, rather than persistent class conflict over institutional construction and reconstruction.

These theoretical shifts reflect an abandonment of the power resource approach to political economy that was once dominant in the field (Korpi 1983). That approach deserves more attention, as Korpi (2006b) has more recently argued, because it problematizes employer preferences and introduces an explanation for the quite rapid shifts in business attitudes toward longstanding industrial relations institutions that we observe empirically. It suggests that preferences are shaped by "the strategic context within which actors operate" (Hacker and Pierson 2004, 193) so that inferring a first-order preference from the behavior of business misses the degree to which support for a policy or institution might reflect acquiescence to a balance of power rather than a particular preference ordering.[4] To exemplify: Firms may have a prestrategic preference for nonmarket coordination (as assumed by early VoC theorizing) or may settle

---

[4] For an exploration of this set of issues, see the fascinating exchange between Peter Swenson on one side and Jacob Hacker and Paul Pierson on the other (Hacker and Pierson 2002, 2004; Swenson 2004a, 2004b).

for coordinating institutions because their first prestrategic preference is ruled out and the alternatives are worse for them. Given appropriate circumstances, the observed outcome will be the same, but there is a world of difference – including for the resilience of the institutions at stake – between a situation in which business is a *protagonist* in some institutional settlement and one in which it merely consents to that settlement in light of its reading of the strategic context (Korpi 2006b).

The difference is crucial because it suggests that employer choices are likely to change as the power resources of actors change. Power resources should be understood in broad terms, encompassing organizational strength, state capacity and also structural power (Block 1987, Chapter 3). As our country cases indicate, the strength of organized labor has declined everywhere, and employer organizations have become more politicized and self-confident. That has taken place within the context of an increase in the structural power of capital that derives in part from greater transnational mobility and the role of financial markets, and in part from the undermining of the ability of states to regulate national economies effectively (Jessop 1990b; Strange 1986). This returns us to the argument made in the last section, that political economy needs to shift from a game-theoretic to a mechanical (*gleichgewichtig*) notion of equilibrium. In the latter, the institutions of capitalism are the product of competing forces. These forces may balance themselves out for some time, but there is no expectation that the resulting equilibrium will be more than a temporary situation. In the contemporary period, understanding institutional change therefore raises the possibility that as the power of organized labor has declined, so a more authentic expression of employer preferences, unconstrained by the need to compromise, has emerged. Capitalists, as Streeck (2009, 41, emphasis in the original) has vividly described them, "are the modern nontraditional economic actors par excellence: they never rest in their perennial rush to new frontiers. This is why they are *fundamentally unruly*: a permanent source of disorder from the perspective of social institutions, relentlessly whacking away at social rules."

We argued earlier that a return to classical political economy, the political economy of Marx, Schumpeter, Keynes and Polanyi, among others, with its emphasis upon the unruly, crisis-ridden dynamism of capitalist growth, is helpful in understanding institutional change in the current. Streeck (2011) has called for political economy to focus analysis upon a *historicized* capitalism, one that pays attention to the changing character of capitalism itself, and suggested that tracing the historical trajectory of capitalism is more enlightening than emphasizing international variation. Our interest is in the dynamic relationship between capitalism and the politically constructed industrial relations institutions that seek to regulate it and to manage its unruly character.

Hence the value of the regulation theory approach to political economy: "regulation politically modifies the economic process to temporarily stabilize, or contain, the contradictory core of capitalism" (Neilson 2012, 161). The central insight of regulation theory is that each growth model of capitalism produces different types of conflict and fundamentally different problems for its stable reproduction. As such, each capitalist model is likely to be accompanied by different sets of regulatory institutions. These institutions serve to stabilize a particular capitalist regime of accumulation temporarily, but there is no grand designer lurking in the back to ensure the adequacy of institutional fitting, and therefore no guarantee that the institutional regime will persist over time.

For the regulationist literature, a Fordist regime rests on a multiplicity of interrelated conditions (e.g., an accommodative monetary regime, limited international economic openness). However, the institutions regulating employment relations play a fundamental role (Boyer 2004). With at least moderately strong trade unions and collective bargaining, real wages become indexed to labor productivity as opposed to being determined solely by competitive forces. This sets in motion two complementary and mutually reinforcing dynamics. On one hand, stimulated by real wages, mass consumption becomes a large and increasingly reliable source of aggregate demand. On the other hand, the expansion of markets stimulates productivity increases through the availability of economies of scale and through alternative mechanisms.

The regulationist literature emphasizes the Keynesian "accelerator," that is, the tendency of investments to expand in response to the increase in demand (e.g., Boyer 2004, 95). New investments in turn incorporate the latest vintage of capital and technical progress and thus stimulate productivity. Other post-Keynesian literature emphasizes the productivity-enhancing role of labor rigidities, including high wages and institutional constraints that stimulate both capital/labor substitution and a more effective use of human resources (for more on this see the discussion in the final chapter of this book, as well as Storm and Naastepad 2012b). The increase in productivity in turn "finances" the increase in real wages, ensuring both healthy growth and a relatively equitable distribution of the proceeds of growth between labor and capital.

The Fordist model was never without problems. Its social foundations were always somewhat precarious. There was a tendency for wage growth to exceed productivity growth, which both undermined capital accumulation and caused inflationary tendencies. For reasons that are not fully understood, the Fordist model ground to a halt sometime in the 1970s as a result of overlapping developments such as trend decline in labor productivity, increase in oil prices and growing militancy of the working class in the 1960s and 1970s (Armstrong, Glyn and Harrison 1991). The liberalization of capital movements has increased the systemic importance of profits for accumulation and has imposed a worldwide floor on returns to capital that acts as a constraint on national actors. The growing trade openness of advanced economies has simultaneously strengthened the current account constraint on wage-led growth – if domestic wages grow too fast relative to trade competitors this will result in an external deficit – and enabled countries with a strong and productive manufacturing sector to pursue export-led growth strategies at the expense of stimulating domestic demand. There has been, over the last thirty years, a veritable growth industry in the effort to understand and characterize post-Fordism: to identify the central elements and core dynamic of the growth model that has replaced Fordism.[5] We will not rehearse this literature here. For our purposes it suffices to say two things: (1) that the weakening of industrial relations has upset a critical condition for the viability of the Fordist growth regime, namely, the ability of unionism and collective bargaining to stimulate productivity increases and then transfer them into household consumption by means of growing real wages; and (2) that the capitalism that has emerged has put a far higher premium than before – for the manufacturing sector as much as for the increasingly dominant service sector – upon flexibility and the ability of employers to respond rapidly and in a differentiated manner. This is what Harvey nicely terms "flexible accumulation" and it is this that makes the expansion of employer discretion a universal feature of the current period (Harvey 2005:, 76).

One can point to a comparatively brief period following the Depression and Second World War when a combination of changed needs on the part of the dominant Fordist element of capital and a new balance of class forces, built largely on the weight of the industrial labor force, produced a temporary and fragile "class compromise." The industrial relations systems of advanced capitalist countries that became formalized during this period reflected that compromise and served to limit employer discretion. Each of our country chapters begins with an account of the form that compromise took and the types of institutions that were constructed to regulate the labor market. While the particular form of those institutions varied from country to country, in each case, by the end of the 1970s, employer discretion was constrained in substantial and important ways. However, the class compromise did not result in an institutional equilibrium in the VoC meaning of the term and was significantly eroded in the following years in all countries, as our country case studies show.

We conclude this chapter by noting that the trajectory of industrial relations is not simply a "sectoral" story relevant only to a particular type of scholars interested in trade unions, labor market institutions and justice at work. The institutions of industrial relations have systemic importance for capitalist countries. They ensured the viability of the whole accumulation regime that was at work between the 1930s and 1970s in advanced industrial democracies. Their erosion and crisis are to a large extent responsible for the instability that capitalism is currently facing everywhere.

---

[5] The literature here is enormous. For a sampling of the most ambitious work see Harvey (1989); Kotz, McDonough and Reich (1994); Lash and Urry (1987); Offe (1985); and Piore and Sabel (1984). For an overview, see also Amin (1994).

3

Quantitative Analysis of Industrial Relations Change

In this chapter we assess the extent of institutional change in European industrial relations by analyzing available data for 15 OECD countries between 1974 and 2011. Previous research of this type has tended to emphasize limited, incremental change and the persistence of distinct national institutional sets (Golden, Wallerstein and Lange 1999, Lange, Wallerstein and Golden 1995, Wallerstein, Golden and Lange 1997). However, such research has covered a shorter time period and relied on a smaller set of variables than we do here.

We focus on the following indicators: the union density rate (the percentage of the eligible workforce who are members of unions); the employer density rate (workers employed by member firms as a percentage of total workers); three indices of collective bargaining centralization and coordination (one of which takes into account the presence of "opening clauses" in multiemployer contracts); an index of social pacting capturing the extent to which trade unions and employer organizations participate in the design and implementation of public policy; and an indicator of the conflict rate. The sample covers 12 Western European countries (Austria, Belgium, Denmark, Finland, France, Germany, Ireland, Italy, Netherlands, Norway, Sweden and the United Kingdom). In addition, to increase the sample of liberal market economies, Australia, Canada and the United States are also included. For ease of presentation, as well as to smooth out short-term variation and to address the problem of missing observations, the yearly data are aggregated into seven five-year averages from 1974 to 2008 and one three-year average for 2009–2011. All data, except on industrial conflict, are from the Database on Institutional Characteristics of Trade Unions, Wage Setting, State Intervention and Social Pacts (Version 4) assembled by Jelle Visser (2013).

The chapter is divided into two sections. The first section presents descriptive trends of the variables. The second section performs a factor analysis on the various indicators to uncover underlying dimensions and then discusses the trajectories of different countries.

3.1 Union Density, Collective Bargaining Structure and Conflict Rates

Data on union density are reported in Table 3.1.[1] They suggest that between 1974–1978 and 2008–2011 union density has declined in 13 countries out of 15. The largest declines have occurred in France (−63 percent); Australia (−59 percent); Austria (−52 percent); the United States (−49 percent); the Netherlands (−48 percent); and Germany (−47 percent). The decline has been minimal in Belgium (−3 percent), while in Norway and Finland there have even been small increases (+2 and +4 percent, respectively). Focusing solely on the period between 1989–1993 and 2009–2011, the greatest declines are registered in Australia (−55 percent), Germany (−44 percent), Austria (−38 percent) and Ireland (−32 percent). From the 1990s on, union density has declined in all countries, even in "Ghent countries" such as Finland, Norway and Belgium, in which union density had remained stable and even increased slightly in previous years.[2]

The data in Table 3.1 show that union decline cuts across coordinated and liberal market economies. The cross-cutting trend is clearly brought out by comparing union densities in Germany and the United Kingdom (Figure 3.1). Union density declined more rapidly in Britain than in Germany in the 1980s. From the early 1990s on, however, the decline has been more rapid in the former than in the latter.

In 2009–11, Sweden, Finland and Denmark (three Ghent countries) still had rates of unionization close to 70 percent, while Norway and Belgium had rates above 50 percent. As shown in Figure 3.2, however, even in these countries, unionization, after peaking in the early 1990s, declined in the 1990s and 2000s. In Ireland, Italy, France, Canada and Norway, union decline appears to have plateaued in the early 2010s. In fact, union density even increased slightly in these countries. This phenomenon may be due to union members being less affected by labor shedding during the crisis years than nonmembers.

The Visser database (Visser 2013) also compiles data on union density by sector from various sources. The series are far from complete and most data are available only from the mid-1990s on, but the information they convey is nonetheless worth considering. In Figure 3.3, union density rates are plotted separately for the following sectors: private; public; industry; manufacturing;

---

[1] For Australia and the United States, the union density series are constructed by splicing two series in the Visser database (2013): one based on administrative data on union membership (available for earlier years) and the other based on labor market surveys (for later years). An adjustment factor has been calculated by dividing the administrative data by the survey data for the period of overlap between the two series. The adjustment factor was then applied to the administrative-source data for earlier years, while for later years the survey-based data have been used.

[2] Ghent countries provide strong selective incentives for union membership, since unemployment insurance is voluntary and managed by trade unions but heavily subsidized by the state (Rothstein 1992, Van Rie, Marx and Horemans 2011).

TABLE 3.1. *Union Density Rates*

Country	74–78	79–83	84–88	89–93	94–98	99–03	04–08	09–11	%11–74	%08–79	%11–89
Australia	44.76	44.98	43.85	40.51	30.75	23.84	20.00	18.37	−58.97	−55.53	−54.66
Austria	58.46	55.44	50.56	45.58	39.98	35.86	31.48	28.30	−51.59	−43.22	−37.91
Belgium	52.42	53.00	51.78	53.98	55.20	50.56	52.98	50.83	−3.03	−0.04	−5.83
Canada	34.50	35.04	34.60	34.78	33.56	30.52	29.68	29.90	−13.33	−15.30	−14.03
Denmark	71.80	79.32	76.74	75.96	76.60	73.70	69.90	68.65	−4.39	−11.88	−9.62
Finland	65.88	68.60	70.22	76.00	79.70	74.44	71.04	68.73	4.33	3.56	−9.56
France	21.40	17.62	12.82	9.96	8.60	8.02	7.66	7.90	−63.08	−56.53	−20.68
Germany	34.82	35.06	33.98	33.06	28.06	24.02	20.72	18.50	−46.87	−40.90	−44.04
Ireland	57.28	58.18	53.88	52.20	45.92	36.92	33.14	35.47	−38.08	−43.04	−32.06
Italy	48.98	47.90	41.60	39.00	37.22	34.38	33.56	35.13	−28.27	−29.94	−9.91
Netherlands	37.20	33.48	26.66	24.56	24.78	22.16	20.72	19.27	−48.21	−38.11	−21.55
Norway	53.66	57.58	56.94	58.14	56.48	54.54	54.36	54.57	1.69	−5.59	−6.15
Sweden	74.98	78.46	82.56	83.30	84.68	78.46	73.10	69.30	−7.58	−6.83	−16.81
UK	47.02	51.24	45.78	39.72	33.34	29.62	27.48	27.20	−42.15	−46.37	−31.52
USA	22.75	20.97	17.06	15.42	14.04	12.82	11.80	11.50	−49.44	−43.73	−25.42

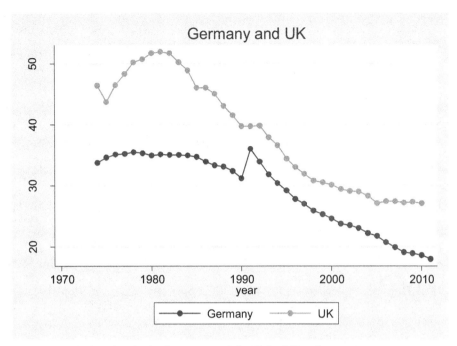

FIGURE 3.1. Union density in Germany and the United Kingdom

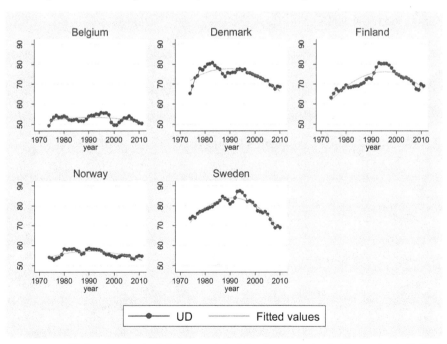

FIGURE 3.2. Union density in Belgium and the Nordic countries (with quadratic fit line)

a) LMEs

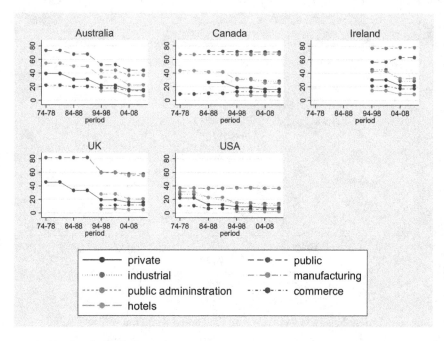

b) Continental Countries

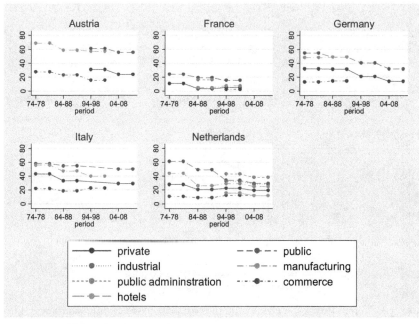

FIGURE 3.3. Union density rates by sector

c) Belgium and Nordic Countries

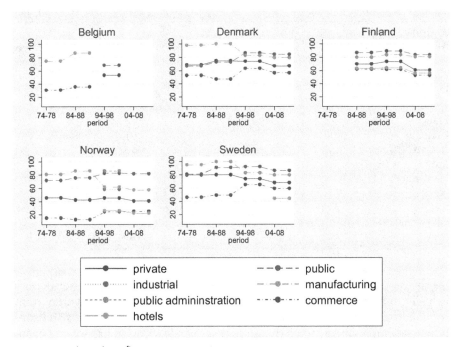

FIGURE 3.3 *(continued)*

public administration (more strictly defined than the public sector at large); commerce; and hotels, restaurants and catering. The latter two service sectors tend to be labor-intensive and low-skilled. The union density rate is everywhere higher in the public sector than in the private/manufacturing sector. In most countries, public sector unionization has not declined (including in the United States), but there are countries, such as Australia, Britain, Austria and Germany, where public sector decline has proceeded in parallel with private sector decline. In the Netherlands, it seems that public sector decline was greater than that in the private sector. Furthermore, union density is everywhere especially low in the labor-intensive service sectors (commerce and hotels, restaurants and catering), with the exception of Denmark, Finland and Sweden (all Ghent countries), where private service unionization is above 50 percent.

If statistics on union density by sector are scarce, even scarcer are statistics on the associational density of employer organizations (as a percentage of employees). Table 3.2 reports the available data in the Visser database (Visser 2013). Although most data are available only from the early 2000s on, and for Australia, Canada and the United States there are no data at all, there is no evidence of a decline in employer association density. In Austria, employer density remains constant at 100 percent throughout the period, while in other countries

TABLE 3.2. *Density Rates of Employer Associations*

Country	74–78	79–83	84–88	89–93	94–98	99–03	04–08	09–11
Australia								
Austria	100.00	100.00	100.00	100.00	100.00	100.00	100.00	100.00
Belgium						82.00		82.00
Canada								
Denmark					58.00	60.00	65.00	
Finland				63.75		66.50	72.70	
France				74.00		74.00	75.00	
Germany						63.00	60.00	
Ireland						60.00		
Italy						62.00	58.00	
Netherlands						85.00	85.00	
Norway					53.50	59.00	65.00	
Sweden					86.00	83.00	84.00	83.00
UK						40.00	35.00	
USA								

the density rate seems to have increased slightly. In general, employer density is higher than union density. A high employer density is especially important for countries in which there is no legal extension of negotiated terms and conditions of employment, and bargaining coverage depends on firms being members of employer associations. A small decline of employer density is found in Germany, Italy, Sweden and the United Kingdom.

Differently from trade union density (but perhaps consistent with trends in employer density), there is no evidence of a cross-country decline in bargaining coverage (proportion of employees who are covered by a collective bargaining agreement). The relevant data are reported in Table 3.3. They suggest shrinking coverage in countries in which bargaining coverage is strictly associated with union coverage, such as the United Kingdom, Australia, the United States and Canada. However, the decline of bargaining coverage is not a peculiarity of the liberal market economies: Germany, too, has seen the coverage rate drop from 85 percent in 1990 to 61 percent in 2010, and the rate is even lower in manufacturing. The decline of bargaining coverage will be discussed in the German chapter. It suffices to say here that in Germany collective bargaining coverage is strictly dependent on the strength of employer associations. Extension clauses, while legally possible, have been used sparingly in recent years. Some German employer associations have been experimenting with "membership without contract" (a form of membership that does not imply firms being bound by the industry contract) as a way to stop membership loss. In other countries, bargaining coverage has increased slightly. Consequently, a gap has opened between union membership coverage and collective bargaining coverage. This gap is particularly wide in France (85 percent), Austria (70 percent),

TABLE 3.3. Collective Bargaining Coverage Rates

Country	74–78	79–83	84–88	89–93	94–98	99–03	04–08	09–11	%11–74	%08–79	%11–89
Australia	88.00	88.00	85.00	76.67	60.00	50.00	45.00			-48.86	
Austria	95.00	95.00	95.00	98.00	98.00	98.75	99.00	99.00	4.21	4.21	1.02
Belgium	90.00	97.00	96.00	96.00	96.00	96.00	96.00	96.00	6.67	-1.03	0.00
Canada	37.60	37.96	37.28	38.10	35.48	32.24	31.68	30.20	-19.68	-16.54	-20.73
Denmark	81.00	82.00	83.00	84.00	84.00	83.00	85.00			3.66	
Finland	77.00	77.00	77.00	85.00	85.00	86.50	88.30	89.50	16.23	14.68	5.29
France	76.00	78.95	88.30	94.50		92.00	92.00			16.53	
Germany	85.00	85.00	85.00	85.00	75.18	68.84	64.70	61.55	-27.59	-23.88	-27.59
Ireland						44.40	41.90	42.20			
Italy	85.00	85.00	85.00	85.00	85.00	85.00	85.00	85.00	0.00	0.00	0.00
Netherlands	78.40	81.80	80.30	80.00	83.40	84.70	84.85	84.30	7.53	3.73	5.38
Norway	65.00	70.00	70.00	70.00	72.00	72.00	73.50			5.00	
Sweden	84.00	85.00	85.00	87.50	91.50	94.00	92.25	91.00	8.33	8.53	4.00
UK	77.30	73.50	64.00	54.00	36.88	35.74	34.22	31.57	-59.16	-53.44	-41.54
USA	26.26	24.78	20.04	18.14	16.26	14.74	13.52	13.23	-49.61	-45.44	-27.05

the Netherlands (65 percent) and Italy (50 percent). It is the result of legal clauses extending the terms and conditions set by the shrinking unionized sector. It generates a worrisome disconnect between a minority of unionized workers and the majority of unorganized workers. As a result, unions become liable to being accused of acting as insider organizations that exploit their privileged position to set terms and conditions of employment to the exclusive benefit of their members while unduly damaging the prospects of outsiders (Lindbeck and Snower 1986, Saint-Paul 2002).

An important dimension in industrial relations is the bargaining structure and specifically the degree of bargaining centralization, which is often measured by recording the main level of bargaining. In the Visser database, there is an indicator capturing the main level of bargaining (thus providing an ordinal measure of bargaining centralization/decentralization), which is coded as follows (Visser 2013: 11):

5 = bargaining predominantly takes place at central or cross-industry level and there are centrally determined binding norms or ceilings to be respected by agreements negotiated at lower levels;
4 = intermediate or alternating between central and industry bargaining;
3 = bargaining predominantly takes place at the sector or industry level;
2 = intermediate or alternating between sector and company bargaining;
1 = bargaining predominantly takes place at the local or company level.

"Dominant level" means that the level accounts for two-thirds of the total coverage rate. Table 3.4 reports the data on bargaining centralization/decentralization based on the above coding scheme. Bargaining decentralization has been fairly dramatic in the United Kingdom. In 1975–78 this country had centralized bargaining, but bargaining was dramatically decentralized afterward. A decline of centralization is also visible in Australia and Canada, while in Ireland bargaining was highly centralized between 1988 and 2008 (Baccaro and Simoni 2007, Roche 2007) and then was decentralized with the onset of the financial crisis (Roche 2011). The U.S. indicator suggests no change, because the American bargaining structure has always been company-based. A process of decentralization seems to have occurred in Denmark and Sweden as well. In these countries wages and working conditions were centrally determined in the 1970s, but bargaining moved to the industry level (with a progressively greater role of company-level bargaining) between the late 1980s and early 1990s (Iversen, Pontusson and Soskice 2000). No change is reported for Germany and Austria, while bargaining centralization seems to have increased in Belgium and slightly in Italy from the 1990s, according to this measure of main bargaining level.

It may be argued that the above measure of bargaining centralization severely understates the extent of true bargaining centralization in Austria and Germany, as well as in Sweden, Denmark and other countries. The country chapters will document that the bargaining structure has changed dramatically

TABLE 3.4. *Collective Bargaining Centralization Scores*

Country	74–78	79–83	84–88	89–93	94–98	99–03	04–08	09–11	%11–74	%08–79	%11–89
Australia	4.00	4.20	4.60	3.20	2.00	2.00	2.00	2.00	−50.00	−52.38	−37.50
Austria	3.00	3.00	3.00	3.00	3.00	3.00	3.00	3.00	0.00	0.00	0.00
Belgium	3.40	4.20	4.80	4.60	4.20	4.60	4.60	4.67	37.25	9.52	1.45
Canada	2.00	1.20	1.00	1.00	1.00	1.00	1.00	1.00	−50.00	−16.67	0.00
Denmark	5.00	3.80	3.80	3.00	3.40	3.00	3.00	3.00	−40.00	−21.05	0.00
Finland	5.00	4.60	3.80	4.20	4.20	4.60	4.20	3.67	−26.67	−8.70	−12.70
France	3.00	2.40	2.00	2.00	2.00	2.00	2.00	2.00	−33.33	−16.67	0.00
Germany	3.00	3.00	3.00	3.00	3.00	3.00	3.00	3.00	0.00	0.00	0.00
Ireland	2.80	2.20	2.60	5.00	5.00	5.00	5.00	1.00	−64.29	127.27	−80.00
Italy	3.40	3.40	2.40	2.80	3.00	3.00	3.00	3.00	−11.76	−11.76	7.14
Netherlands	3.60	3.60	3.20	3.40	3.00	3.40	3.20	3.00	−16.67	−11.11	−11.76
Norway	4.40	4.00	4.20	4.40	3.20	3.40	3.00	3.00	−31.82	−25.00	−31.82
Sweden	5.00	4.60	4.20	3.80	3.00	3.00	3.00	3.00	−40.00	−34.78	−21.05
UK	4.60	3.00	2.40	2.00	1.00	1.00	1.00	1.00	−78.26	−66.67	−50.00
USA	1.00	1.00	1.00	1.00	1.00	1.00	1.00	1.00	0.00	0.00	0.00

in Germany and Sweden, yet such change is not captured by focusing on the main level of bargaining. While the main level of bargaining has remained at the industry level, industry-level bargaining has been subject to erosion since opportunities to bypass centrally negotiated provisions have increased. One way to more realistically assess the extent of change is to factor in the impact of "opening clauses," legal or contractual norms that allow lower-level deviations from the provisions of higher-level agreements.

The Visser database (Visser 2013, 11) includes a time-changing measure of opening clauses (OC), reflecting mostly developments in manufacturing, which is coded as follows:

5 = opening clauses are exceptional (one-off hardship clauses only, related to specific cases of bankruptcy or restructuring);
4 = opening clauses exist, limited use, on work time only;
3 = opening clauses exist, limited use, also on pay;
2 = opening clauses exist, use is widespread, including pay;
1 = opening clauses are generalized; the sector agreement sets only a framework for local bargaining or define only a default in case local negotiations fail;
0 = does not apply (no sectoral or national agreements).

By combining the measures of bargaining level and opening clause, it is possible to produce an adjusted measure of bargaining centralization/decentralization that takes into account the fact that even when bargaining remains formally centralized, opportunities for derogation may increase. The new measure is based on the main level of bargaining weighted by the extent of opening clauses according to the following coding scheme:

level × 1.0 if oc = 5
level × 0.8 if oc = 4
level × 0.6 if oc = 3
level × 0.4 if oc = 2
level × 0.2 if oc = 1
level × 0.0 if oc = 0.

This coding scheme generates a variable equaling 5 (maximum score) if bargaining is highly centralized and opening clauses are exceptional, and 0 (minimum score) if bargaining is decentralized. When the main bargaining level is intermediate or alternating between the sectoral and the company levels (score 2), the opening score weight is divided by two. For example, a country scoring 2 on the level dimension, in which opening clauses are exceptional, obtains an adjusted score of 1. This alternative measure of centralization seems better suited to account for the erosion of formally unchanged bargaining structures. As revealed by Figure 3.4, in the case of Germany the adjusted measure suggests a decentralizing trend that parallels the decline in trade union density, while the measure of main bargaining level registers no change (see Figure 3.4).

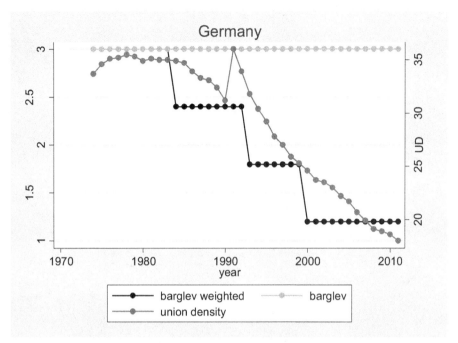

FIGURE 3.4. Bargaining centralization (left scale) and union density (right scale) in Germany according to the weighted and unweighted measures of centralization

With the adjusted measure of bargaining centralization, not only does the extent of decentralization become more clearly visible, but also it is clear that it is a cross-cutting phenomenon. According to this measure, there has been extensive decentralization not only in the United Kingdom but also in Sweden and Denmark. The only countries where the measure reports no change are Canada and the United States, and in both cases the lack of change is due to their having had a decentralized bargaining structure to begin with (see Table 3.5).

A slightly different measure often used to assess a country's bargaining structure is the level of coordination in wage bargaining (Kenworthy 2000, Soskice 1990). The notion of coordination is linked to centralization, but coordination can be also achieved within a formally decentralized bargaining structure when functional substitutes such as strong and cohesive employer associations or union confederations are present. The coordination variable is coded by Visser as follows (Visser 2013: 10):

5 = (a) Centralized bargaining by peak association(s), with or without government involvement, and/or government imposition of wage schedule/freeze, with peace obligation (example: Sweden prior to 1980); (b) informal centralization of industry-level bargaining by a powerful and

TABLE 3.5. *Collective Bargaining Centralization Adjusted for Opening Clauses*

Country	74–78	79–83	84–88	89–93	94–98	99–03	04–08	09–11	%11–74	%08–79	%11–89
Australia	4.20	4.36	4.36	2.68	1.60	1.60	1.52	1.40	−66.67	−65.14	−47.76
Austria	4.00	4.00	3.52	3.40	3.16	2.80	2.80	2.80	−30.00	−30.00	−17.65
Belgium	4.40	5.20	5.24	4.68	4.36	4.68	4.68	4.73	7.58	−10.00	1.14
Canada	1.00	1.00	1.00	1.00	1.00	1.00	1.00	1.00	0.00	0.00	0.00
Denmark	6.00	4.80	3.52	2.80	2.48	2.20	1.60	1.60	−73.33	−66.67	−42.86
Finland	6.00	5.60	4.80	5.20	5.20	5.60	4.96	3.33	−44.44	−11.43	−35.90
France	4.00	2.72	1.80	1.80	1.80	1.80	1.60	1.60	−60.00	−41.18	−11.11
Germany	4.00	4.00	3.40	3.28	2.80	2.32	2.20	2.20	−45.00	−45.00	−32.93
Ireland	2.44	1.96	2.20	4.00	4.00	4.00	4.00	1.00	−59.02	104.08	−75.00
Italy	4.40	4.24	2.28	3.16	4.00	4.00	3.64	3.20	−27.27	−14.15	1.27
Netherlands	4.60	4.12	3.56	3.72	3.40	3.28	2.92	2.80	−39.13	−29.13	−24.73
Norway	5.40	4.84	4.56	5.40	4.20	3.72	2.80	2.80	−48.15	−42.15	−48.15
Sweden	6.00	5.60	5.20	4.56	2.80	2.32	2.08	1.60	−73.33	−62.86	−64.91
UK	3.76	2.80	2.08	1.60	1.00	1.00	1.00	1.00	−73.40	−64.29	−37.50
USA	1.00	1.00	1.00	1.00	1.00	1.00	1.00	1.00	0.00	0.00	0.00

Note: To avoid dividing by 0 when calculating percentages, 1 has been added to all scores

monopolistic union confederation (example: Austria prior to 1983); (c) extensive, regularized pattern setting and highly synchronized bargaining coupled with coordination of bargaining by influential large firms (example: Japan prior to 1998).

4 = (a) Centralized bargaining by peak associations with or without government involvement, and/or government imposition of wage schedule/freeze, without peace obligation (example: Ireland 1987–2009); (b) informal (intra-associational and/or inter-associational) centralization of industry- and firm-level bargaining by peak associations (both sides) (example: Spain 2002–8); (c) extensive, regularized pattern setting coupled with high degree of union concentration (example: Germany most years).

3 = (a) Informal (intra-associational and/or interassociational) centralization of industry- and firm-level bargaining by peak associations (one side, or only some unions) with or without government participation (Italy since 2000); (b) industry-level bargaining with irregular and uncertain pattern setting and only moderate union concentration (example: Denmark 1981–86); (c) government arbitration or intervention (example: United Kingdom 1966–68, 1972–74).

2 = Mixed industry- and firm-level bargaining, with no or little pattern bargaining and relatively weak elements of government coordination through the setting of basic pay rates (statutory minimum wage) or wage indexation (example: France most years).

1 = Fragmented wage bargaining, confined largely to individual firms or plants (example: United Kingdom since 1980).

The coordination scores reported in Table 3.6 suggests that coordination has declined in most countries (particularly in the United Kingdom and Canada) but has also increased in others (particularly in Germany and Belgium). However, it is likely that the measure of coordination, like the unweighted measure of bargaining level/centralization, is biased by the absence of any consideration for the growing diffusion of opening clauses (which hinder the coordinating abilities of both employer organizations and union federations) and thus overstates the real extent of coordination in the bargaining system.

Another dimension of industrial relations institutionalization is the participation of trade unions and employer associations in the design and implementation of public policy broadly defined, particularly in the areas of incomes policies, social policies and labor market policies (Avdagic, Rhodes and Visser 2011, Baccaro and Simoni 2008, Baccaro 2014b, Rhodes 1998). This dimension, known as corporatism or social pacting, was until recently considered to have undergone a process of decline (Streeck and Schmitter 1991), but more recent research suggests that corporatism as an institutionalized mode of policy making never died; rather, it began to be used to implement different types of policies, no longer aimed at redistribution or at the expansion of public consumption, but rather at reducing real unit labor costs and increasing

TABLE 3.6. *Bargaining Coordination*

Country	74–78	79–83	84–88	89–93	94–98	99–03	04–08	09–11	%11–74	%08–79	%11–89
Australia	3.00	2.80	4.00	3.20	2.00	2.00	2.00	2.00	−33.33	−28.57	−37.50
Austria	5.00	4.80	4.00	4.00	4.00	4.00	4.00	4.00	−20.00	−16.67	0.00
Belgium	3.60	4.20	4.60	4.00	4.40	5.00	5.00	5.00	38.89	19.05	25.00
Canada	3.40	1.00	1.00	1.00	1.00	1.00	1.00	1.00	−70.59	0.00	0.00
Denmark	5.00	3.80	3.40	4.00	3.80	4.00	4.00	4.00	−20.00	5.26	0.00
Finland	5.00	4.20	4.60	4.20	4.20	4.60	4.20	3.67	−26.67	0.00	−12.70
France	2.40	2.20	2.00	2.00	2.00	2.00	2.00	2.00	−16.67	−9.09	0.00
Germany	3.20	4.00	4.00	4.00	3.80	3.40	4.00	4.00	25.00	0.00	0.00
Ireland	2.80	2.20	2.20	4.00	4.00	4.00	4.00	3.00	7.14	81.82	−25.00
Italy	2.80	2.80	2.40	2.80	4.00	3.20	3.00	3.00	7.14	7.14	7.14
Netherlands	3.80	3.40	4.00	4.00	4.00	3.40	3.40	3.67	−3.51	0.00	−8.33
Norway	4.80	4.20	3.80	4.40	4.00	4.20	4.00	4.00	−16.67	−4.76	−9.09
Sweden	5.00	4.60	3.60	3.80	3.40	4.00	4.00	4.00	−20.00	−13.04	5.26
UK	3.80	1.60	1.00	1.00	1.00	1.00	1.00	1.00	−73.68	−37.50	0.00
USA	1.00	1.00	1.00	1.00	1.00	1.00	1.00	1.00	0.00	0.00	0.00

competitiveness and at smoothing the process of welfare state retrenchment and labor market liberalization (Avdagic, Rhodes and Visser 2011, Baccaro 2014b).

The measure of social pacting presented here is constructed by combining two variables from the Visser database: whether either a tripartite or bipartite pact was negotiated in the year in question, or whether the wage effects of a previous pact apply even though no pact was negotiated in the year. The resulting measure is displayed in Table 3.7. The measure varies between 1 and 2. A score of 1.2 implies that in one year out of five a social pact was negotiated or the wage effects of a previous pact obtained in the country in question. It should be noted that because this index focuses on explicit negotiation and pacting, it is likely to underestimate the extent of concertation that occurs on a routine basis in countries such as Austria and Germany. The indicator suggests that social pacting has declined considerably in Sweden, Denmark and Norway, in line with accounts emphasizing the decline of corporatism in Nordic countries (Iversen 1996, Swenson 1991), as well as in the United Kingdom. In Ireland, social pacting dominated policy making from the late 1980s until the late 2000s but was dismissed in the postcrisis period (Regan 2011, Roche 2011).

Finally, we consider industrial conflict (see Table 3.8). We use ILO data on days not worked due to strikes and lockouts, which we normalize by the size of civilian employment.[3] The data are available until 2008 (2004 for France) and show a strong declining trend for all countries, including historically conflictual countries such as Italy and the United Kingdom. Strike data may be interpreted in two opposite ways. A low propensity to strike may be a consequence of low labor power, but also of high labor power, if the sheer threat leads employers to cave in. Given socioeconomic circumstances (generalized decline in wage growth relative to productivity, high unemployment, increasing inequality), the decline in industrial conflict is almost certainly not a manifestation of growing union strength.

3.2 Factor Analysis

We now rely on factor analysis to uncover systematic patterns of covariation in the variables presented above. Factor analysis assumes that the data are visible manifestations of underlying hidden constructs and expresses these constructs as linear combinations of the (standardized) observed variables. The indicators used for the factor analysis are union density, collective bargaining coverage (with linear imputation of missing values), bargaining level,

---

[3] The numerator is from the ILO Laboursta database (variable 9C) (ILO various years); the denominator is from the OECD's Annual Labour Force Statistics (OECD various years). The recording of industrial conflict varies somewhat across countries. In particular, the French data exclude general and political strikes and all strikes that involve more than one establishment and thus are likely to underestimate the extent of conflict in French industrial relations.

TABLE 3.7. *Social Pacting*

Country	74–78	79–83	84–88	89–93	94–98	99–03	04–08	09–11	%11–74	%08–79	%11–89
Australia	1.00	1.20	2.00	1.80	1.00	1.00	1.00	1.00	0.00	−16.67	−44.44
Austria	2.00	1.80	1.00	1.00	1.40	1.20	1.40	2.00	0.00	−22.22	100.00
Belgium	1.60	1.60	1.60	1.60	1.60	1.40	1.80	1.33	−16.67	12.50	−16.67
Canada	1.00	1.00	1.00	1.00	1.00	1.00	1.00	1.00	0.00	0.00	0.00
Denmark	1.60	1.20	1.20	1.00	1.20	1.20	1.40	1.00	−37.50	16.67	0.00
Finland	1.80	1.60	1.40	2.00	1.80	1.80	1.60	1.67	−7.41	0.00	−16.67
France	1.20	1.20	1.60	1.40	1.20	1.60	1.20	1.33	11.11	0.00	−4.76
Germany	1.00	1.00	1.00	1.00	1.20	1.00	1.00	1.00	0.00	0.00	0.00
Ireland	1.80	1.40	1.40	2.00	2.00	2.00	2.00	1.00	−44.44	42.86	−50.00
Italy	1.60	1.40	1.20	1.60	1.60	1.40	1.20	1.33	−16.67	−14.29	−16.67
Netherlands	1.60	1.60	1.20	1.60	1.80	1.80	1.40	1.67	4.17	−12.50	4.17
Norway	1.60	1.40	1.00	1.20	2.00	1.20	1.40	1.00	−37.50	0.00	−16.67
Sweden	2.00	1.80	1.60	1.20	1.20	1.00	1.20	1.00	−50.00	−33.33	−16.67
UK	1.80	1.00	1.00	1.00	1.00	1.00	1.00	1.00	−44.44	0.00	0.00
USA	1.00	1.00	1.00	1.00	1.00	1.00	1.00	1.00	0.00	0.00	0.00

Note: To avoid dividing by 0 when calculating percentages, 1 has been added to all scores.

TABLE 3.8. *Industrial Conflict*

Country	74–78	79–83	84–88	89–93	94–98	99–03	04–08	09–11	%11–74	%08–79
Australia	0.59	0.48	0.20	0.15	0.07	0.05	0.02	−96.67	−95.92	−86.90
Austria	0.00	0.00	0.00	0.01	0.00	0.07	0.00	−99.39	−99.35	−99.84
Belgium	0.21	0.11	0.05	0.03	0.02	0.05	0.06	−69.80	−45.41	107.24
Canada	0.89	0.65	0.38	0.23	0.19	0.15	0.13	−85.06	−79.75	−42.57
Denmark	0.07	0.10	0.22	0.03	0.27	0.04	0.03	−61.87	−71.69	−8.45
Finland	0.40	0.29	0.40	0.14	0.16	0.04	0.08	−81.06	−74.27	−45.40
France	0.15	0.09	0.04	0.02	0.02	0.02	0.01	−94.88	−91.53	−67.90
Germany	0.05	0.01	0.04	0.02	0.00	0.00	0.00	−89.38	−11.33	−69.06
Ireland	0.50	0.54	0.28	0.11	0.06	0.06	0.01	−98.66	−98.75	−93.69
Italy	1.01	0.86	0.25	0.18	0.08	0.09	0.03	−96.66	−96.09	−81.16
Netherlands	0.01	0.03	0.01	0.01	0.02	0.01	0.01	−45.31	−78.33	−55.50
Norway	0.07	0.04	0.13	0.06	0.09	0.06	0.03	−51.90	−30.20	−44.51
Sweden	0.03	0.22	0.09	0.06	0.04	0.03	0.01	−78.36	−97.29	−90.58
UK	0.35	0.44	0.35	0.06	0.02	0.02	0.03	−92.73	−94.21	−57.51
USA	0.26	0.17	0.07	0.06	0.04	0.04	0.01	−95.64	−93.22	−80.59

Source: ILO Laboursta and OECD

TABLE 3.9. *Factor Analysis*

Factor	Eigenvalue	Difference	Proportion	Cumulative
Factor1	4.16	3.05	0.59	0.59
Factor2	1.10	0.41	0.16	0.75
Factor3	0.70	0.18	0.10	0.85
Factor4	0.52	0.22	0.07	0.92
Factor5	0.30	0.15	0.04	0.97
Factor6	0.15	0.08	0.02	0.99
Factor7	0.08	.	0.01	1.00

Factor loadings and unique variances

Variable	Factor1	Factor2	Uniqueness
Union density	0.70		0.40
Barg coverage	0.74		0.42
Barg level	0.95		0.10
Barg level weighted	0.93		0.13
Coordination	0.93		0.12
Social pacting	0.71		0.49
Conflict rate		0.96	0.07

Notes: Number of observations: 105. Retained factors (unrotated): 2. Blanks represent abs(loading) < 0.5.

bargaining level weighted by the presence of opening clauses, bargaining coordination, the prevalence of social pacts and conflict rate. Due to poor data coverage, employer density has not been included in the factor analysis. The data are in five-year averages. The method used for extracting the factors is the method of principal components. The results of the factor analysis are reported in Table 3.9.

Two factors with eigenvalues greater than one emerge, jointly accounting for 75 percent of the cumulative variation in the data. Interestingly, the two (unrotated) factors lend themselves to a straightforward interpretation. The first factor is very strongly positively correlated with both indicators of bargaining level (weighted and unweighted) and with the indicator of bargaining coordination (factor loadings greater than 0 .9), and has a strong correlation with union density, bargaining coverage, and social pacting (factor loadings greater than or equal to 0.7). In other words, a country scoring high (low) on the first factor has highly (lowly) centralized and coordinated bargaining, high (low) union density, high (low) bargaining coverage, and high (low) prevalence of social pacts. Hence the first factor captures the dimension of *industrial relations institutionalization*. The second factor has an extremely high correlation with the conflict rate (factor loading of 0 .96) and modest correlation with all other variables (the other factor loadings are below 0.5 and hence not shown

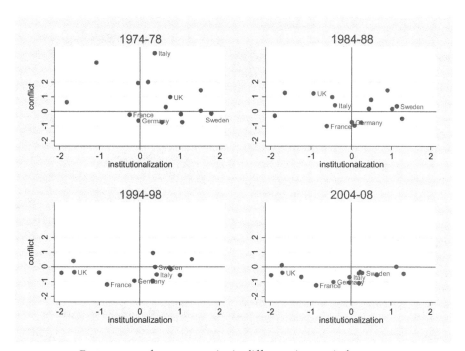

FIGURE 3.5. Factor scores for 15 countries in different time periods

in the table). This factor captures the *level of conflict*. By construction, the two principal components are orthogonal to one another.

Figure 3.5 plots the average *institutionalization* and *mobilization* scores for the 15 countries at ten-year intervals: 1974–1978 (on average); 1984–1988; 1994–1998; 2004–2008. To avoid cluttering the graphs, only France, Germany, Italy, Sweden and the United Kingdom are identified on the graphs. The most evident feature of Figure 3.5 is the generalized decline in conflict for all countries in the sample: the graph seems to have migrated southward progressively over time. Particularly impressive is the decline of conflict in Italy. However, there is no generalized westward shift. Although the de-institutionalization of the UK industrial relations system stands out when 1974–1978 and 2004–2008 are compared, the dispersion of countries has not shrunk over time.

Figure 3.6 plots the evolution of factor scores by country groupings: Nordic countries (Denmark, Finland, Norway and Sweden); (2) continental CMEs (Austria, Belgium, Germany and the Netherlands); (3) LMEs (Australia, Canada, Ireland, the United Kingdom and the United States); and (4) mixed economies (France and Italy). The graphs reveal that all countries follow the same trajectory of change, even though they start from different initial positions. For all groupings the direction of change is from the northeast (higher conflict and institutionalization scores) to the southwest (lower conflict and

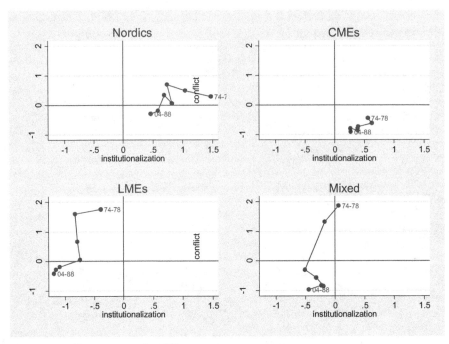

FIGURE 3.6. Factor scores for different country groupings

institutionalization scores). Consistent with common wisdom, Nordic industrial relations systems were more strongly "institutionalized" than others in 1974–1978, followed by CMEs, mixed economies, and LMEs in order; and all country groupings have a lower institutionalization score in 2004–2008 than they had at the beginning. However, although all industrial relations systems have undergone deinstitutionalization, differences across country groupings remain and Nordic countries are still slightly more institutionalized than continental CMEs, as well as considerably more institutionalized than mixed economies and LMEs.

3.3 Assessing the Trajectory of Change

The quantitative analysis presented in this chapter suggests the following conclusions: (1) There has been a generalized decline of union density. For the Nordic countries and Belgium this decline began in the early 1990s as opposed to the early 1980s, that is, later than for other countries. (2) With some exceptions, union decline has been stronger in the manufacturing sector than in the public sector, while unionization in labor-intensive services was and still is lower than in the other sectors. (3) Based on available data, it seems that employer density has not declined to the same extent as union density. In other words, class actors have not undergone the same extent of organizational decline. (4) There is a clear cross-country trend toward the decentralization of collective bargaining. This trend becomes more visible when indicators of bargaining structure take into account the diffusion of opening clauses. (5) Industrial conflict has declined dramatically everywhere.

Arguments trying to determine whether national industrial relations systems are stable or fundamentally changing, and if so if they are converging toward one another, run the risk of falling into what logicians call a sorites paradox. The sorites paradox was first attributed to an ancient Greek philosopher, Eubulides of Miletus. It was stated in various equivalent forms, one of which had to do with a man losing his hair: "Would you say that a man with an arbitrarily high number of hairs on his head is hirsute?" "Would you also say that if a hirsute man loses one hair he is still hirsute?" It would be natural to answer positively to both propositions, but then one would also have to admit, by repeated application of the second premise, that a man who has lost a very large number of hairs is still hirsute. The deduction is perfectly legitimate by the standards of classical logic, as it only involves modus ponens ("if p then q", but "p," so then "q") and the chaining together of individually true propositions, and yet it stands in sharp contrast with common sense.

The paradox applies to all propositions involving slow accumulation or depletion of a particular quality, including propositions such as "an industrial relations system in which a number of companies decentralize their bargaining structures is still fundamentally stable." It is widely acknowledged that the origin of the paradox lies in the vagueness of natural language, which does not permit the precise identification of the boundaries within which a predicate applies. Artificial languages eliminate this kind of paradoxes by introducing predicates with sharp cutoff points at which the propositions' truth values shift from true to false, such as when a diabetic patient is defined in medical language as somebody with a blood sugar of more than 7 mmol/l. However, such cutoff points are often somewhat arbitrary and everyone may not be willing to agree to them. In the absence of sharp cutoff points, trying to determine the truth status of soritical propositions such as the ones reported above is inherently flawed: when looking at what philosophers of language call the *penumbra*, a state where it is not patently clear which predicate should apply, one observer may consider that the balding man has not fundamentally changed his hirsute status and another that he has. In this case, the only nonarbitrary thing to do is to try to assess the direction of the process without seeking to decide the truth value of the soritical proposition. The question becomes, Is the man in question losing or gaining hair?

The factor scores presented above lend themselves rather nicely to the definition of a sharp cutoff point for liberalization. For the five countries this book focuses upon – France, Germany, Italy, Sweden and the United Kingdom – we conventionally identify a threshold score after which industrial relations can be considered liberalized and then compare the various countries at particular

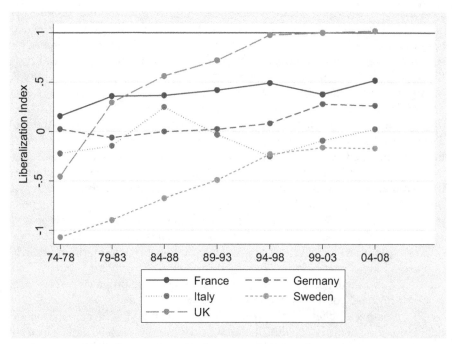

FIGURE 3.7. Liberalization indices for five countries (United Kingdom 1989–1993 = 1)

points in time with this benchmark. We concentrate on the first factor capturing institutionalization and choose the average value of Britain between 1989
and 1993 as a reference point. This choice is a convention but not an unjustified one: In Britain liberalization started earliest and proceeded further than in
the other countries. We consider that by the late 1980s/early 1990s, the British
industrial relations system had been liberalized. Having identified the point of
comparison, we then construct a liberalization index as the ratio between the
institutionalization factor score for each country–period and the anchor. The
liberalization index is growing, and higher values express higher levels of liberalization. The United Kingdom in 1989–1993 has a value of one, by definition.
A value of one or higher signifies that the threshold for a fully liberalized system has been passed. This index provides some indication of where the different
countries stand on the liberalization continuum.

Figure 3.7 displays the liberalization indices for the five countries. It suggests
that all five have been moving in parallel toward the liberalization threshold,
but only the United Kingdom has actually crossed it. At the beginning of the
period (1974–1978), Sweden was the outlier as a highly nonliberal case, with
the other four countries clustered around the middle of the distribution. At
the end of the period (2004–2008), the United Kingdom was the outlier as
a highly liberal case, but the other four cases had all undergone considerable

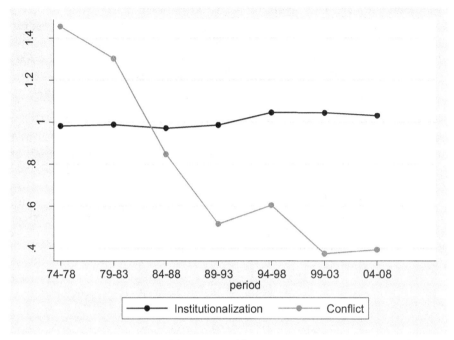

FIGURE 3.8. Plot of the standard deviations of factors 1 (institutionalization) and 2 (conflict) over time

liberalization, although from different initial conditions and without reducing their relative distances.

The factor scores also allow us to produce an operational definition of convergence. We would say that industrial relations systems are converging if the standard deviations of the two factors identified above, institutionalization and industrial conflict, decline over time, in other words, if the distributions of the factors become less disperse over time. Figure 3.8 plots the standard deviations of the two factors across time periods for all fifteen countries. While there is clear evidence of shrinking dispersion on the conflict dimension, no declining trend is visible for institutionalization. Thus, the available quantitative indicators suggest that there has been convergence with regard to industrial quiescence, but not with regard to the composite dimension of institutionalization (which includes bargaining centralization and coordination, social pacting, union membership and bargaining coverage). On this latter dimension, advanced countries continue to differ greatly, although they have all been moving in the same direction.

If the quantitative evidence suggests persistent institutional divergence on the institutionalization axis, why do we insist on using the language of convergence? The answer is that the currently available quantitative indicators are at best suitable to capture liberalization qua institutional deregulation but have little to say about liberalization as institutional conversion. As we argue in the next chapters, we have reason to believe that although the range of institutional diversity may not have shrunk, the outcomes produced by different institutions are increasingly convergent, as they allow an increased level of employer discretion in all cases. In the next five chapters we engage in historical analyses of Britain, France, Germany, Italy and Sweden. These countries provide ample variation in starting points and institutional endowments: Britain and Germany are respectively the quintessential LME and CME; Sweden has often featured prominently in comparative political economy because of the combination of strongly centralized collective bargaining, strong unions and social democratic dominance; France and Italy are notoriously difficult to classify, but they are worth examining in detail because of their size and economic importance and for the particularity of their postwar trajectories. In brief, the five cases seem well suited to test our main claim that behind national peculiarities there has been a common neoliberal direction in industrial relations.

4

Constructing a Liberal Market Economy

The Collapse of Collective Regulation in Britain

The British case fits somewhat uneasily with the others examined in this book. That is not because it refutes our central claim that industrial relations institutions have been subject to transformational change in a neoliberal direction. On the contrary, British industrial relations underwent decollectivization on a massive scale in a relatively short period of time, a process powerfully characterized as "the end of institutional industrial relations" (Purcell 1993). Two factors set the British case apart. First, institutional change occurred primarily through the direct erosion and ultimately the dismantling of existing institutions, rather than the mechanisms of institutional plasticity and reengineering described in other cases; the task of identifying institutional change, in other words, is straightforward and visible to the naked eye.

Second, the last thirty-five years divide into a first period in which decollectivization took place under a series of Conservative governments, and a second in which there was a partial re-regulation of the labor market under the auspices of New Labour governments, offering a rebuff, albeit an extremely limited one, to neoliberalism. Re-regulation took the form not of a return to collectivism – trade union density and collective bargaining continued to decline – but of an enhanced role for the state through legislation and state agencies. Thus, while the trajectory of change has not been uniformly neoliberal, the current resting point for British industrial relations is itself deeply neoliberal, characterized by a highly flexible labor market and decentralized, individualized institutions. The Conservative–Liberal Democrat coalition government elected in 2010, and reelected in 2015 without the participation of the Liberal Democrats, has not disturbed this emerging consensus.

4.1 The Peak of the Collective Regulation Regime

By the end of the 1970s, Britain was widely understood to have an industrial relations system characterized by a very high degree of collective regulation on the part of employers and unions (nicely captured by Otto Kahn-Freund's term "collective laissez faire"), a largely abstentionist state and a powerful labor movement (Howell 2005: Chapter 3). The institutions of industrial relations, and indeed trade unions themselves, were decentralized to the level of the firm and workplace. The result was quite limited employer discretion, as conditions of employment and the organization of work were subject to joint regulation: "It reflected a degree of routine local union influence over the conduct of work that is beyond the dreams of most twenty-first century trade union activists" (Brown and Edwards 2009:7).

An earlier system of industrial relations, inherited from the interwar period, which rested upon industry-level bargaining with limited formal regulatory institutions inside the workplace, began to give way in the 1950s under pressure from Fordist firms seeking to manage economic change and boost productivity (Howell 2005: Chapter 4). The diagnosis of a Royal Commission investigating industrial relations (known colloquially as the Donovan Commission after its chair), which reported in 1968, argued that the formal (industry-level) and informal (decentralized) industrial relations systems were in conflict (Royal Commission on Trade Unions and Employers' Associations 1968: paragraph 149), leading to Flanders' famous conclusion that "managers could only regain control by sharing it" with unions (cited in Kessler and Bayliss 1998: 36). The result, largely complete by the early 1980s, was to transform British industrial relations, as collective bargaining, dispute resolution, joint regulation and union structures all migrated downward to the firm level.

While the institutions of collective regulation were strengthened and decentralized in the 1960s and 1970s, trade union ideology, particularly with regard to the British state, remained unchanged. "Voluntarism" was the label given to this ideology, and it captured the remarkable self-confidence of British unions: their belief in the independent strength of unions and their ability to bargain with employers and extract benefits for their members without the need for extensive statutory protection or regulation on the part of the state. Unions expected (and received) immunities from tort in the case of industrial disputes, but beyond that, strongly preferred collective to statutory regulation. It reflected "the notion that unions have, as it were, lifted themselves into their present position of power and influence by their own unaided efforts" (Flanders 1974:355). This was a view of labor power that was shared by academic analysis; as Kahn-Freund pithily put it, "What the State has not given the State cannot take away" (cited in McCarthy 1992:6). And it was a view that could only be strengthened by the experience of 1969–72 when efforts by two different governments to constrain the right to strike were turned back by labor movement resistance, and indeed a strong case can be made that the 1970–74 Conservative government was brought down by the trade unions.

While this perspective fails to recognize the important role of the British state in constructing, extending the coverage of, and maintaining industrial relations institutions (Howell 2005), it is indisputable that by the end of the

1970s an industrial relations system had come into being that institutionalized collective regulation directly inside the firm, and extended joint regulation – effectively codetermination – beyond pay, hours and dispute procedures to the whole range of issues related to labor productivity; the scope of decentralized bargaining was greatly expanded (Brown and Batstone 1981). Shop stewards, the most visible face of local union power, grew from roughly 90,000 in 1961 to 317,000 in 1980 and spread well beyond blue collar workers in manufacturing (Terry 1983: 67). Growth in trade union membership and density accelerated in the 1970s, reaching a peak of 13.4 million and 55.4% in 1979, with two-thirds of the growth coming from white collar workers (Bain and Price 1983:5). By this point approximately 85% of British workers were covered by collective pay-setting mechanisms of some kind, whether collective bargaining or the Wages Councils set up for low-paid sectors (Milner 1995).

The result was limited employer discretion across the whole gamut of workplace organization and management of labor, but the constraints on that discretion came primarily from the preferences of managers themselves, as we shall see below, and the capacity of trade unions to bring employers to the negotiating table or the joint consultative committees that sprang up inside so many British firms. Statutory regulation remained limited and of recent origin, with, for example, protection from unfair dismissal not appearing until the 1971 Industrial Relations Act (Davies and Freedland 1993).

By 1979, British industrial relations institutions approached the archetype of a collective regulation model: tripartism characterized social and economic policy making through a network of corporatist institutions and practices, including frequent recourse to incomes policies; collective pay setting dominated the industrial relations landscape through a combination of direct and indirect mechanisms; work organization was subject to joint regulation in much of manufacturing and the public sector; and public policy itself unambiguously supported collective regulation.

4.2 Crisis and Change

In retrospect, the end of the 1970s was the peak both of trade union strength and of the collective regulation regime. That system of industrial relations has disintegrated in the ensuing three decades and more, to be replaced by ever smaller islands of collective bargaining threatened by a rising sea of individualized bargaining and unilateral employer discretion, all underpinned by a minimalist framework of rights embedded in labor law. Understanding the rapid turnaround and the scale of institutional change in industrial relations is not straightforward. The expectation of the British academic community in the mid-1970s was well captured by Goldthorpe's claim that "British industrial relations are simply not in any far-reaching way reformable" (Goldthorpe 1974: 452).

What changed was the role of the British state, which ended its almost eighty-year support for collective bargaining, and the interests of employers and thus their investment in the collective regulation regime. This began as a political dynamic rather than an economic one. A political consensus had existed through the early 1960s between the two major parties concerning the public policy benefits of a strong trade union movement and collective laissez faire. This broke down in the context of the highly politicized nature of the "labor question" in Britain, especially with the downfall of the Heath government in 1974, which elements of the Conservative Party blamed on trade union resistance to the Industrial Relations Act, and then the collapse of the "Social Contract" in the wave of public sector strikes during the so-called Winter of Discontent, in 1978–79, culminating in the election of a new Conservative government led by Margaret Thatcher in 1979. To this can be added the perception of union responsibility for what were largely understood to be short-term problems of British capitalism: inflation, balance of payments crises, lack of confidence in sterling and budget deficits.

The degree to which trade unions were in fact responsible for Britain's economic problems (Hall 1986: Chapter 2), or to which the Winter of Discontent reflected union power rather than its opposite, mattered less than the perception, particularly in the context of media hostility to labor and its role in the construction of a narrative of crisis (Hay 1996).

Thus, it was the state that initially took the lead in the reconstruction of British industrial relations. Contrary to the expectations of the academic industrial relations community, trade unions proved to be much more dependent upon resources provided by the state, and the state's support for the institutions of collective regulation, than anticipated. The British labor movement had largely internalized the assumption of its own independent strength embedded in voluntarist ideology, and, in the absence of positive collective rights or an organizing tradition, this made it more vulnerable to the removal of state support. Flanders had argued that "the tradition of voluntarism cannot be legislated against" (Flanders 1974: 365), but the experience of the last three decades indicates that indeed it can, to devastating effect.

Initially employers, and certainly front-line managers, seemed content with the decentralized system of collective bargaining and joint regulation that emerged in the 1960s and 1950s; indeed they drove it, seeking ways of managing change inside the workplace. Managers were the "true disciples" (Clegg quoted in McCarthy 1992: 36) of the Donovan Commission Report, and survey evidence from the end of the 1970s shows strong support among managers for decentralized bargaining with shop stewards (Batstone 1988). Employers were not, for the most part, opposed to the direction of post-1979 industrial relations legislation, certainly the first two packages of legislation in 1980 and 1982. Conflict between the government and employers over industrial relations was limited. But it is also true that state policy was usually ahead of the demands of the bulk of employers; that is, employers tended to approve legislation once enacted, but the legislation itself was not driven by active, enthusiastic lobbying from business. That became more and more true as the 1980s progressed, and the intent of legislation shifted from its initial goals of limiting the circumstances under which legal strikes could take place to the broader decollectivist transformation of industrial relations. The consultative papers issued by Conservative governments prior to legislation were likely, from 1984 onward, to elicit concerns from employers about the disruption of established industrial relations. Yet, once they were implemented, employer concerns tended to disappear.

Thus, the state prodded employers in particular directions and shaped how employers thought about the acceptable limits of their ability to change their industrial relations practices. As time went on, the words and actions of Conservative governments gave employers confidence that their efforts to resist trade unions and collective bargaining would be aided and encouraged by state action; by making strikes less likely and more costly to workers and trade unions, the British state changed the calculus facing employers as they considered changing their industrial relations practices. As Dunn and Metcalf have argued, the real importance of Conservative industrial relations legislation lay in encouraging the "slow build-up in management confidence to resist unionization" (Dunn and Metcalf 1994: 22).

However, while the state created a context in which employers had greater freedom to choose how to deal with their workforces, the fact remains that over time, employers used that freedom to choose very different arrangements. Those choices reflected the changing structure of British capitalism and with it, the changing interests of employers. The series of workplace industrial relations surveys[1] have demonstrated that the transformation in industrial relations was for the most part a result of the difference in the industrial relations practices of dying and new firms, rather than changes in the practices of continuing firms, and Machin (2000) has argued that in the private sector the key variable explaining changes in union strength is the age of the workplace. Union recognition rates are much lower in workplaces that have been set up since 1980, and that effect becomes more marked over time. Thus, the transformation of British industrial relations is primarily the product of newer firms, with different sets of interests, being able, courtesy of Conservative policy and legislation, to choose to avoid collective regulation.

The structural changes to British capitalism are familiar to students of comparative political economy; the processes of international integration, deindustrialization, demographic change and flexibility affected all advanced capitalist economies. Yet when faced with the resultant economic pressures, different countries responded in different ways. It was the interaction of international and domestic economic developments, played out on a field of national

---

[1] Many of the best data on industrial relations developments in Britain come from six workplace surveys, conducted in 1980, 1984, 1990, 1998, 2004 and 2011.

institutions, that generated the specific strategies pursued by the state and class actors in Britain. Many of the distinctive institutional features of British capitalism (Hall 1986) – the absence of employer coordination, of long-term relationships between industrial and financial capital and of the capacity for coordinated wage bargaining – had the effect of encouraging a response to any intensification of international competitive pressure through cost reduction and low wage/low skill strategies (Wood 2001). Under these circumstances, it is no surprise that supply-side flexibility was eventually achieved in Britain in a quite different manner, one associated with unilateral managerial control, the decollectivization of social relations and labor market deregulation. What has been termed "hyperflexibility" in the British case (Amoore 2002), was a natural, though certainly not inevitable, variant of post-Fordism.

This has obvious implications for industrial relations. As Heery (2002) has pointed out, a social partnership model of industrial relations needs large firms, dominant in their markets, able to pursue high quality, high value-added strategies, to thrive. The British economy, characterized by smaller firms in competitive markets, pursuing cost-reduction strategies, was more likely to produce social conflict than social partnership. The role and value of trade unions and collective regulation are less clear under these circumstances.

The significance of the economic shifts noted above has primarily been their effect on the interests of employers. As the internationalization of the British economy, and demands for flexibility, increased, employers sought different relationships with their employees (Boswell and Peters 1997). The greater importance attached to flexibility in this period undermined the collective basis of that system of industrial relations, because employers increasingly wanted to differentiate in the terms and conditions of their employees. This made collective bargaining for large groups less attractive to employers. In the 1960s and 1970s employers sought to buy out restrictive practices in the workplace, and they used collective bargaining as a mechanism for achieving that goal. In the current period, they are more likely to seek an individualization of their relationship with their employees, rendering collective representation problematic.

4.3 The Conservative Onslaught on Collective Regulation

The story of Conservative industrial relations reform between 1979 and 1997 has been told often and in great detail (Davies and Freedland 1993, Howell 2005, Marsh 1992), so its elements need only be summarized in this section. But even a summary must capture the scale of institutional change. By early in the 1990s, a study of workplace industrial relations could conclude that "so great were the changes that it is not unreasonable to conclude that the traditional, distinctive 'system' of British industrial relations no longer characterized the economy as a whole" (Millward et al. 1992: 350).

In place of a system of industrial relations organized around a dominant role for collective regulation, powerful trade unions and two-tier bargaining over not simply terms and conditions but also the organization of work is the unmistakable architecture of a new set of institutions, characterized by the wholesale decollectivization of industrial relations. This has involved the emasculation of collective representation, collective regulation and collective action and thus the individualization of social relations between employer and employee. The simultaneous decline in union membership, union recognition and collective bargaining means that we see the growing dominance of workplaces where management sets the terms and conditions of employment unilaterally, in some cases after consultation with employees, but with only minimal constraint from trade unions, national or industry level agreements or legislation protecting individual workers.

In contrast with earlier periods of institutional change in British industrial relations, which had relied upon administrative action and a more limited role for legislation, Conservative policy accorded primacy to the role of labor law in driving reform. This helps to explain why there were no fewer than six major pieces of Conservative industrial relations legislation, each one comprising several parts and addressing multiple themes, over the course of the eighteen-year-long period of Conservative governance. We will turn to the substance of this legislation below. However, the centrality of legislation should not detract from the importance of other, more indirect elements of policy, all of which pushed in the same direction. These included a contractionary macroeconomic policy that greatly loosened the labor market and accelerated deindustrialization; the opening up of the economy to greater international economic pressures and an expansion of inward investment (often accompanied by different industrial relations cultures); restructuring and privatization of the public sector in ways that encouraged new industrial relations policies; the dismantling of corporatist institutions and practices; and the demonstration effect of absorbing and winning public sector strikes.

Nonetheless, a distinctive feature of this period of industrial relations reform was the extent to which legislation sought to directly restructure industrial relations. When a piece of legislation did not appear to achieve the goals set for it, the response was further legislation, to "add another layer of cement" (Undy et al. 1996:74), rather than to seek nonlegislative solutions or to change the goals themselves. Conservative governments after 1979 had learned two key lessons from the failure of the 1971 Industrial Relations Act. The first was to move slowly, adding new pieces to the architecture of a new system of industrial relations "step-by-step" so that resistance on the part of the labor movement was more difficult than it would have been if the whole system had been visible at the start.

The second lesson was to make the legislation permissive. Government policy did not so much prescribe a particular model or form of industrial relations as remove restrictions (either in the form of legislative obstacles or on the capacity of trade unions to resist) upon the right of employers to choose the industrial relations arrangements that they deemed most appropriate. The

goal was to expand employer discretion. Whereas the 1971 Industrial Relations Act created a set of criminal liabilities for noncompliance, the legislation
of the 1980s and 1990s created only civil liabilities. It was up to employers to
choose whether to use the new legislation. This both minimized employer resistance to the legislation, because employers were not being forced to change their
industrial relations practices, and prevented the creation of trade union martyrs
around whom the labor movement could mobilize support.

That said, by the end of the 1980s, Conservative policy had become increasingly concerned not so much with eliminating abuses of collective bargaining and the collective representation of workers, and permitting employers to
deal with their employees as they wished, as with encouraging an individualization of industrial relations in which trade unions and collective bargaining had a limited role. Conservative ministers and government White Papers
urged unions to get out of the business of collective bargaining and instead
offer individual services to their members, and stressed the merits of individual contracts to employers, promising to support "the aspirations of individual
employees to deal directly with their employer, rather than through the medium
of trade union representation or collective bargaining" (Department of Employment 1992:15). The permissive nature of industrial relations legislation should
not distract from the fact that decollectivization was an explicit state strategy
between 1979 and 1997.

An analysis that emphasized the influence of Hayek on the Conservative legislative program (Wedderburn 1991: Chapter 8) identified its main themes: the
disestablishment of collectivism; the deregulation of employment law; the treatment of trade unions as unique organizations requiring extensive government
regulation, with priority given to the rights of individual members against the
union itself; and enterprise confinement, meaning that where unions operated,
their influence should be confined to the firm, and not extend beyond it. This
last point is also well made by Dunn and Metcalf (1994: 8):

If the first preference [of Conservative legislation] is to legislate collective bargaining
out of existence, diminishing unions to harmless friendly societies and workers' advice
bureaux, then, should that prove too difficult, the fallback position is to cordon off
union enclaves and prevent them contaminating the existing non-union sector and new-
born enterprises...if legislation stops the spread of collectivism among market rivals,
individual unionised companies and their employees have to face up to the costs of trade
unionism in an increasingly non-union world.

Conservative governments made it clear that collective bargaining was no
longer considered a public policy good and that they would support employers
who sought new relationships with their employees. In some cases (the replacement of collective bargaining with personal contracts, for example), legislation legalized employer practice after courts had ruled against that practice. In
short, the climate of industrial relations fostered by the state gave employers the

confidence to experiment with new industrial relations institutions and practices of their own.

The main elements of the avalanche of industrial relations legislation can be summarized under a number of headings. First, those related to industrial action, which in Britain depended upon the provision of immunity from civil and criminal liability. Here Conservative legislation sought to narrow the conditions under which industrial action was protected by immunity. A distinction was made between primary and secondary (or sympathetic) action, and the latter lost all immunity. Similarly, the definition of a trade dispute (for which protection existed) was narrowed to cover only immediate terms and conditions of work. In recognition of the impact of mass "flying" pickets in the mining strikes of the 1970s, picketing was also restricted to only permit picketing of one's own place of work, and to limit the number of pickets. From 1984 onward, industrial action was only protected if a ballot was held in advance. This requirement became progressively more highly regulated. Legislation determined the wording of ballots and the time limits on the use of ballots, and even required that employers be allowed to know the names of those balloted, creating the potential for intimidation. And from 1993 only postal ballots were allowed. Unless these enormously complicated regulations were followed, trade unions opened themselves up to liability for industrial action.

The central point about legislation in this area is that it contributed to the decollectivization of something inherently collective. Legislation sought to limit strike action to the workplace where the dispute arose, and to a narrow range of strictly economic issues. A requirement that a separate ballot be held for each workplace further undermined broader types of collective action. And postal ballots individualized participation on the assumption that a worker would respond differently to the likelihood of a strike when sitting at home filling out a ballot than when at a workplace meeting, surrounded by colleagues.

A second theme of the legislation was the regulation of trade union governance. Prior to 1979 (with the brief exception of 1971–74, when unions were expected to register under the Industrial Relations Act), governments had operated on the presumption that union autonomy in internal governance procedures was more important than external regulation. After 1979, this position was reversed. A high priority was given to enforcing a certain form of democratic process within unions. The legal regulation of strike ballots was part of this emphasis upon external regulation. Legislation also required that key national positions within trade unions, including the principal executive committee (whatever its exact name) and the union president or general secretary, be elected every five years (eventually insisting that postal ballots be used). Furthermore, the ability of unions to discipline their members, or limit their actions, was restricted by legislation. Finally, in a challenge to trade union funding for the Labour Party, in 1984 it was required that any trade union with a political fund should ballot its members on whether they wished to continue to support such a fund every ten years. No equivalent legislation was introduced to give company shareholders a vote on business contributions to political parties; trade unions were regarded as unique organizations.

A third theme was the removal of state support for trade union activity in general and collective bargaining in particular. The institutions of collective regulation of industrial relations in Britain, constructed from the 1890s onward, had always depended upon support of one kind or another from both the state and employers. Legislation in the 1980s and 1990s largely removed any form of state support and limited the statutory duty of employers to provide support for unions and collective bargaining. In 1980, both the short-lived statutory union recognition procedure and provisions for unilateral arbitration were abolished. The latter had been a mechanism for the extension of collective bargaining, permitting unions to sweep up firms that refused to participate in industry bargaining agreements. The Fair Wage Resolution was also rescinded. Successive pieces of legislation after 1979 also chipped away at the closed shop – a mechanism for preventing free riding by employees where unions were recognized – until finally outlawing it altogether in 1990.

Conservative legislation also minimized the effects of the 1975 Employment Protection Act by limiting the range of duties for which employers were required to give time off to union officials and reducing the requirement that union officials be paid for time undertaken for union training. In 1993, government financial support for union training was also phased out. The prior assumption had been that good industrial relations depended upon well-trained and resourced union officials in the workplace, and that the state and employers should, in effect, subsidize these activities. This was reversed after 1979, thereby pushing the cost exclusively onto trade unions themselves.

Finally, collective bargaining lost its imprimatur as a public policy good in itself. This occurred symbolically in 1993 when the Advisory, Conciliation and Arbitration Service's (ACAS) statutory duty to encourage collective bargaining was removed. This was the formal end to a public presumption in favor of collective regulation that had existed since the end of the 1890s. Another provision of the 1993 Trade Union Reform and Employment Rights Act went further, in permitting employers to provide financial inducements to employees to opt out of collective bargaining agreements and adopt "personal" (individual) contracts. Previously it had been accepted that such action would discriminate against union membership and hence be illegal. But a crucial distinction was drawn between union membership, which remained protected, and having a trade union as collective bargaining agent, which was not. This provision reflected an ever more influential discourse in the early and mid-1990s that emphasized trade unions as providers of individual services to members rather than as collective actors representing workers in their collective relationships with an employer or group of employers. As such, it epitomized the decollectivist logic of this period.

A fifth theme was labor market deregulation. Protection from unfair dismissal was watered down by removing the burden of proof from employers and increasing the length of service before employees came under the umbrella of unfair dismissal legislation from six months to two years. The Wages Councils, Britain's only form of statutory minimum wage legislation, first had their powers reduced and then in 1993 were abolished, leaving Britain with no statutory minimum wage. Nevertheless, measures to deregulate the labor market were relatively few in Britain for the simple reason that legislation had never played much of a role in regulating employment relations. The legacy of collective laissez faire meant that trade union strength was the main obstacle to a flexible labor market.

However, it is important to note the passage of some legislation providing new employment rights, partially reregulating the labor market. This apparent contradiction is resolved by noting that the bulk of the new employment rights came to Britain courtesy of European directives. Thus, the 1993 Trade Union Reform and Employment Rights Act contained provisions to comply with the EC Pregnant Workers' Directive, the EC Proof of Employment Directive, the EC Health and Safety Framework Directive and the EC Acquired Rights Directive (Davies and Freedland 2007:28).

The public sector was an important site of industrial relations reform, though here legislation was not alone in shaping the construction of a new set of institutions for the regulation of class relations. The British state had long used the public sector as a "model employer," to provide a demonstration to private sector employers of those industrial relations practices preferred by public policy. Conservative governments after 1979 had a radically different vision of public sector industrial relations. State policy shifted from using the public sector as a model employer to importing private sector best practice to the public sector. In other words, the public sector was now to learn from and emulate the private sector, not vice versa (Carter and Fairbrother 1999). For the most part, the reform of public sector industrial relations took place indirectly as a result of the wider restructuring of the public sector, relying upon exposing public sector managers, trade unions and workers to market forces, in the expectation that this would lead to changes in industrial relations institutions and practices. Where it could, the Conservative government reduced the size of the public sector, in the belief that market forces would impose different industrial relations practices upon the newly privatized firms. For those industries and services that remained in the public sector, market surrogates were introduced, and public sector industrial relations were reorganized (Beaumont 1992, Seifert 1992).

The list of privatized industries included steel, gas, electricity, water, telecommunications, coal and rail. The total number of people working in the public sector fell by one-third, from 7.4 million in 1979 to 5 million in 1998, with the great bulk of the decline resulting from privatization as the workforce of the nationalized industries fell by 83%, from 1.8 million to less than one-third of a million (Labour Research Department 1999: 97).

It is difficult to generalize about the industrial relations practices of newly privatized firms. There was little explicit derecognition of trade unions in privatized firms, not least because unions tend to be well entrenched with large memberships, though the water companies and electricity supply were important exceptions. In practically every case, privatization resulted in the end of national bargaining and instead a decentralization to either regional centers or different business groups (Labour Research Department 1994). Additionally, privatization has almost always been followed by broad-ranging flexibility agreements, including multitasking and performance-related pay.

Restructuring of the public sector itself gathered pace from the late 1980s on, emphasizing greater autonomy for local units of the public sector – hospitals and schools, for example – while also injecting some form of competition into the public sector, such as "contracting out" and then "compulsory tendering," which forced public sector union employees to compete with private contractors in the provision of certain services.

Mention must also be made of a willingness to endure and win strikes in the public sector. Early examples were British Rail and British Leyland, but pride of place must go to the mineworkers' strike in 1984–85. This strike was in many ways the defining moment for Conservative industrial relations policy and a microcosm of the range and scope of state action employed in the restructuring of British industrial relations; even the intelligence services were drawn into the conflict. Once the mineworkers had been defeated, the coal industry was privatized and mine closures and layoffs have to all intents and purposes eliminated the industry.[2]

Finally, in the public sector, pay determination for increasing numbers of public sector employees was removed from collective bargaining and placed instead under the auspices of Pay Review Bodies (PRBs), which make pay recommendations based upon broad comparability criteria. Whereas PRBs established prior to 1979 were used for groups that did not engage in collective bargaining (doctors, dentists, the armed forces), those established after 1979 involved groups that had previously had collective bargaining rights, such as nurses and teachers. Almost one million people were removed from collective bargaining, increasing the number covered by PRBs by two-thirds during the Conservative period in office (Bailey 1994: 123–25). It is worth noting that this was a policy continued and extended by Labour governments after 1997. In 2004 the *Agenda for Change* was implemented, transferring another more than a million employees of the National Health Service to an independent pay review body.

The last theme of Conservative industrial relations policy was the elimination of any vestiges of corporatism in Britain. Tripartism and union access to

---

[2] At the time of the strike, the NUM had 180,000 members employed in 170 pits. By the time Arthur Scargill retired from leadership of the NUM early in 2002, membership was estimated at 3000, with only 13 pits remaining, all privately owned (Wainwright and Nelsson 2002).

government came to an abrupt halt after 1979. High-level contacts between the TUC and Conservative governments were very limited, and the tripartite bodies of greatest importance to the trade unions – the Manpower Services Commission and the National Economic Development Council, probably the most potent symbol of the postwar "British Consensus" – were first weakened and then abolished (Mitchell 1987).

Later in this chapter we will summarize the effects of Conservative industrial relations policy. At this point it suffices to say that almost every institution of British industrial relations was touched by these reforms, and that the consistent direction of change was toward decollectivization, decentralization and deregulation, all with the ultimate goal of expanding employer discretion.

4.4 The Emergence of a New Industrial Relations Consensus After 1997

Something approaching a political consensus on the institutions of industrial relations had existed in Britain from 1894, when the Royal Commission on Labour had first articulated the public policy good of collective bargaining between trade unions and employers' organizations, until the election of a Conservative government led by Thatcher in 1979. The torrent of legislation and associated public policy that sought to undermine collective regulation ended that consensus. The return of a Labour government, one still institutionally linked to the trade union movement, might have been expected to reverse course. In fact, it marked the emergence of a tentative new consensus, one largely endorsed by the Conservative–Liberal Democratic coalition government elected in 2010 and the Conservative-only government elected in 2015.

In 1997, a Labour government returned to power after eighteen years of Conservative rule and survived for thirteen years before losing office in 2010. The Labour party had been transformed during its years of opposition, rebranding itself as "New Labour," pursuing what its leader, Tony Blair, called "the Third Way." Its approach to the labor market was to endorse the necessity of a flexible, minimally regulated labor market with a significant low-wage, low-skill sector; there was no serious effort to reposition Britain within the international division of labor, and indeed any such effort would have been enormously difficult in light of the absence of coordinating institutions, as noted above. Thus, while the industrial relations agenda of New Labour differed in some respects from those of its Conservative predecessor, they were fundamentally convergent with the decollectivist thrust of the Conservative industrial relations reforms (Smith 2009). The distinctiveness of New Labour's approach to industrial relations lay, rather, in the government's emphasis upon the creation of individual rights at work, rather than support (legislative or otherwise) for the collective regulation of class relations.

New Labour had an essentially unitarist conception of industrial relations. Blair argued that the interests of business and labor were not opposed:

"My vision is where the boundaries between management and workforce erode...the government's programme [is] to replace the notion of conflict between employers and employees with the promotion of partnership" (Department of Trade and Industry 1998: Foreword). The role of labor law, then, was to "put a very minimum infrastructure of decency and fairness around people in the workplace" (ibid.). Fairness and competitiveness go hand in hand; there is no conflict between them because "a competitive and growing economy itself requires a culture of fairness and opportunity at work so that Britain can harness the talents of our people" (ibid.). But for New Labour, fairness was in the service of competitiveness, not the other way round. Regulation of the labor market was always to be undertaken with an eye to its effects upon efficiency and competitiveness (Davies and Freedland 2007).

The primary task of industrial relations institutions was not to correct an imbalance of power in the workplace, but to create a context in which the productivity and creativity of workers was properly harnessed for the good of the firm:

> Let us build trades unions and businesses that are creative, not conservative, unions that show they can work with management to make better companies. Let us build unions that people join not just out of fear of change or exploitation but because they are committed to success, unions that look forwards not backwards and that support workers and foster the true adaptability they need to be secure in that competitive and fast changing world. (Blair 1997)

Thus, there has been no return to a public presumption in favor of the collective regulation of class relations. The government has repeatedly argued that trade unions need to demonstrate value to employers. Their role is to provide services to their members and help firms become more competitive, not to protect their members from employers; it is individual rights at work enshrined in legislation, not unions, that serve this protective function. This explains why state regulation under a Labour government remained highly restrictive of the ability to engage in industrial action, but did encourage minimum rights and a voice for workers.

It should be noted that British trade unions, which were utterly marginalized during the years of Conservative rule, did play a more substantial part in making the case for the main directions of New Labour industrial relations reform. The experience of Thatcherism led the labor movement to abandon its long-standing voluntarism and to recognize the value of positive rights and legal support for workers and trade unions. Of most importance in this regard was union support for a statutory union recognition mechanism (Trade Union Congress 1995). Certainly, British unions were disappointed by the timid nature of New Labour reforms and would have liked substantial changes to the law surrounding industrial action. But it was a mark of their weakened and chastened state that trade unions nonetheless now finally understood their dependence upon a supportive framework of labor law.

New Labour pursued four main industrial relations reforms (Brown 2011; Howell 2004). First, a national statutory minimum wage was introduced for the first time in British history. Prior to 1993, when they were abolished, Wages Councils, composed of employer and labor representatives, set minimum terms and conditions in a set of traditionally low-wage industries as a form of embryonic collective bargaining. The use of national legislation to regulate low wages was a departure for a country with a tradition of collective laissez faire. After its implementation in 1999, the minimum wage was increased relative to the median wage (at least until 2008), but it was still set at a level that produced "only limited ripple effects" (Grimshaw and Rubery 2012: 111).

Second, New Labour ended Britain's opt-out from the Social Chapter of the European Union. This has had an accelerating impact on domestic labor law, as European directives have multiplied, particularly in the areas of "family friendly" policy (maternity and paternity leaves) and equal rights for atypical (part-time, temporary, agency) workers. However, it must be said that the New Labour government always chose to interpret these directives in the narrowest possible manner to minimize regulation of the labor market; it sought to limit the impact of directives related to worker consultation, and it won an opt-out from the maximum-work-hours provision of the Working Time Directive. Further, it opted out of the EU Charter of Fundamental Rights in 2007 because it would have given the European Court of Justice new powers to protect employment rights (Grimshaw and Rubery 2012).

The third element of industrial relations reform was the 1999 Employment Relations Act (ERA). This legislation had a number of features, including a new set of individual rights at work: more protection from unfair dismissal; a legal right for individuals to be accompanied by a fellow employee or union official in grievance hearings; protection from blacklisting for union membership; and protection from unfair dismissal during the first eight weeks of a strike. The ERA did contain one major collective right: a right to union recognition if a ballot showed majority support for a union. This right was hedged in important ways, in that it did not apply to small firms and required a turnout threshold on the ballot, but it was nonetheless a significant innovation in British labor law (a somewhat different form of union recognition legislation existed for half of the 1970s).

The fourth and final part of the reform agenda appeared in Labour's second and third terms and involved an overhaul of the employment tribunal system to reduce the number of cases being handled. The goal was explicitly to reduce the financial burden on employers. As part of this reform, the 2002 Employment Act created minimum statutory internal procedures covering dismissal and grievances inside firms (once again replacing a potential form of collective regulation with an individual juridical one). However, even this was considered too burdensome for business and the 2008 Employment Act replaced it with a statutory code of practice overseen by the ACAS.

The election of a Conservative–Liberal Democratic coalition government in 2010 did inaugurate a harsher phase of austerity with quite dramatic implications for public sector employment (Elliott 2010), but it did little to change the trajectory of British industrial relations (for a comprehensive survey see Williams and Scott 2016). It is possible that had the Conservatives achieved an absolute majority, more significant reform might have been envisaged, and certainly the largest British employers' organization has called for further limitations on the ability to engage in industrial action, justified on the grounds that the post-2008 economic crisis might embolden unions to resist layoffs (Confederation of British Industry 2010). However, indications prior to the election suggested that the Conservatives, rebranded under David Cameron, were largely content with the inherited industrial relations settlement (Williams and Scott 2010), and it is striking that the depth of the recession was not used as an excuse for extensive further legislation in this area. Even in the public sector, which bore the brunt of austerity measures in the aftermath of the financial and economic crisis, "most of the institutional architecture of social dialogue remains in place" (Bach and Stroleny 2012: 4); while wages were effectively frozen in the public sector after 2010, and substantial reductions in employment took place, there has been limited effort at an institutional restructuring of industrial relations (Bach and Stroleny 2012).

There were some small changes: an increase in the qualification period for benefiting from unfair dismissal protection and further measures to discourage bringing cases to employment tribunals (Hall 2012). But the coalition government declined to weaken the implementation of an EU directive protecting agency workers (despite CBI lobbying), and remains committed, rhetorically at least, to extending an important right to flexible work time, introduced by New Labour, to all parents. There is little question that there was an instinctive neoliberalism in the approach of the coalition government to economic, social and labor market policy, but one that did not translate into an effort to substantially rewrite the industrial relations settlement of the last two decades. This in part reflects the simple fact that the coalition inherited an already deeply deregulated system of labor law. To the extent that reforms were implemented after 2010, they targeted labor market regulations rather than collective rights, such as the union recognition procedure and what remains of the right to strike (Grimshaw and Rubery 2012).

However, in the run-up to the 2015 elections, and with the prospect of a dissolution of the Conservative–Liberal Democratic coalition, the Conservative Party announced that, if reelected, it would raise the threshold of votes needed for a strike to be legally valid in "core" public services, impose further limits on picketing, permit hiring of agency staff during strikes and create an opt-in mechanism for payment of union dues (Conservative Party 2015: 18–19). In July 2015, the newly elected Conservative government announced a package of legislation delivering on these promises and taking particular aim at strike ballots by introducing a 50% threshold of turnout for any strike ballot and an additional 40% threshold of support from all members eligible to vote in the health care, education and public transport sectors, among others (Department for Business 2015). This was followed by bringing to an end the direct debit of union dues for public sector workers. The changes in industrial relations institutions announced by the Conservative government have largely centered on the public sector because of the need to overcome resistance on the part of public sector unions to harsh austerity, but they also suggest a wider and continuing fixation with limiting collective action on the part of workers and their unions.

The overwhelming majority of Conservative industrial relations legislation dating from the onslaught of the 1980s and early 1990s remains in force and has been endorsed by New Labour and its Conservative–Liberal Democratic successor. To that basic framework of labor law was added after 1997 limited regulation of the labor market. This regulation took the form of individual legal rights, enforceable through labor courts and state agencies, not, for the most part, collective rights designed to strengthen trade unions, which could then take on the role of regulating social relations through collective bargaining. One consequence has been that with more limited recourse to workplace union representatives to advise workers of their rights, there has been a large increase in the use of employment tribunals and the ACAS advisory service as individualized arrangements replace unions (Advisory Conciliation and Arbitration Service 2008).

With few exceptions, any benefits that have accrued to unions – and there is limited evidence of benefit – have come indirectly, by virtue of a more regulated labor market or a new role as enforcers of legal rights. Of the two parallel tracks along which social relations have been regulated in Britain, as elsewhere in the advanced capitalist world – collective regulation by unions and legal regulation by the state – it is the latter that has become the focus of government attention. Thus, the current industrial relations settlement is best understood as a consolidation of, rather than a radical departure from, Thatcherism. It shares a broad acceptance of the current balance of social power in the workplace, a largely unitarist view of industrial relations, and, most fundamentally, an emphasis upon individual rather than collective regulation of social relations. The distinction between the approaches of Thatcherism and its successor governments, whether of the center left or center right, lies in the degree of labor market regulation undertaken by the state, not the agent of that regulation. Both largely reject collective regulation.

4.5 The Architecture of Contemporary British Industrial Relations

To what extent has the institutional architecture of British industrial relations changed in a neoliberal direction in the period since the heyday of collective regulation in the mid-1970s?[3] And given that employer discretion is our primary

---

[3] As noted earlier, a series of six workplace surveys conducted between 1980 and 2011 is a rich source of evidence of institutional change in industrial relations. The size threshold of firms

indicator of neoliberal transformation, to what degree and in what areas have employers expanded their ability to manage terms and conditions of employment, work organization, flexibility in its many forms and so on? Recall that the central obstacle to employer discretion in the 1960s and 1970s was a system of collective or joint regulation with trade unions, one deeply institutionalized at the workplace level, rather than a highly juridified industrial relations system in which labor law was the source of limitations upon managerial prerogative. As such, neoliberalism was always more likely to manifest itself through decollectivization than deregulation, and this indeed is what we have seen. The institutions for the collective regulation of industrial relations, which were central to both public policy and industrial relations practice in Britain for almost a century after 1890, are now almost certainly in terminal decline.[4]

To begin with trade union membership and density, which had been at their peak in 1979, both have been more than halved in the ensuing thirty years. Union membership now stands at 6.5 million with union density at 26.6%, though the density figure is heavily weighted toward the public sector: density in the private sector is only 14.2%, with the corresponding number for the public sector being 56.3% (Achur 2011). Roughly a third of the decline can be attributed to changes in workplace and workforce composition, but the remainder reflects changes in employer attitudes and practices, a preference "to 'go' or 'remain' non-union, or reduce the range of issues for which recognition is effective" (Blanchflower and Bryson 2009:56).

The strongest indicator of the institutionalization of labor power in the workplace, and of union capacity to engage in joint regulation of work, was the dramatic expansion of shop stewards in the course of the 1960s and 1970s. The more recent period has seen an equally precipitous decline, as the total number of stewards fell from about 330,000 in 1980 to an estimated 102,000 today (Charlwood and Forth 2009:79). In 2004, only 23% of firms employing 25 or more workers had any shop steward presence at all (ibid.: 77), and where workplace union representatives still exist, the bulk of their time is taken up by servicing members rather than engaging in negotiation.

Turning to collective bargaining, once again the coverage has collapsed, reflecting both the waning presence of unions and the near disappearance of industry-level bargaining. A once quite sizable gap between coverage of collective pay-setting mechanisms and union density (on the order of thirty percentage points in the 1970s) reflected both a role for industry bargaining (usually as

included has been gradually reduced over time, from firms employing 25 or more workers to those employing 10 or more, and more recently to those employing 5 or more, requiring that some caution be used in comparison across the full three decades of the surveys' existence. However, what is clear is a steady and continuous decline in all institutions of collective representation and collective regulation across that period.

4 The most comprehensive survey of the state of British unions in the contemporary period comes from the three-volume *The Future of Trade Unions in Britain* project (Gospel and Wood) (Fernie and Metcalf 2005, Gospel and Wood 2003, Kelly and Willman 2004).

part of two-tier bargaining) and such mechanisms as the Wages Councils. This gap has all but disappeared, as collective bargaining coverage fell to 30.8% in 2010, with the figure for the private sector being 16.8% (Achur 2011: 32). Multiemployer (industry-level) bargaining was only used for pay determination in 7% of workplaces employing 25 or more workers in 2004, 1% in the private sector (Kersley et al. 2005: 20), and of course the Wages Councils were abolished in 1993. In 2004, 85% of private sector workplaces employing 25 or more workers (and thus a much larger proportion of all workplaces) had wages principally determined unilaterally by management, with no role for collective bargaining (Brown, Bryson and Forth 2009: 34). Collective bargaining has remained stronger in the public sector, but even here there has been a substantial increase in the proportion of workplaces where no employees have their pay determined by collective bargaining, reaching 43% in 2011 (van Wanrooy et al. 2013: 83).

The impact of the decline in trade union membership is particularly important for British industrial relations because of the absence of mechanisms for the extension of collective agreements beyond the workplaces where they are negotiated. Without legal extension, or extension by coordinated employer organizations, the decline in trade union coverage leads directly to a decline in collective bargaining coverage, as the current exceptionally narrow gap between these two levels demonstrates. As one commentary put it: "although the decline of trade union membership may not have been exceptional in international terms, the implications of it are" (Brown, Deakin and Ryan 1997: 75).

The net effect of these simultaneous and substantial declines in union density and collective bargaining has clearly been to reduce the presence of collective regulation within the economy. One of the central features of the 1970s was that collective bargaining expanded not just in scale but in scope, as it came to encompass all aspects of workplace organization and the terms and conditions of work. But it is now "evident that there has been a very substantial decline in union representative involvement in the regulation of employee obligations and work organization" as the scope of bargaining once again shrank, leaving the organization of the workplace as a matter for unilateral managerial prerogative (Brown et al. 2000: 617). Collective bargaining itself now more often takes on a less formal character, resembling consultation rather than negotiation, with the result that the "scope, status and influence of these organisations [firm-level union organizations] had, in all cases, diminished greatly. By implication, the extent of collective regulation had diminished" (Brown et al. 1999: 69). The study concludes, "Thus what [union] recognition means in practice is very much what the employer chooses it to mean" (Ibid.: 75). The 2011 Workplace Employment Relations Survey echoes this finding, indicating a sharp decline even since the 2004 survey in the scope of collective bargaining, and suggesting that pay bargaining often resembles a "hollow shell" (van Wanrooy et al. 2013: 82). It should be no surprise, then, to learn that by 2010, the union wage premium had shrunk to 6.7% in the private sector (Achur 2011: 2).

While the coverage of collective bargaining with trade unions has shrunk and then been hollowed out where it remains, there are alternative forms of consultation and bargaining. Employers can create direct mechanisms for employee participation, and they can create nonunion collective bodies representing employees. Two clear conclusions concerning "employee voice" can be drawn from workplace surveys. The first is that the last three decades have seen a sharp decrease in mechanisms of *union-only* voice, and an increase in *nonunion-only* voice, where the latter includes a range of forms of direct communication between management and employees. In continuing workplaces, union voice mechanisms tended to be supplemented with these other mechanisms to create a dual channel of communication, while new firms would only rarely have any form of union voice, but were more likely to have nonunion voice.

The second, and related, conclusion is that there was a steep decline in the presence of any form of collective representation – union, consultative committee, works council – during this period, a decline that was partially compensated for by an increase in mechanisms of direct participation, through institutions created and controlled by management (van Wanrooy et al. 2013: 56–67). These industrial relations institutions are likely to be much more fragile, less likely to survive an economic downturn or other crisis, than those based either upon a strong trade union presence in the workplace, or upon legal requirements, as is the case for continental European works councils. Since 2005, Britain has been subject to the EU Information and Consultation Directive, but it was introduced into British law in such a way as to put the burden upon employees to trigger its effects, and with a "double hurdle" for challenges to existing, nonstatutory arrangements (Hall 2004).

What then can we conclude about the impact of industrial relations change on employer discretion? At the end of the 1970s, management attitudes were "extraordinarily defensive," with a major survey of manufacturing indicating that two-thirds of managers claimed to negotiate with unions over "internal redeployment of labour, manning levels, redundancy and major changes in production levels" (Brown and Edwards 2009:7). This had all changed three decades later.

The regulatory impact of labor law, even after New Labour's policy emphasis upon the provision of individual rights at work, remains light. There is a statutory minimum wage, but it is not used in an aggressive manner. There are no limitations upon hiring and firing beyond (a now reduced) protection from unfair dismissal. Part-time, temporary and agency workers benefit from EU directives that provide for equal treatment, and the EU is also largely responsible for enhanced parental leave and some limitation on work hours. But in all cases, EU directives have been implemented in weak forms that provide the maximum flexibility to employers. The comprehensive OECD employment protection indicators for 2008 (before the advent of the coalition government) place Britain comfortably at the bottom of our twelve European cases (with only the United States and Canada within the OECD having less strict employment protection); employment protection for temporary forms of employment was particularly weak (Venn 2009: 9, Figure 1).

Thus, collective regulation remains the primary constraint acting upon employers, and here all the evidence is of very high levels of unilateral managerial determination. The 2004 Workplace Employment Relations Survey (in this case looking at firms with 10 or more employees) asked managers if they negotiated, consulted, informed or did none of those things on a range of twelve possible subjects for joint regulation (Kersley et al. 2005: 22, Table 7). In two-thirds of workplaces, there was no engagement of any kind on any aspect of terms and conditions. On each issue, somewhere between 69% and 78% of firms did not engage at all. Negotiation occurred in 15–18% of workplaces on pay, hours and holidays, but not on other issues. Outside the core issues of pay, hours and holidays, the workforce was informed of changes in about 10% of workplaces and consulted in 12–17% of workplaces.

This amounts to a degree of employer discretion across all aspects of managing the workplace that would have been inconceivable at the end of the 1970s. It is hard to disagree with Purcell's judgment that "What evidence we have points to the emergence of a free, unregulated labour market of the sort that predated the birth of collective bargaining 100 years ago" (1993:23).

4.6 Conclusion

The core institutions of collective regulation have been systematically dismantled in the decades after 1979. Decollectivization manifested itself in the decline in trade unionism, the primary collective agent of workers, in both the decentralization of collective bargaining to the firm and workplace and its replacement by unilateral managerial determination of terms and conditions, in the weakening of collective decision-making structures within trade unions, and in the decline in collective action and its replacement with individual legal cases or complaints directed towards state agencies rather than trade unions. As the authoritative series of workplace industrial relations surveys cautiously concluded, the changes that have taken place "in the structures and conduct of British industrial relations can reasonably be regarded as a transformation" (Millward, Bryson and Forth 2000:234).

The apparently autonomous strength of British trade unionism has been overcome by a combination of the scale and scope of state activism, alongside a withdrawal of support for collective regulation on the part of many employers and a period of profound economic restructuring. What began as a political project to limit the political and policy influence of unions and their capacity to engage in industrial action expanded into a wider decollectivist project to create the space and the conditions under which employers could choose how to manage social relations at work. The changing structure of the British economy, the changing interests of employers, and the inability of unions to mount effective resistance ensured that new firms chose nonunion forms of industrial relations, and existing firms scaled back the role of unions to one more of consultation than negotiation. The scope of employer discretion dramatically expanded.

Returning to the mechanisms of institutional change discussed in Chapter 1, the British case is a rare illustration of the wholesale dismantling of existing institutions, with institutional conversion playing a much smaller role. During the Conservative period in office the statutory, juridical or administrative basis for every form of collective regulation was undermined or abolished outright. Little by the way of new institutional construction occurred until the arrival of New Labour in office. Then institutional construction took the form of individual legal rights at work. One result was that the once marginal institution of employment tribunals took on enhanced importance, forced to substitute for the collapse of collective mechanisms for regulating disputes, and rapidly became overwhelmed. To the extent that employers engaged in institutional construction, it was at the workplace level, and it involved the creation of individual direct mechanisms for communication with their employees; they resisted the Continental temptation to accept or create forms of nonunion collective representation. British industrial relations have been thoroughly decollectivized.

5

State-Led Liberalization and the Transformation of Worker Representation in France

French industrial relations at the end of the 1970s appeared an unlikely candidate for liberalization. Extensive state regulation and predominantly industry-level bargaining had combined to ensure a high degree of labor market rigidity and limited autonomy and discretion on the part of employers in the determination of pay and organization of work. After the strikes of May–June 1968, the French state became more and more directly involved in the regulation of the labor market. In effect, the state came to substitute for the weakness of trade unions and collective bargaining through a more aggressive use of the minimum wage, administrative authorization for layoffs, and generous unemployment benefits and public sector wage contracts. Thus, in marked contrast to the British case, the obstacle to greater flexibility lay in extensive state regulation rather than collective regulation of class relations.

And yet by the end of the first decade of the twenty-first century, a remarkable degree of labor market and workplace flexibility had appeared, as firms enjoyed greater autonomy from both state regulation and higher levels of collective bargaining. At the same time, a dense network of firm-level and firm-specific institutions for bargaining, consultation and representation – institutions that were almost completely absent in the private sector twenty-five years earlier – had spread widely through French workplaces. This transformation of the institutional landscape of industrial relations took place through both the creation of new firm-level institutions and the mutation of existing institutions to take on new functions (Howell 2009).

Given that the obstacle to flexibility from the 1980s onward was not perceived to be primarily trade unions and collective bargaining, as in so many other countries, but rather the direct regulatory efforts of the French state, French governments faced a particular problem in their efforts to reconstruct industrial relations institutions: how to withdraw from direct regulation of the labor market in the absence of labor actors at the firm level capable of ensuring that the introduction of flexibility was genuinely negotiated rather than imposed unilaterally by employers. The resulting strategy was to tie opportunities for employers to enjoy greater flexibility in the deployment of labor to a legal obligation to negotiate change at the level of the firm. The important and paradoxical point here is that post-Fordist restructuring of the economy was hostage to a process of institutional reconstruction that only the French state could undertake.

The last three decades have seen a broadly bipartisan effort – as the essential strategy of shifting responsibility for regulating the labor market and workplace to actors inside the firm has been shared by conservative and socialist governments – result in the transformation of the French industrial relations system in a manner that permits a greater degree of employer discretion than existed at the end of the 1970s. Thus, while periodic social explosions, such as those over pension reform or the introduction of temporary youth labor contracts in the last decade, continue to shape the public perception of French industrial relations, the reality is that social mobilization has masked a quiet revolution in industrial relations, one that has contributed to a marked liberalization of the institutions governing class relations.

5.1 Dirigiste Industrial Relations

Postwar French industrial relations were heavily marked by the absence of a strong Fordist dynamic that might have encouraged employers and the state to seek mechanisms to link wages, and demand more generally, to productivity. The process and goals of indicative planning made the construction of industrial relations institutions inside the firm a low priority. Add to this the well-known organizational weakness of trade unions and the dominance of conservative governments after 1958 and you have the recipe for France's particular labor exclusionary postwar settlement (Jefferys 2003: chapter 3, Ross 1982).

The first feature of note in this postwar industrial relations regime was the weakness of collective bargaining, especially within the firm. The cornerstone of French labor law in this early period was a 1950 law that established a strict hierarchy, giving priority to legislation over collective agreements, and agreements reached at higher levels over those reached inside the firm. Since firm-level agreements were not permitted to derogate from (undercut) legislation or sectoral or national agreements, employers had little incentive to reach them, and there was no institutional mechanism inside the firm to achieve flexibility. The 1950 legislation also permitted the state to extend sectoral or regional agreements beyond the scope of their original signatories, making them still more rigid instruments of social regulation. It is no surprise, then, that collective bargaining grew only fitfully in the postwar period, and then almost exclusively at the sectoral level (Reynaud 1975: chapter 7).

The second, and related, feature of this period was the weakness of trade union organization. Trade union membership declined after 1945 to a low of around 17% in the early 1960s. It then recovered in the wake of the strike wave of 1968 to reach a peak of almost 25% in 1974 before beginning a long, slow decline that has continued to the present (Amossé and Pignoni 2006: 407). French unions are also divided along ideological and confessional lines, have competed for members, and have only rarely been able to work together. French postwar legislation bestowed representative status on at least five different confederations, meaning that only these union confederations could sign national agreements and stand candidates in the first round of workplace elections. Furthermore, until 1968, trade unions enjoyed no legislative protection inside the firm, making union organization especially vulnerable to employer hostility.

The strike wave of May and June 1968 altered the trajectory of French industrial relations. Initially, at least, it appeared that the legacy of that surge in labor mobilization would be to strengthen both trade unions and collective bargaining inside the firm, the two primary weaknesses of the postwar industrial relations system. The Grenelle Accords that settled the strike wave produced legislation that for the first time provided legal protection, along with some rights and resources, for union "sections" (locals) inside firms employing fifty or more workers. There were also a number of government reforms throughout the 1970s, particularly Chaban-Delmas's "New Society" project, which attempted to kickstart collective regulation (Howell 1992: chapter 4).

There was some limited evidence of an increasing institutional presence of union sections inside the firm, albeit unaccompanied by any surge in union membership, and of a rise in firm-level bargaining (*Liaisons Sociales* 1971: 8). However, French unions simply were not strong enough to take on the burden of social regulation; they could neither force employers to the bargaining table nor exercise the kind of control over workers that might encourage employers to seek agreements. Under these circumstances one prominent academic jurist argued, "Negotiation is only a pretense. The employers make suggestions; one either subscribes to them or one doesn't...if there is no balance of power one cannot speak of collective bargaining" (Lyon-Caen 1980: 8–9, translation by the author).

But something did change. The real legacy of May 1968 was an even more interventionist state in the sphere of industrial relations and a more highly regulated labor market. In essence, the French state came to substitute for the weakness of trade unions and collective bargaining, expanding juridical and administrative regulation in the absence of collective regulation. In part, this reflected a recognition on the part of the conservative governments that followed the resignation of De Gaulle that the planning process needed to be complemented by greater social investment and attention to expanding demand and linking it to growth in the economy (Hall 1986: chapter 7). But it was also a self-protective response on the part of a regime that had barely survived the events of May 1968. From that point onward, continuing to the present, governments sought to prevent future bouts of social mobilization by a combination of labor market protections and industrial relations institutions that, it was hoped, would channel and dissipate labor grievances.

After 1968, the statutory minimum wage was indexed both to the cost of living and to the general wage level in the economy, and it was used more aggressively, through annual discretionary increases, exerting more upward pressure on the wage scale. Further, beginning in public sector collective agreements, but diffusing rapidly to the private sector, came the widespread use of price indexation as an automatic element of wage contracts. It was estimated that by 1973 about six million workers benefited from cost-of-living safeguards, ensuring an increased rigidity of wages (Mery 1973). In addition, the procedure by which the Ministry of Labor could extend collective agreements was eased in 1971.

Looking beyond wage determination, state intervention affected other parts of the labor market as well. In October 1974, an additional unemployment benefit worth 90% of the previous wage for one year was created, and the following year, legislation required that administrative authorization be sought before layoffs for economic reasons. French labor law also strictly regulated employment contracts, limiting recourse to temporary or fixed-term contracts, and making permanent, open-ended contracts the norm (Le Barbanchon and Malherbet 2013: 10).

Thus, by the end of the 1970s, France had an industrial relations system that combined hierarchical collective bargaining, emphasizing the primacy of the sectoral and national levels while remaining underdeveloped inside the firm, with statist regulation of the labor market. The result was low employer discretion in the ability to hire and fire and a wage determination process that was constrained by sectoral agreements, indexation clauses, government extension beyond the industry or region of the original signatories and aggressive use of the minimum wage at the low end of the pay scale (Contrepois and Jefferys 2006). However, the weakness of trade unions and collective bargaining inside the firm, coupled with the limited powers available to works councils, did grant employers greater discretion in the organization of work.

5.2 Social Actors Face the Challenge of Post-Fordist Restructuring

Awareness of the implications of France's highly regulated labor market for employment and the dangers of highly politicized class relations encouraged efforts to "re-launch" collective bargaining in the second half of the 1970s (Howell 1992: chapter 5). But it was not until the 1980s that, in the context of an acceleration of economic restructuring, rapidly rising unemployment and the perceived failure of traditional dirigiste and Keynesian policies, the imperative of labor market and workplace flexibility moved to the top of the agenda of employers and politicians (Culpepper 2006). After 1981, compatibility between the industrial relations system and post-Fordist restructuring of the French economy became of central political importance, and institutional reform of industrial relations has appeared on the agenda of every government in the intervening thirty or more years.

This shift coincided with the abandonment of the initial Socialist economic project in the face of domestic and international constraints and the subsequent "conversion" of the French Socialist Party to the merits of market-friendly policies (Singer 1988). It is hard to exaggerate the traumatizing effect that the early years of governing had upon French socialism, and the persistently high unemployment of the last two decades and more has reinforced a sense of perpetual economic crisis. During this period, there has been little political disagreement about the goals of monetary stability, labor market flexibility and privatization of state-owned industries. Rather, the questions became how industrial relations institutions could contribute to this form of economic restructuring and what precise balance between social protection and flexibility was appropriate. The result has been that industrial relations reform was essentially a political project shared across the major political parties, albeit with small differences in emphasis.

As Mériaux (2000) argues, the two core elements of post-Fordism in France have been the "emancipation" of the firm from juridical regulation and a shift from a focus upon bargaining over the wage relationship to bargaining over the management of employment. There is a distinctiveness to French neoliberalism, however. Neither the Socialists nor the Gaullists, their main political opponents, seriously contemplated Thatcherism *à la Française*. In part, this reflected different ideological heritages, and in part, the fear of social upheaval in response to unemployment and economic restructuring, a fear periodically reinforced by paralyzing strikes. Just as the economic crisis of 1982–83 profoundly marked Socialist thinking about labor markets and macroeconomic policy, so strike waves in 1987 and 1995 encouraged timidity on the part of Gaullists. Jacques Chirac inaugurated his first term as President with appeals to heal the "social fracture" of French society, and President Nicolas Sarkozy emphasized his intellectual debt to the "Third Way," despite his reputation as a free marketeer. With regard to the labor market, the result has been a more than two-decade-long bipartisan commitment to increasing the ability of employers to manage their workforces as they wish, with limited government regulation, but to do so in a way that cushions the social impact on workers. That cushioning includes the greatly expanded use of social policy as a form of "social anaesthesia" (Levy 1999) and the repeated attempts, detailed below, to ensure that the introduction of flexibility is at least negotiated.

The central problem facing the French state in its efforts to reconstruct industrial relations institutions in a manner appropriate to post-Fordist economic restructuring was how to deregulate the labor market in the absence of developed institutions of collective regulation inside the firm that would permit negotiation rather than managerial unilateralism. The core of the state's strategy, under both Socialist and Gaullist governments, was to create legal obligations inside the firm that would have the effect of generating autonomous and self-sustaining social dialogue that would in turn permit deregulation of the labor market. Opportunities for employers to enjoy greater flexibility in the deployment of labor were tied to a legal obligation to negotiate change at the level of the firm. Given the weakness of trade unions inside the firm, this obligation in turn required a redefinition of who could legally bargain with the employer, or at least formally ratify workplace change. Thus, the three consistent elements of industrial relations reform after 1981 were the decentralization of bargaining to the firm, the creation of new institutions of worker representation, and linkage between the use of these micro-corporatist institutions and practices and the achievement of flexibility.

This shared strategy captures the central paradox of institutional change in the recent past (Lallement and Mériaux 2003): the goal was to shift responsibility for the regulation of class relations to business and labor themselves – to empower those actors – but the context of labor weakness required that the state remain heavily involved. The state could not withdraw from the process of reconstructing industrial relations institutions because private industrial actors were too weak to respond to the challenge of post-Fordism alone, and because its own juridical regulation of the labor market was the primary obstacle to labor market flexibility. Furthermore, there is a sense in which the French state *invented* the social partners at the end of the 1960s (Couton 2004), bestowing representative status, and thus legitimacy, upon class actors in order to have someone with whom to negotiate an end to social disruption. After 1981, the weakness of trade unions limited the ability of the French state to promote autonomous collective bargaining, and in response, governments came to redefine who represented labor, shifting legitimacy from unions to nonunion institutions inside the firm, reprising its earlier role in the creation of social interests.

The French state did not, of course, act in a vacuum, and to the extent that the goal of successive governments has been to reduce labor market regulation in order to provide more flexibility, but to do so in a way that is negotiated and limits the social cost of flexibility for workers, this has required cooperation from labor and business (Vail 2004). France's social partners have become more willing to bargain over critical issues. Still, this evolution has been contested on both the labor and employer sides.

On the labor side, the Confédération Générale du Travail (CGT) finally broke with the Communist Party in the early 1990s, ending its long-term institutional ties and its isolation from other unions at both the international and national levels. Bernard Thibault, its general secretary between 1999 and 2013, pursued a more pragmatic strategy, showing himself willing to seek compromise with other French unions and to sign collective agreements more frequently. The national agreement on professional training in 2003 was the first significant interconfederal agreement the CGT had signed since 1971. Meanwhile, the Confédération Française Démocratique du Travail (CFDT) emerged as the privileged partner of employers and the state. The CFDT pursued a strategy that has been labeled "hyper-reformism" (Pernot 2005), involving an acceptance of the constraints imposed on bargaining by employers and the state and an emphasis upon negotiation as almost an end in itself. It has proven much more willing to support the reform of the welfare state than other unions, an approach that culminated in the CFDT breaking ranks with other unions in 2003 to endorse the pension reform of the Raffarin government, thereby averting a crisis like that of 1995, the last time public sector pension reform was attempted.[1]

Nonetheless, for all the increased willingness to engage in social dialogue, the core dilemma facing unions remained: in a period of declining membership, when dialogue meant, in practice, bargaining concessions, what independent role could unions have? French trade unionism can be usefully characterized as "virtual unionism," (Howell 1998) in which the influence of organized labor rests not upon class power (in the sense of the collective capacity of labor), nor upon any of the conventional measures of labor strength, but rather upon two functions: as a vehicle representing labor interests to the state (deployed by workers, who are rarely union members, to bargain with the state during moments of social crisis); providing the state with an institution to legitimize economic policies that cause social dislocation. In this latter function, French governments have tended to seek out trade unions during moments of industrial conflict and economic crisis to negotiate the terms of change. Thus the paradox of the French trade union movement: it simultaneously displays tremendous organizational weakness and yet a continued ability, right up to the present, to put itself at the head of grand social mobilizations (Béroud and Yon 2012).

The main employers' organization became radicalized and politicized in the course of the 1980s and 1990s, particularly in response to two Socialist reform initiatives: the Auroux laws of the early 1980s and the Aubry laws instituting the thirty-five-hour week at the end of the 1990s. The result was the creation in 1998 of a new organization, the Mouvement des Enteprises de France (MEDEF), with a much stronger neoliberal prescription for France's economic ills and a greater combativeness when it came to its relationship with both the state and the unions (Woll 2006). In 1999, MEDEF launched what it called a *refondation sociale* and invited the trade unions to join it. At its core, the *refondation sociale* was an appeal for the state to stay out of regulating the labor market and instead to leave the social partners free to negotiate reforms as they saw fit (Lallement and Mériaux 2003). It involved derogation writ large, as firms would be granted greater flexibility than legislation currently allowed, as long as change was negotiated. MEDEF had a schizophrenic attitude toward collective bargaining, however, championing it in order to urge deregulation on the part of the state, but also espousing the benefits of the individualization of labor contracts. The *refondation sociale* was predicated upon at least

---

[1] For the CFDT, the result was massive internal dissent that manifested itself in the disaffiliation of several prominent federations, losses in professional elections and a decline in membership.

one major trade union being willing to support a call for greater autonomy of industrial relations and the labor market from the state, despite the attendant risk that autonomy in the context of weak labor organizations would translate into a flexibility that benefitted employers more than workers. Thus, the CFDT's strategic shift toward "hyper-reformism" enabled this new employer strategy and ensured that the CFDT would be the MEDEF's privileged interlocutor.

However, the importance of the radicalization of the main French employer organization should not be overstated. MEDEF is organizationally weak (Woll 2006), and there is evidence of a gap between its pronouncements and the interests, and certainly the actions, of employers (Moreau 2004: 36). MEDEF is more important as a lobbyist than as a representative of business. The more significant shift, as Mériaux (2000) has noted, is the transformation of French capitalism, as an older "patrimonial culture," which tended to tolerate state regulation so long as firms were protected from trade unionism, increasingly gave way to modern firms competing in European or global markets, for which great flexibility was an imperative.

5.3 Projects of Industrial Relations Reform

The institutions of French industrial relations had experienced remarkable stability in the thirty-five years after World War II. Certainly, as described above, the state became more interventionist, but when the Socialist Party won the presidency and control of the National Assembly in 1981, it inherited the same core elements of the collective bargaining system and labor law put in place soon after 1945. The last thirty years, in contrast, have seen rapidly accelerating institutional change. Successive governments have reformed industrial relations to encourage both decentralized collective bargaining with unions and also social dialogue (by which we mean here forms of consultation and participation that fall short of formal bargaining) with nonunion, firm-specific representatives of workers. The goal of these efforts has been to permit the state to withdraw both from active management of industrial relations and from substantive regulation of the labor market. Thus, there has been an intimate link between institutional reform and the provision of greater flexibility, both elements often appearing in the same pieces of legislation.

As time went on, and evidence that French trade unions could take the strain of collective regulation dimmed, attention passed to the creation and legitimation of nonunion, firm-specific institutions. As it did – and this was increasingly also true of weakened union sections inside the firm – the extent to which agreements could genuinely be considered the result of negotiation, backed up by countervailing power, eroded, to be replaced by something much closer to consultation, or the ratification of unilateral employer initiatives. It should be no surprise, then, that this period of industrial relations reform has been accompanied by an expansion of employer discretion and labor market flexibility.

This section of the chapter will focus upon three moments in the reconstruction of industrial relations institutions: the Auroux laws in the early 1980s, which first breached the strict collective bargaining hierarchy and encouraged firm-level bargaining and dialogue; a period of transition and experimentation in the 1990s, when the association between flexibility and the obligation to bargain appeared; and the codification of a new industrial relations system centered on the firm and permitting a much expanded role for nonunion institutions of worker representation in the first decade of the twenty-first century.

The *lois Auroux* (Auroux laws), passed in 1982–83, during the early years of the new Socialist government, rewrote fully one-third of the French labor code and represented the most thoroughgoing state industrial relations reform project since 1936 (Gallie 1985, Howell 1992: chapter 7). There were diverse inspirations for the reforms, and Delors, the first economics and finance minister of the 1981 Socialist government, had also, in an earlier incarnation, been the architect of Chaban-Delmas' New Society project of industrial relations reform. Thus, the Auroux Laws combined some fairly conventional (though nonetheless radical in scope) measures aimed at encouraging decentralized collective bargaining with a series of elements that can be characterized as "microcorporatist": strengthening firm-specific industrial relations institutions that were largely autonomous from, and unarticulated with, sectoral or national institutions of labor regulation.

The central elements introduced by the Auroux Laws, for our purposes, were as follows. First, a right of self-expression was established for workers, in the form of regular meetings to discuss social relations within the firm. Second, works councils received new rights of mandatory consultation over a wide range of economic issues, greater resources including the right to hire outside experts, and, in very large firms, a special economic delegation was created. Third, trade union delegates received legal protection in all firms, not simply those employing 50 or more workers, as had been the situation since 1968. Unions also gained greater resources (office space, time off for union duties) in firms employing 50 or more workers. Fourth, an obligation to bargain annually (though not to conclude an agreement) at both the firm and branch levels was created in firms employing 50 or more workers and having a union delegate. In addition, under narrow circumstances, firm-level agreements could now derogate from legislation and higher-level agreements. There were also a series of equivalent reforms of public sector industrial relations.

In understanding the legacy of the Auroux laws for the liberalization of industrial relations institutions, a number of points are worth noting. The first is that the emphasis upon, and obligation to engage in, bargaining created, for the first time in France, a public policy presumption in favor of collective bargaining as the primary form of social regulation, something that has only become stronger in the ensuing three decades. And it occurred at almost exactly the same time that this presumption was being overturned by a Conservative government in Britain. Furthermore, with the right of derogation (albeit still tightly constrained), this marked the first breach is the strict hierarchy (or "favorability principle," in the sense that firm-level agreements could not be less favorable than legislation or higher-level agreements) that had existed since 1950.

The second point of note is that while the Auroux laws did very little to strengthen French trade unions directly (the hope was that unions would be strengthened indirectly by the increased powers given to workers' councils), they did contain a whole series of micro-corporatist elements, whose logic pointed away from articulated collective bargaining between independent trade unions and employers: more powers of consultation for works councils; the right of self-expression; and the right to derogate. The reforms encouraged an assortment of forms of social dialogue inside the firm, involving company-specific institutions of worker representation, unconnected to either outside trade unions or higher levels of collective bargaining. For example, the expression groups were made mandatory at a time when managerial practices that emphasized direct communication with the workforce, unmediated by trade unions, were spreading within French firms, and an assortment of institutions such as quality circles and worker–management groups were appearing (Jenkins 2000: chapter 3). Thus, the legislation had the effect of a forced modernization of managerial practices, extending their reach beyond the leading edge of French firms to the rest of the economy.

The results of the Auroux reforms for the industrial relations institutions of France were made clear by an exhaustive study ten years after their implementation (Coffineau 1993). While sectoral-level collective bargaining had stagnated, there had been a substantial increase in the scale of firm-level bargaining, to the point that it had become "the privileged mode of social regulation" (Coffineau 1993: 93, translation by the author). But at the same time, the decline of trade unionism had not been reversed and indeed appeared to have accelerated. In practice, employers were signing agreements with union delegates who represented very few actual members, in order to gain dispensation from legislation or branch agreements. At the same time, the distinction between union delegates negotiating collective agreements and works councils or worker self-expression groups consulting over work reorganization collapsed in the context of an acceleration in the process of economic restructuring. As one study of the application of these laws to small and medium-sized firms concluded: "[B]argaining always takes place with the works council, even if some union representation exists" (Bodin 1987: 195, translation by the author).

The impulse for reform efforts throughout the 1990s was a deepening sense of economic crisis. As the unemployment rate remained high by international standards, employment policy came to drive industrial relations policy, giving an urgency to reform projects and tying them more closely to the introduction of flexibility. Certainly the linkage was there in the 1980s; in fact, the right of derogation first appeared in the 1982 legislation reducing the work week before being incorporated into the Auroux laws later that same year. The Socialist government had sought to permit firms more flexibility in the use of work time in return for the reduction in the work week. In the 1990s, however, innovations in industrial relations practice were more likely to originate in agreements between employers and unions explicitly designed to permit flexibility. This gave the decade an experimental quality, as new institutions and practices were created for quite narrow purposes before being expanded, extended and embedded in legislation.

In the context of sluggish growth and high unemployment, employer organizations and some of the trade union confederations publically pledged support for decentralized bargaining and greater autonomy from the state for the regulation of class relations. For employers, the appeal of bargaining either with quite weak unions or with firm-specific labor representatives was fairly straightforward: it was a way of achieving flexibility. For trade unions, the calculus was more complicated. Some union confederations never supported these changes – the CGT was a consistent nonsignatory – while for others, the hope was that, in the context of declining membership, new forms of labor representation would help unions get access to smaller firms and eventually lead to the creation of more union delegates inside the firm. Interunion jockeying for influence also played a role in the different positions taken by each union confederation.

In October 1995, employers and several of the trade union confederations (though only one of the three largest) issued a general statement calling for the autonomy of collective bargaining from the state and signed a national agreement on collective bargaining (EIRR 1995). It proposed a three-year experiment during which firm-level agreements could be signed by either an elected employee representative (a member of a works council, or the employee delegate, both of which have existed in French labor law since the immediate postwar period) or an employee mandated by a national trade union in small firms in which there was no union delegate. This constituted an important innovation, but was also a recognition and post hoc legitimization of a practice that had evolved since the Auroux legislation; in the absence of actual union representatives inside the firm, employers needed someone with whom to negotiate flexibility. The agreement also extended the right of derogation more broadly. The 1995 accord was sanctioned by legislation in 1996, and extended for another five years in 1999, when the initial experiment expired.

What was the link between industrial relations reform and the quest for firm-level flexibility during the 1990s? Its best illustration comes in the sphere of work time reduction and flexibility (Askenazy 2013). For two decades after 1982, the recipe for modifying work time remained remarkably consistent, regardless of which party was in power: greater flexibility in the use of work time was offered to employers in return for a reduction in overall work time and a requirement that changes in work time be negotiated. Laws in 1993 and 1995 had this formula embedded in them, permitting derogation for work time flexibility if it was the product of a firm-level agreement and created or saved jobs through work time reduction.

But the most extensive work time reduction experiment was contained in the *lois Aubry*, which implemented the 35-hour work week between 1998 and 2002 (Hayden 2006, Rouilleault 2001, Trumbull 2002). This series of laws sanctioned the use of union-mandated worker representatives and other alternatives to traditional collective bargaining in the negotiation of the reduced work week. In smaller firms where there was no union delegate, firm-level agreements either could be signed on behalf of employees by a worker who was mandated to sign by one of the national trade union confederations or, if no worker was mandated, the resulting agreement had to be approved by a majority vote of employees and approved by a local labor–business commission. The mandating procedure was widely used for firm-level work-time agreements (Rouilleault 2001: chapter 7), and the smaller the firm, the more likely it was to reach agreement without the signature of a union delegate. In the context of trade union weakness, the price of achieving work time agreements was to create new industrial actors on the labor side to ratify those agreements.

It will be recalled that a requirement that mass layoffs for economic reasons receive administrative authorization was introduced in the 1970s, and it rapidly became a symbol among employers of rigid bureaucratic obstruction to economic restructuring. This requirement was abolished in 1986, but what emerged in its place was a greater emphasis upon the obligation of employers to provide alternatives to layoffs or compensation through a social plan presented to the works council. The 1995 *loi Robien* required that social plans include work time reduction as one option for avoiding layoffs. Once again, deregulation, in this case related to numerical flexibility, was accompanied by the obligation to engage in social dialogue at the firm level. In the words of Jenkins (2000: 140), this legislation fostered "a more proactive HR [human resources]" approach. In practice, this obligation was likely to encourage the negotiation of flexibility in order to minimize job losses. And, since any employer plan to avoid layoffs would likely touch on a wide range of aspects of compensation and the organization of work inside the firm, the result was further blurring of the line between the legitimate monopoly bargaining role of trade unions and the consultative role of work councils and other employee representatives.

Following the electoral loss of the Socialist Party in 2002, and accelerating with the election of Sarkozy as president in 2007, French labor law came to generalize and codify the experiments of the 1990s. This appeared primarily in two pieces of legislation, in 2004 and 2008, but there were other important developments that also helped give shape to an emerging decentralized, firm-centric, increasingly nonunion set of industrial relations institutions.

The most substantial incorporation of formerly piecemeal reforms of collective bargaining into French labor law took place in the 2004 *loi Fillon*. This legislation, building upon the 1995 national agreement between employers and unions, and a further such agreement in 2001, incorporated two important sets of changes. The first part of the changes did involve a significant modification of the favorability principle, essentially ending it by permitting derogation unless explicitly denied in collective agreements or legislation. Only in four areas, including the minimum wage, did the legislation prevent derogation. Thus, industry agreements could now be less favorable to workers than national agreements, and firm agreements could be less favorable than industry agreements. Furthermore, in firms without a union delegate, firm-specific bodies such as the works council could be authorized to sign agreements, and in the absence of any elected employee representative, a union-mandated worker could sign an agreement and the workforce then ratify it by referendum. Thus, practices such as derogation and ability of nonunion actors to ratify agreements that had previously been permitted on single issues or to take advantage of specified financial benefits were now extended throughout the industrial relations system. The expanded scope of derogation has encouraged what Rodière has nicely characterized as "l'émiettement dérogatoire" (translated as "crumbling by derogations," Moreau 2004: 10), as labor law is undermined by a "multiplication of special dispensations" to provide flexibility for firms.

A second set of changes attempted to incorporate the so-called "majority principle" into bargaining. The majority principle referred to the extent to which signatories to agreements on the labor side represented a majority of some kind (a majority of union confederations or a majority of workers). Prior to this point, under French labor law, an agreement could be valid if only a single union, possibly representing a small minority of workers, signed. The *loi Fillon* recognized that if the possibility of reaching firm-level agreements that undercut higher level agreements and labor law was to be extended, there should be some assurance that these derogatory agreements would be signed by organizations or institutions that were plausibly representative of workers. However, this part of the law was implemented in a weak fashion, and it will not be examined in detail here, because it was largely superseded by 2008 legislation (for details see Moreau 2004: 27–32).

The result of the *loi Fillon* was both to enhance the autonomy of the firm from the wider industrial relations system and to encourage the shift in worker representation from trade unions to nonunion, firm-specific institutions (Jobert and Saglio 2005). French trade unions had lost their formal monopoly on signing collective agreements in 1996, and this legislation ratified that loss. The *loi Fillon* reflected the central dilemma facing decentralized bargaining in the absence of strong, well-implanted unions. It embodied at least four different notions of labor representation: a union delegate representing union members in the workplace; employee representatives (such as works councils and employee delegates) chosen through workplace elections; an employee mandated by a trade union confederation that had no formal union representation inside the firm; or a referendum of all employees in a firm. As Mériaux has pointed out (2004, personal communication with the author), the referendum procedure, as with the ratification of agreements signed by mandated employees, introduces direct democracy as a parallel, possibly rival, principle to representative democracy: employees are asked directly whether they support contract agreements that may not have been negotiated at all, but rather proposed unilaterally by management.

The widening opportunities for derogation and greater use of collective bargaining for the implementation of social policy (see below) made "representativeness" or, more properly, legitimacy a more pressing political issue. The larger union confederations, in particular, wanted to close off the possibility of small, unrepresentative unions signing concessionary firm-level agreements or those weakening terms and conditions for workers. Employers had less of an interest in ensuring the representativeness of their labor-side partners, though doing so reduced the possibility of resistance to agreements on the part of workers. Further, the legitimacy of the new decentralized industrial relations regime depended upon some clarification of the rules of representation.

The 2004 *loi Fillon* had begun this process, but the election of Sarkozy in 2007 led to intense negotiations between unions and employers' organizations with an eye to further legislation. The result was a 2008 law on firm-level representation in collective bargaining (Ministère du Travail 2013, Robin 2008).[2] The two main provisions required that henceforth a union delegate would only be recognized for collective bargaining purposes if that union won at least 10% of the vote in the most recent professional election inside the firm (usually a works council election), and further that valid firm-level agreements must now be signed by a union or unions receiving at least 30% of the vote in those elections (and not opposed by unions winning more than 50% of the vote). Initially, smaller unions could reach the 10% threshold by running joint lists, though that practice ended in 2012. This raises the possibility that some smaller union confederations, particularly the Confédération Française des Travailleurs Chrétiens, may eventually be eliminated from many workplaces in both the public and private sector (Turlan 2012), though that did not happen in the first postreform workplace elections, which took place in 2012.

Two further modifications were introduced in the legislation. First, on issues of work time, the traditional bargaining hierarchy was actually reversed: a sectoral agreement could only be reached if no firm-level agreement existed. This went well beyond derogation to privilege firm agreements. Second, the ability of elected representatives and mandated employees to sign agreements in place of union delegates was extended to all workplaces employing 200 or fewer workers. Note the linkage here: as thresholds of representativeness were introduced, making it less likely that union delegates would be recognized in firms and be able to sign agreements, the opportunity for nonunion signatories was expanded. If this legislation has the effect of reducing the coverage of union sections and delegates inside firms, it remains to be seen whether that reduces the overall quantity of bargaining or simply shifts more of it to elected

---

[2] The Ministry of Labor report cited here is both the most comprehensive account of the provisions of the legislation and the first report on its effects, five years after it went into effect.

representatives rather than unions. What is certain is that voting in professional elections, rather than membership or national organization, has now become the ultimate arbiter of union legitimacy. This has profound implications for worker representation in France.

In the last decade and a half, and accelerating over time, a practice has emerged on the part of the French state of using collective bargaining as the primary form of implementing social policy. Moreau (2004: 58) has noted a "quasi-systematic practice to turn to multi-sectoral bargaining before legislating," and the *loi Fillon* incorporated a "solemn commitment" on the part of legislators to let the social partners bargain before the resulting agreement was turned into legislation. This reflects a search for "a greater flexibility in the norms of work" than is possible to achieve with labor law or sectoral agreements (Naboulet 2011b: 6, translation by the author). The result is a hybrid form of *loi négociée* in which legislation reflects the results of bargaining. But it is important to understand that this is not simply the state stepping aside and mutely accepting the product of bargaining. Rather, the state has increasingly set the agenda for that bargaining through legal obligations and financial incentives. Naboulet counted more than ten such obligations just since 2005 (Naboulet 2011b: 1), and a practice emerged during the Sarkozy presidency of the government laying out an agenda for national bargaining each year, urging unions and employers to bargain on a specific range of issues. The presidency of François Hollande, who was elected in 2012, began its term with a "grande conférence sociale" to set the social agenda for the entire five-year span of the new government (Noblecourt 2012).

While the practice has become more formal in recent years, it is part of a longer lineage in which flexibility and liberalization are introduced through national agreement rather than legislation, or more accurately, national agreements legitimize deregulatory or liberalizing legislation. In practically every case since the end of the 1990s, the initiative for negotiation has come from the state or from employers and involved concessions on the part of workers. Indeed, this was a central plank of MEDEF's *refondation sociale*: the reform of labor market practice and the comanaged social insurance schemes through national bargaining. For the state, the public sector was of particular interest – hence the 2003 agreement on public sector pensions, which successfully prevented the surge of strikes that had blocked a similar plan in 1995. Both the sickness insurance and unemployment insurance systems were also reformed in the same manner. The year 2009 saw the government propose a social agenda of bargaining on flexibility of employment contracts and a simplification of unemployment benefits, both of which found their way into legislation following national bargaining (Rehfeldt 2011).

The point here is that the revival of national bargaining in France (Freyssinet 2010), at the same time as trade unions are experiencing historically low membership levels, reflects a dynamic similar to that of contemporary social pacts elsewhere in Europe: the search to legitimize neoliberal reforms of the social and industrial spheres (see Baccaro 2011b, and the chapter on Italy later in this book).

5.4 The Changed Architecture of French Industrial Relations

At the end of the 1970s, French industrial relations were marked by some collective bargaining at the sectoral level, but institutions were most underdeveloped inside the firm, where collective bargaining was rare and unions weak and precarious. Most important was highly statist regulation both of the labor market and of social relations between employers and unions: sectoral agreements were extended by the state; the ability to hire and fire was constrained; the representative status of union confederations was officially legitimized by legislation; price indexation and the minimum wage shaped wage determination. The result was that the primary obstacle to labor market flexibility and the ability of employers to organize the firm as they wished was the French state. In the ensuing three decades, this system of industrial relations has been transformed as the state has steadily deregulated the labor market, a dense network of firm-level institutions has appeared, and collective bargaining inside the firm has become widespread and regularized (for good overviews of this process see Duclos, Groux and Mériaux 2009 and Amossé, Bloch-London and Wolff 2008).

The central paradox of this transformation is captured in Lallement's identification of two discordant tendencies: on one hand, the "contractualization" of society as collective bargaining becomes an increasingly important form of social regulation; on the other, the delegitimization of trade unions, whose membership and organizational strength have collapsed (Lallement 2006). The question becomes, then, what does it mean to reconstruct industrial relations at the firm level without unions, or perhaps more accurately, with unions that lack members? What in turn do these developments mean for the scope of employer discretion and the liberalization of French industrial relations?

To start with collective bargaining, it is important to recall the point made above, that the social role of bargaining has expanded as governments are now much more likely to use bargaining – through a combination of legal obligations, financial incentives and broad policy statements – as *the* mechanism by which social policy is implemented in order to permit greater flexibility in its application (Duclos, Groux and Mériaux 2009: Part Four). Law and public policy are still central to "the enabling of social dialogue" (Naboulet 2011b: 1, translation by the author), in the sense that they establish tasks for the representatives of employers and workers, but they create considerably more discretion and flexibility at the firm level.

Sectoral bargaining continues to ensure near universal coverage of French workers, over 97% (Combault 2006: 1), but coverage reflects the state's determination to extend agreements rather than the strength or presence of trade unionism across the economy. More importantly, sectoral agreements are increasingly minimalist, setting a minimum wage, hours and vacations, and managing the procedures for firm-level bargaining.[3] There is evidence of employers either terminating sectoral agreements (as in banking) or minimizing their importance (chemicals, automobiles, iron and steel, aeronautics) in order to achieve greater flexibility through firm level agreements (Moreau 2004: 61–62).

The primary development with regard to collective bargaining has been the expansion of firm-level bargaining since 1981, with moments of exceptional growth in the aftermath of the *lois Auroux* and the *lois Aubry* (Ministère de l'Emploi 2004: 111). The number of firm-level agreements rose almost ninefold between 1984 and 2011 (Castel, Delahaie and Petit 2013: 21). While approximately 2 million French workers were covered by firm-level agreements in 1984, by 2002 that had doubled (Andolfatto 2004: 115). By the second half of the 2000s, Naboulet (2011a: 19–20) estimates that 61.3% of workers, or about 7 million, engaged in some form of firm-level bargaining each year, and between 2005 and 2010 the number of firm-level wage agreements signed increased by 43%.[4]

The capacity to use firm-level bargaining to undercut either legislation governing the labor market or sectoral agreements, beginning with a small breach in the established "favorability principle" in 1982, is now very broad indeed (Martin 2011), something that in no small measure explains the greater recourse to firm-level bargaining on the part of employers and their willingness to shift attention from the sectoral to the firm level. Derogation is both inherently decentralizing and deregulatory: it involves a shift downward in social regulation and a withdrawal of the state from its regulatory role. As Moreau has noted in a comprehensive survey of collective bargaining in France, its *function* has changed over the last four decades, from a mechanism for acquiring rights and benefits for workers to a practice of mutual concession (what the French refer to as *donnant–donnant*), and "finally as a process of bargaining a way towards deregulation ... a management tool introducing a measure of flexibility which would not have been possible under statute law" (Moreau 2004: 5–6).

Understanding the function of bargaining, but also the extent to which the resulting agreements involve an expansion of employer discretion, requires an examination of who is signing firm-level agreements. Recall that until the end of the 1990s, recognized unions had a formal monopoly on bargaining, though there was increasing recourse to illegal agreements with works councils or other

---

[3] Castel, Delahaie and Petit (2013) have examined the relationship, or "articulation," between sectoral and firm-level bargaining. They conclude that there is a broadly complementary relationship, with sectoral agreements serving to regulate the wage determination process, while it is at the firm level that wages are actually determined.

[4] This is calculated using the figure for 2005 (Ministère de l'Emploi, du Travail et de la Cohésion Sociale 2006: 204) and the figure for 2010 (Ministère du Travail, de l'Emploi et de la Santé 2011: 456).

employee delegates from the passage of the *lois Auroux* onward. The categorization of firm-level agreements is complicated in France, and the data are not fully comparable prior to the 1990s. That said, a survey of bargaining in the mid-2000s found that a little over a third (37%) of all firm-level agreements were signed by union delegates or a union section, with a further 9% signed by elected representatives (Naboulet 2011a: 52). The remaining more than 50% of agreements were the product of either unilateral employer signature or an employer decision ratified by a referendum of employees. After 2002, with the decline of new work time agreements and the activation of the *loi Fillon*, agreements signed by employees mandated by an external union shrank to less than 2%. The great majority of formal wage agreements, encompassing wages, hours and working conditions, are still signed by union delegates, but it is increasingly the case that a range of agreements, narrower in scope, implementing savings or profit-sharing plans, for example, are signed by elected representatives or subject to employer signature or referendum. This becomes more common in smaller firms, where union delegates are rarer.

Furthermore, Naboulet (2011a) has made a strong case for a blurring of the lines between union delegates and elected employee representatives, as the two are often the same people, or elected representatives participate in bargaining alongside a union negotiator. This is unsurprising given that the boundary between the competence of collective bargaining and that of dialogue and consultation inside the firm has become "more and more porous" (Naboulet 2011a: 55) in the context of the negotiation of flexibility. There is no hard and fast line between wage bargaining, the province of unions, and firm-specific forms of profit-sharing, or consultation over changes in work organization, subject to discussion with a works council and employee delegate, or unilateral employer action. Thus, an essential continuum exists between a wage agreement signed with a recognized union and a savings plan implemented unilaterally by an employer and perhaps ratified by employee referendum. The result is that, as firm-level negotiation has spread and become more important, it is less and less the exclusive province of trade unions, particularly in smaller firms, and the line between union bargaining, consultation with firm-specific institutions and extra-legal action on the part of employers has blurred.

The place of French trade unions within the emerging decentralized institutions of industrial relations presents something of a puzzle (Béroud and Yon 2012, Wolff 2008b). On one hand, unions have fewer and fewer members. On the other, there has been a trend toward greater institutional presence of unions within firms over the last two decades. The rapid decline in membership that occurred during the 1980s, a decline that saw union density cut in half to 9.4% in 1993, has stabilized somewhat since, but unions continue to lose members, and more recent figures indicate a density of 7.6%, with something close to 5% in the private sector (Amossé and Pignoni 2006: 406).

The argument for a "resyndicalisation" rests on two recent trends. The first is the greater electoral success of union lists in professional elections since the mid-1990s (Dufour and Hege 2008, Jacod and Ben Dhaou 2008), and the second is the greater implantation of union sections inside firms. The REPONSE workplace industrial relations surveys, conducted in 1992/3, 1998/9, 2004/5 and 2010/11, indicated an increase in the presence of union delegates in firms over the period of the four surveys, with the result that by 2011, 67% of firms employing 50 or more workers and 35% of firms employing 20 or more workers had a union delegate (Pignoni and Raynaud 2013: 5). What then does it mean for the functioning of the industrial relations system to have "syndicats sans syndiqués" (Pernot and Pignoni 2008: 147, translated as "unions without members")?

Unions themselves, as noted above, have become more dependent upon the votes they receive in professional elections, especially since the passage of the 2008 law on union representation. Dufour and Hege (2008) note that for most of the postwar period, works councils occupied a marginal position in the industrial relations system and were clearly subordinate to unions, but as works councils received more legal powers from the *lois Auroux* onward, and as union membership collapsed, unions have become the junior partners, dependent upon works councils for legitimacy: "union structures become dependent upon [works council] electoral results to justify their representativeness and thus their survival. This marks a reversal of representative roles" (Dufour and Hege 2008: 35, translation by the author). More important, it fundamentally changes the nature of union strength from class power – the ability to withdraw labor and halt production – to electoral influence in workplace elections.

Trade union delegates inside the firm have come to be absorbed by firm-level representative institutions (works councils, employee delegates, health and safety committees), resulting in a "generalized slippage from collective bargaining toward social dialogue under the control of management" (Pernot and Pignoni 2008: 161, translation by the author). Thus, union delegates are delinked from the national unions to which they formally belong, serving to sign agreements with employers but exercising little independent power. Indeed, early in 2015, as part of negotiations encouraged by the Socialist government on the "modernization of social dialogue," MEDEF proposed the creation in small and medium-sized firms of a "Conseil d'Entreprise" that would merge all the firm-level representatives, including union delegates, employee delegates and the works council, into a single body that would in turn be authorized to sign firm-level collective agreements (Ouest France 2015). If implemented, this would have been the final erasure of the trade union bargaining monopoly; however, the final legislation in July 2015 allowed the merging of all *nonunion* representative institutions in firms employing 50–299 workers to create a "délégation unique du personnel," while also creating a new form of worker representation external to the firm in those employing less than 11 workers (Assemblée Nationale 2015).

It is perhaps no surprise, then, that surveys of workers indicate limited confidence in the capacity of unions to protect their interests (Pignoni and Tenret

2007: 5), and studies examining the "quality" of work time agreements found that those signed by mandated employees were stronger – contained more benefits for workers – than those signed by union delegates (Thoemmes 2009). This appears to be because unions at the sectoral level could exercise more control over the terms of the bargaining using the mandating mechanism than relying on increasingly autonomous firm-level union delegates. The virtual disappearance of mandating since 2002 reinforces, then, the growing weakness of union organization inside the firm. Union organization at the firm level in the absence of membership has produced something more akin to enterprise unionism than independent trade unionism.

The strategy on the part of the French state of creating legal obligations to bargain at the firm level in return for permitting greater flexibility required, given the weakness of trade unions, the creation and legitimization of nonunion forms of worker representation. The result has been an increase in the number and influence of nonunion worker representatives, including works councils, employee delegates, a new form of delegate who fulfills the duties of both works council and employee delegate in small firms, and mandated employees, though these were used primarily to implement work time reduction (Wolff 2008a: 91). By 2010/11, fully 75% of firms employing 20 or more workers had some form of elected, designated or mandated employee representative, with that figure rising to 94% in firms employing 50 or more workers (Pignoni and Raynaud 2013: 5).[5]

The density and range of workplace institutions, where once firm-level industrial relations institutions had been underdeveloped, reflects the need on the part of employers and the state to bring partners into existence in order to negotiate flexibility. As increasingly with union sections, these are firm-specific institutions, with limited capacity, autonomy from management or independent power resources. Small wonder that only a little over one-third of workers (36.9%) believe that employee representatives are able to influence the decisions of management (Amossé 2006: 6).

The transformation of French industrial relations over the last three decades has been driven by the search on the part of governments and employers, with limited support from some of the union confederations, for mechanisms that would permit the controlled and negotiated introduction of a more flexible labor market, even if the weakness of labor representation has made for largely one-sided negotiation: "This organised decentralisation of collective bargaining aims to allow an enlargement of negotiated flexibilities. *Firm level bargaining is becoming the place of flexibilities and even of negotiated de-regulations*" (Moreau 2004: 23, emphasis in the original).

[5] It is worth noting that the REPONSE surveys showed a secular increase in all forms of worker representative (union and elected) from 1992/3 to 2004/5, but that the 2010/11 survey indicated a small decline in both works councils and union delegates. This suggests a stabilization of workplace industrial relations institutions in the period since the peak of state-mandated or encouraged workplace social dialogue (Pignoni and Raynaud 2013).

The decentralization of industrial relations and generalization of social dialogue encouraged flexibility and an expansion of employer discretion by obligating bargaining on some issues, by creating opportunities for derogatory agreements, by ensuring that employers had relatively weak partners on the labor side and by legitimizing deregulation on the part of the state. As Jenkins has noted (2000), over the space of 30 years, state projects of reform have "have catalyzed a search for *broader organizational flexibilities*" (Jenkins 2000: 166, emphasis in the original). The institutional reconstruction of industrial relations went hand in hand with the introduction of flexibility.

The last twenty years have thus seen a remarkable increase in flexibility in work organization and the labor market (for a comprehensive overview of the 1990s see Jenkins 2000). Askenazy concludes (Askenazy 2013: 242) that "the progressive adjustment of French labor law and the inventiveness of firms' human resources departments offer a labor market that is increasingly flexible." The spread of flexibility has been apparent across a range of areas: the diffusion of individualized payment arrangements;[6] the spread of total quality programs of various types; increases in contractual flexibility that have led to an expansion in the number of workers on part-time, temporary or fixed-term contacts; and opportunities for reorganizing work made possible by flexible work time. The proportion of employees working part-time increased from 8% in 1980 to 18% in 2003, and those on fixed-term contracts increased by almost two percentage points to 11.1% between 1996 and 2003 (IRES 2005: 9–10). Work time reduction is a good example of a legislative obligation that produced broad organizational flexibility because of the requirement that it be bargained. As Askenazy notes (2013: 324): "The 35-hour working week policy appears as an exchange of more leisure for a more flexible and intensive organization of work." Firms took advantage of the wide range of options for how to calculate reduced work time to experiment with different kinds of shift work and with scheduling that corresponded better to demand (Askenazy 2013: 341–343). And by creating a greater financial disincentive to use overtime, the Aubry 35-hour week legislation forced employers to contemplate a more fundamental reorganization of work (Hayden 2006).

The state was also more willing to withdraw from direct regulation of the labor market in the presence of firm-level provisions for social dialogue over layoffs. As noted above, administrative authorization for layoffs was abolished and replaced by a provision that a social plan be presented to the works council. The first decade of the twenty-first century ushered in the introduction of new kinds of work contracts that subsidized employers for hiring, made it easier to fire recently hired workers, or both. It rested upon the assumption that the fastest way to reduce unemployment, especially for young people and the

---

[6] The 2004–05 REPONSE workplace industrial relations survey found that fully 76% on non-supervisory employees received individual raises, with 56% receiving individual performance bonuses (Castel, Delahaie and Petit 2013: 35).

long-term unemployed, was to make it easier and cheaper for employers to hire and fire new workers. Thus labor market deregulation became more explicit. The result was the introduction of a dizzying array of work contracts, aimed primarily at young workers and new hires, and offering lower wages and less job protection (Le Barbanchon and Malherbet 2013: 18). The *contrat nouvelle embauche*, for example, introduced in 2005, targeted new hires in small firms and permitted employers to unilaterally fire a worker without cause and without the usual separation costs, during the first two years of the contract.

In 2008, the government translated a national agreement (which the CGT had refused to sign) into law, providing for a trial period during which new employees could more easily be fired, a new form of fixed-term contract, and the option for mutually agreed employment termination (what employers somewhat misleadingly termed "séparation à l'aimable") that would not require consultation with a works council. Evidence from late 2010 indicated that this procedure was used for 11% of all layoffs (Tissandier 2011).

Among the earliest actions of the socialist presidency of Hollande was to inaugurate national negotiations on the "sécurisation de l'emploi," conceived as a grand bargain to increase competitiveness and flexibility while offering some protection to laid-off workers. The wide-ranging agreement, reached in January 2013 (though not signed by the CGT and FO) and subsequently incorporated into legislation, made it easier for firms to dismiss workers and reduced the compensation paid to those workers. And in an effort to reduce labor market dualism, it reduced the employer unemployment insurance contributions for hiring permanent workers while increasing them for hires of temporary workers (Turlan and Cette 2013). Following losses in local elections and a reshuffling of the Socialist government in 2014, and in the context of stubbornly high unemployment, a further package of labor market reforms, focused upon easing hiring and firing regulations upon small business, was unveiled in June 2015 (Melander 2015), followed by another, the *loi El Khomri*, in March 2016. The latter proposed a range of new possibilities for flexibility with regard to work time, overtime, compensation for unfair dismissal and layoffs (Bissuel 2016). In doing so, it follows a familiar path: much of the flexibility is subject to firm-level negotiation.

At the end of the 1970s, the primary constraints upon employer discretion came from the state, in the form of legislation directly regulating the labor market, but also supporting sectoral or national standards that limited firm-level flexibility. Those constraints now weigh much less heavily upon employers. The ability to hire and fire has been substantially deregulated, and work organization, never heavily regulated, has seen the widespread introduction of flexibility, in part under the impulse of work time reduction. In the 1970s, employers faced standardized wage increases from sectoral agreements, usually with built-in price indexation, and upward pressure from the minimum wage. This has been transformed by the widespread introduction of individualized wages and the replacement of part of across-the-board increases with elements of profit sharing and other financial participation schemes (Brochard 2008). While firm-level agreements must respect sectorally bargained minimum wage levels, they can modify the wage structure as long as overall wage increases are maintained (Martin 2011); in the sphere of wage determination, individualization has accompanied decentralization and deregulation, expanding the scope of employer discretion.

5.5 Conclusion

Liberalization follows different pathways in different countries, depending in part upon the inherited institutional legacies of the earlier postwar period and the strength of class actors. While, in Britain, collective regulation had to be dismantled to permit an expansion of employer discretion, in France the limits upon employer discretion came not from unions and collective bargaining but from a dirigiste industrial relations system. Thus, paradoxically, a shift from statist regulation to the construction of institutions of bargaining and social dialogue inside the firm was the pathway taken by liberalization, and the mechanism by which the state was able to withdraw from active regulation of the labor market and permit flexibility and expanded employer autonomy and influence in managing the firm.

Starting with the *lois Auroux* and accelerating in the late 1990s and 2000s, successive governments of the Left and Right have sought to balance the perceived imperative of liberalizing the labor market to reduce chronic and persistent unemployment against the fear of social mobilization and a "bloody" post-Fordism. Social mobilization has not been entirely avoided, but, contrary to the international perception of France as a blocked society, unable to reform itself, recent years have seen a remarkable neoliberal transformation of the labor market and industrial relations institutions.

The method of implementing liberalization, applied consistently for the last three decades, was to promise deregulation – either formal legislative change or the ability to exempt oneself from the effects of legislation – in return for a commitment to engage in some form of social dialogue – bargaining with unions if possible, consultation with firm-specific institutions of worker representation if not – over the terms of the resulting flexibility. "Contractualization" and the decentralization of industrial relations was the price of deregulation. This process required the creation of new labor-side actors inside the firm or the investing of new responsibilities in existing ones. But neither French unions, increasingly hollow shells within the firm, or these newer actors have had sufficient independence or capacity to act as effective counterweights to a resurgent, self-confident employer class. The result has been a one-sided liberalization.

The transformation of French industrial relations, as previous lacunae in collective regulation were filled in through extensive experimentation and the emergence of a dense network of firm-level and firm-specific institutions, took place through a range of forms of institutional change. It included the construction of entirely new institutions, the mandating procedure, for example, but more important has been the mutation of existing institutions to take on new functions, such as works councils and employee delegates, or the use of national bargaining to negotiate flexibility, and the expanded scope and usage of the mechanism of derogation. Indeed, derogation represents a new form of the "exceptionalism" beloved by French planners in the 1960s, in which high levels of flexibility and autonomy can be enjoyed by firms even as the formal institutions of industrial relations appear rigid and constraining. As we have noted throughout this book, the functioning of institutions can be transformed even as elements of their form remain unchanged.

6

Softening Institutions

The Liberalization of German Industrial Relations

Germany has long been a crucial case for debates about the resilience of non-liberal capitalism. As the prototypical *coordinated market economy* within the varieties of capitalism (VoC) literature (Hall and Soskice 2001a), it has been exhibit A in the claim that Anglo-American capitalism is not the only viable model of capitalism and that a more equitable, but no less economically efficient alternative exists and continues to be viable even in a globalized world, resistant to neoliberal drift.

A respectable research tradition inspired by the VoC perspective expects Germany's political economic institutions to be subject to at most incremental change along a broadly coordinated market economy path. This expectation is based on the strong degree of complementarity among financial institutions that provide patient capital, industrial relations institutions that provide employee voice and flexibility at work while taking wage costs out of competition, and a training regime that ensures high levels of industry-specific skills. Those institutions in turn provide German employers with a comparative institutional advantage in what Streeck (1991) once termed "diversified quality production" (DQP). The result is an employer preference for existing institutions (Soskice 1999, Thelen 2000) and the expectation that employers will be the staunchest defenders of the model's institutions rather than seeking to dismantle them.

In fact, as we argue in this chapter, the German model is unraveling. Certainly in the sphere of industrial relations, and possibly in other functional spheres as well (Höpner 2001), German institutions have been subject to quite dramatic levels of change. This has taken place not so much through a frontal assault upon core industrial relations institutions, although there was some of this too, but through a combination of the plasticity of institutions, primarily a change in the practice and functioning of works councils, and the erosion and retreat of collective bargaining coverage, trade unions and employer associations.

Geographic escape routes have permitted employers to opt out of once dominant industrial relations practices without being forced to dismantle them.

In this chapter, we document how the German manufacturing firms' need to
cut costs spurred liberalization, through company-level initiatives at first, and
then through legislative change as well. These dynamics led to deep modifications in the functioning, if not the form, of German industrial relations institutions. As we argue in the concluding chapter, the erosion of industrial relations institutions weakened household consumption as a driver of economic
growth and contributed to shifting the German growth model toward export-
led growth. This in turn weakened the role of domestic consumption as a driver
of German growth, adding further momentum to the process of institutional
transformation.

It should be noted at the outset that the focus of this chapter is on the manufacturing sector, which is the remaining bone of contention in the literature
on the German model. While the most recent VoC-inspired literature on German industrial relations acknowledges liberalization, it continues to argue that
the manufacturing sector remains strategically coordinated, while it is in the
service sector that a logic of market coordination prevails (Hassel 2014, Thelen 2014). In other words, liberalization is essentially a compositional effect,
according to this argument: as deindustrialization shrinks the size of the manufacturing sector and increases the size of the service sector, the importance of
market coordination increases in the economy as a whole (see Thelen 2014).
In contrast with this argument, in this chapter we argue that the liberalization
process deeply affects the manufacturing sector as well.

The chapter is organized as follows: In Section 6.1, we discuss the golden age
of German industrial relations. In Section 6.2, we provide a historical account
of the liberalization process. In Section 6.3, we present data on collective bargaining coverage, works councils and wage dynamics. Section 6.4 concludes by
providing an interpretation of the German trajectory.

6.1 The German Model as It Once Was

The German model of textbook fame was a fairly rigid system. Employer discretion in hiring and firing was limited by high levels of employment protection. The ability of firms to adapt wage rates to local labor and product market
conditions was constrained by industry-level collective bargaining. While functional flexibility at the workplace level was high in comparative perspective, as
a result of cooperative relationships between management and elective worker
representation structures (works councils), every major change in work organization had to be negotiated (Thelen 1991, Turner 1991).

According to Streeck's seminal argument (Streeck 1997a), Germany's institutional rigidities were a source of dynamic efficiency that helped German manufacturing move away from cost competition in mass production industries and
make the shift toward DQP. This in turn allowed German firms to successfully

weather competition from new Asian competitors (Jürgens, Malsch and Dohse 1993, Sorge and Streeck 1987). Institutions simultaneously constrained and enabled German employers, nudging them toward competitive strategies they might have not chosen if left on their own. Unable to compete on costs due to the presence of strong unions and encompassing industrial relations institutions, firms were encouraged to boost their quality and productivity levels by investing in technology and innovation (Hall and Soskice 2001a, Sorge and Streeck 1987, Streeck 1991).

The vocational training system contributed to German economic success by producing an ample supply of worker skills. Co-financed by employers and the state and co-managed by unions, employers and public authorities, it combined schooling and practical experience over a period of two to three years. The key professional degree in the manufacturing industry – the *Facharbeiterausbildung* – provided workers with sector-specific occupational skills that were recognized across companies. Skilled workers (*Facharbeiter*) had a "broad-based knowledge of materials, tools and products" and were able to perform independent work without close supervision (Roth 1997: 117). Thus, they could cope with the complex technologies and functional flexibility necessary for DQP. During the eighties, vocational training was expanded to reduce unemployment, and this led to an even greater supply of skilled workers than usual (Streeck 1997b: 247).

The DQP arrangements were supported by strong works councils with codetermination rights and encompassing sectoral bargaining institutions. An additional element in the institutional landscape was the high level of employment protection, which incentivized employers and workers to invest in skill-specific training (Estevez-Abe, Iversen and Soskice 2001). Protected by strict employment protection legislation (EPL), permanent employment relationships were the dominant contractual form in the manufacturing industry and created a hospitable environment for work organization systems based on mutual trust (Iversen and Soskice 2001, Streeck 1992: 32).

Works councils were actively involved in the organization of vocational training and in the implementation of non-Tayloristic forms of work organization; furthermore, they fostered cooperation between labor and management. Although formally autonomous, works councils were organizationally dominated by trade union members, and this prevented them from adopting company-oriented logics at odds with the union goal of setting homogenous industry standards (Streeck 1984). The union membership rate of works council members reached a peak of over 90 percent in the steel industry (Niedenhoff 1981: 27–30). Union density in the metal sector, although not very high by international standards, was around 40–45 percent, 10 percentage points higher than the overall (Hassel and Schulten 1998: 499, ICTWSS 2011). Metal sectoral agreements covered around 80 percent of the workforce. This high coverage rate was due both to IG Metall's strength and to high employer cohesion. In 1979, the employers' organizational density was around 58 percent, covering over 77 percent of employees (Silvia 1997: 193, Silvia and Schroeder 2007: 1440). IG Metall and the employers' association Gesamtmetall negotiated collective agreements at the regional level in Baden-Württemberg, and these were then extended to the other regions. Metal collective agreements set high wages and limited wage dispersion across workers. These constraints on labor costs were functional for the development of DQP. In particular, low wage differentials across skill categories encouraged employers to invest in broad training (Streeck 1992: 32).

Collective bargaining institutions contributed to high wage levels and low wage dispersion not only for manufacturing workers but across the economy. Indeed, among OECD countries, Germany had one of the lowest rates of intersectoral wage dispersion, after Belgium and the Scandinavian countries (Hassel and Schulten 1998: 487). Even though the productivity rates and the strength of industrial relations actors were lower in the service than in the manufacturing sector, wages grew at a comparable pace across different sectors because IG Metall oriented its bargaining policy toward the productivity rates of the economy as a whole instead of the (higher) sectoral rates of manufacturing, setting a floor for the negotiations of other sectoral unions (Schulten 2001: 5). Furthermore, the overall coverage of collective bargaining in the economy as a whole was over 80 percent in 1980 (Streeck 1997b: 244). The high rate was also due to the frequent declarations of collective agreements as generally binding. In West Germany, between 500 and 600 collective agreements per year were declared generally binding in the period 1977–1987, with a peak of 608 in 1980 (BMAS 2013: 7).

If the industrial relations system was highly institutionalized at the workplace and sectoral levels, national-level tripartite policy making was not a central feature of the German model. The most relevant and explicit experience of coordination in this sense was the *Konzertierte Aktion* in the 1970s, a nonbinding institutional forum set up to achieve price stability, economic growth and high employment. The *Konzertierte Aktion* fostered information exchange and consultation among unions, employers' associations, Federal states and the Bundesbank (Adam 1972: 8 f., Scharpf 1987: 153). It was abandoned in 1977 when unions refused to discipline their wage claims according to the suggestions of the government's Advisory Council (*Sachverständigenrat*) (Testorf 2011: 313 f.).

Although most analyses of the German model emphasize its supply-side characteristics and the role it played in enabling the development of DQP, German industrial relations institutions, particularly the collective bargaining system and the associated intersectoral redistribution, played an important role on the demand side as well. In particular, they supported the development of private domestic demand by ensuring that productivity increases fed into wage increases (Schulten 2004: 5). Coordinated sectoral bargaining based on the principle of pattern bargaining redistributed from workers in more productive companies to workers in less productive ones. Thanks to pattern bargaining,

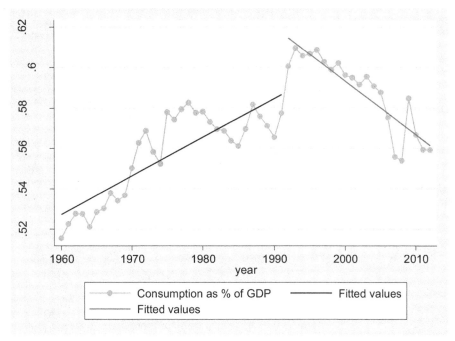

FIGURE 6.1. Trajectory of private consumption as a percentage of GDP *Source:* AMECO Database

the productivity of the manufacturing sector was redistributed to low-value-added sectors (e.g., services). At company level, works councils ensured that the sectoral contract was applied to all workers in the firm along the value chain. Thus, in a manufacturing company, workers employed in services, such as logistics, catering and cleaning services, were covered by the same collective agreement as their colleagues in more "productive" business units such as the assembly line or forging and were paid comparable wages.

As we articulate more fully in the concluding chapter, the German growth model changed over time. Domestic demand, and particularly household consumption, progressively came to count for less than export growth. Germany has always been very successful in exports, but until the 1990s its growth model was pulled both by household consumption and by exports. From the 1990s on, however, consumption fell and exports became the sole drivers of German growth.

Figure 6.1 presents the trajectory of private consumption as a percentage of GDP. The graph shows a rising trend until 1990, a step increase corresponding to the shock of unification around 1990, and then a steady decline from 1990 on. The slack in private consumption was not picked up by investments. In fact, investments declined until the late 1980s, followed by a short-lived improvement until the late 1990s (corresponding to the unification effort), followed by

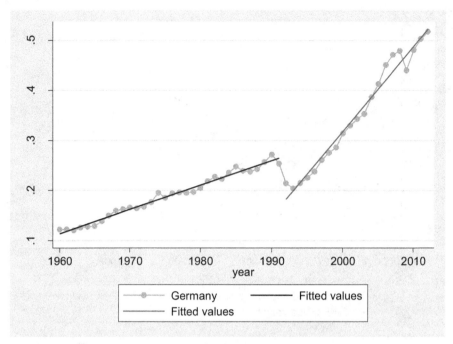

FIGURE 6.2. Exports as a percentage of GDP *Source:* AMECO Database

a new decline in the 2000s. Figure 6.2 displays the trend of exports as a percentage of GDP. Exports grew steadily between 1960 and 2010. However, the growing trend is markedly steeper from 1990 on. Germany has become a much more open economy in the 20 years since unification: Exports as a percentage of GDP increased from 20 to more than 50 percent. Imports grew as well, but less rapidly. Imports are partly linked to exports because they include imported intermediate goods that are incorporated into the final phases of domestic production. According to data reported in Stockhammer et al. (2011: 14), in 2000 the import content of German exports was 38 percent and had been growing for the previous 40 years. Figure 6.3 shows the trajectory of the wage share of GDP. This graph shows a modest increase until 1980, followed by thirty years of continuous decline until 2008. The period following the crisis of 2008 saw a modest increase in the wage share, but it was largely insufficient to make up for lost ground.

Overall, four trends stand out in the trajectory of the German economy: compression of domestic consumption from 1990 on; acceleration of exports (and imports) as a percentage of GDP in the same period; a positive trade balance; and a decline in the wage share.

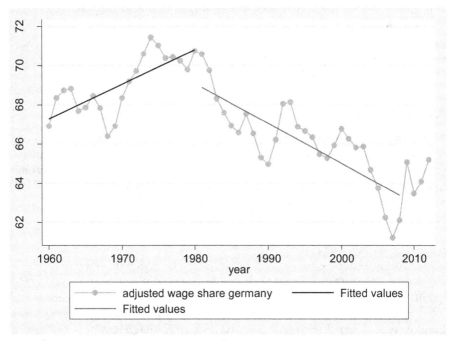

FIGURE 6.3. Trajectory of the wage share *Source:* AMECO Database

In related work (Baccaro and Benassi 2014), we analyze these trends econometrically. Here we summarize the main conclusions of the analysis: the German economy has been shifting from a balanced growth model, in which both household consumption and exports act as stimulants for growth, to an exclusively export-led model, in which increases in domestic consumption negatively affect the competitiveness of exports, and through this channel undermine growth. Furthermore, German exports seem to have become more price-sensitive in the post-1990s period than they were before. When exports are price-sensitive, they are negatively affected by real effective exchange rate appreciation, that is, by domestic wages and prices growing faster than foreign wages and prices, leading to declining cost competitiveness in international markets. This makes wage moderation – specifically, keeping unit costs below those of trade competitors – a functional requirement for export success. Beginning from 1999, membership in the Euro has accentuated the economic effects of price-sensitive exports. The Euro has been for Germany a structurally underappreciated real exchange rate regime in which German wage moderation has directly translated into real exchange rate gains because trade partners have been unable to compensate for it with nominal exchange rate adjustments. More importantly for the purposes of this chapter, in an export-led growth model in which exports are price-sensitive, export-oriented companies are under a lot of pressure to contain costs and boost competitiveness to expand their market share. As argued in the next section, this promotes the liberalization of industrial relations institutions.

6.2 The Trajectory of Liberalization

This section documents the progressive erosion of German industrial relations institutions. The reconstruction begins in what may seem an unlikely place: the unions' work time offensive of the 1980s, possibly the apogee of German trade unions' power. Despite appearances, the work time reduction offensive set in motion a decentralizing trend in German industrial relations that was to continue in later years (Streeck and Hassel 2004).

6.2.1 The Work Time Offensive

In the 1980s, unions were pushed by declining growth and increasing unemployment to moderate their wage demands. Bargaining increasingly addressed qualitative issues such as the work–life balance and the implications of work reorganization and rationalization processes occurring at company level. Employers welcomed the qualitative turn of collective bargaining because it shifted the focus of negotiations from "hard" issues such as wages to "soft" ones such as work time and work organization, and because the shift increased the importance of company-level bargaining (Artus 2001: 87 f.).

In line with the new qualitative orientation, in the 1983 bargaining round IG Metall demanded a work time reduction to 35 hours a week. This bargaining strategy was also meant to tackle high unemployment rates through work redistribution (Artus 2001: 88). A compromise solution was found after a seven-week strike. IG Metall and Gesamtmetall agreed on a work time reduction in steps starting from 38.5 hours a week. In exchange, the unions agreed to the negotiation of work time flexibility at the workplace level. The figure of 38.5 hours was a sectoral average; in reality, works councils could bargain for a weekly number of work hours between 37 and 40 hours (French 2000: 203, Hinrichs and Wiesenthal 1986: 280).

As workplace agreements varied, the formulation and implementation of standard work time reduction policies became difficult. Big manufacturing companies took advantage of increased flexibility. Thanks to their advanced technologies and scientific work organization arrangements, they were able to counterbalance higher hourly costs with increased productivity. Small companies, however, stuck to a standardized working week (Hassel and Rehder 2001: 14). Thus, the attempts to bring about a generalized work time reduction failed, and the goal of 35 hours per week was achieved only in the western metal industry and in the printing industry in the Nineties. In turn, the selective reduction of work time in establishments affected by economic downturn spread massively in the post-unification period, especially during the crisis of 1993–94 (Lehndorff 2001: 19 ff.). Overall, the conflict over work time reduction increased the relevance of workplace bargaining and initiated the erosion of industry-level bargaining.

6.2.2 The Impact of Unification

German unification was a giant governmental attempt at institutional transplantation, which involved inter alia the transfer of industrial relations and social protection institutions to the new regional states (Jacoby 2000). Unions and employers' associations supported the extension of industrial relations institutions to eastern Germany (Paster 2012: 163 f.). In 1991, a staged agreement (*Stufenplan*) was signed in the metal sector, linking eastern wage rates to western rates. The goal was to achieve wage parity by 1994 despite large differences in productivity. Employers agreed to wage increases in eastern Germany for three main reasons. First, they could pass on the negative effects of higher wage costs to the state, as the government was subsidizing the unification process (French 2000: 204). Second, they thought productivity rates would catch up with the rates in western Germany thanks to the investments in high technology supported by the West German government (Sinn and Sinn 1994: 153). Third, low wages in the east would have damaged western employers by diminishing the disposable income of eastern consumers and leading them to orient their consumption choices toward cheap products for which German producers had no comparative advantage (French 2000: 204).

However, the rapid rise in unit labor costs undermined the competitiveness of East German firms, contributing to the collapse of the eastern economy. Between 1989 and 1991, the East German GDP shrank by 40 percent. In 1992, the unemployment rate in eastern Germany was around 14.8 percent – twice the western German rate of 6.6 percent – and it reached almost 20 percent in 1997 (Ritter 2007: 119–21). In this context, eastern metal employers became increasingly critical of the *Stufenplan*, and many small and medium-size enterprises left or failed to join Gesamtmetall to avoid having to comply with the *Stufenplan* (Silvia 1997). In response, Gesamtmetall adopted a more aggressive bargaining policy aimed to regain support among eastern German employers. After the failure to revise the *Stufenplan* in 1993, Gesamtmetall suspended its application and asked for new negotiations.

The bargaining round started with employers offering a 9 percent wage increase – one- third of the previous rate – and asking for the introduction of opening clauses at company level to be applied not just to eastern companies but to western ones as well. Not surprisingly, IG Metall strongly opposed this proposal and mobilized workers in opposition throughout the spring of 1993. The agreement that was signed on 14 May set a wage growth rate of 26 percent and maintained the goal of wage parity between east and west, but delayed it to 1996. The price of the agreement for IG Metall was the introduction of opening clauses. These were allowed until 1996, exclusively under the control of the social partners. Employers and works councils had to request the approval of hardship status from a commission constituted by representatives of IG Metall and Gesamtmetall (French 2000: 206 ff.). The use of hardship clauses was more strictly regulated for companies with a number of employees below five. Between 1993 and 1995, the commission got 181 applications for hardship status in the metalworking sector in eastern Germany, and rejected 83 of them (Bahnmüller, Bispinck and Weiler 1999: 60 f.). The other economic sectors in eastern Germany experienced similar developments. The hardship clauses spread quickly, and many firms used them to introduce work time reduction and wage cutting or freezing to avoid redundancies (Bahnmüller, Bispinck and Weiler 1999: 57). They became a common instrument also in western Germany when the recession hit in 1992. Thus, the response to the unification shock led to the introduction and progressive institutionalization of exceptions to the principle of rigid sector-level collective bargaining.

6.2.3 *The Cost Problem of the German Model*

The economic crisis of the early 1990s revealed a new dimension of the German economic model: although the country competed in high market niches, cost considerations seemed to have become a more pressing concern for the viability of exports (Herrigel 1997: 178 f.). As argued in the previous section, a common theme in the literatures on DQP and VoC is that institutional rigidities, especially encompassing and redistributive IR institutions, contributed to the success of the German economy. However, with the new competitive strength of US and Japanese manufacturers, and with the emergence of new East Asian producers, there were now alternative and cheaper ways to manufacture quality products (Jürgens 2004).

In the 1990s, the German economy experienced unusually high unemployment and lagging growth. A consensus emerged (even in progressive economic circles such as the Max-Planck Institute in Cologne) that high costs and rigid wage determination rules were at least partially to blame for economic stagnation. The debate focused on two channels: the negative effect of social security contributions on employment creation in the service sector (Scharpf 1997a) and the incentives for offshoring in the manufacturing sector (Sinn 2006).

The first line of argument held that rigid wage determination rules and the high compulsory social security contribution rate made employment creation economically unattractive for firms in the private service sector. At a time in which the manufacturing sector was shedding employment due to deindustrialization, private services were supposed to compensate, but they were unable to play this substitution role adequately due to the combination of high (and fiscally regressive) social security costs and low productivity. Differently from the Scandinavian countries, where the public sector expanded employment and compensated for slack private demand (Iversen and Wren 1998), in Germany public sector expansion remained politically unfeasible. Until the end of the eighties, expanding vocational training, work time reduction and early retirement attenuated the rise of unemployment (Streeck 2001: 89–93). However, these solutions were unsustainable in the long run given the high burden they placed on the public budget (Jürgens 1997: 112).[1]

The second argument emphasized the restructuring of manufacturing supply chains. Companies responded to cost pressure from international markets by introducing lean production techniques and by reorganizing their value chains into modules that could be outsourced at lower cost to suppliers both in Germany and abroad. As a result, the value chains of big manufacturing companies became increasingly disintegrated and fragmented (Doellgast and Greer 2007, Greer 2008, Jürgens 2004: 419); new markets in Eastern Europe provided companies with easy access both to new production sites geographically close to the German border, and to a qualified labor force that was cheaper than the domestic one (Jürgens and Krzywdzinski 2006: 3).

According to a survey by the Fraunhofer Institut, between 1999 and 2001 over 40 percent of companies in core manufacturing sectors outsourced part of their production abroad. For over 75 percent of these companies, the reason for outsourcing was the reduction of production costs (Kinkel and Lay 2003: 4). Another survey by the Cologne Institute for Business Research reported that around 60 percent of enterprises between 1000 and 5000 employees had set up new plants in countries outside the old EU member states (Sinn 2006: 1160). Value added as a share of production value of the biggest automotive companies decreased from 41.3 to 34.8 between 1989 and 1998 (Greer 2008: 187). A measure of the extent of outsourcing is the import content of German exports, which was around 25 percent until the beginning of the nineties and had increased by 13 percentage points by 2004 (Ludwig and Brautzsch 2008: 177).

The massive outsourcing to Eastern European countries, especially to the Czech Republic and Poland, reduced low-skill employment in the manufacturing sector (Geishecker 2002, Sinn 2006). Given the high unemployment rate from the 1990s until the mid-2000s, the issue of job losses through outsourcing dominated political discourse in this period and contributed to build a consensus around the need for industrial relations and labor market liberalization (Silvia 2010: 223, Upchurch 2000: 76).

6.2.4 Pacts for Employment and Competitiveness
In the first half of the nineties, the employer associations' support for sectoral bargaining institutions dwindled. In particular, small and middle-sized companies complained vociferously about the high wage levels set by sectoral collective agreements, not just in eastern but also in western Germany (Hassel and Rehder 2001: 5). Some firms withdrew from employer associations altogether. The organizational density of the metal industry employer association fell from

---

[1] What may be referred to as the "Max Planck Institute" proposal aimed to reduce social security contributions for low-wage workers by financing them with a general "green tax."

77.4 percent in 1984 to 71.6 percent in 1991 in West Germany, while density stood at 65.7 percent in eastern Germany in 1991 (Silvia and Schroeder 2007:: 1440).

To stem the organizational hemorrhage, Gesamtmetall introduced the option of membership without application of the sectoral agreement (*Ohne Tarif-bindung (OT)-Mitgliedschaften*). Furthermore, the organization's bargaining policies became less willing to accommodate the union's wage demands. In September 1993, Gesamtmetall announced that the sectoral agreement in western Germany would not be renewed after its expiration in early 1994 and asked for a wage reduction of 10 percent and for greater work time flexibility at the workplace level (Turner 1998: 102).

IG Metall responded by mobilizing its members. The decisive industrial action was undertaken in Lower Saxony, where 92 percent of IG Metall members voted to strike. This unlocked the negotiations with Gesamtmetall. The final agreement froze wages for one year and allowed companies to bargain with works councils over work time reduction up to 30 hours/week in exchange for employment security. It was then extended through pattern bargaining to all federal states (Turner 1998: 104–6).

This outcome came at a moment when works councils were under pressure due to the threat of disinvestment from German locations and of high unemployment (Turner 1998: 100). After the agreement in 1994, the so-called Pacts for Employment and Competitiveness (PECs) (*Betriebliche Buendnisse zur Beschaeftigungssicherung und Wettbewerbsfaehigkeit*) quickly spread across sectors. The companies with a more internationalized product strategy made greater use of company-level pacts, making works councils co-responsible for the economic viability of production sites (Rehder 2003: 113–16). The PECs mainly included measures regarding work time, work reorganization, early retirements and wage cuts or freezes (Seifert and Massa-Wirth 2005). Differently from the company-level pacts signed in the eighties, the PECs were not subordinated to the sectoral agreements but could amend and derogate their provisions (Hassel and Rehder 2001). The PECs were presented as responses to an exceptional economic situation and were initially intended to cover a maximum period of three years. From the late nineties on, however, the company agreements contained more long-term provisions and became more institutionalized, bringing the decentralization of collective bargaining a further step forward (Rehder 2003: 118).

In 2003, the unions' attempt to equalize work-time conditions between east and west (at 35 hours) was decisively defeated by the employers. This union defeat is noteworthy because metalworking employers proved willing to sacrifice labor peace and sabotage industry-level bargaining in order to gain a strategic advantage over IG Metall. According to Raess's account (2006), metalworking employer associations encouraged firms to shift to OT membership, large players such as BMW and Siemens threatened to move production abroad, and a rift opened between works councils (concerned with job security) and IG

Metall (concerned with equalization). The use of aggressive bargaining strategies by employers (see also Kinderman 2005) is difficult to reconcile with claims in the VoC literature about large firms backing German industrial relations institutions (Soskice 1999, Thelen 2000).

To regain a modicum of control over centrifugal tendencies, IG Metall signed the Pforzheim Agreement in 2004. The agreement made derogations to collective agreements possible, but only if employers offered concrete measures for safeguarding jobs, such as new production investments. Also, unions and employers' associations were to be actively involved in the negotiations (Haipeter 2009).

6.2.5 The Alliances for Jobs

Parallel to the diffusion of PECs, attempts to reduce wage costs and alleviate the problem of unemployment were also made at the national level, where the actors sought to negotiate European-style social pacts. In 1995, the Head of IG Metall, Klaus Zwickel, proposed the Alliance for Jobs (*Bündnis für Arbeit*) – a tripartite agreement covering all economic sectors. IG Metall would agree to wage increases in line with inflation (with no productivity-related increases) and also to authorize the employment of long-term unemployed workers at lower wage rates. In exchange, IG Metall required employers to provide employment guaranties and new job positions for long-term unemployed and trainees. The government, in turn, was asked to step up its financial and political commitment to vocational training and to reduce social security contributions (Bispinck 1997: 64).

The unions' initiative was supported by the federal government, which started consultations with representatives of unions and of employers' associations in January 1996. The employers' associations saw the Alliance for Jobs as an opportunity to push through their demands for labor cost reductions. In accordance with employer preferences, the consultations focused mainly on labor market and welfare reforms rather than on investments in innovation and policies for promoting new business and employment. This cooled the unions' enthusiasm for a tripartite solution and the negotiations broke down when the unions refused the package of cuts proposed by the government, a relaxation of employment protection for small companies, cuts to health care and to unemployment benefits, and the extension of the maximum duration of fixed-term contracts. The unions' counterplan included work time reductions and measures promoting part-time work instead of overtime work.

The unions reacted to the government's proposed reforms by organizing protests and demonstrations. Despite these, the Parliament approved the package of cuts in September 1996 (Bispinck 1997: 66–71). Even though the attempts at tripartite negotiations failed, the collective bargaining rounds running parallel to the consultations achieved some results: wage increases were set at modest rates in all sectors, but the agreements included provisions on training and work time reductions (Bispinck 1997: 74).

A new attempt at tripartite social pacting was made a few weeks after the elections in 1998, when the new coalition government formed by the SPD and the Green Party initiated renewed tripartite consultations. The strategic landscape had changed dramatically: If in 1995, faced with an "unfriendly" government, the unions had been keen to negotiate at the national level, now, faced with a supposedly more "friendly" government (whose electoral campaign had included the promise to repeal the Kohl government's welfare state cuts), the unions were more inclined to simply collect the rewards of their electoral support (Streeck 2003). The new Alliance for Jobs, Training, and Competitiveness covered a broad range – from vocational training and pensions to work time and fiscal policies. Employers' associations pushed for long-term wage restraint in bargaining negotiations. The advisory council of economic experts supported their position. The unions refused to make wage policy a bargaining issue within the Alliance, but could not find a common position on alternative policies. While IG Metall wanted early retirement at 60, the chemical union IG BCE preferred improving the partial retirement scheme. Other unions – for example, in the service sector – criticized these measures, which privileged male workers in a permanent employment relationship, and asked instead for a collective reduction of weekly work time (Bispinck and Schulten 2000: 197–201).

Given the divergence among and within the bargaining parties, negotiations were difficult and long. Courting the unions' favor, the government introduced an environmental tax to reduce nonwage labor costs and started a special program for job seekers. However, the government simultaneously further relaxed employment protection in small companies to satisfy one of the employers' requests (Hassel 2001: 319). In 2000, the Alliance agreed on a national document setting a general framework for future bargaining rounds: Wage policies should reflect available distributive margins based on productivity growth and should facilitate job creation. Still, the positions of the bargaining parties were difficult to reconcile in the following bargaining round: IG Metall asked for a wage increase of 5.5 percent and for early retirement at 60. Employers, instead, stuck to the figures of the advisory council, which suggested an optimal wage rate increase of around 2.6 percent. After the chemical union IG BCE negotiated an agreement in line with the guidelines of the Alliance document, IG Metall, too, had to accept modest wage increases; moreover, it gave up on its demands for an early retirement scheme and agreed instead to some improvements in the already existing partial retirement scheme (Bispinck and Schulten 2000: 201).

Thus, while the first Alliance for Jobs achieved few concrete outcomes, since the package of cuts could partly be "corrected" through collective bargaining, the second Alliance did manage to restrain unions' wage claims (Hassel 2001). Nonetheless, in the eyes of key actors, the limited results that had been reached through the negotiated approach signaled the need for more incisive unilateral action by the government, thus paving the way for legislative labor market liberalization in the early 2000s.

6.2.6 The Hartz Reforms

In the early 2000s, the continuing employment crisis (unemployment reached 11 percent in 2005) and the shift to the right in both the Social-Democratic and the Green Party camps led to the emergence of a more decisive governmental approach to reform. Essentially, the negotiated approach was cast aside and the government intervened unilaterally. An important role in the government's strategic shift was played by the failure of the second Alliance for Jobs and by developments in the political sphere: With the electoral defeat in the regional elections in Niedersachsen in January 2003, the Red–Green government had lost its majority in the Federal Council (Bundesrat) and thus was compelled to pursue an economic policy the political opposition (sensitive to business interests) would be able to agree to (Streeck 2003). The package of labor market, tax and welfare reforms (*Agenda 2010*) launched by the head of the Red–Green government, Gerhard Schröder, reflected this new political orientation. The drivers of these reforms were German employers, who were actively engaged in the public debate to promote neoliberal reforms (Menz 2005: 199 f.). The most famous employer initiative was launched by the "New Social Market Initiative" think tank, funded by Gesamtmetall. The goal of the initiative was not just institutional reform but also, and more fundamentally, changing the social norms and values surrounding the concept of a "social market economy." For instance, the campaign promoted the idea that free markets offer chances to everyone and that "badly paid jobs are better than none at all" (Kinderman 2005: 440 f.).

Schroeder's Agenda 2010 was mostly based on the proposals of the "Commission for Modern Labor Market Services," composed of 15 members and chaired by Peter Hartz, who was the head of personnel at Volkswagen at the time. The proposals of the Commission aimed to decrease the unemployment rate by 50 percent over three years by reforming active and passive labor market policies and by deregulating the labor market (Menz 2005: 204). The reforms were approved between 2003 and 2005 and had a strong impact on both the welfare system and labor market regulation.

The Hartz I and II reforms deregulated the use of atypical work. Hartz I focused on agency work, setting up staff agencies for the unemployed at every local employment office. Limitations on the use of agency work were lifted. Companies could use agency contracts without specifying the reason and without offering any guarantee of a permanent job afterward. Dismissal protection was lowered, as agencies could employ workers on contracts of the same duration as their assignments at the hiring company. Furthermore, the principle of equal pay for regular and agency workers could be waived by collective agreement. Hartz II created mini- and midijobs, that is, employment contracts with reduced social security contributions and tax rates with a maximum income of 400€ and 800€ a month respectively. The reform lifted the limitation of 15 hours/week that used to apply to this type of employment (Weinkopf 2009: 13). Furthermore, Hartz II created subsidies for self-employment (Ich-AG) (Jacobi and Kluve 2006: 21).

Hartz III restructured the unemployment offices, merging the Employment Offices and the Social Welfare Offices and creating Job Centers with the goal of increasing the efficiency of labor market services. Hartz IV overhauled the system of unemployment insurance. This had previously been divided into three tiers: The first tier (*Arbeitslosengeld*) was social security contribution-based, income-related and time-limited. The second tier (*Arbeitslosenhilfe*) was tax-based, income-related (at somewhat lower levels than the previous tier) and time-unlimited. It was often used as a transition to retirement. The third tier (*Sozialhilfe*) was tax-based, means-tested and set at a subsistence level. Access to this third tier involved a set of hurdles such as prior liquidation of the recipient's savings and sale of the recipient's house. Hartz IV shortened the period of full wage-related unemployment benefits (now referred to as *Arbeitslosengeld I*) to a maximum of 12–18 months depending on age. In addition, it merged *Arbeitslosenhilfe* and *Sozialhilfe*, setting the new benefit (*Arbeitslosengeld II*) at approximately the level of the former *Sozialhilfe* (i.e., non-wage-related). In addition, access to *Arbeitslosengeld II* was made contingent on asset availability, and recipients were required to engage actively in job search (Hassel and Schiller 2010: 26–34). This reform, which was implemented at a time of high unemployment, forced workers to accept available jobs independent of qualification and increased the willingness of Works Councils to make concessions to strengthen job security.

The employers' associations welcomed the Hartz reforms, while the unions harshly criticized them, especially with regard to the shortening of unemployment benefits and to the pressure on the unemployed to accept jobs. However, the unions were too weak and divided to resist the liberalizing offensive of employers and government. Works councils in big manufacturing companies did not prioritize the defense of the unemployment insurance institutions because they had already developed social policy instruments at the enterprise level (e.g., early or partial retirement) that made the outcomes of restructuring and downsizing more sustainable (Hassel and Schiller 2010: 129–33).

Furthermore, different unions had different positions. The chemical union, the catering unions and the railway union were willing to bargain over the reforms. IG Metall – whose Head had changed from the reformist Zwickel to the more militant Jürgen Peters – and Ver.di (the service sector union) had a more radical position and did not want to negotiate with the government. The DGB (trade union confederation) tried to set up a common platform by publishing an alternative proposal, but without success. The reformist unions started an initiative shortly after, called "The future of the Welfare State: Yes to Reforms," supporting dialog. After the limited success of a mass demonstration called by IG Metall and Ver.di in May 2003, these two unions, too, agreed to negotiate with government (Hassel and Schiller 2010: 265–9).

The poor outcomes of the bargaining round over agency work are emblematic of the power imbalance during the negotiation of the Hartz reforms. As mentioned earlier, Hartz I introduced the possibility of derogating from the equal pay principle through a specific collective agreement for the agency sector. Employers broke up the bargaining monopoly traditionally reserved to the DGB unions, and a small agencies' association (IZA) started bargaining with the Christian Federation of Trade Unions (CGZP),[2] a union that is renowned for undermining DGB collective agreements (Dribbusch and Birke 2012: 6, Vitols 2008). As a result, the pay differential between an agency worker and a regular worker in the metal sector was between 30 and 40 percent in 2009 (Weinkopf, 2009). In 2012 and 2013, the main staff agency associations and the unions signed collective agreements in nine industries with a view to reducing the wage gap between permanent workers and agency worker. These agreements set sector-specific surcharges that apply after a surcharge-free period (four to six weeks) and gradually increase up to 50 percent of the agency worker's salary over nine months (Spermann 2013).

For the unions, the Hartz reforms were a clear signal they should no longer expect political support from a "friendly" government. The coordination between sectoral unions, concerned with equality of working conditions, and works councils, primarily concerned with job security, and between sectoral and company-level agreements became more difficult. Shorter unemployment benefits and more stringent criteria for eligibility increased the willingness to make concessions at the company level. These trends put works councils and unions under pressure (Dörre 2012, Urban 2010). In addition, the diffusion of contract forms to which the sectoral collective agreements do not apply (e.g., agency work, minijobs) further contributed to labor market segmentation and to the diffusion of precarious forms of employment.

6.3 The New German Model

In this section we present new data on the current state of the German industrial relations system.[3] Although the organizational erosion of German class actors has been documented by previous research (Bosch et al. 2007, Hassel 1999), the extent to which industry-level collective bargaining has been affected by the liberalizing trends illustrated above, including in manufacturing, is often underestimated. Our analysis relies on data from the Establishment Panel of the Institute for Employment Research (IAB). Figure 6.4 reports data on collective bargaining coverage rates for manufacturing and service sectors as well

[2] The special body of the Christian Unions on agency work has been declared unable to negotiate collective agreements by the rulings of the Berlin Labor Court and Federal Labor Court in 2011.
[3] This section relies on data from Baccaro and Benassi (2014).

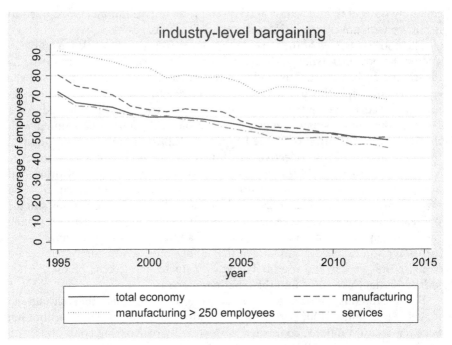

FIGURE 6.4. Worker coverage of industry-level bargaining *Source:* IAB, own elaborations

as for the economy as a whole.[4] Industry-level collective bargaining coverage has shown a steep and uniform decline across sectors: In 1995 collective bargaining covered 72 percent of workers in the economy as whole, 80 percent in manufacturing, 92 percent in manufacturing establishments with more than 250 employees and 72 percent in services. In 2013 the coverage rates were 49, 50, 67 and 45 percent, respectively. The decline in industry-level bargaining has not been compensated for by an increase in company-level bargaining, whose coverage has remained limited, especially in services. The only exception is manufacturing establishments with more than 250 employees, for which the coverage of company bargaining increased from 6 to 17 percent between 1995 and 2013 (see Figure 6.5). The most notable trend has been the increase in the proportion of workers not covered by any contract. In 2013 this proportion was 42 percent for the economy as a whole, 37 for manufacturing, 15 for

---

[4] We include in manufacturing the following industries: pulp, paper, paper, printing and publishing; chemical, rubber, plastics and fuel; other nonmetallic minerals; basic metals and fabricated metal; machinery, NEC; electrical and optical equipment; transport equipment; manufacturing, NEC; recycling, food processing; textile. Services include retail trade, except of motor vehicles and motorcycles; repair of household goods; hotels and restaurants; and the category "other personal services."

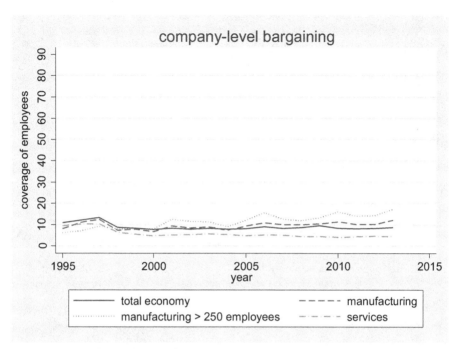

FIGURE 6.5. Worker coverage of company-level bargaining *Source:* IAB, own elaborations

manufacturing establishments with more than 250 employees and 50 percent for services, up from 17, 12, 2 and 19 percent in 1995, respectively. Even more impressive is the proportion of establishments not covered by any collective bargaining agreement (Figure 6.6): In 2013 this was 70 percent in manufacturing and 66 percent in services. Even in establishments with more than 250 employees, 26 percent of establishments (and 14 percent of workers) were not covered by any type of agreement in 2013.

There has been a loss of worker coverage of 20 to 30 percentage points in 18 years, with no dramatic differences between manufacturing and services. Furthermore, between 2005 and 2007 (the two years for which data are available), over 20 percent of the manufacturing establishments covered by sectoral agreements made use of opening clauses, which, as argued above, can amend the provisions set by collective agreements. Overall, the above evidence suggests that industry-level bargaining is still the main type of bargaining in Germany, but it is full of holes, and only about 30 percent of German manufacturing establishments are now covered by a collective agreement of any type.

Also based on IAB data, Figure 6.7 reports the proportion of workers covered by works councils in manufacturing, services and the economy as a whole. Here the coverage is considerably higher for manufacturing than for services (higher than 60 percent vs. lower than 30 percent). Furthermore, while there

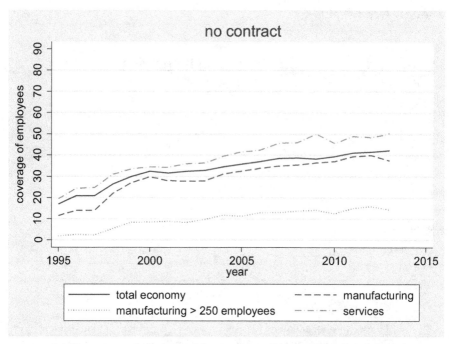

FIGURE 6.6. Percentage of workers with nocontract *Source:* IAB, own elaborations

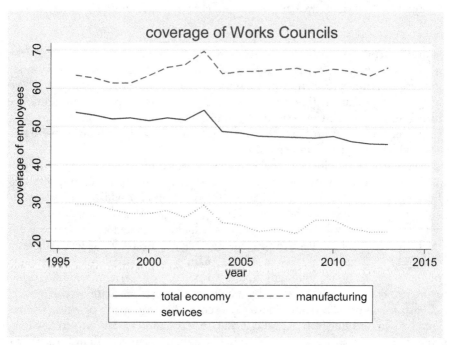

FIGURE 6.7 Worker coverage of works councils *Source:* IAB, own elaborations

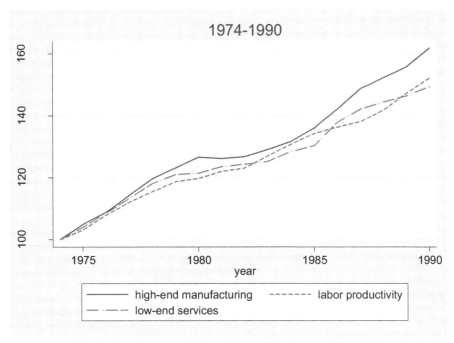

FIGURE 6.8. Trends in real wages (high-end manufacturing and low-end services) and labor productivity (total economy) in 1974–1990 *Source:* Own elaborations on EU KLEMS data (for the definition of sectors see text)

is no declining trend in manufacturing, a small declining trend is visible for services.

These data suggest that the main institutional changes affecting industry-level collective bargaining have been erosion of coverage and derogation. In contrast, the diffusion of works councils has not declined, but their role has changed considerably. Work councils have gone through a process of conversion. In the golden age, they implemented the unions' policy of uniform work standards; in the last 20 years, they have focused on the defense of employment for core employees. To achieve this goal, they have increasingly been willing to make concessions and have contributed to weakening industry-level bargaining.

The softening of industry-level collective bargaining has had important consequences for the ability of collective bargaining institutions to redistribute productivity growth within and across sectors, and to stimulate domestic demand. Figure 6.8, based on data from the EU KLEMS database,[5] shows that intersectoral redistribution and balanced wage growth were indeed key features of

[5] See http://www.euklems.net/ (March 2008 release).

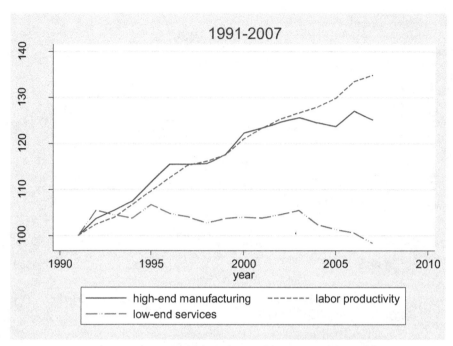

FIGURE 6.9. Trends in real wages (high-end manufacturing and low-end services) and labor productivity (total economy) in 1991–2007

the German model in the period 1974–1990. The graph compares real wage growth in high-end manufacturing and low-end private services with economywide labor productivity.[6] The three sectors grew at approximately the same rate in this period. However, as shown in Figure 6.9, the situation changed dramatically from 1991 to 2007: only high-end manufacturing was able to keep pace with economywide productivity growth, and even in this privileged sector, wages trailed productivity from the mid-2000s on. Service sector wages were instead flat and even slightly declining in real terms. Considering that the employment share of high-end manufacturing declined by approximately 30 percent in 35 years, while the share of low-end private services increased by 40 percent (based on EU KLEMS data), this situation implies that only a shrinking share of workers saw their real wages grow in proportion to productivity. Wage repression depresses domestic consumption and contributes to lock in export-led growth.

---

[6] High-end manufacturing includes NACE codes D21 through D37: paper and pulp, petroleum products, chemicals, rubber and plastics, nonmetallic mineral products, metal products, machinery, electrical and optical equipment, transportation equipment, and manufacturing NEC; low-end services include retail trade (NACE code G52) and hotels and restaurants (H).

6.4 Conclusion

In this chapter, we have provided a historical reconstruction of the liberalization of German industrial relations. The process of collective bargaining decentralization began in the 1980s as an unintended consequence of the trade unions' offensive for work time reduction. It continued in the 1990s in response to the unification shock and employers' attempts to reduce costs and aim for more flexible contractual provisions. The threat of offshoring and outsourcing led worker representatives to agree to deviations from sectoral standards and opening clauses. Attempts were made during the 1990s to govern the process of concession making through social pacts, but these attempts were unsuccessful. In the early 2000s, substantial labor market liberalization was accomplished through unilateral government reform, while the erosion of the collective bargaining system – in the form of dramatic reduction of coverage and the spread of opening clauses – continued unabated. The new German model of industrial relations is very different from the golden age: with a coverage rate of 50 percent of workers and 30 percent of establishments in the manufacturing sector, industry-level collective bargaining is much less encompassing then it once was. Furthermore, the decline of industry-level collective bargaining is not simply a peculiarity of the service sector, but affects the manufacturing sector as well.

The liberalization process has brought about an increase in employer discretion. Rules for the determination of wage increases were adapted to the economic conditions of particular firms through contractual mechanisms such as opening clauses or simply by abandoning collective bargaining coverage altogether. In the 2000s, the German economy experienced wage repression, with wage increases trailing productivity increases and a declining wage share, especially but not exclusively in the service sector. These trends have resulted in growing wage inequality, especially in the bottom half of the wage distribution, and higher proportions of low-wage jobs (Antonczyk, Fitzenberger and Sommerfeld 2010, Bosch and Weinkopf 2008, Dustmann, Ludsteck and Schönberg 2009). Employer discretion in the determination of work time has also increased. Indeed, the ability to adapt work time regimes to specific firm conditions through company-level bargaining has been used first to counter the effectiveness of the work time reduction offensive of the 1980s and then to weather company crises while minimizing employment losses. While employment protection for regular workers has not decreased, it has become considerably easier for employers to hire workers on a temporary basis, and the wage comparability requirement has been weakened.

The argument developed here differs from recent VoC accounts of the evolution of the German model. This literature no longer contests that German industrial relations have been considerably liberalized in the past 20 years, but insists that the manufacturing core remains fundamentally coordinated (among others, Hall 2007, Hassel 2014, Palier and Thelen 2010, Thelen 2014). According to this literature, it is incorrect to talk about liberalization *tout court*. What has occurred instead is not a dismantling but rather a shrinking of coordination, mostly as a result of deindustrialization, that is, of the shrinking of manufacturing and the expansion of services (Thelen 2014). This process has generated a dual equilibrium with a coordinated manufacturing core and a deregulated service periphery. According to the argument, this is a new type of dual equilibrium.

We do not deny that a dualization trend is clearly visible in the German political economy. However, we have no reason to believe it represents a stable equilibrium. In our reconstruction, the impetus for liberalization does not come from an impersonal process of deindustrialization, but from the export sector itself. Export-oriented firms have aimed to reduce costs and in so doing have dramatically changed the way industrial relations institutions work.

This is not the first time that the category of dualization has featured in political economy debates. Dualism between "primary" and "secondary" workers was a prominent feature of debates on internal labor markets in the US and elsewhere (Doeringer and Piore 1971, Osterman 1994). Thirty years ago, John Goldthorpe explained the trajectory of contemporary capitalism by introducing a dichotomy between "corporatist" and "dualist" systems (Goldthorpe 1984). Corporatist countries such as Germany and the Nordic countries had strong collective actors and centralized institutional capacities which allowed them to produce more "inclusionary" outcomes. In contrast, in countries such as the US and the UK, a divide had emerged between the "core," in which internal labor markets predominated, and the "periphery," in which labor market standards were eroded by market forces and an increasing proportion of workers were experiencing commodification. Thirty years later, the process of commodification seems to have reached the final stage in the United States and the United Kingdom, and the discourse on dualism has shifted to the former corporatist countries.

Qualitative evidence suggests that the German manufacturing sector is far from equilibrium: liberalizing reforms put pressure on core workers to agree to concessions (Eichhorst and Marx 2010); core workers and atypical workers perform similar jobs and thus are potentially substitutable (Holst, Nachtwey and Dörre 2010); and unions believe that agency work is a way to replace stable employment with precarious employment (Benassi and Dorigatti 2015).

One implication of the argument developed in this chapter is that dualism may be an intermediate step in the process of liberalization rather than a new equilibrium. Short of a reversal in the actors' balance of power, there is no reason to believe in the resilience of a coordinated core in the long term.

7

"Well Burrowed, Old Mole!"

The Rise and Decline of Concessionary Corporatism in Italy

Looking at the Italian industrial relations system at the end of the 1970s and thirty-five years after is like looking at pictures from two different geological eras. At the end of the 1970s, the key problem for government was persuading trade unions to moderate their militancy so that it would not destabilize the Italian economy. In the early 2010s, faced with the sovereign debt crisis, government no longer sought to strike deals with trade unions, but rather made it very clear that it could do without union support.

In the late 1970s, the Italian industrial relations system was still reeling from the consequences of the Hot Autumn wave of worker mobilizations. The Hot Autumn had dramatically increased the power of trade unions both at the workplace and in society at large. Unions demanded higher and more equally distributed wages and shorter work times, limits on management discretion through rigid work rules, more industrial democracy, more generous social policies and more influence on economic policy in general. Combined with the effects of two oil crises, the growth in union power had led to wage militancy and union control over the workplace in large industrial factories.

In the subsequent thirty-five years, a steady erosion of trade union power and institutional rigidities ensued. Until the early 2000s, most changes were driven through national corporatist pacts in which government played a key role. Corporatist bargaining underwent a process of conversion over time and became increasingly concessionary. In the late 1970s–early 1980s, it was entered into sporadically and reluctantly by trade unions, which required hefty compensation for every concession they made. In the 1990s, it was used as an emergency device to facilitate the flexible restructuring of the Italian economy. In the 2000s, the government continued to seek union cooperation through corporatist pacts, but the largest union confederation became increasingly reluctant to concede it. In the early 2010s, the Italian government shifted to unilateral reform. Being able to prove that it was able to pass reforms against the unions' will became a sign of distinction and increased the government's credibility in international financial markets.

The Italian case stands out among the countries examined in this book because it shows that the liberalization of industrial relations does not need to involve formal bargaining decentralization. In fact, the collective bargaining structure was recentralized in Italy, and there is no evidence that the coverage of decentralized bargaining increased. Liberalization was instead a result of the changing balance of power between unions and firms and of the shift of government policies against organized labor. When the liberalizing potential of centralized bargaining was exhausted, unilateral labor market reform reduced employment protection and expanded the ability of lower-level bargaining to derogate from higher-level regulations.

The chapter is organized as follows: The next section provides a stylized account of Italian industrial relations at the end of the 1970s and of the attempts that were made to reform them. Section 7.2 analyzes the trajectory of corporatist agreements. Section 7.3 concerns the evolution of collective bargaining structure. Section 7.4 examines labor market reforms. The concluding section provides an interpretation of the Italian trajectory.

7.1 Italian Industrial Relations at the End of the 1970s

Up until the 1960s, the Italian industrial relations system was characterized by trade union weakness and employer dominance (Romagnoli and Treu 1981, Turone 1992). Collective bargaining was mostly centralized. This allowed *Confindustria*, the main business association, to link labor cost developments in the most dynamic industrial sectors to the economic conditions prevailing in more backward sectors such as agriculture. Also, trade unions generally lacked the organizational infrastructure needed for decentralized collective bargaining. Their plant-level representation structures were either weak or nonexistent.

This situation began to change in the 1960s, when labor market conditions became more favorable to labor (especially in the northwest of the country), first in the early years of the decade and then dramatically with the so-called "Hot Autumn," a massive wave of strikes initiated by popular demonstrations over pension reform in 1968 and continued during the 1969–72 collective bargaining round (Pizzorno et al. 1978). In many industrial plants, and especially in the metalworking industry, the three main union confederations – the *Confederazione Generale Italiana del Lavoro* (CGIL), the *Confederazione Italiana Sindacati dei Lavoratori* (CISL) and the *Unione Italiana dei Lavoratori* (UIL) – experimented with unity of action. In 1972, these grass-root experiments led to a partial reunification of the Italian labor movement with the signing of a federative pact that established the so-called *Federazione Unitaria CGIL–CISL–UIL*.

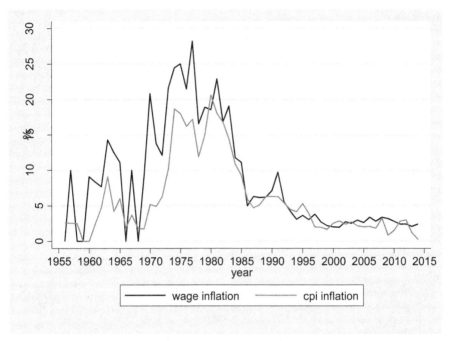

FIGURE 7.1. Wage and price inflation *Notes:* Wage inflation: annual percentage change of hourly manufacturing earnings. Price inflation: annual percentage change of consumer price index *Source:* OECD

The Hot Autumn introduced a variety of innovations into collective bargaining that severely limited employer discretion at the workplace level. For example, it led to the unification of blue- and white-collar job classification schemes (*inquadramento unico*); the abolition of territorial differences in wage levels (the so-called *gabbie salariali*); equal wage increases for all workers regardless of skill levels; improvements in health and safety conditions; and reductions in the speed and duration of work. In 1970 a new labor code, the Workers' Statute, introduced limits on the employer's ability to redeploy workers across production units and job classifications (Art. 13) and made firing decisions in establishments of more than fifteen employees dependent on the existence of "just cause" (Art. 18), in the absence of which employers would be forced to reintegrate the laid-off workers.

These developments led to declining competitiveness vis-à-vis other countries. Particularly worrisome was the rapid increase in wage and price inflation (see Figure 7.1). Italy's real effective exchange rate (a measure of cost competitiveness vis-à main trade partners) appreciated throughout the 1970s (see Figure 7.2). Faced with a worsening macroeconomic situation, all actors, and

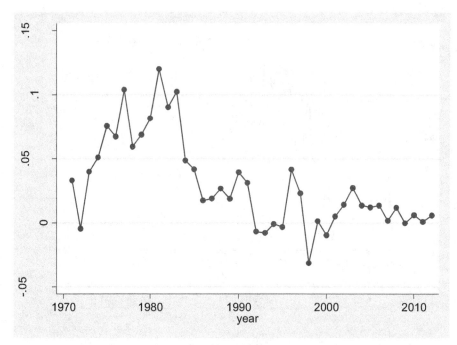

FIGURE 7.2. Real effective exchange rate based on comparison of labor costs with EU-15
Source: AMECO Database

particularly the three union confederations, were forced to rethink their strategies. The process of strategic rethinking was favored by an important political
change: for the first time since 1947, the Italian Communist Party (PCI) was
close to the governmental majority with the so-called governments of "national
solidarity" (Ginsborg 1990: 351–58, Vacca 1987).

   The PCI's (indirect) participation in government was considered of fundamental importance by the Italian labor movement, and especially by the CGIL,
the largest union confederation, because it provided a guarantee that workers'
voluntary wage moderation would be compensated with structural economic
policy reforms favoring the working class (see Lama 1978: 16).

   The unions did not want to facilitate economic restructuring on management terms. They had a vivid recollection of the recession of the mid-1960s:
there had been an upsurge in wage settlement in 1962–63, followed by wage
moderation, which had restored profit margins but had failed to create the
conditions for renewed growth and employment because Italian enterprises
had preferred exporting their capital to investing in Italy.[1] The events of the

---

[1] On this see Salvati (1984: 93). Notwithstanding the decline in nominal wages in the early to
    mid-1960s, investments fell sharply from 27.7 percent of GDP in 1963 to 21.7 percent in 1966
    and never regained their previous level (see EC 1997: Tables 19 and 19).

mid-1960s were interpreted by the Italian union movement as proof that economic adjustment could not be left to the invisible hand of the market but needed to be politically and socially steered. Consistent with economic policy orthodoxy at the time (Shonfield 1965), the unions demanded a new policy of economic planning aimed to correct geographical and sectoral imbalances in the national economy. This new policy should include projects to industrialize the South, sectoral plans for the industrial reconversion of ailing companies, a new energy policy aimed to reducing dependency on oil imports, and the large-scale modernization of Italian agriculture. In exchange for these policy reforms, the confederal unions were ready to accept some wage moderation and slightly increased labor mobility. All of these intents were formalized with the unions' adoption of the so-called "EUR policy" at an organizational conference in February 1978 (Golden 1988, Lange and Vannicelli 1982).

The EUR policy produced a lively debate on the need for unions to moderate their wage demands and become more responsible actors. Its concrete outcomes were, however, rather limited (see Locke 1995: 77–88). Furthermore, most results predated the official adoption of the EUR policy. In January 1977, the three major union confederations (CGIL, CISL and UIL) and Confindustria signed a national agreement that transformed seven previous holidays into regular working days, introduced controls on absenteeism and facilitated flexible shift work and internal mobility. Perhaps most important, the agreement contained a mini-reform on the *scala mobile* (the national wage indexation mechanism), as the indexation of the seniority-based components of pay was eliminated. All in all, the 1977 accord turned out to be little more than a joint declaration of intents (see Cella and Treu 1989: 179). Seniority pay, which as a result of the agreement would no longer be indexed to inflation, only amounted to 1 percent of the average pay of blue-collar workers (CERISS 1980: Table 20, p. 52).[2]

Notwithstanding their limited impact, the EUR line policies met with widespread opposition from within the union movement. The metalworkers, Italy's most powerful and militant industrial workers, mobilized against them (Golden 1988). On December 2, 1977 (even before the EUR policy was officially adopted), the metalworkers organized a national strike that saw the participation of approximately 200,000 people. The strike sent a clear political signal to the Communist Party (which supported the government through parliamentary abstention and actively pushed for trade union restraint) that the strategy of national solidarity was not appreciated by the working-class vanguard. The metalworkers' opposition was instrumental in bringing about a strategic shift within the Communist Party. Influenced by the metalworkers' critique, the PCI began revising its strategy of "historical compromise" and in

---

[2] The figure reported above refers to a blue-collar metalworker employed in the province of Milan in 1977. Seniority pay was more important for white-collar workers and counted for approximately 10 percent.

the early months of 1979 withdrew from the national solidarity governments altogether.

In the late 1970s, Italy's collective bargaining structure was weakly institutionalized and highly dependent on the actors' bargaining power, which ebbed and flowed with labor market conditions (Cella 1989, Cella and Treu 1989). The most important locus of bargaining was the industry level, which set uniform wage and working conditions for all workers, including in the South, where productivity levels were lower. However, in firms where unions had a strong presence, that is, in large manufacturing establishments in the North, company-level bargaining led to wage gains in excess of sectoral standards as well as more favorable working conditions. There was a tendency for the subsequent round of sectoral bargaining to generalize the outcomes of company-level bargaining, thus generating an inflation of demands. In the 1980s, Italian experiments with corporatist bargaining sought to reduce wage militancy and to increase the predictability of the Italian bargaining structure.

7.2 The Checkered Trajectory of Italian Corporatism

After the second oil shock of 1979, the economic policy debate in Italy became less concerned with structural reforms and economic planning and much more focused on bringing inflation under control (see Carrieri and Donolo 1986, especially 119–44, Ferri 1982). Many economists and opinion-makers, including those close to the labor camp, argued that defeating inflation should take precedence over all other policies (see Napoleoni 1982: 7). Given the highly inertial nature of Italian inflation and the role of expectations in reproducing it, fighting inflation essentially meant reforming the *scala mobile*, the national mechanism of wage indexation.

The government had to work hard to bring about the first incomes policy agreement of Italy's postwar history in January 1983. The differences to be bridged were not just across the bargaining table but also within the union camp. The government managed to find a compromise by providing generous compensation for both parties involved. The unions obtained the abolition of bracket creep (to stabilize disposable incomes), while organized employers obtained the subsidization of social security contributions. As a result, this incomes policy accord proved extremely expensive for the Italian state: its cost for the public coffers was estimated to be almost 3 percent of Italy's 1983 GDP (Carrieri and Donolo 1986: 133). Nonetheless, it was hailed as a historic turning point in Italian industrial relations (Treu 1984). With it the unions consented to a 15 percent cut in wage indexation. The accord also established wage ceilings for industry-level collective bargaining (so that inflation could be brought down to the targeted levels of 13 percent in 1983 and 10 percent in 1984). It also introduced an eighteen-month ban on plant-level collective bargaining on wage issues. Finally, it established the principle that the same bargaining issues could not be negotiated at different bargaining levels more than once, thus increasing the stability and predictability of the wage bargaining system (Altieri, Bellina and Carrieri 1984, Ferri 1984).

While inflation declined between 1983 and 1984, possibly as a result of the tripartite agreement (see Figure 7.1), it remained well above 10 percent. In 1984, the new government was determined not just to renew the agreement but to strengthen it substantially. However, the three confederations had different views about the content of a new deal. For the CGIL, it was time for unions to "cash in the price of past sacrifices" (Militello 1984: 10). The other two confederations (CISL and UIL) were, instead, willing to consider a new round of concessions, including a reform of the *scala mobile*.

Eventually, the government and two union confederations, CISL and UIL, converged on a reform proposal formulated by the economist Ezio Tarantelli, who was to pay with his life for this proposal, as he was assassinated one year later by the Red Brigades (a left-wing terrorist group). His ingenuous proposal sought to transform the *scala mobile* from an institution reproducing inflationary expectations into an anti-inflationary device. According to Tarantelli, Italian inflation could be reduced without increasing unemployment if the *scala mobile* was no longer used ex post to recover the lost purchasing power of wages and salaries, but ex ante to predetermine nominal wage growth and hence future inflation. This implied that for one period (which was initially quantified as one year, and later as six months) there would be a cut in nominal wages as a result of predetermination, but this cut would be compensated for by a lower inflation rate at the end of the period so that real wages would remain unchanged (Tarantelli 1986a). The end result would be a cut of nominal wages, that is, of the inflation rate, but not of real wages.

The CISL and the UIL embraced the predetermination proposal, but a split occurred within the CGIL: The Socialist Faction accepted it while the larger Communist faction refused it. The Confindustria also agreed to sign. To give the agreement *erga omnes*, that is, generalized, validity and bypass the CGIL's (and Communist Party)'s opposition, the government included the key parts of the accord in a government decree. With this decree, four *scala mobile* points (corresponding to 27,000 lira) were cut (see Faustini 1986: 411).

The CGIL was under a lot of pressure from some of its members. Even before the union break-up, a few factory councils in Northern Italy began mobilizing against the emerging agreement. These factory councils argued that the confederal unions put too much strategic emphasis on centralized negotiations at the expense of decentralized collective bargaining and industrial conflict.

The "dis-agreement" of 1984 and the subsequent referendum of 1985, whose results were favorable to government and its union allies, had durable consequences for Italian industrial relations. Only twelve years after the birth of the *Federazione Unitaria*, unity of action among the three major union confederations dissolved. Relationships among the three main confederations (especially the CGIL and the CISL) became extremely sour, and national bargaining lost the key role it had played in the previous years. There were no major national agreements until the end of the decade.[3] At the local level, however, the unions continued to cooperate informally with management and local political authorities. These cooperative relations developed not only in industrial districts, but also in large industrial firms previously characterized by adversarial industrial relations (Barca and Magnani 1989, Locke 1995, Regini and Sabel 1989, Trigilia 1986).

In the early 1990s, the government and the social partners were pushed by deteriorating macroeconomic conditions to take up once again the thorny issue of the *scala mobile*. As a result of both (semi-)fixed nominal exchange rates (the lira was tied to the European Monetary System) and positive inflation differentials between Italy and all other major international competitors, Italy's real exchange rate experienced a constant appreciation from 1985 on (Modigliani, Baldassari and Castiglionesi 1996: 38) (see also Figure 7.2). This dampened exports and increased import penetration, producing a balance-of-payments problem. It also contributed to the formation of expectations about a forthcoming devaluation of the lira. These expectations were initially countered by the Bank of Italy through a policy of high interest rates. In September 1992, however, a wave of financial speculations forced the lira (together with the British pound) out of the EMS (Vaciago 1993).

Before this happened, the social partners were pushed by the government to sign an agreement on July 31, 1992, that abolished the *scala mobile*. This agreement was intended to signal to international financial markets that Italy would be better able to keep its inflation rate in check in the future. It also included a one-year moratorium on both firm-level wage negotiations and public sector collective bargaining and a freeze on industrial wages and salaries, government rates, as well as administrative fees for the rest of 1992.

Unsurprisingly, the July 1992 accord stirred wide-ranging internal discontent within the Italian union movement, especially within the CGIL. For almost 20 years, the *scala mobile* had been *the* symbol not only of union power but also of egalitarian ideals in Italy (Locke and Thelen 1995). The Italian confederal unions went very close to replicating the 1984 split. As in 1984, the CISL, the UIL, and the Socialist faction within the CGIL were favorable to the accord. A significant minority faction within the CGIL, however, not only was opposed but even theorized the impossibility of unions engaging in "concession bargaining" with government (Trentin 1994: 166). In turn Giuliano Amato, the head of government, announced that it would resign if the unions refused to sign the accord. Unwilling to bear responsibility for both political instability and

---

[3] On December 18, 1985, the three major confederal unions and government signed a new accord to reform the *scala mobile*. The new wage escalator was divided into two parts: one (580,000 lira) was fully indexed, the other (corresponding to the difference between total remuneration and this fixed part) was only 25 percent indexed. This reform was initially negotiated by the public sector unions. With the implicit assent of the Confindustria, it was later extended to the private sector as well. For more on this reform, see Patriarca (1986).

renewed union division at a time of great political–economic turmoil, Bruno Trentin, the Secretary General of the CGIL, signed the agreement, but simultaneously offered his resignation (which he later withdrew).

The climate of emergency and Trentin's resignation were not sufficient to prevent the emergence of a new wave of grass-roots protest. The timing of the accord, signed on 31 July – the day before the beginning of summer holidays in most industrial factories – was perceived as a *coup de théâtre* designed to preempt rank-and-file opposition. In September, protest exploded in several northern factories and at public rallies.

The mobilizations continued well into the spring of 1993. In the meantime, CGIL, CISL and UIL went on to negotiate with government and Confindustria at the national level. The bone of contention was the bargaining structure. According to Confindustria, wages and salaries were to be determined at a single bargaining level and not multiple levels. The employer association preferred the industry level. In the course of the negotiation, however, Confindustria also threatened to dismantle national collective bargaining altogether and push wage determination to the enterprise level – which is what organized employers were trying to accomplish in other countries (Katz 1993, Katz and Darbishire 2000, Locke 1992, Locke, Kochan and Piore 1995). The unions wanted wage bargaining to take place at both the industry and company levels (or at the territorial level for small and medium-sized firms).

After a long negotiation, delayed *inter alia* by the fall of the Amato government and the formation of a new "technical" government headed by former Bank of Italy governor Azelio Ciampi, the parties finally reached agreement in July 1993. The parts of the agreement devoted to industrial relations confirmed the abolition of the *scala mobile* and established tripartite consultations (in May and September) that would link wage increases to the government macroeconomic targets as stated in its yearly budget. The agreement also modified the structure and timing of national industry contracts. The clauses of the national contract that governed hiring and firing procedures, job classifications and career trajectories were to be renewed every four years, whereas more strictly wage-related clauses were to be renegotiated every two years.

It was also decided that wage bargaining should take place at both the industry and company (or territorial) levels – in the latter case every four years. Company (and territorial) bargaining could only take place on issues not already regulated by the national contracts. Moreover, wage increases deriving from company-level bargaining were to be financed through productivity increases or performance improvements. By closely linking local wage increases to profit- and gain-sharing schemes, the July 1993 accord sought to reduce the inflationary potential associated with local wage drift. Also, to create incentives for more flexible forms of remuneration, social security taxes were partially subsidized, provided that contingent pay schemes were negotiated with the unions.

In the following years, the confederal unions were involved in new episodes of corporatist concertation. In 1995, unions and government negotiated a reform of the Italian pension system. This reform involved a long transition period, in which a mixed system of pre- and postreform rules would apply. When functioning fully, it would radically change the conditions for eligibility and benefit entitlements, as pension benefits would no longer be set, as it had previously been the case, as a function of past income (*defined benefit*) but would be determined in accordance with accumulated social security contributions (*defined contribution*). Also, the so-called "seniority pensions" (i.e., pensions paid before the minimum retirement age was reached, based on the worker's seniority) would be gradually phased out (Aprile 1996, Aprile, Fassina and Pace 1996, Castellino 1996, Cazzola 1995). In the short run, the reform introduced cuts in seniority pensions, even though these cuts were, according to various economists, not as incisive as they should have been.

In 1996, a tripartite "Pact for Labor" relaxed the rules regulating flexible and contingent forms of labor. In particular, this agreement introduced agency work into Italy, eliminated the public administration's monopoly of labor intermediation and facilitated the use of part-time and fixed-term work through bureaucratic simplification of procedures and tax incentives. While the agreement made it easier for employers to have recourse to nonstandard employment, it maintained a series of limits on its use: for example, it introduced a requirement for collective bargaining to set a ceiling on the use of agency work. A tripartite agreement of 1998 set this ceiling at 8 percent of indeterminate duration contracts.

In 1998, a so-called "Christmas Pact" confirmed the structure of collective bargaining established in 1993 and introduced a contractual obligation for government to consult with the social partners on all social policy issues and even to devolve decision-making authority to the social partners. The various centralized agreements of the 1990s helped the Italian economic authorities rally the necessary popular consensus for fiscal austerity measures needed to qualify for the second phase of EMU (Modigliani, Baldassari and Castiglionesi 1996, Salvati 2000), allowing the government to reduce public deficit below the 3 percent threshold of the Stability and Growth Pact.

At the end of the 1990s, the newly emerged corporatist system seemed well on its way to being institutionalized, and there was even talk of including a reference to it in the Italian constitution (Carrieri 1997). Also, the three main confederations seemed very close to merging into a single organization. However, this opportunity was missed: the CGIL and the CISL, in particular, had different views on a number of key issues such as union democracy (with the CISL opposing widespread use of worker referenda and the CGIL favoring it) or the decentralization of collective bargaining (with the CISL being much more open to it than the CGIL). These differences led in some cases to agreements signed only by the CISL and the UIL and not the CGIL.[4]

---

[4] This happened, for example, with the metalworking contract of 2001 and with the proposed "Pact for Milan" in early 2000, which was signed only by the CISL and UIL. This was a local-level

In turn, Confindustria became increasingly disenchanted with tripartite negotiations and, on the eve of national elections in 2001, struck a strategic alliance with the center-right coalition. The new government's labor program emphasized labor market deregulation, criticized concertation as an empty rite that blocked much-needed structural reform, and emphasized the need to move from job protection to employability (Biagi et al. 2002). In 2002, another tripartite agreement was signed. This time, however, the union front split. These tripartite negotiations started with the ambitious objective of boosting employment creation with a comprehensive reform of both EPL and economic shock absorbers. Eventually, however, the scope of the agreement shrank and the proposed text ended up exchanging the promise of tax reductions for a less rigid regulation of individual dismissals (Article 18 of the Worker Statute). The CGIL refused to sign this agreement and called for workers to mobilize in opposition. This call was largely heeded and the policy reform stalled. As a result, the government never implemented the new rules on dismissals it had negotiated with the other two confederations.

Corporatist policy making returned in 2007. The opportunity was once again a pension reform. While the reform of 1995 had fundamentally altered the future structure of the Italian pension system, it had had only a limited impact on the transition phase affecting workers who had matured pension rights under the old regime. To prevent a short-term increase in pension expenditures, in 2004 the center-right government had unilaterally increased the minimum age for seniority-based pensions. However, it postponed the introduction of the reform to 2008 to avoid political problems with its electoral base. The new center-left government abolished the unilateral reform and negotiated with the unions a gradual increase of the minimum age for seniority-based retirement. Leftist parties in the government opposed the agreement and appealed to Italian workers to reject it. As had been done previously both in 1993 and in 1995, the three confederations organized a massive information campaign among the workers, followed by a binding referendum. The workers approved the agreement by an overwhelming proportion and thus contributed to bolster both the unions and the government's credibility (Baccaro 2014a).

In 2008, the center-right coalition returned to power. Strategic divisions among the three confederations resurfaced and the unions split again. The crux of the matter was this time the updating of the 1993 agreement and the reform of the collective bargaining structure. This was a topic that had been tabled repeatedly in the past, including during the 1998 negotiations, but had never been settled, due to the parties' inability to converge on a mutually agreeable solution. The January 2009 agreement confirmed the 1993 articulation of collective bargaining on two levels (industry and company), but changed some minor elements (see below). All the major employer organizations signed the

concertation agreement aimed at allowing municipal authorities a more flexible use of fixed-term contracts in exchange for employment creation.

agreement, and so did CISL and UIL, but not the CGIL. The CGIL's refusal was motivated by the agreement's inadequate protection of the wages and salaries' purchasing power.

Over time, the sequence of negotiated agreement or unilateral government interventions began to follow a predictable pattern: when the center-left coalition was in power, all three confederations shared responsibility for the final agreement; when the government was in the hands of the center-right coalition, CISL and UIL (as well as other union confederations) signed the agreements, while the CGIL refused to sign. The CGIL, and especially its metalworker confederation, FIOM, increasingly found it difficult to negotiate centralized agreements with a government it did not trust.

7.3 The Evolution of Collective Bargaining

One of the outcomes of the 1993 tripartite agreement was the institutionalization of a bargaining structure on two levels.[5] The Italian collective bargaining system has traditionally focused on the industry-level contract (Cella and Treu 2009). This contract has often had a symbiotic relationship with enterprise bargaining. After the Hot Autumn, enterprise bargaining (in large firms) became the channel through which innovations in collective bargaining emerged, and the role of the industry contract was to generalize and diffuse them (Cella and Treu 2009). In the 1980s, there was a trend toward collective bargaining decentralization, which Italy shared with all other advanced countries (Katz 1993, Katz and Darbishire 2000), and the industry agreement lost some of its significance (Locke 1992). However, with the tripartite agreement of 1993, it was restored to its focal place (Regalia and Regini 1998).

As far as remuneration was concerned, the 1993 agreement introduced a clear division of labor across bargaining levels: industry-level negotiations had the function of keeping inflation expectations in check by linking wage increases distributed at the industry level tightly with the expected inflation rates decided by the government. Also, they would compensate ex post for any positive difference between anticipated and actual inflation (the adjustment would be net of terms of trade changes). According to the new bargaining architecture, productivity increases were not to be redistributed at the industry level, but only at the enterprise or territorial level. This particular bargaining structure had the potential to determine a growth of real wages below productivity increases. Unless the coverage rate of enterprise bargaining increased dramatically to cover most if not all workers, productivity increases would not be redistributed. To obviate this situation, from 2006 on, the metalworking contract began to include an additional (small) wage element to be paid to workers to whom a company-level contract did not apply.

[5] This section draws on Baccaro and Pulignano (2011).

The collective bargaining structure introduced in 1993 represented a delicate equilibrium among different interests and views (Mascini 2000). This made it difficult to reform it, notwithstanding repeated attempts. The employers were, in principle, against collective bargaining at two levels, and argued instead for a single bargaining level. Initially, they had favored the industry contract (see above), but over time, they came to favor the enterprise contract. The unions vocally defended the complementary nature of the industry and enterprise levels of bargaining and argued for the need to keep both. When push came to shove, however, the CISL and the UIL were often willing to experiment with institutional solutions increasing the weight and importance of decentralized levels, while the CGIL acted as staunch defender of the industry contract.

Divisions on the proper role of the industry level did not just pit different organizations against one another, but often also reflected specific sectoral traditions and peculiarities. For example, the chemical sector agreement of May 2006 allowed greater autonomy to company-level bargaining and even introduced an opt-out clause for companies in distress. Very different was the January 2008 metalworking contract, which in many ways recentralized labor relations at the industry level. A significant innovation was introduced only for artisanal, craft-based companies in March 2004. For these companies, the role of compensating for differences between anticipated and actual inflation was moved from the national to the regional level of bargaining. This reduced the importance of the industry agreement.

After years of fruitless discussion and failed negotiations, in January 2009 a national agreement explicitly set out to reform the architecture of Italian collective bargaining. Hailed as a historic event, it did not fundamentally alter the existing system but confirmed the dual structure introduced by the 1993 accord, increased the duration of industry-level agreements from two to three years, linked industry-level wage increases no longer to Italy's expected inflation but to an EU-wide index, reiterated that decentralized bargaining should take place only on issues explicitly delegated by the industry contracts and should not concern topics already negotiated at other levels, and affirmed the need for government to favor the diffusion of decentralized bargaining by introducing special tax advantages. The CGIL refused to sign this agreement because it introduced the principle of opening clauses, that is, the possibility for second-level contracts to derogate *in peius* from provisions stipulated at the national level.

In September 2010, at the insistence of Fiat (see below), an amendment to the 2009 agreement was added. It contained an explicit opt-out clause that allowed employers to conclude derogatory company agreements to counter the effects of a company crisis. Unsurprisingly, the metalworking union FIOM, affiliated to the CGIL, was strongly critical of this initiative, while the other trade unions found it helpful to safeguard employment in company crises (Sanz 2011).

The possibility of derogation was dramatically extended by the government in 2011 when, with an urgent measure (Article 8 of Law 148/2011), it introduced the possibility of company- and territorial-level contracts ("proximity agreements") signed by a majority of trade union representatives to derogate not just industry-level contracts but even legal provisions (Garilli 2012). The government's unilateral intervention came despite the signing by all confederal unions, including the CGIL, of a national agreement with Confindustria in June 2011 providing ample guarantees for opening clauses at the company level. With the 2011 agreement, company-level agreements were allowed to derogate from the provisions of industry-level contracts with respect to various contractual matters such as hours and work organization in case of crisis.

It would appear from the most recent reform initiatives aimed to increase the role of decentralized agreements that collective bargaining would have shifted to the company level in Italy. Yet there is little evidence to substantiate this claim. As in many other domains, the tripartite protocol of 1993 was of key importance in establishing the role of company-level bargaining in Italy. It introduced for the first time in Italian history a series of rules regulating decentralized bargaining. These were contractual rather than legal rules; thus institutionalization was weaker than it could have been. However, compared with the previous situation, when decentralized bargaining had depended on voluntary recognition and on the balance of power between the parties, the 1993 accord was an important step forward. In addition, it established an institutional link between unions negotiating at the national level and worker representative structures at the company level (*Rappresentanze Sindacali Unitarie*) (Baccaro 1999). Last but not least, the 1993 protocol attributed to enterprise-based bargaining the role of productivity redistribution.

Although the available evidence does not provide definitive answers – some studies are available, but they are based on specific sectors and/or geographic areas, are limited to enterprises of a particular size (e.g., with at least fifty employees) or lack a longitudinal dimension, and their results are often not comparable – the extension of company-level bargaining does not seem to have happened. A survey conducted in 1995–6 by the Italian statistical agency based on a representative sample of private-sector enterprises with at least ten employees estimated that company bargaining involved only 10 percent of relevant enterprises and covered 39 percent of private-sector employees (ISTAT 2002). Based on various sources of data, Rossi and Sestito (2000) concluded that company bargaining in 1995–7 had been less diffuse than in 1988–9 and approximately as diffuse as in 1985–6. There had been a peak of enterprise-based bargaining in 1996, presumably as a result of the 1993 accord, but it had not been sufficient to bring the coverage rate back to previous levels. Overall, the time trend was negative. The propensity to negotiate at the enterprise level was strongly positively correlated with company size (see also Bordogna 1997, 1999) and company-specific union density. Hence, the decline in decentralized bargaining appeared to be due both to a decline in average size and to a decline in union density. This analysis also showed that there had been no increase in the relative importance of wage increases negotiated at enterprise level. Instead, increases decided unilaterally by management had become more important.

A more recent analysis of decentralized bargaining trends confirmed the findings reported above and revealed that bargaining propensity had declined between 1998 and 2006 for a sample of private enterprises with at least 100 employees. The decline had been greater for companies of smaller size (CNEL 2007). Thus, it seems that the institutionalization of enterprise negotiations in 1993 did not increase the diffusion of this form of bargaining. Two forces possibly operated at cross purposes: on one hand, the 1993 protocol provided unions with a "right to access" that was previously unavailable; on the other hand, due to the decline of density rates, unions were increasingly unable to act on this right.

In this context, it is important to mention the shift in the collective bargaining strategy of Fiat, Italy's largest private sector employer. In the early 1980s, this company had launched an attack against trade unions (Collidà and Negrelli 1986, Locke 1995: ch. 4, Romiti 1988). Management prevailed in a highly publicized strike in 1980 (Golden 1997) and managed to restore managerial prerogative in its factories. While the Fiat initiative was a clear signal that the balance of power was shifting against the unions, it remained more the exception than the rule in Italian industrial relations. These remained largely cooperative in other large companies, especially in state-owned ones (Cella and Treu 1989, Negrelli 1991, Regini and Sabel 1989) and in the industrial districts of the "third Italy" (Bagnasco 1977, Trigilia 1986).

In the late 2000s, Fiat acted again as a vanguard of the Italian employer front. Convinced that the company had to break free of the constraints imposed by the industry-level contract in order to regain competitiveness vis-à-vis other automakers, in 2010 the Fiat management signed plant-level agreements at two of its Italian factories (Pomigliano and Mirafiori). The content of these agreements, which were negotiated under management's threat to relocate production to foreign factories if the unions did not agree to concessions, was not compatible with provisions in the metalworking sectoral agreement. This led Fiat to leave both Confindustria and the industry agreement and to introduce its own separate company agreement. The main goal was to avoid having to negotiate with the most representative union in the metalworking industry, the FIOM CGIL, which had refused to agree to the required concessions.

In accordance with the Workers' Statute (Law 300 of 1970, as modified by a popular referendum in 1995), only trade unions that are signatories to a collective agreement that is applied in the relevant workplace can set up workplace representation structures. Thus, by exiting from the employer organization and terminating all existing collective agreements, Fiat thought it would be able to exclude the FIOM both from collective bargaining and from workplace representation. So far, labor courts have ruled that the exclusion is an unfair labor practice according to Italian law. Nonetheless, Fiat's initiative was perceived as a major threat to the established structure of collective bargaining and union representation in Italy. As a result, in June 2011 an intersectoral agreement was signed by Confindustria and CGIL, CISL and UIL to introduce new criteria (based on union representation) for participation in industry-wide bargaining and for the signing of valid company deals. With this agreement, Confindustria signaled that it did not share Fiat's radical approach to collective bargaining decentralization and derecognition. Some of the tensions between CGIL on one side, and CISL and UIL on the other, were lowered. However, longstanding differences remain.

7.4 The Reform of Employment Protection Legislation

The 2000s saw a series of legislative initiatives aimed to relax labor market regulation. Legislative activism took two forms: liberalization of labor market contracts over and beyond what had already been achieved with the 1996 social pact and associated law, and attempts to modify Article 18 of the Workers' Statute. Article 18 stated that employees in establishments of more than 15 employees who were found by a judge to have been fired without just cause (serious disciplinary infringement) or justified (subjective or objective) reason (disciplinary or economic reasons) could choose between monetary compensation (approximately equal to 15 months plus any lost wages) and reinstatement in their previous jobs.

The Italian economy is characterized by a majority of small firms. According to the Italian statistical agency, less than 3 percent of Italian firms (excluding agriculture) have more than fifteen workers. However, firms with more than fifteen workers employ 65 percent of Italian employees.[6] For workers in establishments of up to fifteen employees, the protection of Article 18 did not apply; there was no right to reinstatement in case they were illegitimately fired, but only a monetary compensation of between 2.5 and 6 monthly wages (Baccaro and Simoni 2004).

According to scholarly analyses, Article 18 has a statistically significant but quantitatively small impact on reducing the probability that small firms would grow above the fifteen-worker threshold (Garibaldi, Pacelli and Borgarello 2004, ISTAT 2001, Schivardi and Torrini 2004). However, its symbolic dimension goes well beyond its direct economic impact. For trade unions, and especially for the CGIL, the abolition of Article 18 meant a dramatic reversal in power balance, since in their eyes this article guaranteed the fundamental workers' right to be protected against arbitrary dismissals and hence made possible the fruition of all other rights, both individual and collective, including the right to effective voice. The Italian employers perceived Article 18 as a bridgehead of great strategic importance, whose conquest would have enabled additional

---

[6] Data reported by Pietro Ichino, "Una lettura errata dei dati ISTAT nel dibattito sulle cause del precariato" (http://www.pietroichino.it/?p=17248, accessed June 20, 2013).

victories in the fight to liberalize the Italian labor market. For center-right governments, first, and later for center-left governments as well, eliminating Article 18 meant sending a clear signal about their ability to pass unpopular reforms against trade unions. For a number of intellectuals on both the (moderate) left and the right of the political spectrum, Article 18 was responsible for the inability of Italian firms to grow dimensionally and for the dualism between protected insiders and unprotected outsiders in the Italian labor market. Furthermore, the high costs and long duration of judicial proceedings discouraged foreign direct investment (AAVV 2002, Boeri and Galasso 2007, Ichino 1996, Ichino 2011, Simoni 2012, Treu 2001).

In the year 2000, the Radical Party, a small libertarian party, took the initiative to launch an all-out attack on Article 18 by organizing a popular referendum for its abolition. However, the referendum did not reach the required threshold of 50 percent of potential electors necessary for legal validity.

After the electoral victory of the center-right government in 2001, Article 18 returned to the center of political debate as part of the new government strategy for labor market reform (Biagi et al. 2002). The government proposed a comprehensive package of policy measures aimed to further liberalize the typologies of flexible contracts and reduce the influence of trade unions in policy making by shifting from "concertation" to "social dialog." Social dialog meant that the government would inform and consult with the social partners but would make decisions autonomously.

With regard to Article 18, the government proposed its experimental suspension for three years for firms that passed the threshold of fifteen employees as a result of new hires. For new hires alone, the full protection of Article 18 would not be applied for a limited period of time and the new hires would have a right to monetary compensation but not to reinstatement in case they were fired. The government wanted to examine the impact of this measure on unemployment before generalizing it. However, the unions, and especially the CGIL, mobilized against this proposal and refused to sign the 2002 Pact for Italy, in which the proposal was included. In March 2003, three million workers marched in Rome to show their support for Article 18. As a result, the reform of Article 18 was never implemented. However, with the so-called "Biagi Law" of 2003, named after a consultant of the Labor Ministry who had contributed to elaborating the government proposals and had been murdered for this reason by the Red Brigades in March 2003, the government further deregulated flexible contracts. As a result of both the 1997 and 2003 liberalization of atypical contracts, the incidence of these forms of work increased dramatically in Italy in the 2000s (see Figure 7.3).

Also, in 2003, Article 18 was the target of another political initiative of opposite sign. A group of radical political forces, including the FIOM, launched a popular referendum to extend its application to all workers, including those employed in firms below the threshold. This extension was a logical corollary of the argument that Article 18 was a fundamental right of workers. As such, all

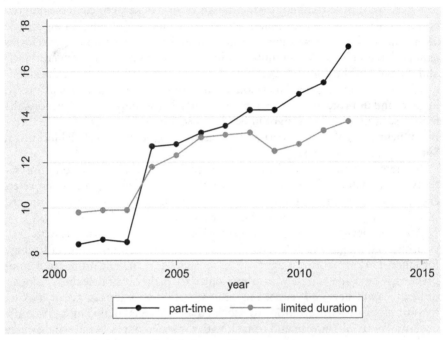

FIGURE 7.3. Atypical forms of work *Source:* Eurostat

workers should benefit from it. This referendum, too, failed to reach the quorum for legal validity, even though a majority of voters (more than ten million) voted for the extension (Baccaro and Simoni 2004).

In 2012, the reform of Article 18 featured prominently in the Monti government's attempt to regain the confidence of international financial markets (Sacchi 2012). The Monti government, an executive of technocrats supported by a three-way grand coalition among center-left, center and center-right forces, was put in power to reassure the international policy-making elites, most importantly the European Central Bank and the European Commission, that Italy was ready to implement a program of "structural reforms" (involving labor and product market deregulation) and fiscal adjustment to boost international financial market confidence. The government's policy style shunned concertation with the social partners and emphasized the ability to pass reforms unilaterally. These reforms were presented as necessary to increase economic efficiency and to rebalance the scales between "insiders" and "outsiders" in the Italian labor market.

The government managed to pass a draconian pension reform that increased retirement age, abolished seniority pensions and imposed the application of the pro rata method of capitalized contribution to calculate the pension benefits of retirees who had entered the labor market before the reforms of the 1990s.

When it came to Article 18, however, the government had to modify its original proposal – which would simply have abolished the possibility of reinstatement for workers fired for economic reasons – due to opposition from within its own parliamentary majority and had to reintroduce the principle of judicial discretion. With this reform, judges had the possibility of choosing between monetary compensation and reinstatement when faced with an economic firing decision that they deemed unjustified.

It looked as though not even a technocratic government operating under conditions of extreme external urgency (a sovereign debt crisis) would be able to decisively reform Article 18. However, the government's twenty-year attempts came to fruition in the spring of 2015. With the strong support of Confindustria and against the opposition of all trade unions, the Renzi center-left government eliminated the possibility of reinstatement for illegitimate economic firings. The new norm would apply to new employment contracts, while previous ones would still be protected by the old Article 18. The new employment protection regime would thus cover the entire Italian labor force only in due time. This reform was part of an ambitious program of labor market reform aimed to shift the center of protection away from the job and toward workers and their employability. However, while some measures have been taken to extend unemployment insurance to previously excluded categories of workers and to strengthen active labor market policies, efforts to institutionalize Nordic-style flexicurity in Italy have so far been hindered by the limited availability of public funds, a consequence of the need to keep public deficits in check.

7.5 Conclusion

As argued at the beginning of this chapter, if one were to take two snapshots of Italian industrial relations, at the end of the 1970s and thirty-five years after, one would be more likely to be impressed by the differences than by the continuities. In the late 1970s, unions were strong both at the workplace level and in society at large; collective bargaining was carried out both at the company level (in large and medium-sized industrial factories) and at the industry level, and the industry-level contract was used to generalize the innovations of the most advanced company-level contracts; and corporatist bargaining was a rare event and every union concession was on a strictly quid pro quo basis. In the early 2010s, unions were much weaker; industry-level bargaining was under attack, and the role of company-level bargaining was reconfigured to allow for derogation from upper-level regulatory provisions; and corporatist policy making was unceremoniously abandoned after having been used extensively in the preceding years to institutionalize wage restraint, as well as to liberalize the labor market and reform the pension system.

Comparing various dimensions of employer discretion also reveals dramatic differences over time. In the late 1970s, employers' discretion in work organization was limited both by statutory provisions and (at least in large firms) by the formidable power and mobilization capacity accumulated by the unions in the years of the Hot Autumn. The employer's discretion in wage flexibility was limited by the *scala mobile*, which redistributed in favor of low-wage workers, and by the unions' commitment to wage egalitarianism. Employers were forced to choose their new hires from bureaucratic lists that could be bypassed only in special circumstances. Their ability to fire was constrained by Article 18, which imposed reinstatement in case of unjustified decisions.

In the early 2010s, the *scala mobile* had been abolished, and compression of wage differentials across skill categories was no longer a union goal. The employers' ability to hire whoever they wanted was essentially unlimited. Their ability to fire the growing number of atypical workers was full. For unlimited-duration workers in establishments with more than fifteen employees, the protection of Article 18 was lifted for new hires in 2015. At a time of declining trade union strength, growing unemployment and increasing work precariousness, job security had become a key priority, and in the name of this all-important goal, workers and unions were willing to accept the worsening of work conditions, as happened with the Fiat agreements at Pomigliano and Mirafiori in 2010.

Strangely enough for a country known for its vibrant periphery and less than fully functional center, most changes were driven from the top down. Corporatist policy making underwent a gradual process of conversion from a tool to extend the unions' social power from the labor market to the political sphere into a mechanism to extract and generalize union concessions. While employers have also been active in the process of liberalization (see Fiat's two offensives in 1980 and 2010), the key actor has been the government, sometimes with the open support of organized employers.

Italian policy-making authorities responded to the crisis of the late 1970s with attempts to build a domestic variant of the neocorporatist systems prevailing in the more "mature" Northern and Central European countries (Bruno and Sachs 1985, Flanagan, Soskice and Ulman 1983, Tarantelli 1986b). However, this early phase of neocorporatist concertation was short-lived and did not produce any dramatic changes. Trade unions were willing to contribute to disinflation, but expected "structural reforms" in exchange, by which they meant a stronger role of government in economic planning, investments and labor market policy and the redressing of territorial asymmetries between North and South.

The second half of the 1980s was characterized by decentralized industrial relations and was accompanied by higher growth than the OECD average. There was, however, in all likelihood no causal association between the two. Higher growth was rather due to the economic stimulus associated with growing public deficits and debt. The unsustainability of this model of debit-led growth became clear in 1992, when the consequences of the EMS crisis forced the Italian policy-making authorities to hurriedly introduce a series of restrictive measures aimed to bring about both disinflation and fiscal adjustment. In these years, the country was faced with a multifaceted political and economic crisis, and national-level pacts on wages, bargaining structure and pensions were used to tackle the emergency while minimizing popular backlash against unpopular policy measures.

After the abolition of the *scala mobile* in 1992, the 1993 agreement put in place the institutional conditions for a decline of the wage share by establishing that productivity increases would be redistributed only at the enterprise level through second-level contracts, but no longer at the national level through industry-level ones. However, since second-level bargaining only covered a minority of Italian firms and workers, productivity was not redistributed. In the second half of the 1990s, a corporatist pact was also used to liberalize employment contracts at the margin, that is, to make it easier both to hire and fire workers on atypical contracts, but not workers on independent-duration contracts.

In the 1990s and 2000s, the Italian policy-making authorities, regardless of their political affiliation, pursued (with few marginal differences) essentially the same labor market policy aimed at increase the degree of flexibility of the economy and undo the rigidities introduced by the Hot Autumn. The shared assumption was that in order to be competitive, Italian firms had to be able to enjoy greater discretion in hiring and firing, in the internal deployment of workers and in their ability to derogate from industry-level contracts. Not surprisingly, this program met resistance from trade unions, although not from all of them: there were strategic differences among union confederations, and some of them did not oppose flexibilization as a matter of principle but asked for it be negotiated. The program of liberalization was pursued through negotiated national agreements when the unions accepted the terms proposed to them and through unilateral reform when they did not.

When reform was pursued through negotiated agreement, the unions fought hard to defend their core constituencies, for example, through the introduction of long transition rules that exonerated senior workers from the effects of pension reform or through reforms of EPL that liberalized atypical forms of work only. The end result was that policy change overwhelmingly affected outsiders and increased labor market segmentation. Recently, however, the sense of urgency created by the sovereign debt crisis has created the conditions for a reform of EPL that targeted workers on undetermined-duration contracts.

The sovereign debt crisis of the early 2010s has inaugurated a new phase of the relationship between governments and the social partners characterized by government unilateralism. Before resigning in late 2011, the Berlusconi government delivered what may turn out to be the most disruptive of all legislative changes: the possibility of second-level contracts derogating from both industry-level contracts and law provisions if signed by a majority of workplace trade unions. For the governments that followed, such as the Monti government and the Renzi government, being able to pass reforms against trade union opposition became a sign of distinction.

The trajectory of Italian industrial relations is without a doubt one of liberalization. Differently from other countries, however, there has been little formal decentralization of the bargaining system. On the contrary, the collective bargaining structure has in many respects been recentralized and there is little evidence that company-level bargaining has expanded its coverage. The limited coverage of company-level bargaining allowed real wages to grow more slowly than productivity increases in the 1990s. In the 2000s, reform initiatives gave decentralized bargaining the ability to derogate from higher-level collective bargaining agreements or even laws. The Italian case demonstrates clearly that changes in institutional form do not fully capture the liberalization process and that formal institutional analysis has to be complemented by an examination of the way in which institutions function and of the balance of power among actors that operate within and through them.

8

The Conversion of Corporatism

Reengineering Swedish Industrial Relations for a Neoliberal Era

For most of the postwar period, Swedish industrial relations have anchored one end of a spectrum from individual to collective regulation of class relations, characterized by high levels of labor strength, near-complete collective bargaining coverage and centralized collective bargaining between the peak organizations of business and labor. It was, until the early 1980s, one of the best examples of stable and successful corporatist bargaining. As such, Sweden was long considered a model of the kinds of political and industrial gains that could be made by social democratic parties and labor movements willing to engage in political exchange.

The luster came off the Swedish model, and indeed it appeared close to collapse, for a period from the mid-1980s until the mid-1990s. For reasons that will be discussed below, the annual centralized bargaining rounds broke down, Swedish employers withdrew from the main corporatist institutions, and, between 1990 and 1993, the Swedish state was forced to intervene to an unprecedented degree in the regulation of industrial relations. Yet somehow, collective regulation survived this period of crisis, and employers, unions and state actors reconstructed a system of industrial relations that, in many ways, looks very familiar: multisectoral coordinated bargaining; self-regulation by employers and unions; high collective bargaining coverage; and low strike levels.

As such, Sweden is a difficult case for the argument of this book, perhaps the most difficult of the five cases we examine in detail. On the surface at least, Sweden appears to have largely resisted the liberalization of industrial relations institutions. It would be straightforward and plausible to interpret recent developments in Swedish industrial relations through the lens of path dependence, incremental institutional change and approaches to comparative political economy that emphasize the continued resilience of national models of capitalism, even in the face of liberalizing and globalizing pressures. In such a narrative the main Swedish class actors fell back upon a familiar toolkit of institutions and practices in order to manage crisis and, in so doing, reinvented the past.

This chapter offers an alternative interpretation of the recent evolution of Swedish industrial relations, one that signals a fundamental change in the manner in which Swedish class relations are regulated and that identifies an important convergence in institutional trajectory with other industrialized countries in the practice of industrial relations, even as many of its institutions remain distinct. As such, this account contributes to a growing body of scholarship that sees liberalization in Sweden – across all spheres of the political economy – since the early 1990s as not limited, incremental and grudgingly conceded but extensive, transformational and embraced by the state and employers (Andersson 2015). In comparative accounts, while starting from a lower base, to be sure, liberalization in Sweden has been swift and wide-ranging. The comprehensive survey of liberalization policy across 21 OECD countries and 5 domains by Höpner et al. (2014) saw Sweden drop from first place in terms of state intervention in 1985 to eighth by 2002 (Hopner et al. 2014: 21) and to show the greatest degree of liberalization among a series of liberalization indicators in the sample between 1990 and 2002 (Hopner et al. 2014: 27).[1]

Swedish industrial relations have in fact been transformed in the last fifteen years, in part through the creation of new institutions, but more through a shift in the interests and behavior of class actors and the state and changes in the practice and functioning of existing industrial relations institutions; Swedish collective bargaining institutions have been subject to a remarkable degree of institutional conversion as they have come to permit, and even to encourage, decentralized wage setting and a high degree of individualization and labor market flexibility. This shift has occurred as a consequence of an accumulation of strains within the postwar industrial relations regime, changed economic circumstances, greater activism and radicalism of the part of employers, more innovation and interventionism on the part of the state and a traumatized labor movement willing to experiment with new bargaining practices.

8.1 The Saltsjöbaden Era of Swedish Industrial Relations

Important elements of the Swedish model remained in place for fifty years after 1938, the point at which the main employer federation, *Svenska Arbetsgivareföreningen* (SAF), and the blue-collar union confederation, *Landsorganisationen* (LO), agreed that unions would be recognized in return for mechanisms to ensure industrial peace and respect managerial prerogative inside the workplace. But the centerpiece of that model was in place for only half that period,

---

[1] This study defines liberalization more narrowly than we do, limiting it essentially to deregulation and disengagement on the part of the state. As such, it understates the extent to which liberalization can result from changes in collective regulation that have the effect of expanding employer discretion.

from the second half of the 1950s until the early 1980s (Murhem 2003, Pontusson 1992, Steinmo 2010, Stephens 1979). That core revolved around centralized wage bargaining based on two principles: wage moderation on the part of workers in high-productivity sectors in order to ensure the competitiveness of the export sector, and wage solidarism, understood to mean that workers were paid on the basis of the job they did, not the ability to pay of the firm or even the entire industry in which they worked. Centrally determined wage levels were imposed across the economy regardless of the profitability of individual firms, something that also served as a crude industrial policy. National wage agreements incorporated a peace obligation, preventing legal strikes for the life of collective agreements.

This was the Rehn–Meidner bargaining model, named after two LO economists, which had the effect of compressing the wage scale through "wage moderation at the top and wage immoderation at the bottom" (Alexopoulos and Cohen 2003: 343). Workers in high-productivity sectors, such as metal and engineering, experienced substantially lower real wage gains than those in low-productivity sectors, such as textiles (Alexopoulos and Cohen 2003: 346–347). This was designed both to moderate wages in exposed sectors and to reduce labor supply problems in those same sectors by encouraging labor release from low-productivity firms unable to afford wage solidarism. Hence its strong support among the leading export-oriented firms that dominated the SAF (Swenson 2002: chapter 6).

At its simplest, this was a compromise between powerful class organizations, involving wage restraint for a small, highly export-dependent economy and relatively untrammeled managerial power in return for the social democratic goals of full employment, a high social wage and relative income equality. While centralized wage bargaining provided the wage moderation and solidarism, the Swedish state, in the hands of the Social Democratic Party continuously from 1932 until 1976 (occasionally in coalition), contributed to full employment and the social wage through an extensive active labor market policy, a generous welfare state and a taxation policy that encouraged reinvestment (Pontusson 1992: chapter 3). Thus, despite the limited role of labor law (see below), the state played a crucial supportive role in the Swedish model. By managing an active labor market policy and serving as employer of last resort, it assured workers that the solidaristic wage policy would not lead to widespread unemployment in firms and sectors with limited productivity and profitability.

The institutions of industrial relations underpinned these essential principles. Central to this institutional configuration were centralized and encompassing peak organizations with substantial formal and informal power over affiliates, including financial resources and control over the strike and lockout weapons. On the labor side, unions were strengthened by a single track of labor representation, ensuring that trade unions had no rivals either inside or outside the firm, and a Ghent-style system that funneled unemployment insurance through union organizations, encouraging membership. Swedish unions benefited both from centralization in the form of confederal power and from decentralization in the form of workplace organization (Kjellberg 2009). In addition, while the blue collar LO was hegemonic within the labor movement until the 1970s, white collar and professional confederations, the *Tjänstemännens Centralorganisation* (TCO) and *Sveriges Akademikers Centralorganisation* (Saco), also grew rapidly, and organization on the basis of collar ensured a degree of within-confederation homogeneity that appears, at least initially, to have encouraged union density and solidarism.

Like that of Britain during the same period, though to an even greater degree, the Swedish model emphasized collective self-regulation: governments were committed to allowing the social partners to use collective bargaining to regulate the labor market, with only limited recourse to labor law. Sweden has no extension mechanism or statutory minimum wage, there are very few legal limits on strikes (the peace obligation and limits on strikes in essential services are the result of negotiation, not legislation), and labor law is "semimandatory," meaning that collective agreements can contain elements that derogate from legal standards (Nyström 2004). It is worth noting that the absence of a statutory extension mechanism made the ability of unions to engage in sympathy and secondary strikes in order to enforce and extend collective bargaining coverage of particular importance.

While these core elements remained, Swedish industrial relations evolved in important ways in the late 1960s and 1970s, so much so that some scholars have referred to this period as the "conflict regime" or "legislation regime" (Murhem 2003: 21–22), terms signifying emerging characteristics of class relations. Sweden's enviable postwar record of industrial peace eroded first through unofficial strikes over wages and working conditions in a small number of industrial sectors and then through official strikes in the public sector and among white collar workers (Stokke and Thörnqvist 2001). The response of Social Democratic governments during the 1970s has been characterized as "left-reformist" (Ryner 2002), involving a departure from self-regulation through greater recourse to legislation as a mechanism for benefiting workers. The 1974 Employment Protection Act (expanded in 1982) regulated atypical employment and created the expectation that permanent employment contracts, concluded for an indefinite period with dismissal difficult, would be the norm (Murhem 2013: 626). The 1976 Codetermination Act both codified and replaced all previously existing legislation regulating industrial relations and also created broad new powers of information and consultation in the firm. With Sweden's single track of labor representation, these new rights accrued to unions. Last, plans (ultimately unsuccessful) for wage-earner socialism were discussed within the Swedish Social Democratic Party (SAP) in the 1970s and legislated in watered-down form in 1983 (Pontusson 1992: chapter 7). These pieces of legislation challenged the principle of self-regulation, imposed limits on the quite broad managerial prerogative that had been an element of the Saltsjöbaden regime, and provided important labor market protection to Swedish workers.

At the same time, the nature of wage bargaining was changing. Some degree of wage drift and local bargaining had always characterized bargaining in Sweden. It was never static, nor as rigidly centralized as the depiction of peak-level wage bargaining above suggests; there was always some degree of wage drift, serving to manage economic pressure and defuse conflict at the firm level (Swenson 1989). But wage drift became steadily more important as time went on. By the 1970s it averaged 40% a year for blue collar workers and 20% for white collar workers, growing to 50% a year for each category by the 1980s (Elvander and Holmlund 1997: 13). In the 1960s, LO bargained for wage supplements for low-paid workers who did not benefit from wage drift, something that initially contributed to the egalitarianism of the industrial relations system. White collar unions responded in the 1970s by bargaining for supplements for their members who did not benefit from wage drift, to which LO in turn responded by arguing for compensation for the individual merit bonuses enjoyed by many white collar workers in a form of wage leapfrogging (Oliver 2011). The white collar bargaining cartel, *Privattjänstemannakartellen* (PTK),[2] championed "non-wage-level-increasing increments," which functioned as a form of seniority increase (Elvander and Holmlund 1997: 15). By the 1980s, wage agreements had a wide range of indexation and compensation guarantees that provided supplements to account for prices, wage drift and seniority; a system of centralized wage bargaining initially designed to moderate wages now incorporated a complex set of wage provisions independent of the wage norm set by the needs of the export sector.

In principle, the limited role of labor law and the permissibility of derogation in the Swedish industrial relations system provided an important degree of flexibility to employers. But by the end of the 1970s, and in the context of powerful labor organizations at both the national and local level, employer discretion had become severely constrained across all three dimensions discussed in Chapter 1. Wage bargaining was centralized and followed a pattern set by large firms in the export sector rather than the profitability of individual firms, and employers faced rigid wage supplement provisions that were also independent of their ability to pay or need to recruit. Codetermination provisions coupled with the workplace strength of unions imposed limits on managerial control over the organization of work, and statutory regulation of the labor market limited recourse to fixed-term employment and made dismissal difficult. Thus a combination of labor's collective and political power served to restrict employer discretion.

---

[2] Composed of a number of TCO and Saco white collar unions, PTK was formed in 1973 and began bargaining with SAF. This took place in parallel to the annual SAF–LO negotiations.

8.2 The Crisis of the Swedish Model

This industrial relations regime contained multiple tensions within itself. The Swedish model involved a difficult balancing act resting both upon compromises between capital and labor and upon compromises within each of the class organizations. Small changes in the relative power or perceived interests of actors could unravel the political and economic calculus that tied the elements of the model together. This balancing act became all the harder when the Swedish economy faced first exogenous economic shocks in the form of the collapse of the fixed exchange rate system and the oil crisis in the early 1970s, and then new forms of international competitive pressure resulting from European integration and the globalization of financial markets (Murhem 2003, Ryner 2002).

The Swedish economy experienced many of the same broad structural changes as other advanced capitalist countries: deindustrialization; the exhaustion of a Fordist intensive regime of accumulation; and greater international integration, bringing with it new competitive pressures and an enhanced emphasis upon flexibility in wage setting, work organization and the labor market more generally, all areas where employer discretion had weakened significantly by the end of the 1970s.

The impact of internationalization, through trade, foreign direct investment, the liberalization of financial markets and the accelerated pace of European integration, has been of particular importance in Sweden (Bergholm and Bieler 2013). During the Saltsjöbaden era, Sweden had already been heavily export-dependent, and industrial relations institutions reflected external constraints with their emphasis upon wage moderation and industrial peace. Nevertheless, large Swedish firms retained an attachment to and interest in the expansion of the domestic market; indeed, the early transition to intensive growth was one reason the depression of the 1930s was relatively mild in Sweden (Edvinsson 2010: 469).

There was a qualitative shift in the significance of trade and capital mobility from the late 1970s. Exports as a proportion of GDP almost doubled in the quarter century after 1980, reaching over 50% by 2006 (Edvinsson 2010: 468), and after remaining stable from 1960 to 1980, foreign direct investment as a proportion of GDP rose from 5.8% in 1980 to almost 40% in 1999 (Edvinsson 2010: 470). Outward FDI had long been a feature of the Swedish economy, but after 1990, inward FDI saw a massive increase of 1800% by 2006, a far higher growth rate than in other OECD economies (Jefferys 2011: 296). This went hand in hand with an almost tripling of the market capitalization of Swedish business between 1990 and 2005 as firms shifted away from bank loans to the equity and bond markets for financing (Peters 2011: 78).

The initial steps toward completion of the Single European Market after 1985 gave Swedish export firms an incentive to relocate outside Sweden but within the EU, delinking their interests from those of the domestic economy

(Sheldon and Thornthwaite 1999). After Sweden's accession to the EU in 1995, and especially after the accession in 2004 of low-wage former eastern European economies, social dumping emerged as a challenge to existing industrial relations institutions, as did the issue of the movement of foreign capital and labor into Sweden. The absence of a statutory extension mechanism or minimum wage put a premium upon maintaining high collective bargaining coverage as a means of taking wage costs out of competition. This became increasingly difficult, especially with a series of European Court of Justice decisions, discussed in the next section, that privileged free movement of capital and labor over national regulatory institutions (Malmberg and Bruun 2006).

The new international environment has certainly influenced Swedish industrial relations, but it has done so in a path-dependent manner, as employers were both constrained by an organizationally powerful labor movement and empowered by the institutional capacity to achieve wage moderation, labor market flexibility and industrial peace through coordinating institutions; we will see this dynamic at work in the next section, which traces the reemergence of coordination in the later 1990s.

Nonetheless, it remains the case that employer dissatisfaction with the existing Saltsjöbaden industrial relations regime has been the primary driver of its mutation since 1980. A common theme of the cases examined in this book is a resurgence both in the political activism of employers and in their interest in experimentation and innovation in industrial relations institutions. This has certainly been true in the Swedish case. The existing tensions within the Swedish model, plus the threat of new, more labor-oriented institutions constructed in the 1970s, had the effect of mobilizing and radicalizing employers so that many were now willing to challenge the core institutions of Swedish industrial relations. The benefits of the Saltsjöbaden regime for employers had weakened: it no longer served to contain inflation, as wage drift accelerated and assorted forms of wage indexation proliferated; it no longer produced social peace, as strikes increased; and it no longer protected managerial prerogative, as co-determination expanded bargaining to almost every aspect of workplace organization. The second half of the 1970s saw "the most severe crisis of profitability for manufacturing in modern times" (Edvinsson 2010: 476). Add to this the potential threat to the private ownership of capital posed by the wage earner funds proposals, and the sources of employer dissatisfaction with the existing industrial relations regime begin to come into focus.

There were multiple causes and emphases within the generalized employer dissatisfaction with the operation of the Swedish model, and scholars disagree about the balance of economic need and political opportunism in employer activism and the extent to which wage rigidity or industrial conflict was the biggest concern for employers (Pontusson and Swenson 1996, Sheldon and Thornthwaite 1999, Thörnqvist 1999). And, of course, these interests and imperatives differed among firms in different sectors and of different sizes; indeed, growing internal differences among industry associations within SAF were one source of the breakdown of centralized bargaining. Murhem has noted (personal communication with the author, Uppsala, October 11, 2006) that the radical industrial relations innovators tended to be large firms, particularly those in manufacturing, while smaller firms were more likely to see the benefits of coordination. But for all the different emphases and interests, the result was "an ideological offensive without precedent" against the Swedish model (Thörnqvist 1999: 80). From an employer perspective, it was the "legislative rage" of the labor movement and its political allies in the 1970s that moved away from the Swedish model. As a result, the SAF concluded that the main elements of the Swedish model were irretrievably broken and moved to both end centralized bargaining and undermine corporatism by withdrawing from the tripartite institutions in which it had been represented. Thus, the employer response in the 1980s was not to try to restore that model but to challenge its central elements.

The attack on corporatism, meaning the tripartite agency boards that played a central role in regulating the labor market, was led by an "activist" group within the SAF that believed that employers had become hostages on these boards (Johansson 2005). Beginning in the late 1970s, this group followed a long-term strategy of shifting resources away from the boards toward the political sphere, where lobbying and opinion-shaping were deemed more viable mechanisms for exercising influence. The formal withdrawal from the agency boards in 1991 was based on the (correct) calculation that employer withdrawal would lead to the ending of all interest group representation on the boards and the "decorporatization" of the Swedish model. This activism remained the hallmark of the main Swedish employers' organization even as the SAF transformed itself into the *Svenskt Näringsliv* (Confederation of Swedish Enterprise, SN), which styled itself much more explicitly as an organization of entrepreneurs than as an employer organization.

The origins of the attack upon centralized, solidaristic bargaining, the centerpiece of the postwar Swedish model, are to be found in the changing interests of employers, particularly those of large engineering firms, with the Association of Swedish Engineering Industries (*Verkstadsföreningen*, or VF) taking the lead role in pushing for a decentralization of bargaining. For these firms, as centralized bargaining could no longer deliver industrial peace, its costs became increasingly clear. Wage drift at the industry and firm levels, combined with a wages floor set by centralized bargaining, created additional wage costs, leading employers to seek to opt out of centralized bargaining, preferring "two levels of bargaining to three" (Sheldon and Thornthwaite 1999: 521). Meanwhile, the wage structure that had developed in the course of the late 1960s and 1970s, with interoccupational leveling, wage drift guarantees and assorted forms of indexation, responded neither to sectoral needs in heavily export-dependent engineering nor to the microeconomic role of wages in recruiting skilled labor and rewarding individual performance (Pontusson and Swenson 1996. 235-39). Thus for "engineering employers as a whole, the choice was between increasing rigidities on management at the microlevel or high inflation at the macrolevel" (Pontusson and Swenson 1996: 234–35). There was a further desire to disconnect bargaining in the traded goods from that in the public sector and to "quarantine" the former from the later (Sheldon and Thornthwaite 1999: 522).

The result, then, was a crisis of the institution of centralized, confederal-level collective bargaining in the 1980s. The engineering sector concluded a separate agreement in 1983. There was no central agreement at all in 1984, and separate engineering agreements were reached in 1988 and 1989. Finally, in 1990, the SAF shut down its bargaining unit and withdrew from any role in centralized bargaining, implicitly endorsing a new decentralized bargaining regime. What was unclear then, and remains murky today, is the extent to which the ultimate goal of employers is decentralization to the sectoral (or multisectoral) level or to the firm level; whether some degree of coordinated bargaining is the first preference of employers or simply the second-best option so long as a powerful labor movement has recourse to a largely unrestricted strike weapon. This question would reemerge after the election in 2006 of a bourgeois coalition government, and it will be discussed in the next section.

While employers were the prime agents of change in the industrial relations regime, labor and political actors also played their part. After all, VF would not have been able to conclude separate sectoral agreements without the willingness of its opposite number, the engineering union *Metall* (now *IF Metall*), to join it in breaking away from centralized bargaining. Skilled manual workers in highly profitable engineering firms could see the benefits of decentralized bargaining, and there was resentment at the wage guarantees that ensured that white collar workers and public sector "pay parasites" would benefit from solidaristic bargaining and wage drift in the private sector (Pontusson and Swenson 1996: 234). Evidence of a resulting decline in morale among skilled workers comes from rising absenteeism and the effort of employers to compensate for the inability to increase wages through new forms of work organization, perhaps best exemplified in Volvo's Kalmar plant (Alexopoulos and Cohen 2003: 358).

The collapse of centralized bargaining also reflected growing fissures within the labor movement and the declining hegemony of the LO over its own affiliates and within the union movement as a whole. In 1945, almost 80% of union members belonged to LO unions; two-thirds still did in 1970. By 2009 it was down to 47%. Since 1980, about a third of union members have belonged to the white collar TCO unions, while a growing proportion, 16% in 2009, now belong to Saco (Kjellberg 2011a: 54). Further, the homogeneity of each union confederation has declined as the line between blue and white collar work has blurred and cross-collar union cooperation within sectors has challenged within-collar solidarity (Mahon 1999). Thus, as employers have increasingly sought to defect from centralized bargaining, unions have found themselves divided in defending bargaining at that level. Decentralization was an inevitable consequence.

Finally, some brief mention of the role of the Swedish state should be made here, though its role becomes more significant during the economic crisis of the early 1990s and the reconstruction of industrial relations discussed in the next section. Ryner (2002) exaggerates somewhat in characterizing the crisis facing the Swedish model in the 1970s as one primarily of legitimation rather than profitability; the Swedish economy faced very real problems, as outlined above. But he is right to emphasize the extent to which, when the Social Democratic Party returned to power in 1982, it had internalized a "compensatory, disciplinary neo-liberalism" (Ryner 2002: 166) and proved willing to largely give up on industrial policy and the regulation of capital mobility, and to deem Keynesian policy ineffective in the new international environment.[3] As a result, many of its traditional policy tools were replaced by neoliberal ones, combined with the familiar elements of social protection and incomes policy designed to compensate for the costs of a more open and deregulated economy. This was accompanied by both privatization of public utilities and a "new managerial discourse" within the public sector, emphasizing flexibility and performance-related pay, all with important consequences for industrial relations in the public sector (Thörnqvist 2007).

8.3 Reengineering Coordination for a Neoliberal Era

By the end of the 1980s, the Swedish industrial relations regime was in crisis: inflation; historically high unemployment; higher strike levels; and an empty seat at the employer end of the bargaining table. But it did not collapse. It was out of that crisis, and the Stabilization Drive between 1990 and 1993 that served as the immediate response to it, that the seeds of a new industrial relations regime emerged (Elvander and Holmlund 1997). The early 1990s played a key role in altering the calculus and strategies of industrial actors, making the reconstruction of industrial relations institutions possible (for a good overview see Thelen 2014: 181–82).

The role of the Swedish state in the gestation of the new industrial relations regime was crucial, not least because many of the elements of the new regime were inaugurated by the state during the Stabilization Drive. As Ahlberg and Bruun note, employer and union willingness to reconstruct coordinated bargaining was in part "a conversion on the way to the gallows" (Ahlberg and Bruun 2005: 124) as the social partners anticipated increased state intervention and regulation in the event of nonaction on their part. The state had become more activist in a legislative sense in the course of the 1970s, but it had still largely respected the principle of collective self-regulation that was at the heart of the postwar Swedish model. In response to the economic crisis, however, it

---

[3] Then SPD finance minister Kjell-Olof Feldt claimed in his memoirs that the government elected in 1982 was the first social democratic government elected on a promise to restore profits (cited in Bengtsson 2013, paper 1).

became activist in a different sense, seeking to shape a post-Saltsjöbaden set of industrial relations institutions and practices. This involved both a direct role in inaugurating a set of new bargaining practices and an indirect role in pressuring employers and unions to bargain in new ways. By the end of the 1990s, a new industrial relations regime had emerged and "the starting point of this reform process was the most comprehensive and centralized state intervention in the labour market in Swedish history" (Elvander 2002: 214).

The initial response of the minority Social Democratic government to the economic crisis and the withdrawal of the SAF from centralized bargaining and corporatist institutions was to propose a wage freeze and a ban on strikes. Rank and file rebellion within the labor movement and the party thwarted these efforts, and the government then created the so-called Rehnberg Group of former chief negotiators to implement a wage settlement for 1991–93 through "*de facto* reinforced mediation" (Elvander and Holmlund 1997: 22). That mechanism was kept in place by a bourgeois coalition government elected in 1991. Collective bargaining between employers and unions took place in 1993, but it was closely supervised by state mediators and followed the outlines of the Rehnberg wage settlement. This agreement set a wage pool through centralized bargaining but left most of its distribution to local, firm-level bargaining, and it removed all wage guarantees and forms of indexation – the main forms of wage rigidity that had crept into wage bargaining in the 1960s and 1970s – out of sectoral agreements. Thus, elements that appeared during the Stabilization Drive and then emerged in full-blown form after 1997 included the use of technocratic criteria to create wage norms as the basis for a renewal of coordinated bargaining, the enhanced use of mediation to both limit conflict and adhere to the wage norm, the stripping out of all wage guarantees and forms of indexation from collective agreements, and greater local wage determination. The last two elements set the scene for the decentralization and individualization of wage setting that followed.

The next bargaining round, in 1995, was far more conflictual. Engineering employers opened with a radical bargaining agenda that involved the complete decentralization of wage bargaining to the firm level, with a central agreement serving only to impose a peace obligation on unions during negotiations, and with an expanded right of firm-level agreements to derogate from both the Employment Protection Act and centralized collective agreements. Unions rejected this approach, and an overtime ban and a series of strikes followed. The eventual agreement permitted half of the central wage increase to be distributed locally but did not expand derogatory agreements at the local level.

The experience of 1990 to 1995 proved crucial to the reconstruction of the industrial relations regime after 1997, in two senses. First, and as noted above, a set of innovative bargaining practices emerged which were subsequently integrated into the new regime. Second, employers and trade unions looked into the abyss and stepped back. Trade unions were traumatized by the experience of

the stabilization period,[4] but also by the knowledge that real wages for manufacturing workers had risen only 1% between 1970 and 1995 (Ibsen et al.
2011: 327). If the old bargaining system was failing to produce wage gains,
unions proved more willing to contemplate changes in wage bargaining, meaning primarily greater decentralization. One further consequence of the 1995
bargaining round for labor was greater sectoral cooperation across union confederations, which both weakened the influence of the LO and presaged new
forms of "cross-collar" coordination (Mahon 1999).

Employers, meanwhile, faced with the prospect of much higher levels of conflict, backed away from the more radical elements of their reform program
(Ahlberg and Bruun 2005). Employers could only make fully decentralized bargaining work if there were limits on strikes. In the absence of a reversal of
Swedish labor law's very limited regulation of strikes, the second-best solution
for employers was their opening demand in the 1995 round: sectoral agreements that left all wage bargaining to the firm, but imposed a peace obligation
on bargaining at that level. This was a nonstarter for unions, so employers fell
back upon coordinated sectoral bargaining that linked some decentralization
of bargaining with mechanisms to limit industrial conflict. It was, ultimately,
the inability to achieve industrial peace in any other way that drove employers
back to coordinated bargaining (Sheldon and Thornthwaite 1999). However,
a more complete decentralization of collective bargaining to the firm level has
remained a "dormant wish" of employers (Ibsen et al. 2011: 336), reappear-
ing periodically in subsequent years, with highest intensity in the 2010 to 2012
bargaining rounds.

A new industrial relations regime was put in place between 1997 and 2000.
Its building block was an "Industrial Agreement" reached between eight unions
and twelve employers' organizations in 1997 to provide for coordinated bargaining in the private manufacturing sector. It was followed by two similar
agreements in the public sector, one for central government and the other for
local government. The latter agreement was somewhat thinner than either the
Industrial Agreement or its central government counterpart, but both state sector agreements accepted that their wage norm would follow the lead of that in
the competitive, export-oriented sector. The result was that 60% of the Swedish
labor force, or about 2.2 million workers, was covered by this type of agreement, with the only significant gap being the private service sector (Elvander 2002: 204). In 2009, a similar agreement covering four unions and one
employer organization in the service sector was reached, taking total coverage
to 2.6 million workers or 71% of the labor force (Kullander and Häggebrink
2009). The final piece of the new system was a 2000 law that created a new
National Mediation Office (NMO) which essentially applied some of the core

---

[4] Trauma was the preferred term of trade unionists, used in interviews with the author by Ingemar
Göransson (Stockholm, October 9, 2006) and Tommy Öberg (Stockholm, October 6, 2006), both
of the LO.

elements of the industrial agreement to those parts of the economy that did not have their own industrial agreement equivalent. Thus, a large portion of the Swedish economy is now once again entwined in coordinated bargaining.

Since the original 1997 Industrial Agreement is the model for this new industrial relations regime, it is worth looking at it more closely. It has, broadly three elements. First, it establishes multisectoral coordinated bargaining for those industries that are signatory to the agreement. This is not peak-level bargaining of the kind that characterized the Saltsjöbaden regime, but neither is it simply industry bargaining. Each industry formally bargains separately, but multisectoral employer and labor cartels coordinate contract lengths and wage increases ahead of industry-level bargaining. For example, on the labor side coordination, is carried out by the cross-collar "Unions in Manufacturing," the core of which is *IF Metall* (LO), *Unionen* (TCO) and the Swedish Association of Graduate Engineers (Saco).

Second, the Industrial Agreement relies upon the technocratic construction of a wage norm that becomes the basis for bargaining. An independent Economic Council for Industry composed of academic economists produces the economic analysis from which a wage norm can emerge (though it does not specify a precise figure). The Industrial Agreement also contains a whole series of joint committees designed to create shared policy views on a wide range of issues. Third, it incorporates an enhanced use of mediation to encourage the acceptance of the wage norm and the economic analysis upon which it is based. The OpO-group of mediators, made up of experienced negotiators, serve as impartial chairs of the various bargaining committees. In the event of nonagreement, they can impose mediation and a two-week cooling-off period before strike action can take place. In addition, agreements are longer (initially lasting three years) and bargaining on a new agreement starts earlier in order to further reduce the likelihood of industrial conflict. But the role of these mediators extends beyond simply helping to find compromise, seeking rather to encourage the spread of the common wage norm and length of contract across all the industries covered by the Industrial Agreement (Ibsen 2012: 23).

It was these latter elements that were incorporated into the 2000 legislation creating a National Mediation Office (NMO). Sectors covered by a voluntary agreement, such as the Industrial Agreement, were exempt from this legislation. The NMO can appoint mediators without the consent of the parties concerned if no agreement has been reached a month before an existing agreement is to expire. These mediators were also able to impose a fourteen-day cooling-off period; in a country where the right to strike is almost entirely unabridged by legislation, this was a significant departure. The important innovation, however, is that the NMO is authorized to promote "well-functioning wage formation" (Ahlberg and Bruun 2005: 129). The initial form of the legislation creating the NMO had explicitly given it is a role in enforcing an incomes policy. That was too much for the unions, but what has survived is the use of state mediators to use the wage norm set in the Industrial Agreement as the basis for bargaining in other sectors. Ibsen refers to this a "dual mediation system" (Ibsen 2012:23) in which the OpO-group mediators use a wage norm in the manufacturing sector and then state mediators promote that same norm across the rest of the economy. The NMO cannot enforce that norm elsewhere, but in practice they will not propose higher wage agreements as part of their mediation work: "Defending the cost norm becomes the primary purpose of NMO mediation" (Ibsen 2012: 23).[5]

The Industrial Agreement regime of industrial relations put in place after 1997 was a system of multisectoral, cross-collar coordination, organizing unions and employer associations in a small number of agreements, each covering a broad swath of the economy. The leading role in this regime went to the manufacturing sector, where a wage norm consistent with export competitiveness became the basis for bargaining both within the industrial sector (through the Industrial Agreement) and in the protected private and public services sectors. It incorporated an integral role and enhanced powers for mediators, with the dual goal of limiting industrial conflict and promoting the wage norm. The agreements, the content of which will be discussed in considerable detail in the next section, were for the most part minimalist framework agreements – in some cases "agreements without numbers" at all – which set broad procedures and guidelines for bargaining and imposed a peace obligation on lower-level bargaining, but otherwise left broad scope for local bargaining, often permitting a high degree of individualization at the firm level.

This set of institutions, building on mechanisms and practices introduced during the Stabilization Drive, and responding to the experience of much higher levels of industrial conflict, constituted a delicate balancing act. On one hand, it partially recentralized bargaining through coordination agreements in order to achieve wage moderation, enforced through mediation. Employers could reasonably expect fewer strikes – something they were unable to achieve without such agreements – and not only was the export sector quarantined from the protected sector, but also in fact the export sector drove wage increases in the protected sector. Labor got the opportunity to negotiate for wage-leveling elements in the framework agreements, in the form of additional increases for low-paid workers, mostly women. On the other hand, the minimalist quality of these framework agreements permitted wage flexibility at the firm level, which, combined with the stripping out of the catch-up clauses that had institutionalized wage drift across the economy, gave employers considerably more discretion in wage setting than had existed in the 1970s and 1980s.

It is worth noting that this industrial relations regime had at its heart a tension between two forms of coordination. One was formal multisectoral

---

[5] This practice was highlighted in the spring 2012 bargaining round, when unions in the retail sector wanted to go above the wage norm set in manufacturing to add a low-wage component for female workers, and received no support from mediators. It led to accusations from labor that the NMO was interpreting its role too narrowly (Jacobsson 2012a).

coordination, in which the labor side included unions from more than just a single confederation. Thus, the Industrial Agreement included unions from all three confederations in a cross-collar bargaining cartel. The other was informal coordination organized by peak organizations, particularly the LO and SN, attempting to coordinate bargaining across all the agreements to which its affiliates were party. Coordination on the part of employers has been strong, with the SN largely successful in preventing its sectoral agreements from breaking the wage norm set in the manufacturing sector (Kjellberg interview with the author, Lund, October 2, 2012; Öberg interview with the author, Stockholm, October 4, 2012).

Coordination has been more problematic on the labor side. To the extent that wage solidarism, or, more accurately, compensation for the low-paid, was a goal, it was the LO that sought to encourage its affiliates to introduce such supplements ("kitties" or "pots") into their respective agreements. The post-1997 industrial relations regime privileged the former type of coordination and exacerbated tensions within the LO over common confederal goals. Trade unions "served two masters" (Göransson interview with the author, Stockholm, October 9, 2006), both their confederation and their sectoral bargaining partners, each with somewhat different interests. Ibsen (2015) has noted the institutional weaknesses of labor actors in their ability to achieve coordination and catalogued the scale of defections from the Industrial Agreement pattern (Ibsen 2015: 47). This cleavage was superimposed upon other strains within the labor movement: between the confederations themselves over the degree of individualization and flexibility in employment protection permitted in contracts; between unions in exposed and traded sectors; between unions organizing low-paid female workers and others.[6] In short, finding common interest within each union confederation, let alone across the entire labor movement, has been far more difficult in recent years. Indeed, for the first time, the LO did not coordinate the 2016 bargaining round because of the inability of industrial unions to agree with public sector and domestic service sector unions on a common wage norm (Wallin 2016). This explains the pessimism of some union observers about the future of the Industrial Agreement regime.[7]

This industrial relations regime has now been used for eight bargaining rounds, in 1998, 2001, 2004, 2007, 2010, 2011/12, 2013 and 2016. Each round covers the vast majority of Swedish workers, roughly 3.3 million. At least until 2010, when more difficult bargaining led to shorter and more variable contract lengths, contracts were generally synchronized to last three years.

---

[6] The author is indebted to the members of an LO delegation for highlighting many of these differences at a seminar on the Swedish model, held at the School of Management and Labor Relations, Rutgers University, March 31, 2014.

[7] Öberg has argued that an industrial relations system that is designed around the interests of 15% of the labor force (those in manufacturing) at the expense of the remaining 85% cannot long survive (interview with the author, Stockholm, August 26, 2011).

The first four rounds were considered broadly successful by the social partners (though internal employer coordination broke down in the 2007 round): the dispute resolution procedures worked to minimize industrial conflict, and the contracts provided real wage gains for workers (Ibsen et al. 2011: 327), but wage increases that were in step with the EU average.

The economic crisis that hit in 2008 complicated matters, and the 2010 bargaining round was both drawn out and more conflictual. The loss of jobs in manufacturing that resulted from the economic crisis led unions to accept opening clauses for the first time in modern Swedish history. IF Metall, in particular, had gone along in 2009 with a "crisis agreement" that permitted firm-level agreements to protect jobs by reducing hours and wages. It is worth noting the sharp break here with postwar solidarism: the Saltsjöbaden era saw unions prepared to sacrifice firms in order to maintain a solidaristic wage; this was reversed in the crisis agreement (Ottosson, personal communication with the author, Uppsala, October 3, 2012).

Subsequent bargaining rounds have, to a certain extent, been about how permanent the changes introduced as part of the crisis agreement should become; issues such as seniority rules for layoffs and the role of temporary work agencies remain contested bargaining issues (Säikkälä, personal communication with the author, Stockholm, January 20, 2015). In 2010, employers in manufacturing sought both a wage freeze and to make that agreement permanent. Unions saw space in the recovery for real wage gains and additional increases for the low-paid, and wanted an end to the use of temporary agency workers in place of rehiring permanent workers. Coordination collapsed over differences among unions. The LO saw opportunities for a larger wage increase if the retail sector produced the wage norm, and disagreements about the importance of low pay or gender pots emerged. The result was that white collar workers in engineering settled before a wider agreement could be reached, multiple agreements with different termination dates were reached, and strikes occurred in two sectors. In response, the engineering employers briefly withdrew from the Industrial Agreement, complaining that it has been "re-institutionalized to become a tool for the protected domestic industries' demands for higher wage increases" (quoted in Kullander and Eklund 2010: 1).

Employers did rejoin the Industrial Agreement when its mediators were given new powers and unions made a renewed commitment to the norm-setting role of the export sector. In the 2011–12 bargaining round, manufacturing once again settled first and established the wage norm. Yet these tensions are inherent, and likely to become more severe, in a system that privileges a declining sector. The result is that the wage-leading role of manufacturing has been challenged by white collar unions and by unions representing large numbers of low-paid workers (Kjellberg 2011a: 68–73).

The recent trajectory of Swedish industrial relations has been shaped by developments in domestic and international labor law as well as bargaining agreements between employers and labor (Malmberg and Bruun 2006). As noted earlier, the absence of a statutory extension mechanism or statutory minimum wage puts the onus upon Swedish unions to use pressure to ensure the extension of agreements to firms that are not part of employer associations or signatory to collective agreements. The few limits upon strikes have historically permitted unions to use sympathy strikes and secondary boycotts to achieve that end. Sweden's membership in the EU, and in particular the accession of relatively low-wage eastern European countries in 2004, meant that Sweden now faced easier entry by foreign firms and foreign workers, and it increased the importance of the strike weapon to extend the coverage of collective agreements. Lindberg (2011) has noted that even as the number of strikes has declined since the mid-1990s, now most strikes are concentrated in a few key sectors that are especially vulnerable to low-wage competition – construction and transportation – and have changed in form, with fewer wildcat strikes and more recourse to secondary boycotts designed to pressure employers to abide by existing agreements (Lindberg 2011: 13–14). Similarly, the Swedish Labour Court has seen an increase in cases of this kind, particularly those involving the use of temporary agency workers, posted from outside of Sweden (Bengtsson 2013: paper 4).

It is in this context that recent decisions by the European Court of Justice have intruded. In a series of rulings, most notably the Laval case, the ECJ ruled that the right to strike against firms using foreign workers temporarily posted to another country is limited to core elements of an agreement (Woolfson, Thörnqvist and Sommers 2010); a union cannot strike to demand wages above those required by law, which is problematic in a country like Sweden that largely does not regulate terms and conditions by law. In response, the Swedish government legislated in 2009 to limit recourse to secondary boycotts.

In 2006, the Social Democrats lost power and were replaced by a coalition of centrist and right-wing parties, a coalition that was reelected in 2010, before a minority Social Democratic government returned to power in September 2014. The main employers' organization called on the new government to legislate to limit strikes, emphasizing "disproportionality": the easy recourse and low cost to unions of sympathy and secondary (Svenskt Näringsliv 2006). The government declined to legislate in this area in the absence of agreement from the social partners (other than the legislative response to the ECJ noted above), following Sweden's longstanding tradition of self-regulation. Talks between labor and employers, with the goal of a grand "Saltsjöbaden II" agreement, failed in 2007. Labor was prepared to agree to greater decentralization of bargaining, but not limits on strikes or an easing of employment protection, as demanded by the SN (Henriksson and Kullander 2011: 2).

Nonetheless, there was important industrial relations legislation following the election of the bourgeois coalition. Most immediately consequential were changes to the Ghent system that coupled access to unemployment funds to trade union membership. Sharp increases in unemployment insurance fees and the elimination of tax breaks for union dues and unemployment insurance led to a rapid and drastic decline in union membership by a quarter of a million workers, with the result that union density fell from 77% to 71% between 2006 and 2008 (Kjellberg 2011b: 67). These changes have also accelerated a longer-term delinking of union membership and unemployment fund membership and contributed to a substantial increase in the proportion of workers not covered by the funds; in 2005, 16% of workers were outside the unemployment funds, a figure that rose to 30% by the end of 2008 (Kjellberg 2011b: 87). Combined with a series of further legislative changes in 2007 and 2008 designed to make unemployment benefits more insurance-based and to phase out the benefit for the long-term unemployed, the result has been a dramatic fall in the proportion of the unemployed receiving benefits, from 70% in 2006 to 36% in 2012 (Murhem 2013: 632). These changes contribute to greater low-wage pressure on the Swedish labor market.

Finally, in this section on recent industrial relations developments, it is important to note a progressive easing of employment protection over the last two decades (Emmenegger 2015: 111, Rönnmar 2010). It will be recalled that the 1982 Employment Protection Act, building on its 1974 predecessor, strictly limited the ability of employers to fire workers and made recourse to fixed-term employment contracts difficult. In 1996, a new kind of fixed-term contract was introduced and the EPA, which already permitted derogation subject to a sectoral agreement, was amended to allow derogation from the law if negotiated in a local agreement, giving greater flexibility to employers at the firm level. Then in a major legislative change in 2007 the list of acceptable reasons for being permitted to use fixed-term contracts was replaced with a new "general fixed-term contract" that did not require a specific reason. The overall impact of these changes in labor law has been to "normalize the fixed-term contract" (Rönnmar 2010: 64) while attempting to limit the scope of successive use of the contracts.

8.4 Decentralization and Decollectivization in Swedish Industrial Relations

Following the crisis of the Saltsjöbaden regime of centralized solidaristic bargaining in the 1980s, marked most noticeably by the withdrawal of employers from confederal bargaining and the tripartite agency boards and a period of intense state activism during the Stabilization Drive of the early 1990s, a new system of multisectoral coordinated bargaining emerged. That process was outlined in the last section. An evaluation of the Industrial Agreement regime that focused upon formal institutions would identify elements of both institutional continuity and innovation. Continuity is expressed in the return to coordinated bargaining (albeit of a more patchwork quality), the wage-setting role of the export sector and the continued reliance upon self-regulation. Innovation comes in the use of technocratic criteria for establishing a wage norm and new collective bargaining rules that give a larger role to mediation. It would not be difficult to interpret these developments through the lens of fundamental institutional continuity with incremental change around the periphery of the industrial relations regime. The period since the late 1990s has, after all, seen a resuscitation of coordinated bargaining, the centerpiece of the postwar Swedish class compromise.

However, this would confuse continuity in form with continuity in function. It would miss the truly important innovations in Swedish industrial relations of the last decade or so and the qualitative shift in the nature and functioning of collective bargaining through which "Sweden has experienced major changes in its wage-setting system" (Granqvist and Regnér 2008: 501). This has involved a decentralization, flexibilization and individualization of wage bargaining. The agreements that are the focus of coordinated bargaining are now minimalist framework agreements, establishing procedures for bargaining, sometimes setting some limited wage targets, but permitting wide discretion at the firm level. There has been a "controlled decentralization of wage setting" (Ibsen et al. 2011: 326). A focus upon the bargaining institutions themselves misses the manner in which these institutions have come to function as mechanisms for permitting local variation. In other words, something dramatic has changed under the hood of Swedish industrial relations institutions since the 1970s, as powerful liberalizing tendencies have transformed class relations and expanded the scope of employer discretion at the firm level.[8]

Comparative studies of the decentralization of collective bargaining have noted its multidimensional character and the extent to which decentralization has taken different forms in different countries (Karlson and Lindberg 2010). In Sweden, it took the form of a decline in confederal involvement in bargaining, much greater scope for local bargaining and higher levels of differentiation and individualization in wage setting, particularly for salaried and professional workers. To be clear, there was always space in postwar Swedish industrial relations for some degree of local bargaining, which is why wage drift emerged as so significant an issue from the late 1960s onward. But prior to the 1990s, it took place within limits and was accompanied by a series of guarantees for groups of workers unable to benefit from wage drift. Furthermore, while some decentralized wage bargaining was possible, it was *collective* bargaining, on behalf of an entire group of workers, rather than individualized bargaining. As Ahlberg and Bruun note (2005: 130), the typical agreement in 1980 had a whole series of minimum wage clauses for every conceivable category of worker, provided

---

[8] One problem with identifying the precise scale of change at the firm level is the absence of systematic workplace industrial relations surveys of the kind regularly conducted in Britain and France. There are certainly case studies, but the firm remains something of a black box for researchers.

for minimum guaranteed raises and set clear rules for how to distribute any local wage pool.

Starting in the 1990s and codified after 1997 in the practice of Industrial Agreement-type bargains, central collective agreements became thinner and more minimalist, establishing a set of principles and procedures for predominantly local bargaining. The first "agreements without figures," referring to sectoral agreements that provided for no general increase and simply devolved bargaining to the firm level, were signed by white collar unions, particularly those belonging to Saco, in the early 1990s, and they subsequently spread widely (Nyström 2004: 21). These agreements permitted not only decentralization to the firm level but also individualization within a given workforce as collective components declined as a proportion of the wage pool (Granqvist and Regnér 2008).

Central agreements under the new industrial relations regime tend to have many fewer minimum wage categories, or none at all, some guarantee of a wage increase, usually as a fallback provision in the event that local agreement cannot be reached, and a local wage pool to be distributed subject to firm-level bargaining, accompanied by a set of general principles for its distribution, such as that increases be directed towards low-paid workers (Ibsen et al. 2011: 327).

Public sector and professional workers have the most extreme form of these agreements, with few or no minimum wages or guarantees, and the entire wage pool determined and distributed through local bargaining. A study of professional workers organized into Saco unions, where this process has gone the furthest, indicated that 60% of workers received no guaranteed wage increase whatsoever, 21% had a fallback guarantee if no local agreement was reached, and the remainder had a guaranteed increase stipulated in a sectoral agreement, but it was left to local bargaining to determine its distribution (Granqvist and Regnér 2008: 503). Further, there is a high degree of individualization, as pay is determined either by a pay review process between employer and employee monitored by the local union, or simply by individual bargaining with no union role at all. The result is "a substantial devolution of pay determination to local management" (Granqvist and Regnér 2008: 517).

While this degree of individualization has progressed furthest among white collar workers and the public sector, it is increasingly important for blue collar workers in manufacturing. The 2012 central agreement covering metalworkers, for example, left almost half of the local pool for individualized wage setting (Kjellberg 2012: 1). IF Metall has local wage systems covering over 80% of its members; these typically have 20% or more of the wage determined by the nature of the work and the manner in which the worker carries it out (Kjellberg 2012: 2–3).

There were no consistent time-series national data on degrees of bargaining decentralization prior to the creation of the National Mediation Office in

2000.[9] However, the data available since confirm "a shift towards a greater degree of local wage formation...and greater emphasis on delegation to local parties" (National Mediation Office 2011: 5). This can be observed in 2013, the most recent major bargaining round[10] for which data are available (National Mediation Office 2014: 143, Table 8.8).[11] In central and local government, no employees received a general increase, with all wages determined at the local level. In the private sector, 64% of employees received no general increase from a sectoral agreement at all, and 85% of employees had either the level of their wage increase or the manner in which that increase was distributed determined to some degree by firm-level bargaining. Thus, economywide, only about one in ten employees received his or her entire wage increase from a sectoral agreement, while more than three-quarters received no general increase of any kind. It is also worth noting a substantial increase in "figureless agreements" in the 2013 bargaining round, that is, those with no guaranteed increase of any kind, with any wage increase to be determined entirely through local bargaining. In 2012, approximately 11% of workers were covered by collective agreements that set no minimum wage increase, rising to 20% in 2013, with the Mediation Institute estimating that the figure for 2015 will be 30%, mostly in the public sector (Kullander and Talme 2014).

Decentralization and individualization of wage bargaining have not simply been imposed upon the trade union movement. It should not be surprising that economic actors with market power – whether business or labor – would favor liberalization, though certainly debates about wage determination systems have been more anguished on the labor side. Some unions, primarily in the public sector, even championed the individualization of wage bargaining in the belief that productivity gains would translate into higher wages for their members. *Kommunal*, the Swedish Municipal Workers Union, adopted a new wage-setting system that emphasized individualization as early as 1993, citing member support and opportunities for higher wages, though it is worth noting that there is scant evidence for that support from the membership (Lapidus 2015: 11–13) and there is growing disquiet with the policy even at the leadership level (Öberg 2014).

---

[9] The main Swedish employers' association has some data available for the 1990s, but they are not comparable with those collected by the National Mediation Office after 2000 (Svenskt Näringsliv 2012).

[10] Some agreements are reached every year, but major bargaining rounds are either every two or three years, when the great majority of agreements are reached.

[11] One result of the decentralization of wage bargaining in Sweden has been a proliferation of wage setting models incorporated into sectoral agreements, ranging from those that contain only a general increase to those leaving everything to local bargaining. In between are agreements that leave wage determination to local bargaining but provide for a wage guarantee or fallback provision in the event that local bargaining fails. I am indebted to personal communications from Bjorn Lindgren and Kerstin Ahlberg for help in interpreting the National Mediation Office data.

Thus, the reemergence of multisectoral coordinated bargaining in Sweden since the late 1990s, something that might be interpreted as either a return to past practice or a recentralization of collective bargaining, has in fact gone hand in hand with a fundamental decentralization and individualization of bargaining to the firm level. Central agreements offer principles and procedures for bargaining, sometimes determine local wage pools, and often provide for a guaranteed minimum wage increase, but real wages are now negotiated at the firm level. One result has been that, despite the vastly expanded role of local bargaining, wage drift has been negligible since the late 1990s because the sectoral agreements no longer determine actual wages (Anxo and Niklasson 2006: 365, Figure 7).

The impact of newly decentralized collective bargaining depends both upon the institutional matrix within which it is introduced and upon the strength of the industrial actors. Several longstanding features of Swedish industrial relations take on new relevance in the present period. The framework of labor law and the organization and strength of trade unions are of particular importance. Collective bargaining in Sweden takes place under a peace obligation, meaning that strikes and lockouts are illegal while an agreement is in force. Central agreements (of the Industrial Agreement type) extend that peace obligation to the firm-by-firm bargaining that follows signature of the central agreement. Thus, local unions are unable to strike, or plausibly threaten to strike, in the course of bargaining with the management of a firm.[12] Further, as part of the widespread commitment to self-regulation, Swedish labor law is "semimandatory," permitting collective agreements, including firm-level agreements, to contain provisions less favorable than those found in legislation. In recent years, the scope of permitted derogation from law has expanded, as noted in the previous section. Thus, Swedish labor law is compatible with a high degree of flexibility, so long as it is bargained for, raising the stakes of firm level bargaining and expanding the opportunities for greater variability in wages and working conditions across firms.

In keeping with the power resources approach of this book, the relative balance of class forces is likely to determine the extent to which decentralization expands employer discretion. The outcome of such bargaining will depend in large part on the capacity of organized labor to exercise leverage inside the firm. And Swedish unions remain, by any comparative standard, strong. Overall, union density is currently 70% and unions have long been marked by a combination of centralized (confederal and industrial) and decentralized (workplace) strength (Kjellberg 2009). Thus, it is no surprise that the more minimalist central agreements have been signed in sectors where unions are particularly strong.

---

[12] Sofia Murhem (personal communication, February 13, 2014) has drawn attention to the negative impact for unions of limitations on the right to strike in the public sector in the context of highly decentralized bargaining.

That said, there are some disturbing signs and the trajectory of labor move-ment strength is unquestionably towards decline. There has been a long-term decline in overall union density, from a peak of 85% in 1993 to just below 70% in 2014 (Kjellberg 2015, Appendix 3, Table A). That decline reflects the changing composition of the labor force and of industry and a more critical view of unions among workers (Kjellberg 2011b: 69–72), but also a failure on the part of most trade unions to invest heavily in organizing (Öberg, interview with the author, Stockholm, October 6, 2006). To this long-term decline must be added the fall in union density that resulted from the changes to the Ghent system introduced in 2007. Density had drifted down between 1993 and 2006, but the rate of decline after 2007 was historically unique. Only in 2012 did union membership begin to stabilize. In the last decade, private sector union density has declined by almost 10 percentage points, while private employer membership of SN rose by 5 percentage points. But during the same period, collective bargaining coverage in the private sector has remained largely stable, dropping from 90% to 87% (Jacobsson 2012b). This suggests that, increas-ingly, it is employer organization that is sustaining the high level of collective bargaining, rather than organization on the labor side.

There have been declines in union density for all categories, but most trou-bling for the future has been the scale of decline among young workers (aged 16–24), where union density dropped 34 points between 1993 and 2014 for a union density of 35%, half the overall rate (Kjellberg 2015, Appendix 3, Table D). While density in the public sector remains high, at 82%, it has declined to 64% in the private sector (Kjellberg 2015: Appendix 3, Table B), with density substantially lower in sectors such as retail and wholesale trade and the hotel and restaurant industry.

Of particular relevance to the impact of decentralization is the coverage and vitality of workplace union clubs that do the actual bargaining inside the firm. It was the combination of centralized and decentralized trade union strength that marked the period of labor hegemony in Sweden. The total number of union representatives declined by about a third between 1998 and 2006 (Kjellberg 2011a: 77). While the ratio of union representatives to members has remained stable in LO, it has dropped quite substantially for the white collar and pro-fessional unions affiliated with TCO and Saco (Kjellberg 2011a: 77). Studies by individual unions also show declining membership participation in union meetings and weakening organization; in 2002/2003, only 40% of Union of Clerical and Technical Employees in Industry (SIF) members had a union club or union representative with bargaining powers at their workplace, half the figure in 1990, and in 2001 one-third of *Kommunal* workplaces had no union representative (Kjellberg, personal communication with the author, Stockholm, October 2006).

Union decline has wider implications for the future of the Swedish model of collective self-regulation. There will come a point, if union membership con-tinues to decline, at which union coverage is sufficiently low so that the state is forced to introduce statutory protections for those not covered by a collective agreement, through a statutory extension mechanism, national minimum wage and the like. The growing importance of EU directives, and the recent decisions of the ECJ making it harder for Swedish unions to use strike action to extend collective agreements, point in the same direction, because Sweden has an obligation to ensure that all workers benefit from European social rights, and if collective bargaining cannot guarantee that, legislation will have to substitute (Malmberg, personal communication with the author, Stockholm, October 2006). At that point, the balance between self-regulation and state intervention is likely to change.[13]

The greater variability in wages and working conditions produced by decentralization and individualization undermines the essential solidarism that formed the ideological underpinning of postwar Swedish industrial relations; small wonder that LO coordination has become so fraught with difficulty. Granqvist and Regnér's study of professional workers indicates the emergence of significant wage differentials among union members as a result of individualized wage-setting (Granqvist and Regnér 2008: 501). Unsurprisingly, the wage gap between blue and white collar workers has widened in recent years, and between 1993 and 2008, wage increases for white collar workers in the private sector were higher than those for blue collar workers in all but four of those years (Oliver 2011: 556). This is true even within those sectors covered by the Industrial Agreement, indicating the decoupling of coordination and wage leveling.

It is certainly the case that wage leveling remains an important priority for the LO as a whole and for unions that organize low-paid, usually feminized sectors in particular. The LO has sought agreement on special supplements in the course of bargaining designed to provide additional wage increases to low-paid and female workers, though there have been disagreements even within the blue collar confederation as to how to define and implement these supplements (Kullander and Björklund 2011). These efforts are contested within the labor movement and have met with mixed results; the collapse of LO coordination, in part over the issue of how to close the gender wage gap, in late 2015 may indicate that the union confederations no longer have the capacity to perform a wage-leveling function (National Mediation Office 2016). Employers were also more willing to agree to the supplements prior to the onset of economic crisis in 2008. But in any case, the simple reality is that even where implemented, the egalitarian effects of these small pots of wages have been swamped by the inegalitarian consequences of decentralization and individualization. Oliver (2008, 2011) has noted that, more importantly than overall

---

[13] Indeed, in 2013, the President of the Transport Workers Union floated a proposal for the legal enforcement and extension of collective agreements as a response to the growing difficulty of unions in enforcing industry-wide agreements, particularly in light of the Laval decision (Öberg 2013).

labor movement strength, the particular organization of Swedish unions – separate blue and white collar confederations; the absence of general wage scales – has contributed to rising wage inequality. Wage setting for white collar and professional workers has an individualized logic that emphasizes seniority and performance, while blue collar workers are more likely to see collective increases. And even where wage leveling principles are agreed at the sectoral level, they are likely to be contested and undermined at the local level, where most wage bargaining now takes place (Oliver 2008: 1560). Paradoxically, the forms of union organization that helped to produce egalitarian outcomes in the 1950s and 1960s have evolved in such a way as to exacerbate rivalries and undermine solidarity and egalitarianism today.

At the end of the 1970s, employer discretion was constrained across the board. The codetermination law required that employers negotiate over most aspects of work organization with trade unions (rather than with weaker, more firm-centric works councils, as in many other countries with codetermination legislation). A combination of powerful unions and EPL severely curtailed recourse to atypical employment, made permanent contracts the norm and required just cause for dismissal. And the centerpiece of the postwar Swedish industrial relations system was a form of centralized, confederal-level wage bargaining that set wages based on the nature of the job rather than the ability of firms to pay, used wage leveling as a mechanism for industrial restructuring and, as the 1960s and 1970s progressed, made wage setting increasingly rigid as automatic catch-up and indexation clauses became common elements of collective agreements. The obstacle to flexibility was only to a limited extent legislation. Swedish labor law was semimandatory, permitting derogation subject to collective agreement. It was the strength of the labor movement combined with institutions of centralized bargaining that served to limit employer discretion.

What has changed in the intervening three decades is also not primarily changes to labor law. Employment protection has been amended several times to make recourse to atypical employment easier and to shift the opportunities for derogation down to firm-level bargaining, and the ability of unions to strike against the use of foreign workers in order to pressure an employer to respect collective agreements has been limited. But the Swedish system has always permitted, in principle at least, "negotiated flexibility" (Anxo and Niklasson 2006: 32). It is changes to trade union strength and collective bargaining institutions that have been the real source of expanded employer discretion. Thus, Swedish unions have been willing to negotiate on a range of flexibility issues (Nyström 2004: 30–33), for example, signing comprehensive agreements allowing the use of temporary workers, so long as pay is comparable to that of permanent workers. In 1990, 10% of Swedish employees were on fixed-term contracts; the comparable figure for 2008 was 16.1%, two points above the EU average (Rönnmar 2010: 55).

Most important of all has been the decentralization and individualization of wage bargaining. Automatic indexation and catch-up clauses were stripped from wage agreements in the early 1990s, and the primary locus of wage bargaining is now overwhelmingly at the firm level, whereas it was once at the national or sectoral level; sectoral agreements now serve as minimalist framework agreements, limiting recourse to industrial action and serving to moderate wages, but permitting a high degree of wage flexibility inside the firm. For salaried and professional workers, wage determination is also highly individualized, allowing local managers to set wages based on individual performance criteria. This is not unilateral managerial discretion; local unions oversee and monitor wage setting. But the twin processes of decentralization to the firm and individualization do represent a vast expansion in the flexibility available to employer in the area of wage setting.

8.5 Conclusion

Sweden emerged largely unscathed from the financial and economic crisis that began in 2008, and there is little evidence that the crisis substantially changed the broader political–economic trajectory, or indeed the role of neoliberal ideas and discourses (Schnyder and Jackson 2013). Broadly neoliberal reforms in the financial sector, the welfare state and macroeconomic policy were introduced from the early 1990s onward, to accompany those in the industrial relations sphere outlined in this chapter. There is good reason to suggest that these reforms, complementing traditional strengths in education and gender equality, have made Sweden "once again a model" (Pontusson 2011) among advanced capitalist economies.

Certainly, we would be the first to admit that Sweden is a difficult case for an argument about neoliberal convergence. No one would mistake Swedish industrial relations at the end of the first decade of the twenty-first century for those of Britain or another archetypal liberal market economy. Almost nine out of ten Swedish workers are covered by collective agreements, union density is comparatively high, negotiation remains the hegemonic mechanism for managing class relations, and governments of the Right have not sought to dismantle industrial relations institutions, even as employers' organizations float radical proposals for limiting the right to strike and fully decentralizing all bargaining to the firm.

But nor is it possible to mistake the current Swedish industrial relations regime for that of the 1950s, 1960s and 1970s. As detailed above, it has been transformed along an unambiguously liberalizing trajectory involving the familiar processes of decentralization, individualization, decollectivization and the consequent expansion of employer discretion. Swedish unions retain real strengths that most of their counterparts outside of Scandinavia would envy. But decentralization has undermined the collective power of labor and both the material substance and ideological power of solidarism. The postwar model of solidaristic wage bargaining rested upon the principle of equal pay for equal work, regardless of the profitability of individual firms or the strength of the local union club. That has been replaced by a decentralized logic in which workers and their local unions are encouraged to think about the needs of their particular employers and to respond flexibly. As a former LO negotiator put it (Göransson, interview with the author, Stockholm, October 4, 2012), this has permitted "blackmail to protect jobs," with the result that Swedish workers have acceded to high levels of flexibility in work time and to use of temporary contracts in order to protect those jobs.

It is legitimate to ask what it means to decentralize bargaining when unions are unable to strike during the negotiation process, when there is an absence of trained and experienced workplace union representatives, when derogation is possible at the firm level and when union membership is declining, especially among the next generation of workers. Combined with the spread of individualized wage-setting arrangements, this suggests that in many places the role of unions is one of "monitoring" the implementation of workplace agreements rather than actually doing the negotiating (Ahlberg and Bruun 2005:131).

The industrial relations regime put in place in Sweden over the last fifteen years combines two main elements. First, sectoral coordination, enforced primarily by employer organizations and the state mediation apparatus, operates to implement a tight wage norm derived from the competitive needs of the export sector across the bulk of the economy. Coordinated bargaining serves to realize wage moderation and transmit that moderation to the protected sector. It is striking, for a country that retains a strong labor movement, that Sweden experienced the largest decline in wage share in the quarter century after 1980 in a study of 13 OECD economies (Peters 2011: 92).[14] Second, a decentralization and individualization of bargaining has displaced solidarism and permitted both greater variation in wages among workers and firms and greater flexibility available to employers in the deployment of labor and the organization of work. This process has gone furthest in the public sector and among white collar workers, but is present also for blue collar workers in manufacturing.

Institutional change has not primarily taken place through the wholesale destruction of existing institutions and construction of new ones. Confederal level bargaining and the main tripartite corporatist institutions were subject to frontal assault from employers at the end of the 1980s, and largely disappeared.[15] There has also been some change in the hierarchy of institutions, as mediation, long a part of Swedish industrial relations, has come to occupy a more centrally important role. But for the most part, institutional change has come about through conversion, as the function of coordinated bargaining was

---

[14] See also Bengtsson (2013, paper 1) for further evidence of declining labor share of net value added after 1980.

[15] In the absence of tripartite institutions, union and employer confederations do still periodically negotiate over nonwage issues such as labor market flexibility.

transformed into an institution to impart flexibility into wage determination through decentralization and individualization.

Coordinated decentralization – embedding decentralized bargaining in framework agreements – has tended to be the mechanism for liberalizing industrial relations in coordinated market economies and/or where the consent of organized labor is required for liberalization to take place (Traxler 1995). Sweden is no exception, and in Sweden, as elsewhere, coordinated decentralization has involved a tradeoff between the goals of wage flexibility, wage moderation and wage leveling (Ibsen 2012). The evidence of this chapter is that substantial decentralization has indeed taken place, and further, that the form it has taken – the Industrial Agreement regime – has tended to privilege wage flexibility and wage restraint over wage leveling.

Thelen (2012: 146) has argued that contemporary Scandinavian political economy exemplifies a particular trajectory of liberalization – "embedded flexibilization" – one that produces, or perhaps permits, a more egalitarian form of capitalism.[16] Certainly it remains the case that Sweden enjoys lower levels of inequality and poverty than most of its advanced capitalist counterparts, though it is also worth noting the rapid increase in inequality in the last two decades. In 1985 Sweden had the lowest 90:10 and 80:20 income ratios in the OECD, yet it had the fifth highest rate of increase in income inequality between 1985 and 2002 (Oliver 2008: 1563–4). Between the early 1980s and the late 2000s, household incomes in the bottom decile grew substantially more slowly than the OECD average (0.4% annually compared to 1.3%), while they grew faster in the top decile (2.4% annually compared to 1.9%) (OECD 2011: 23, Table 1). The increase in inequality of market income was sharpest in the period from the mid-1980s until the mid-1990s before stabilizing in the period since (OECD 2011: 270, Table 7.3).[17]

However, the important point for our purposes is that industrial relations institutions no longer have the same egalitarian properties that they once did. At the same time, the extent of "inequality cushioning" in the form of taxes and transfers (to offset market income inequality) has declined since the mid-1990s, primarily because of changes to the tax system (OECD 2011: 271). Nonetheless, Sweden still exemplifies "flexicurity" with expansion of the market domain and employer discretion in the labor market, and social protection from and material compensation for the consequences of the market outside. Baccaro and Pontusson (2015: 28) have suggested that Sweden has developed a particular growth model, one that combines consumption-led growth courtesy of a strong public sector and export-led growth courtesy of the wage moderation

---

[16] For a more nuanced account, which distinguishes between the Danish and Swedish experience and is more pessimistic about the egalitarian prospects for the Swedish political economy, see Thelen (2014), especially Chapter 5.

[17] The authors are indebted to communication with Jonas Pontusson for help in understanding the timing and source of Sweden's growing inequality.

in that sector. It is a growth model that rests upon the institutional transformation described in this chapter. The period since at least 1990 has seen the center of gravity of Swedish industrial relations shift from centralization to decentralization and from rigidity to flexibility, along an unmistakable liberalizing trajectory.

9

Actors, Institutions and Pathways

The Liberalization of Industrial Relations in Western Europe

The five countries reviewed certainly reveal an impressive diversity of institutional forms and paths of institutional evolution, but there seems to be a common directionality behind the national peculiarities. This chapter analyzes the evidence concerning mechanisms of institutional change and the roles of labor, business and the state exhibited across our five country cases.

9.1 Pathways of Institutional Change

As the previous five chapters have demonstrated, our country cases show a common neoliberal trajectory of institutional change, and in each case, substantial liberalization of industrial relations institutions occurs, with the effect of expanding employer discretion across the three domains of wage setting, work organization and hiring and firing. But each country moved toward liberalization in a somewhat different manner, even if there were also common elements (the decline in union density, for example). To some extent, these differences reflect the different obstacles to employer discretion faced in each country: whether it came primarily from legislation and state regulation or from collective regulation on the part of unions and employer organizations, and if the latter, whether the strength of collective regulation derived more from national organization or embedded power at the workplace. And faced with different sources of rigidity and constraint upon employers, the partisan hue of the government, the fear of social and industrial conflict and above all the power resources still wielded by class actors all influenced the willingness of those wanting institutional change to launch a frontal assault on industrial relations systems as opposed to finding alternative mechanisms of change.

One can identify three broad approaches to institutional change adopted by the countries we examined in detail. The first involves deregulation through changes to legislation that had once supported collective regulation and limited employer discretion. One thinks of Britain during the Thatcherite period, when deregulation came without any compensating benefits for workers or unions. During the New Labor period, the collapse of collective regulation was partially offset by the provision of limited legal protections to workers. In other cases, Italy for example, peak-level bargaining was used as a mechanism for gaining acquiescence for deregulation, while in France it was the expansion of workplace bargaining that was used to legitimize deregulation. This approach involved not only deregulation of the labor market but also the removal of legislative support for unions, collective bargaining, and the ability of workers to engage in collective action, such as weakening the Ghent system in Sweden and reducing subsidies and workplace resources available to unions in Britain and France.

A second approach, which was used quite widely in our cases, was the use of derogation to permit a liberalization of industrial relations without having to formally end or replace existing institutions. It was often more palatable than a frontal attack on institutions and could be justified as an emergency measure, or as institutional change under carefully controlled conditions. The advent of opening clauses in Germany, the linking of flexibility, achieved via exemption from labor law, to workplace social dialogue on France, and the ability of sectoral and eventually firm-level agreements in Sweden to derogate from legal limits on atypical employment are all examples of expanding employer discretion without the need to formally reconstruct industrial relations institutions. And they are also all examples of practices that originally appeared for quite limited conditions or time periods but rapidly became permanent features of the industrial relations landscape.

The third approach, one that was prominent in several of our cases, is institutional conversion, whereby formal institutional continuity masks a change in the function of institutions so that they become more discretion-enhancing for employers. A good example would be the role played by works councils in both Germany and France. Once subordinate institutions, supportive of the dominant role of trade unions in collective regulation, under conditions of weakened unions and changes to labor law they increasingly served to detach firms from the wider industrial relations system and tie worker interests more closely to those of their employers, encouraging *de facto* enterprise unionism. Similarly, peak-level concertation, once a mechanism for solidarism and achieving worker gains, came to encourage a decentralization of bargaining in Sweden and to legitimize austerity and deregulation and overcome entrenched worker power at the firm level in Italy. In both cases, centralized bargaining became discretion-enhancing for employers, a mechanism for overcoming obstacles to liberalization.

A different array of mechanisms of institutional change was on display in each of our country cases. In France, the main obstacle to liberalization was the state in the form of legal regulation of the labor market and legal support for collective bargaining; despite spasms of labor protest, labor strength remained poorly institutionalized. The key problem was to ensure that work-place restructuring retained a shade of legitimacy in the eyes of the rank and file, whose active collaboration was rendered necessary by the new forms of work organization. The mechanism of institutional change used was to encourage a decentralization of bargaining to the firm, both by offering greater flexibility in return for negotiated change and by the creation of legal obligations inside the firm. Given the endemic weakness of French trade unions at the workplace level, the state stepped in to create new collective actors ex nihilo who would negotiate and legitimize workplace change. At the same time, the state extended the possibility of derogation from legal and contractual rules and in so doing increased the heterogeneity of the various workplace-based regulatory systems. As time went on, the micro-corporatist elements of the industrial relations system – works councils, employee referenda – became more important as unions continued to weaken. The French state employed both derogation at the firm level and concertation at the national level as mechanisms for achieving a liber-alization of industrial relations. More so than in our other cases, institutional change in France involved the construction of a largely new set of industrial relations institutions located inside the firm.

In Britain, in contrast, the primary obstacle to liberalization was not the state but rather the system of collective regulation put in place since the 1890s and increasingly decentralized to the firm level from the late 1950s onward. Labor law played a relatively light role in directly regulating the labor market. The mechanism for liberalizing industrial relations was an active dismantling of the institutions of collective regulation and the means of their enforcement. This involved above all decollectivization – weakening trade unions themselves – and an individualization of relations between employers and employees. The industrial relations system was deregulated and liberalized by Conservative governments in the 1980s through a combination of labor law reforms, restric-tive macroeconomic policy, restructuring and privatization of public services. Britain is the clearest example among our cases where the institutions of indus-trial relations themselves were wholly reconstructed, involving the destruc-tion in quite short order of an existing system of collective regulation and its replacement by a largely individualized system of industrial relations. The Labour governments that followed did not fundamentally alter the legislative and policy framework of the previous regime but simply adjusted it at the margin by strengthening workers' individual rights in the workplace through legislation, a process that was aided by the European Union, which became an important source of individual rights at work. No attempt was made to strengthen collective rights also, with the exception of the introduction of statu-tory provisions for union recognition. Even this right to organize was, however, interpreted in liberal terms as a compromise between positive and negative freedom (the latter implying the freedom not to join a trade union) and was subordinated to obtaining a majority in workplace elections (similar to the US case).

In Germany, the obstacle to liberalization of industrial relations was partly legislative, in the form of employment protections, but primarily the system of collective regulation, with the sectoral agreement at its core. It was a system that provided functional flexibility, but numerical and pay rigidity. The mechanism for institutional change was not a frontal assault, or even the construction of new institutions – the characteristics of the French and British experiences – so much as erosion, deregulation, conversion and the creation of escape hatches for firms to opt out of sectoral bargaining: nonjuridical derogation, as it were. All indicators point to a severe erosion of the system of collective regulation. Collective bargaining coverage and membership in trade unions have declined. Employer associations, traditionally the bulwark of the German model, although also declining, have been able to fare marginally better than unions because they have allowed firms to retain their membership without having to abide by wage rates negotiated at the industry level. In addition, a number of practices, both legal and illegal, have further decentralized collective bargaining to the firm level and allowed firms to opt out of collective bargaining provisions. The functioning of works councils has undergone conversion, undermining rather than supporting the system of sectoral bargaining. Even the German state played a role, through unilateral labor market deregulation in the Hartz reforms of the mid-2000s. The German experience is not primarily one of deindustrialization, drift and dualism, as traditional industrial relations arrangements survive in the manufacturing core but disappear or never appear in the first place in the service sector. Rather, the system of sectoral bargaining has become increasingly threadbare, full of holes and empty of content in the manufacturing core, while even its form is absent in the remainder of the economy.

Even in the two countries, Italy and Sweden, that might at first sight seem to buck the liberalization trend, having experienced a recentralization of collective bargaining, the new centralized institutions have different features and, more importantly, very different functions from those of the past. Governments and employers in Italy were faced with labor market rigidity put in place after the Hot Autumn and maintained in part by working class strength at the workplace level. Few firms, Fiat being the rare exception, were willing to challenge these forms of rigidity by taking on local unions. As a result, the route to liberalization was top-down, using national peak-level bargaining to bring about system-wide institutional change in a manner that neutralized local labor strength. In the 1980s, this focused upon reducing wage rigidity. In the 1990s, the type of centralized bargaining that emerged was an emergency corporatism intended to help governments drive through a host of largely market-conforming and strongly unpopular macroeconomic, social policy and labor market reforms. It should have been accompanied by the further extension of a dual system of collective bargaining at the company and industry levels, but the plant-level extension of bargaining never materialized because trade unions were too weak to pull it off. Thus, paradoxically, centralized bargaining was the mechanism

by which a liberalization of industrial relations took place in Italy; concertation was repurposed from its original function, as an instrument of worker and
trade union gains, in the 1970s. However, by the 2000s, and especially after the
economic crisis hit in 2008, attention turned to deregulating the use of atypical work, decentralizing bargaining and expanding the use of derogation; under
the impact of economic crisis, even concessionary corporatism was abandoned,
to be replaced by decentralization.

By the middle of the 1980s, the obstacles to a liberalization of industrial
relations in Sweden lay both in restrictive labor market regulation and in a
form of collective regulation that put severe limits upon employer discretion in
wage determination and work organization. That system of collective regulation rested upon a trade union movement that was strong at both the national
and local levels and labor law that imposed few limits upon the right to strike.
In Sweden, institutional change took place through a recentralization of the
collective bargaining system in the late 1990s, the construction of new institutions for mediating industrial conflicts and some limited legislative deregulation
of the labor market. The renaissance of coordinated multi-industry bargaining,
however, did not have the intent or the result of the solidaristic wage bargaining
of an earlier era. Rather, the new coordinated bargaining featured a minimalist role for the center – setting a wage ceiling and imposing a peace obligation
upon local bargaining – while permitting a much greater role for decentralized
and even individualized bargaining than was ever the case in the heyday of the
"Swedish model." This was the very opposite of solidarism, as wages became
more and more determined by local conditions.

We would argue that the basic thrust of developments in the industrial relations systems of advanced capitalism, involving the generalized weakening of
unions or even the substitution of other collective actors for unions, the erosion of bargaining coverage and the transfer of ever more regulatory matters
to the firm level and the increase in the heterogeneity of negotiated provisions
to match a similar heterogeneity in market conditions, all with the effect of
expanding employer discretion, is unequivocally neoliberal in character despite
differences in institutional form. In three of our cases, the British, French and
German, industrial relations liberalized primarily through processes of formal or *de facto* institutional deregulation (with derogation producing *de facto*
deregulation). In our other two cases, Italy and Sweden, industrial relations liberalized more through a process of institutional conversion than through one
of institutional deregulation; centralized or coordinated bargaining institutions
were reengineered to enable neoliberal policy orientations and greater flexibility at the firm level.

9.2 Employers and Trade Unions

The period since the end of the 1970s has seen a marked shift in the balance
of class power and influence between the primary class actors across Western

Europe, as weakened and divided trade unions face resurgent and radicalized employers. Collective organization has always been more important for labor than capital, as workers require collective action and collective organization not only to sanction employers but also to define a labor interest in the first place (Offe 1985: Chapter 7); for employers, on the other hand, collective organization has secondary benefits, but interests are fed back to employers through the market, and the simple act of not hiring or not investing is sufficient to sanction workers. Employers, after all, can encourage a decentralization of bargaining by simply dissolving their peak-level or sectoral organizations and leaving an empty seat at the bargaining table. As a result, a general process of decollectivization, as has occurred across our country cases, is more damaging for the exercise of power on the part of workers than it is for employers.

That said, there has also been a general tendency toward greater politicization and a greater willingness to challenge industrial relations institutions inherited from the past on the part of employer organizations. Streeck has recently reminded us (2014: 18) that while social scientists were quick to recognize labor as a political and strategic actor, as well as an economic one, and studies abounded of union strategy, "political exchange" and party–union ties from the 1970s on, that same recognition for employers has been slower, not least because – as noted above – collective organization is less crucial for the exercise of business power. The period under review in this book has seen, in almost every case, the emergence of a more self-confident, more political employer class willing to seek substantial change in national industrial relations systems, and always in a more liberalizing direction. In two of our cases, France and Sweden, this shift was symbolized by a renaming and rebranding of the main business organization, away from a primary function as employer representative and collective bargaining agent, and toward an organization emphasizing the entrepreneurial function of business and the role of lobbying the state. But even where a formal organizational change did not take place, employer organizations adopted a more overt neoliberal discourse, proved much more willing to revisit and challenge longstanding elements of the industrial relations landscape, and where unable to negotiate the changes that they wanted with trade unions, sought state support for liberalization.

As noted in Chapter 1, this is not what the VoC approach anticipates; its expectation is that rational employers will defend those institutions that offer comparative institutional advantage, leading to different behavior on the part of employers in LMEs and CMEs, and at best incremental institutional change rather than a wholesale assault upon industrial relations institutions. As we argued earlier in the book, there are reasons for skepticism about that expectation, both because changes to growth models have changed employer interests (in particular, reducing their attachment to and investment in institutions of collective regulation) and because it misconstrues the general interests and behavior of employers (Kinderman 2014). "Contra varieties of capitalism," argues Emmenegger (2015: 90), "job security regulations fundamentally shape the balance of power between capital and labor," and his detailed historical survey of such regulations in Western Europe shows clearly that their restrictiveness is primarily determined by the power resources available to employers and unions (Emmenegger 2014). From the same power resources standpoint, we anticipate that employers will generally seek a liberalization of industrial relations institutions, operationalized as an expansion of their discretion at the firm level, unless constrained from doing so by the power of trade unions or the state. Thus, the relative balance of power between labor and capital is likely to be determinative of the pace, scale and scope of liberalization.

The evidence from our country case studies is consistent with the argument that the first-order preference of employers is usually a liberalization of industrial relations institutions: deregulation, decentralization, individualization and the conversion of existing institutions to function in a manner that expands employer discretion. This was the "dormant wish" of employers (Ibsen et al. 2011: 336), and once the political opportunity structure and the ability of labor organizations to resist changed, that wish rose to the surface. Contrast Britain and Sweden in this regard. In Britain, the main employers' organization was initially hesitant to risk conflict with the trade unions and worried publically about the more radical Thatcherite initiatives in the realm of industrial relations. But once the government made clear its willingness to intervene repeatedly to protect the ability of employers to reshape industrial relations, and unions proved too hesitant and enfeebled to resist, both the CBI and employers rapidly took advantage of the situation to marginalize collective regulation. In Sweden, the employer preference for decentralization to the firm level and deregulation of the labor market periodically bubbled up, but in the absence of a government – even a bourgeois coalition – willing to limit the right to strike, and faced with a still powerful labor movement, business settled for relatively incremental deregulation and the Industrial Agreement system of multisectoral agreements to set a wage ceiling, coupled with extensive decentralization of actual wage determination.

A central part of the changing landscape of industrial relations over the last three decades is, of course, the weakening of labor movements. The quantitative data presented in Chapter 2 illustrated the near-universal decline in trade union density in Western Europe, albeit at different paces and with different starting points; Pontusson (2013: 800) has identified at least three waves of union decline, each associated with a different group of countries. Decline has extended beyond membership figures to challenge each of the main power resources of labor: its organizational power, political power and economic power. Labor movements suffered disorganization, disillusionment and division. The description of unions in Sweden – which remain, after all, among the strongest in Europe – as "traumatized" is a fair descriptor of the more general condition.

The literature on union decline is extensive, and a number of comparative volumes, appearing at regular intervals, have charted both its scale and the efforts of national trade unions to respond effectively (for a sampling see Ferner and Hyman 1992, Frege and Kelly 2004, Gumbrell-McCormick and Hyman 2013, Martin and Ross 1999). With each successive volume, the space for effective strategic response appears to have narrowed and the areas of concrete gain have shrunk. Our country cases indicate national trade union movements that are invariably on the back foot, struggling to defend existing industrial relations institutions and usually failing. Organizationally weaker, even those labor movements with traditionally voluntarist outlooks, such as those in Britain and Sweden, they have found themselves forced to turn to the state for protection, but social democratic and center-left governments have been less and less willing to defend collective regulation. In Germany, Italy and France, even center-left coalitions have proved willing to deregulate the labor market and encourage derogation and decentralized bargaining.

Labor movements have also been weakened in their ability to respond to more aggressive employer and state efforts to liberalize industrial relations institutions by internal division. In part this reflects the greater heterogeneity of unionized labor forces – as with the growing influence of white collar union confederations in Sweden, thus diminishing the voice and coordinating role of the LO – in part the different interests of workers in exposed and sheltered sectors – as with divisions among German and British unions – and in part the legacy of ideologically divided labor movements that prevented both Italian and French unions from acting collectively and allowed employers and states to divide and conquer. Whatever the reason, national trade unions have faced profound challenges over the last three decades to the industrial relations systems that they helped build.

In France, the radicalization and politicization of French employers was driven in part by the perceived threats of the lois Auroux and lois Aubry; as the CNPF transformed itself into the MEDEF, it adopted an increasingly neoliberal discourse. Dating from the start of the 2000s, its *refondation sociale* was a statement of, and a policy agenda for, the insulation of industrial relations from the traditionally dirigiste state, which was to get out of the way and permit employers to reach derogatory agreements with unions that were all but bereft of members in the private sector. The growing recourse to signing firm-level agreements – sanctioned by the state – with nonunion labor representatives only added to their one-sidedness. But even in national bargaining, where unions were present, division ensured that governments and the MEDEF were usually able to obtain enough union confederation signatures to endorse an agreement. The "hyper-reformism" of France's second largest union, when allied with the more traditional reformism of the two smaller nationally representative union confederations, permitted a range of national agreements on industrial relations, labor market and social welfare reform that were subsequently turned into legislation.

Surveys of employers in Britain in the 1970s indicated a fair degree of satisfaction with decentralized, firm-level joint regulation and a fear of provoking conflict with workers. The Donovan diagnosis, after all, had looked to strengthen unions and formal bargaining institutions inside the firm as a mechanism for limiting wildcat strikes and regaining control of the workplace. But as the 1980s went on and package after package of Conservative industrial relations reform was implemented and bedded down, employers gradually gained the confidence to reshape their relations with their employees. Evidence from regular workplace industrial relations surveys suggests that the predominant employer preference is for employer-controlled direct communication with employees unconstrained by legal or collective regulation. From the 1990s onward, the CBI also underwent a radicalization similar to that of its French counterpart, calling for further limits on strikes and on the reach of EU directives and emphasizing individualization of industrial relations as the preferred trajectory of change.

Meanwhile, Britain's trade unions discovered that their strength had been far more dependent upon nearly a century of public policy support for collective regulation than the dominance of a voluntarist ideology implied. Faced with a determined state, and unable to act collectively because of the weak confederal structure of the labor movement, the decentralized nature of national unions, and divisions over tactics and strategy (most evident in the response to the 1984–85 miners' strike), trade unions proved unable to resist the onslaught against them.

Germany has in many ways been Exhibit A in the case for the VoC approach to political economy, exemplifying the coordinated market form of economy. The evidence presented in Chapter 5 suggests a far greater degree of liberalization of industrial relations – in the manufacturing core as well as the service sector – than anticipated by VoC theory. The German experience also casts doubt on the expectation that employers will defend existing political economic institutions. While employers did not lead the shift in the 1980s toward greater emphasis upon bargaining over qualitative issues, they welcomed it because the shift effectively decentralized elements of bargaining to the firm level. By the middle of the 1990s, employers' associations, in part responding to developments in the eastern part of the newly unified country, moved to give individual firms greater flexibility within sectoral agreements. Most importantly, the German metalworking employers' association – representing those very firms that VoC theorists anticipated would defend those institutions that seemed to undergird the comparative institutional advantage generated by DQP – launched an ambitious political and public relations campaign to deregulate the labor market through the New Social Market Initiative (Kinderman 2014), an effort that bore fruit in the Hartz reforms.

There is some parallel to the German experience in Italy, where *Confindustria* also proved willing to abandon a bargaining route to industrial relations reform in the 2000s when it appeared possible that a friendly government might unilaterally deregulate the labor market. But for most of the period under review, the employer goal was to overcome entrenched labor power in the workplace, and the mechanism for doing that was peak-level bargaining. The first-order preference of Italian employers for decentralized firm-level bargaining periodically appeared, but overcoming wage rigidity, multiple bargaining levels and expensive nonwage labor costs was best achieved in a top-down manner. The key to the success of liberalization via concertation, however, was division among the trade union confederations. After the *Federazione Unitaria* collapsed in 1984, periods of interconfederal unity were few and far between; employers and governments were usually able to win the support of two of the three confederations to enable liberalization to move forward.

Sweden is the clearest case of employers defecting from the postwar model of industrial relations and then constructing a new model. Beginning with large engineering firms seeking separate sectoral agreements in the early 1980s, through the withdrawal of the SAF from corporatist institutions in 1990 to its more politicized and radical role as the rebranded SN, employers led and unions followed. However, as in Italy, while employers periodically demanded a full decentralization of bargaining to the firm level, that preference was constrained by the capacity of the trade union movement to engage in industrial action. The result was the Industrial Agreement bargaining regime, which provided a high degree of *de facto* decentralization, but within a framework that created a wage ceiling and a peace obligation. Divisions within and among unions were also important in Sweden, permitting unions in manufacturing to break from LO efforts at coordinating a common response to employers, and the LO, TCO and Saco to develop very different wage strategies, with the latter two pioneering decentralized and individualized wage determination. By the end of our period, the coordinating role of union confederations had been largely replaced with that of employers and loose interconfederal organizations of unions.

9.3 The Role of the State

Our cases provide ample evidence that the liberalization of industrial relations institutions has not emerged out of spontaneous market processes, or even as the result of bargaining among class actors alone. Certainly, as the previous section elaborated, a newfound employer radicalism and the declining organizational strength of trade unions created a context in which liberalization was possible. However, it is striking to what extent states have acted as the midwives of this process of institutional change. This might seem paradoxical in a neoliberal era. And yet in practice, while neoliberalism ultimately advocates the retreat of the state and the exclusive use of the market to regulate social relations, it requires active state intervention to bring the required changes about (Levy 2006).

There was certainly national variation in the degree and form of state intervention and legal regulation in employment relations across Western Europe in the first thirty postwar years (Gourevitch et al. 1984, Lange et al. 1982). Under conditions of prosperity, full employment and working class mobilization, most states came to provide basic legal rights that protected collective action and the fundamental ability of unions to engage in collective bargaining, but otherwise encouraged collective self-regulation on the part of unions and employers as a public policy good; in that sense, states for the most part withdrew from active regulation of class relations. However, in a minority of cases, relatively weak, poorly institutionalized labor movements invited a more interventionist role on the part of the state. Furthermore, an important exception to collective self-regulation was recourse to incomes policies of various kinds, particularly in the late 1960s and 1970s, when stagflation led governments of all political stripes to seek either voluntary or statutory wage regulation (Flanagan, Soskice and Ulman 1983).

For all the national variation during the first three postwar decades, it is clear that in the subsequent three decades state intervention and legal regulation have once again become central features of employment relations (Rubery 2011). All of our cases, though to differing degrees, saw a more active role on the part of the state in the regulation of class relations in the period from the early 1980s onward, compared with the earlier period. Neoliberalism does not imply the retreat of the state and its replacement by pure market regulation, at least in the sphere of class relations. Polanyi (1944) long ago argued that creating market society requires an active state role to overcome resistance to the creation of "fictitious commodities," of which labor is a prime example. In a similar vein, Gamble (1988) suggested, in his classic study of Thatcherism, that there is an affinity between "the free economy and the strong state" for modern New Right political parties. For Gamble and for Polanyi, since it is natural for society to protect itself from commodification, the neoliberal project requires a strong state, in Gamble's phrase, "to unwind the coils of social democracy and welfarism which have fastened around the free economy" (Gamble 1988: 32). The German tradition of ordoliberalism also anticipates a strong and continued role of the state in regulating market economies, though less because of resistance to commodification than because of the need to prevent powerful economic interests from undermining competition and economic freedom (Bonefeld 2012).

The neoliberal transformation of advanced capitalist political economies since the mid-1980s – always acknowledging the different timing, pace and scale of that transformation in different countries – has encouraged states to become more interventionist in employment relations as they have sought to accelerate the restructuring of the labor market in the interests of post Fordist flexibility. While states have become more interventionist in the sphere of industrial relations everywhere, the manner of intervention has varied, and what is striking about the forms of intervention in the last three decades is that cross-national differences are more important than differences among political parties within countries. That is, the ways in which states have become more interventionist tend to reflect responses to national institutional legacies and obstacles to liberalization more than ideological proclivities. There are partisan differences, to be sure. The Thatcherite and Blairite approaches to industrial relations differed in their attention to individual employment protection, just as French Socialist governments sought greater legal protection for workers than their Gaullist opponents. Center-right coalitions in Italy were somewhat more likely to engage in unilateral deregulation of the labor market than center-left coalitions, which sought the same goal but preferred to achieve it through concertation.

However, stepping back from differences in approach, it is remarkable that similar national industrial relations projects have been shared across ideological divides and pursued quite consistently over time. Socialist and Gaullist governments in France both encouraged decentralized bargaining inside the firm as a mechanism for deregulating the labor market; Social Democratic and Bourgeois Coalition governments in Sweden both followed a strategy of using government mediation and an external wage norm to encourage new, more flexible bargaining practices; peak-level concertation as a mechanism for liberalizing industrial relations institutions, deregulating the labor market and legitimizing austerity was a shared project of all governing parties in Italy; in the recent past, coalition governments in Germany, including a brief return of a grand coalition government, have sought incremental labor market liberalization; even in Britain, the common policy element between Conservative and New Labour governments has been a commitment to a largely deregulated labor market and a rejection of collective industrial relations institutions.

The restructuring of employment relations institutions in a neoliberal direction across Western Europe has been something that could not take place without a more interventionist state. This is for three overarching reasons, though there are also nationally specific sources of a wider and deeper role for the state in industrial relations. First, states have a set of distinctive capacities when it comes to the construction and "embedding" of new institutions, capacities not shared by private industrial actors. Overcoming resistance to institutional liberalization often requires that the state become more interventionist, just as Polanyi predicted. As existing employment relations institutions come under pressure in the context of changed economic conditions and a change in the balance of class power, states find themselves drawn into the process of reconstructing those institutions. Substantial institutional change is difficult in the absence of state action. Private industrial actors may be timid, divided or concerned with short-term interests, have sunk costs in existing institutions or be generally unwilling to challenge existing institutions. Even when they are willing, change may require action on the part of the state, in the form of changes to labor law. Attempts to challenge existing employment relations institutions are also likely to generate high levels of industrial conflict, which draws the state in either to limit disruption or to manage legitimacy (Kelly 1998, Shorter and Tilly 1974). Thus, we can expect the role of the state to be most significant in the movement from economic and social crisis to a new set of institutions designed to manage crisis.

State actors play a central role in the construction of employment relations institutions by virtue of a set of unique public capacities (Howell 2005: Chapter 2): enforcing and systematizing institutional change; narrating an authoritative interpretation of crisis; solving the collective action problems of employers and unions; redefining the very notion of worker representation, in the process bestowing legitimacy upon new forms of employee representation; anticipating and crafting alliances among private industrial actors – and it is important not to forget the state's overt coercive power. The state can serve as midwife of class compromises by acting as guarantor of agreements, preventing defection through legislation, boosting the associative power of labor and providing side payments to encourage agreement. The state is often best positioned to select successful regulatory experiments, institutionalize them and extend them throughout the economy (Jessop 2002: Chapter 1); through its legal authority, the state alone can create a system in place of a set of scattered experiments.

Examples of state intervention of this kind – to overcome obstacles to liberalization of industrial relations institutions – abound in our cases and are elaborated in our country cases. The Thatcher government limited recourse to secondary and sympathy strikes and made clear its support of employers in their restructuring relations with their employees; in the public sector, those relations were directly restructured or entire industries were privatized; unionized firms were forced to bear the costs of unionization. In France, industrial relations reform was first and foremost a state project; of especial importance was the role of the state in creating and legitimizing new labor actors. In Germany, the Hartz Laws sought labor market and social insurance liberalization directly through legislation. In Sweden, state actors solved collective action problems for powerful collective industrial actors, who were unable to create new institutions and practices on their own; it anticipated the outlines of potential compromise and agreement between labor and capital and used crisis strategically at a crucial moment in the early 1990s to encourage the reconstruction of industrial relations institutions. This involved both a direct role in inaugurating a set of new bargaining practices and an indirect role in pressuring employers and unions to bargain in new ways.

The second source of greater state intervention in industrial relations, related to but analytically distinct from the institution-building role of the state, involves the substitution of legal regulation for collective regulation in the face of the decline in power and influence of national labor movements. Direct legal regulation of the employment relationship has expanded and deepened as the willingness of states and industrial actors to respect collective self-regulation has collapsed. Labor law has come to substitute for collective regulation on the part of employers and trade unions. This reflects the attempt, often by center-left governments, to walk a fine line between flexibility and security in an era of labor decline. This practice is not exclusively the province of center-left governments, but it is closely tied to the transformation of social democracy in Western Europe (Anderson and Camiller 1994, Cronin, Ross and Shoch 2011).

Whereas social democratic governments during the long postwar boom largely vacated employment relations to collective regulation at a time of union strength, the "modernization" of European center-left parties took place at a time of weakening labor movements. This posed a dilemma for these governments: how to manage new economic risks and insecurities and protect workers when unions could no longer be relied upon to do so? At the same time, many of these center-left parties were also becoming more market-friendly and prepared to encourage greater labor market flexibility in a post-Fordist world. This made the dilemma even more acute, because protection for workers had to be balanced against the apparent imperative of flexibility.

The policy response to this dilemma can be thought of as a distinctively "Third Way" of organizing work and employment relations, not least because the period of New Labour government between 1997 and 2010 was a particularly good example of it (see Chapter 4 and also Crouch 2001). It involves juridical protection for workers in the form of minimum rights in the labor market (for example, a minimum wage, some form of job protection, rights for atypical workers and consultation rights within the firm), but protection carefully gauged to be compatible with expanded labor market flexibility. This approach also emphasizes "voice" (Freeman and Medoff 1984: Chapter 1) as a public policy good. Thus, New Labour encouraged the voice function of unions and enlarged consultation rights in nonunion firms but did nothing to restore the rights to collective industrial action removed during the Thatcher era. It is a model of industrial relations centered upon the provision and enforcement of individual rights in the workplace by the state, with only a peripheral role for collective representation and collective bargaining.

This approach has a wider applicability than just Britain. One could argue in fact that it is a policy adaptation specific to center-left governments in weakly coordinated political economies (Howell 2004) where the institutional preconditions for collective coordination are absent and so the state has to step in in its place. It is an approach that captures important elements of the French experience over the last three decades, as governments either sought not to strengthen collective regulation of employment relations, or failed in that effort, and instead fell back upon attempting to regulate the labor market through the provision of individual rights, often as a fallback in the event that social dialogue failed. The emphasis upon voice, as expressed through weak nonunion forms of labor representation, was also central to industrial relations reform efforts in France.

It is worth noting here the similarity to an argument made with specific reference to the United States. Piore and Safford argue that as collective regulation has weakened, it has been replaced "not by the market but by an employment rights regime, in which the rules of the workplace are imposed by law, judicial opinions and administrative rulings" (Piore and Safford 2006: 299). While we would argue that the market has indeed come to play a much larger role in the regulation of the workplace, the labor market and class relations, Piore and Safford are right to emphasize the extent to which collective rights to workers qua workers have been replaced with piecemeal rights of specific categories of workers, based upon either noneconomic identities (race, gender) or some assumption of particular vulnerability (those in precarious employment, for example). The result is to expand the role of legal regulation and state agencies in industrial relations, even as collective regulation collapses.

The same approach is also apparent at the supranational level. As the next section will discuss, the Maastricht Treaty responded to the more business-friendly implications of the Single European Market and Economic and Monetary Union with some protection against "social dumping" under the heading of the Social Chapter. Yet what is striking is the similarity of the strategy chosen to that of Third Way parties; it privileges the provision of individual rights, enforceable through European and domestic courts, in place of attempts to strengthen the collective power of trade unions, which would in turn protect workers. In other words, legal regulation, on behalf of a supranational semistate, was preferred to strengthening labor movements at either the national or supranational level.

The third source of a more interventionist state in the employment relations systems of Western Europe has come in the form of a revival of corporatism since the late 1980s, but corporatism of a different kind, with a different purpose and often in different countries from those traditionally associated with social democratic and social market economies in the Fordist era. What these more recent forms of concertation have in common is an effort on the part of states to use peak-level bargaining to gain acquiescence to neoliberal macroeconomic and social policies from labor movements. The goal has been, fundamentally, to legitimize austerity. States seeking to implement neoliberal macroeconomic and social policy have often attempted to implement and legitimize those policies with the cooperation of labor movements. The late 1980s and 1990s saw the spread of national-level concertation, in which trade unions were invited to endorse austerity measures. Commentators have captured this new reality by adding descriptors to the term corporatism: "lean corporatism" (Traxler 2004); "competitive corporatism" (Rhodes 2001).

The general conditions that gave rise to these social pacts were a combination of the erosion of national competitiveness in the context of heightened international economic integration and the imperative for many European countries of reducing public deficits and inflation rates in order to meet the convergence criteria for the Economic and Monetary Union. This explains both the timing of the revival of concertation – clustered from the late 1980s until the early 2000s – and the range of countries – particularly, though not exclusively, those of southern Europe – that had recourse to social pacts (Baccaro 2003). Among our cases, Italy stands out as an exemplar of this form of "liberalization through concertation," though there are also elements of it in the practice of French governments, both Socialist and Gaullist, in the 2000s in setting out national priorities for labor market and industrial relations reform, then convening peak-level bargaining sessions to achieve those goals, and finally embedding the resulting agreements in binding legislation.

The range of elements incorporated into these agreements varied from country to country, depending upon the particular national obstacles to liberalization: wage restraint to reduce or stabilize wages; institutional reforms to limit wage indexation or deregulate the labor market; social policy reform to slow the rate of growth of government spending and reduce budget deficits. What they had in common was that they were predominantly concessionary on the part of trade unions, offering "least-worst" outcomes with only limited gains for workers (Gumbrell-McCormick and Hyman 2013: 103). Trade unions went along because they were divided, feared worse or just sought to emerge organizationally intact.

9.4 The European Dimension

We wish to briefly draw attention to one further aspect of contemporary political economy that shapes the trajectory of industrial relations institutions among our cases, namely the impact of European integration. This is not the place for a comprehensive discussion of the impact of European integration upon industrial relations (Martin and Ross 2004, Ulman, Eichengreen and Dickens 1993); our country chapters discussed how, and to what extent, developments at the European level influenced national industrial relations institutions. Our point here is simpler and speaks only to the issue of how European integration contributes a convergent, liberalizing trajectory to European political economies.

The acceleration in European integration that dates from the second half of the 1980s, with Delors' arrival at the head of the European Commission, the adoption of the project to complete the Single European Market and the Single European Act, closely overlaps with the period of our study. For all the false starts, aborted projects, U-turns and internal crises, the process of European integration over the last three decades has operated to deepen and institutionalize broader neoliberal projects and the forces of liberalization that shaped the context within which European industrial relations systems have been transformed. European integration adds an explicitly political narrative to understanding liberalization. As with the Polanyian argument of the last section, the removal of obstacles to market liberalization across the European continent was strongly encouraged by the concerted action of national governments and European Union institutions as they pursued the Single European Market and then Economic and Monetary Union.

Indeed, building off a discussion of Hayek's classic statement on the economic impact of federalism (Hayek 1939), Streeck has argued that "*federation inevitably entails liberalization*" (Streeck 2014: 100, emphasis in the original) because it exacerbates the heterogeneity of interests that stand in the way of common regulatory action. Along similar lines, Scharpf (2010) has force-fully argued that there is an asymmetry in the politico-legal mechanisms by which European integration takes place that has "a liberalizing and dereg-ulatory impact on the socio-economic regimes of European Union member states" (Scharpf 2010: 211). While European legislation requires a high degree of consensus among member countries – which themselves have very different labor movement strengths and government political orientations – the Euro-pean Court of Justice (ECJ) is able to act without achieving political consensus and has tended to privilege individual rights to enter and exit market exchanges over collective and national systems of social solidarity. The asymmetry mani-fests itself thus: "the liberalizing effect of judicial decisions may be systematized and, perhaps, radicalized by European legislation. But given the constitutional status of ECJ decisions interpreting Treaty-based liberties, political attempts to use legislation in order to limit the reach of liberalization are easily blocked" (Scharpf 2010: 227).[1] The result is that the liberalizing impact of the ECJ will have little effect on the institutions and practices of liberal market economies, but far more upon coordinated and social market economies, encouraging a common trajectory.

The impact of European integration upon national industrial relations sys-tems and institutions has been uneven, affecting some more than others. Broadly, it has affected least those countries that deregulated their labor mar-kets and liberalized their industrial relations institutions early – Britain would be a good example in this regard – and affected most those countries that had the hardest work to do in remaking their political economies in preparation for Economic and Monetary Union – here Italy stands out among our cases. By and large, the effects of EU-inspired or required macroeconomic policy have been more important and consequential for industrial relations than social directives or European Court of Justice (ECJ) decisions that directly impact industrial relations institutions themselves, though there have certainly been instances such as the Laval decision in Sweden that have shaped national industrial rela-tions systems.

The European project influenced national industrial relations institutions in a number of ways. As noted above, the most important has also been the most indirect. It has been the impact of Economic and Monetary Union on those countries that signed up for EMU (which does not include two of our cases, Britain and Sweden). EMU entailed the loss of a national currency, control over monetary policy transferred to the European Central Bank (designed to be even more independent than the Bundesbank), removal of all barriers to capital mobility and achievement of convergence criteria with regard to inflation rates and public sector debt. For those countries with the most work to do in this

---

[1] For an illustration of this asymmetry, see the dispute over the proposed directive on the use of collective action around the issue of posted workers (Broughton 2012).

regard, social pacts bore much of the burden of permitting and legitimizing austerity. In the Italian case, social pacts performed other functions and predated EMU; nevertheless, they were invigorated and their importance enhanced in the course of the 1990s, in light of the imperative of preparing for EMU. In Italy the European Monetary System crisis in 1992 created the conditions for agreement to end the *scale mobile*, and central agreements in the middle of the 1990s helped build support for the fiscal austerity required to enter the Euro. Furthermore, the EMU had, and continues to have, implications for national systems of wage-setting, as those countries with coordinated wage-setting mechanisms may be better able to make wages a macroeconomic policy variable (Dumka 2014).

But more generally, the manner in which European integration has taken place over the last 30 years – institutionalizing a strong commitment to price stability, constraining recourse to demand management, eliminating devaluation as a policy tool, removing barriers to the free flow of capital, outlawing industrial policy perceived to distort competition and opening up public utilities and procurement to competition – has created a macroeconomic environment that is largely unfriendly to labor and renders impossible or infeasible a wide range of policy tools that labor-friendly governments once used to tighten labor markets or offer protection to workers. It is unsurprising that policies to create more flexible labor markets and interest in active labor market policy (policy that adjusts workers to markets rather than the other way around) have gained such widespread currency; other, more traditional policy tools are no longer available.

The full consequences of this new context became clear during the recent and ongoing crisis, dating to 2008 and morphing through at least three distinct crises (Scharpf 2013). The literature on the Eurozone crises is voluminous (for a small sampling see Blyth 2013: Chapter 3, Streeck and Schäfer 2013), and not the subject of this book. The consequences of managing the European version of the Great Recession within this macroeconomic environment have been high unemployment across the Eurozone, but particularly among the largely southern European economies that were forced into massive internal devaluation in place of external devaluation, and savage cuts to public sector employment and a range of social policies as part of deficit-cutting exercises. In this context, as Verdun notes, "the social dimension has been all but forgotten" (2013: 33).

All our cases, though clearly to different degrees, show evidence of a further liberalization of industrial relations institutions as a consequence of economic crisis (for further evidence see the cross-European surveys Degryse, Jepsen and Pochet 2013, Heyes and Lewis 2014, Marginson and Welz 2014). Marginson (2015) has usefully distinguished between the experience of two groups of countries. The first is made up of continental European and Scandinavian countries, where economic crisis led to further decentralization and disarticulation of bargaining, but where that process was largely negotiated. The other comprises mostly southern European countries, where the equivalent processes were imposed from outside by European institutions as part of restructuring programs.

A further consequence of the Eurozone crisis has been to tighten the deflationary architecture of the European Union and introduce new levels of surveillance of national finances through a series of measures introduced as part of a fiscal compact in 2011 and 2012 that "amount[s] to a constitutional revolution" (Scharpf 2013: 136) overturning the hitherto existing balance of national and EU competences. It should be noted that the new economic governance architecture put in place since 2010 has no formal role for business or labor organizations (Verdun 2013); they are free to lobby at the national level, but national policy making is increasingly constrained from above. The manner in which debt restructuring and bailout programs have been implemented in many of the southern European countries has specifically targeted coordinated collective bargaining: "initiatives through 2011 and 2012 saw the European Council and Commission intervening to an unprecedented extent in wage movements, and also wage-setting mechanisms" (Marginson 2015: 108), with the result that "where articulation mechanisms were already poorly specified, a series of largely imposed changes have progressively detached the company level from multi-employer bargaining arrangements, and most recently cemented the priority of company agreements" (Marginson 2015: 106). This has been liberalization of industrial relations from above.

Adding to the deregulatory and liberalizing logic of European integration has been the impact of the free movement of labor and capital, and of particular importance for industrial relations, a series of European Court of Justice (ECJ) decisions that explicitly privileged free movement over national industrial relations practices. The Laval decision, among others, limited recourse to national constraints upon social dumping. Specifically in the Laval case, it was recourse to strikes in Sweden as a mechanism to enforce national standards of pay and conditions that was outlawed. Swedish industrial relations institutions had largely weathered the first two challenges of Europeanization – being outside the Single Market after 1987 even as Swedish firms saw advantages to locating outside of Sweden to take advantage; being inside the Single Market after Sweden joined the EU in 1995 – intact; indeed, those institutions were to a large extent designed to retain the competitiveness and flexibility of Swedish firms. However, the challenge posed by the accession of low-wage, poorly regulated former Eastern European countries in 2004 was far more serious, affecting a range of sectors that were vulnerable to competition from low-wage, highly mobile workers, such as truck drivers and construction workers.

Responding to social dumping, in the context of ECJ decisions, poses particular problems for industrial relations systems that are heavily dependent upon collective regulation, with a limited role for labor law in enforcing minimum standards of pay and work. It leaves trade unions hamstrung, with the result that either standards are undermined or states are encouraged to play a more interventionist role. Small wonder that some isolated voices inside the Swedish labor movement have called for consideration of government extension and enforcement of collective agreements, while in the last 15 years both Britain and German have for the first time introduced statutory minimum wages, no longer confident that collective regulation can protect workers.

The so-called Social Chapter of the European project, first introduced as part of the Maastricht Treaty in 1993, was understood precisely as a response to the deregulatory logic and danger of social dumping embodied in the Single Market project. It predated the expansion of the European Union to the east, which accentuated the dangers of social dumping, but even prior to 2004, the ability of European firms to relocate more easily within the EU made the risks for existing national labor standards clear. The Social Chapter was subsequently consolidated and incorporated into the Lisbon Treaty as Chapter IV.

Again, this is not the place for an examination of the European dimension of industrial relations as it has emerged over the last two decades (Gumbrell-McCormick and Hyman 2013: Chapter 7); our focus is the liberalization of national industrial relations institutions. Nonetheless, as noted earlier in this chapter, social developments at the European level have been broadly congruent with a Third Way approach. That is, they have emphasized the creation of minimum rights and standards at work, enforced by state agencies and courts, rather than buttressing collective rights or collective regulation. Pay and trade union rights, including the right to strike, were specifically excluded from the Social Chapter. Some limited rights of consultation for firm-specific forms of worker representation, such as works councils, did appear (emphasizing the importance of voice over collective power), but little that would strengthen unions. What has followed in the intervening almost two decades has been the passage of a series of directives offering protections to specific categories of workers considered particularly vulnerable in the labor market, based either on the type of work – part-time, temporary and agency work – or the type of worker – female workers, migrant workers and the disabled.

European-level social protection, because of its focus on creating floors of minimum rights against the dangers of social dumping, has had the most impact upon those countries with already weakly regulated labor markets. But even here, national governments have been given wide leeway to implement social directives flexibly. Britain is the archetypal case in this regard. The Conservative government of John Major obtained an opt-out from the Social Chapter in 1993. The New Labour government of Tony Blair ended the opt-out, but nonetheless was able implement social directives, such as the work time directive and the worker information and consultation directive, in such a manner as to be minimally disruptive to existing industrial relations practices and institutions. And when the Treaty of Lisbon was negotiated, incorporating the Charter of Fundamental Rights, Britain (and Poland) negotiated an opt-out protocol stating that economic and social rights embedded in the treaty were not judiciable under the ECJ, thus ensuring the predominance of national labor law.

9.5 Employer Discretion from the 1970s to the Present

In this section, we summarize the changes in employer discretion across our five country cases in the three domains of wage determination, personnel management and work organization and hiring and firing over the period from the late 1970s until the present. In all cases, there were substantial limits on employer discretion in one or more of those domains at the beginning of our period, and in all cases, discretion had expanded across all three domains by the end of our period. The focus of liberalization varied from case to case, reflecting the specific area and cause of constraint at time 1, but the trajectory of greatly expanded discretion on the part of employers was always the same.

In Britain at the end of the 1970s, while labor law had come to play a larger role in the regulation of industrial relations and the labor market in the 1960s and 1970s, it was primarily the decentralized workplace strength of trade unions that served to limit the flexibility of employers. By this point close to 85% of British workers were covered by some form of collective pay-setting mechanism, and joint regulation by shop stewards and managers inside the firm – the model advocated by the Donovan Commission – had become deeply implanted in both the private and public sectors. Thus, employers were forced to negotiate over pay and work organization, and while labor law regulated hiring and firing quite lightly, they were subject to informal negotiation inside the firm. In short, employer discretion was severely limited.

By the end of our period, most of the shackles of joint regulation had been broken, and legal regulation of the labor market, already limited in 1979, and despite some enhanced role as a result of New Labour's time in office, had receded still further. The collapse of trade union strength and collective bargaining coverage had opened up the large majority of firms to unilateral employer determination of pay and conditions. Only 30% of firms have any collective bargaining at all, slightly more than half that figure in the private sector. The leading edge of joint regulation in the 1970s, shop stewards, have also seen their numbers dwindle and have disappeared from most firms. Even where collective bargaining remains, it is narrowly limited to pay, leaving employers much greater discretion over the organization of work. EU directives have provided some limited individual rights for workers, but limits on hiring and firing are accompanied by reduced protection against unfair dismissal. Britain has the weakest employment protection among our cases. Across all three domains, employer discretion has expanded and faces limited legal and contractual constraints.

In France, the decade after the mass strikes of May and June 1968 saw a significant expansion in government regulation of the labor market and industrial relations, as both the Gaullist and post-Gaullist Right sought to quell the likelihood of another mass mobilization. Regulation primarily constrained employer discretion in terms of pay determination and the ability to hire and fire, though in the public sector and large manufacturing firms, forms of joint regulation of work organization operated through works councils and other firm-specific bodies. Aggressive use of the minimum wage, wage indexation mechanisms, legal extension of collective agreements and administrative authorization for layoffs all limited the flexibility available to employers. Collective regulation with trade unions certainly played a role, but one that was limited to the afore-mentioned sectors of the economy, as unions by and large failed to capitalize on the events of 1968 to expand their reach beyond core centers of strength.

Thirty-five years later, most areas of legal regulation of the labor market have been rolled back either directly or in the form of opportunities for dero-gation from labor law if negotiated at the firm level. Legislative packages that increase the flexibility afforded employers have become an almost annual event over the last decade, with the Left participating as enthusiastically as the Right. Most affected has been employer flexibility with regard to hiring and firing and employment of atypical workers, but greater flexibility in work organization was catalyzed by both new opportunities afforded by work time reduction and the enhanced role of works councils. Individualized wages and profit-sharing schemes have also spread widely. In short, the expansion of employer discretion took place in part through deregulation and in part through decentralization to the firm level. Decentralization to the firm level would not necessarily imply greater flexibility on the part of employers, but in the French case, the feeble-ness of trade unions has meant that employers either face weak firm-specific representatives of labor or are able to unilaterally determine pay and working conditions.

At its peak in the early 1980s, the postwar German model imposed impor-tant limits on employer discretion, and deliberately so as part of an institutional matrix which encouraged diversified quality production. Rigidity came from both legal and contractual regulation and was felt particularly in the area of hiring and firing, where there were high levels of employment protection, and pay determination, where sectoral bargaining played the central role. There was greater flexibility in work organization by virtue of the structure of codetermi-nation, which permitted decision-making at the firm level, but nonetheless all change had to be negotiated, and during this period, trade unions dominated the codetermination bodies.

By the end of our period, employer discretion had expanded across all three domains. This came in part as a result of some limited deregulation on the part of governments, particularly with regard to recourse to atypical employ-ment as part of the Hartz reforms. It also came from the transformation of the collective bargaining model as union strength and collective bargaining coverage collapsed, leaving large swaths of the economy – including parts of manufacturing – not subject to collective bargaining at all, and where it remained, the practice of opening clauses permitted employers to decentralize pay determination to the level of the firm. Even in the area of work organization, employer discretion has expanded as firms have gained greater flexibility in managing work time regimes in response to both union demands for work time reduction (which had the unintentional effect of expanding the scope of firm-level bargaining) and persistently high levels of unemployment. To this it must be added that with the inversion of the once subordinate position of works councils with regard to trade unions, it has become more difficult for trade unions to implement sectoral bargaining policies that may limit the flexibility of individual employers and threaten job losses.

By the early 1980s, Swedish employers had come to see the Swedish model as fundamentally flawed, primarily because it no longer offered protection from strikes and inflationary wage settlements, while at the same time it imposed severe limits upon employer discretion. Those limits came both from legal regulation, in the form of strict limits on recourse to atypical employment and codetermination legislation that effectively provided for joint regulation of the firm, and contractual regulation, in the form of increasingly cumbersome wage contracts that incorporated a range of indexation mechanisms and supplements unrelated to the needs of firms. Across all three domains, a combination of labor law and the dual national and local strength of trade unions hemmed in the flexibility of employers.

The system of industrial relations that emerged out of employer defection from the Rehn–Meidner model and the economic and political crisis of the early 1990s is now almost two decades old, and looking increasingly threadbare. Yet its achievement has been to contribute to the liberalization of the Swedish political economy through the expansion of employer discretion, particularly with regard to wage determination and hiring and firing. The multisectoral coordinated wage agreements that have been in place across most of the economy since 1997 impose a wage ceiling set by the needs of the export sector and an industrial peace obligation, while permitting widespread decentralization and individualization of wage setting, a process that has gone furthest in the public sector and among white collar workers, but is universal. Some weakening of union organization inside firms has also contributed to employer discretion. Meanwhile, modest deregulation of labor law to allow more recourse to atypical employment, combined with a greater willingness on the part of unions to negotiate "crisis" agreements that give employers greater flexibility in the use of temporary and agency workers, has increased discretion in that domain as well. To be sure, collective regulation with trade unions remains the norm across the economy, so that unilateral employer action is limited, but deregulation, decentralization and individualization have all served to ensure a substantial expansion of employer discretion.

The consequences of the Hot Autumn in Italy had, by the end of the 1970s, produced a set of significant impediments to the exercise of employer discretion. These came from both the Italian state, in the form of labor market regulation, and the mobilizational and organizational capacity of trade unions, which were strong at the national level and also, at least in some sectors and parts of the country, at the firm level. Thus, the ability to hire and fire was constrained by Article 18 and legal regulation on the use of bureaucratic hiring lists.

Flexibility in wage determination was limited by the *scala mobile*, the use of industry bargaining to generalize a pattern based on agreements reached in larger manufacturing firms, and a commitment to wage solidarism on the part of unions. And even in the area of work organization, the workplace strength of labor – again limited to certain sectors of the economy – imposed limits on the discretion of employers.

At the end of our period, the situation had been transformed, with deregulation on the part of the state and declining trade union strength combining to expand employer discretion across all three domains. The abolition of the *scala mobile* and the abandonment of wage solidarism on the part of unions served to increase flexibility for employers in wage determination. The weakness of unions at the local level and changes to labor law, such as Article 18, ensure that employers now have wider discretion in hiring and firing, particularly for atypical workers, but also more recently for workers on regular contracts as well. In the postcrisis period, faced with high unemployment and critical economic conditions, trade unions at the national and industry levels accepted derogation for firms from contractual regulations that constrained employer discretion over work organization, and unions at the firm level accepted worsening work conditions in return for job security.

9.6 Conclusion

Liberalization of industrial relations institutions has been a universal tendency among our cases. The precise mechanisms of institutional change have differed from country to country, reflecting different starting positions and obstacles to liberalization, as well as different configurations of class power. Deregulation has been the preferred mechanism of liberalization in some countries, while derogation or conversion has been more important in others. Yet what is striking is the degree to which, across a range of domains, employer discretion has expanded everywhere, most obviously through the retreat of collective regulation and statutory regulation and their replacement by decentralized or individualized bargaining, often with firm-specific worker representatives, some of them newly created for just this purpose. Even where local unions still take on the role of bargaining over pay and conditions, they are likely to be more detached from national labor organizations and higher levels of bargaining. Where national-level institutions of collective regulation remain, actors at the firm level have been given wider permission to opt out of national or sectoral agreements, or even to derogate from statutory labor law. In some cases, national institutions have been repurposed to encourage local bargaining or legitimize austerity.

There remains a wide range of trade union densities and forms of employer organization across Western Europe, and no one could confuse the degree of union influence over the economy and the polity in Sweden with that in Britain. And yet everywhere the representatives of workers are weaker than they were three decades ago, in some case dramatically so, and unions bargain over concessions rather than gains; it is hard to think of a significant area of social progress in any of our cases that has resulted from labor pressure in recent years. Employer organizations, on the other hand, have become more politicized, more self-confident, more committed to neoliberal formulations and more willing to challenge existing industrial relations institutions. In this task they have increasingly been joined by governments, including those of the center left. States have proved more interventionist in industrial relations even as they have retreated from direct regulation of the labor market. All this has taken place in the context of a reinvigorated project of European integration that has institutionalized a deflationary and deregulatory economic logic, simultaneously creating a harsh macroeconomic environment for labor while closing off opportunities to use any residual national political influence.

From Industrial Relations Liberalization to the Instability of Capitalist Growth

Having arrived at this point of the book, the reader will hopefully be clear about the central message we have tried to convey: industrial relations institutions have undergone a process of liberalization in all countries; this process manifests itself first and foremost as an increase in employer discretion everywhere; and it is more easily discernable in the function than in the form of institutions. The last point implies that analyses that focus on some formal properties of industrial relations systems across countries, such as the degree of centralization or decentralization of the bargaining system – the most common form of comparative analysis in both the political economy and industrial relations fields – are likely to underplay the *allomorphic* common neoliberal drift that is taking place in all countries we are aware of.[1]

In this chapter, we set for ourselves a different but complementary task: we wish to demonstrate that the historical process we have analyzed in this book is not just relevant for scholars who care about industrial relations, labor movements and labor rights, but also is crucial for a proper understanding of the evolution of capitalism and of the pervasive instability of its current forms. Returning to themes we alluded to at the end of the first chapter, we will argue that the liberalization of industrial relations that has taken place over the last three decades and more has undermined the institutional foundations of what was in all likelihood the best-performing – in terms of growth – and most equitable – in terms of income distribution – growth model capitalism has produced so far: the Fordist/wage-led model; and that this has ushered in an era simultaneously of "secular stagnation" (Summers 2014) and of high-end inequality

---

[1] This chapter draws on ongoing collaborative work between one of us and Jonas Pontusson (see Baccaro and Pontusson 2016). However, Jonas Pontusson is not responsible for the content of the chapter nor, a fortiori, for any errors contained in it.

(Piketty 2013). Furthermore, we will argue that the growth models that have replaced the Fordist/wage-led one are all inherently unstable and crisis-ridden because, unlike the Fordist growth model, they lack a well-functioning institutional mechanism ensuring that aggregate demand grows in tandem with aggregate supply.

In making these points we will draw freely on the regulationist and post-Kaleckian literatures in heterodox macroeconomics (see Baccaro and Pontusson forthcoming). We make no claim to be true to either the nomenclature or the specific arguments advanced in these literatures. In our view, they are largely convergent, but they adopt different terminologies and styles of analysis. These differences will not concern us here. With this final chapter we wish to emphasize, again, that our argument about neoliberal convergence is a nuanced one: it is compatible not only with remaining differences in institutional forms (something we hopefully have established in the country chapters), but also with the emergence of different accumulation regimes across countries. Thus we don't think we can be accused of treating liberalization as the "night in which all cows are black."

In this chapter, we also offer an answer to the question of what causes what in our argument about industrial relations liberalization. Although the causal links are complex and, as we argue later in the chapter, it seems more appropriate to talk of "coevolution" than of unidirectional causation, we argue that industrial relations institutions were an essential component of the Fordist growth model and key for capitalist stability *tout court*. However, the Fordist model began to collapse sometime in the 1970s due to a combination of international economic shifts (trade liberalization and capital account liberalization) and internal contradictions (wage inflation and deindustrialization). In turn, the crisis of Fordism facilitated a shift in the balance of class power that permitted the liberalization of industrial relations institutions through changes in state policy, a decline in labor's capacity to resist and capital's greater ability to push for its first-order preference, which was ensuring as much discretion for itself as possible. The liberalization of industrial relations contributed to undermining Fordist growth further and closed off a return to the old wage-led growth model, but also created the conditions for the emergence, in some cases, of a new set of post-Fordist growth models, characterized by the following common features: industrial relations were no longer of paramount importance in the regulatory architecture of capitalism; labor markets were much closer to being competitively regulated than ever before in the postwar period; and the resulting growth models were all unbalanced because they lacked an institutional mechanism ensuring that aggregate demand would grow in tandem with aggregate supply.

The chapter is organized as follows. First, using the Regulation School literature as a point of departure, we discuss the crucial role that industrial relations institutions once played in the stability and viability of the Fordist/wage-led model.[2] Second, we analyze the main features of different growth models, drawing on the post-Kaleckian literature in heterodox macroeconomics. We believe that this approach has important implications for the dominant stream of comparative political economy, of which we have been critical in the course of this book. As such, it deserves an extended explication. Third, we analyze the features and the inherent instability of the growth models that have emerged after the crisis of Fordism, focusing in particular on export-led and debt-led growth. We conclude by examining the growth profiles of the five countries this book has focused upon.

10.1 The Regulation School's Analysis of Fordism[3]

One of the attractions of the French Regulation School for the type of political economy that has inspired this book is its conception of capitalism as a historically specific institutional order as opposed to a natural order. Capitalism is not the same as a market economy. In a market economy, coordination between supply and demand is ensured by a system of freely forming prices. But a capitalist economy is more than that. There is not just a market in which goods and services are exchanged, but also economic units (firms) in which one class sells its labor and stands in a relation of subordination to another class.

The Regulation School argues that capitalism does not emerge spontaneously from man's innate disposition to truck and barter, but is simultaneously made possible and regulated by historically specific institutions. Institutions shape the process of wage formation, the process of price formation, the supply of money and its price (interest rate), the role of the state in the economy and the modalities of insertion in the international economy. Following Marx, institutions regulate the possible tension between the forces of production and the social relations of production (Marx 1970[1859]), or, to use the language of macroeconomics, between the supply potential of the economy and effective demand (Keynes 2007[1936]). With the benefit of hindsight, it is possible to identify fit and complementarity among institutions, but these can only be ascertained a posteriori. In reality, there is no grand designer lurking in the back. Neither the durability nor the functionality of a given institutional setup is guaranteed. Institutions change in response both to endogenous dynamics and to exogenous shocks.

The institutions of capitalism are not all at the same level, but each capitalist configuration is characterized by a particular hierarchy of institutions. The institutions regulating industrial relations play a crucial role in the configuration known as "Fordism." Fordism emerged in the period after World

---

[2] A wage-led growth model and a Fordist one overlap to a large extent, as discussed later in the chapter, and we often use the terms interchangeably.

[3] This section draws freely on Boyer (2015).

War II as the evolution and replacement of a previous mode of regulation (prevailing in the interwar period) in which, while it was technically possible for capitalist firms to generate sizeable productivity increases by engaging in mass production, insufficient aggregate demand constrained the productive potential of the economy. Insufficient aggregate demand was due to the balance of power between capitalists and laborers in the interwar period. In this period, wages were formed in competitive labor markets and were generally low and highly sensitive to economic fluctuations and unemployment. As a result, consumption out of wages remained limited and consumption out of profits was insufficient to generate economies of scale, causing accumulation to remain below its potential. To the extent that there were productivity gains, they were mostly appropriated by profits, which had (and still have) a lower propensity to consume than wages and a greater propensity to save, i.e., to spend income to acquire financial assets (including cash) as opposed to goods and services. This in turn lowered demand relative to potential and stimulated the search for returns and financial speculation. To use Marxian language, there was a "contradiction" between the technical potential of the economy and the balance of social forces determining the distribution between wages and profits. As will be discussed later in the chapter, there are some similarities between the mode of regulation of the interwar period and that of the current period.

The key innovation that ushered in the Fordist era was the institutionalization of collective bargaining and the increase in trade union power that went with it. Collective bargaining transformed the process of wage formation: wages were no longer flexible and responsive to labor market conditions, but downwardly rigid and indexed to labor productivity. In this period, advanced capitalist countries saw the emergence of a "historical compromise" between unions and employers, whereby unions recognized the capitalist order, setting aside any attempt to transform property relations, and employers acknowledged the legitimacy of unions and agreed to share the fruit of technical progress with them (Korpi 1983). To be sure, the historical compromise was struck at different times in different countries and was more solid in some countries than others. For example, it may be argued that this type of compromise was reached only in the mid-1970s in Italy and was always internally contested (see Chapter 7). Nonetheless, the indexation of real wages to labor productivity added the link that was missing from the previous regulatory mode: mass consumption emerged as a counterpart to mass production.

All the country chapters in this book begin their narratives at a time (the late 1970s) at which the Fordist compromise had already begun to unravel. However, it is important to be clear about the systemic importance of Fordist industrial relations institutions for capitalism. They eliminated the demand side constraint that had hindered growth in the interwar phase. As a result, growth took off in the "glorious" thirty years after WWII (Armstrong, Glyn and Harrison 1991). As has been argued repeatedly in this book, it was not the presence of collective bargaining per se that ensured the viability of Fordism; rather it was the balance of social power surrounding the institution of collective bargaining in this historical period, which allowed trade unions to turn collective bargaining into an institutional conduit to transform productivity increases into real wages. In addition to collective bargaining, other institutional innovations contributed to producing an adequate level of effective demand, particularly the introduction of shock absorbers such as unemployment insurance and counter-cyclical budget policies.

Changes in the sphere of wage-setting unleashed changes in other institutional spheres as well. Once wages began to be taken out of competition, prices, too, had to be established in noncompetitive fashion. Perfect competition is a theoretical abstraction. As soon as one allows for the possibility of economies of scale or other types of heterogeneity across firms, some firms grow in size, others go bankrupt, and the market changes from competitive to oligopolistic. A competitive market exists if explicit state intervention enforces a competitive order (see Foucault 2004). In the Fordist period, markets were predominantly oligopolistic, and prices were set through mark-up on costs. As argued in the previous chapter, the liberalization of product markets was aided considerably by the European single market project.

Monetary and exchange rate policy had to adapt to the changes in the wage and price formation regime. The gold-standard system had linked the money supply to the external balance of payments and thus had forced wages and prices to adjust in case of disequilibrium. If a country had a current account deficit it lost gold; this in turn reduced the money supply and brought the economy back to equilibrium through a painful process of deflation of wages and prices. This monetary system was, however, incompatible with a regime in which wages were rigid and unable to adjust. It had to give way to a more accommodative monetary system and more flexible exchange rates.

It is interesting to compare the Fordist growth model as characterized by the regulationist literature with the mainstream neoclassical growth model: the Solow–Swan model, which assumes that markets are perfectly competitive and that each factor of production is paid its marginal productivity (see Carlin and Soskice 2006). In other words, the neoclassical growth model assumes away the historical process sketched above, that is, the emergence of institutions allowing the transformation of productivity increases into real wages. This comparison brings out one of the defining traits of the regulationist approach, and in general of the post-Keynesian approach: macroeconomic parameters are not "constants of nature" but are summaries of social relations that change with the ability of social groups to mobilize effectively for their interests.

Despite its attractive features, the Fordist model was not without problems. Its first main vulnerability was the difficulty of ensuring an acceptable rate of profit. Although real wages stimulated demand, wages that were too high and profits that were too low per unit of output reduced capitalists' incentive to invest. The Swedish Social Democrats sought to address the problem of "capital strike" in the 1970s with the ultimately unsuccessful wage-earner fund experiment, which sought to compensate for faltering private investment by institutionalizing collective investment by workers (Pontusson 1992).

The second vulnerability had to do with nominal wages and inflation. Although the whole heterodox macroeconomic literature assumes that there is spare capacity in the economy – such that increases in demand are accommodated by expanding quantities as opposed to rising prices (Lavoie 2009) – this was clearly an idealization. In reality, the Fordist model had a problem of endemic inflation. Part of the problem was that monetary policies had to be accommodative, since wages were inflexible. In addition, when trade unions pushed for high nominal wage increases and the economy was already at full employment, even in some sectors, the push resulted in higher inflation. The problem of high inflation was a generalized feature of the 1970s and resulted from the simultaneous occurrence of both militant wage demands by trade unions and large increases in oil prices (Armstrong, Glyn and Harrison 1991). It was dealt with differently by different countries depending on the specific institutional features of the wage-formation system, and with different degrees of success (Flanagan, Soskice and Ulman 1983, Tarantelli 1986a). Disinflation generally involved the institutionalization of incomes policies (Bruno and Sachs 1985). However, wage restraint worked better in relatively centralized or coordinated bargaining systems such as Germany and Sweden than in relatively decentralized systems such as France, Italy and the United Kingdom (Cameron 1984, Soskice 1990). In the United Kingdom, inflation was eventually defeated through a shift to monetarism (Tarantelli 1986a). The inability of the Fordist industrial relations system to address the problem of inflation contributes to explaining its demise (Glyn 2006).

If some of the factors leading to the erosion and demise of the Fordist model, such as the oil shocks, could be considered exogenous, other processes were clearly endogenous. For example, Fordist firms reaped productivity increases through the expansion of markets. Once national markets became saturated, it was natural for the most efficient firms to try to tap into foreign demand. Although the early stages of trade liberalization probably helped to reproduce the Fordist model for some time, they eventually ended up destabilizing it. Trade liberalization reinserted wage competition into the regulatory picture. Wage moderation has negative growth consequences for a closed Fordist economy, but in an open economy, wage moderation relative to trade partners makes domestic products cheaper than competitors' products, thus boosting the net export component of aggregate demand (see the discussion below).

Another source of endogenous erosion for the Fordist model was deindustrialization. In a path-breaking article, Baumol (1967) explains how deindustrialization was a feature of unequal productivity growth across sectors. To the extent that the manufacturing sector is successful in generating productivity increases, and to the extent that productivity grows more slowly in the service sector – which is plausible, because the mechanisms for Fordist productivity gains, economies of scale and capital deepening, are unlikely to play a big role in the service sector – there is a tendency for employment to decline in relative terms in the high productivity sector and to increase, again in relative terms, in the low-productivity sector (assuming plausibly that the law of one price ensures comparable wage levels across sectors). Thus, the very success of manufacturing – the core of the Fordist model – planted the seeds of its own decline.

To summarize, the Fordist model generated rapid growth with high wages and a highly institutionalized industrial relations system in in the "glorious thirty years" after WWII, an era characterized by limited trade openness and controls on capital movements. However, its long-run viability was limited both by endogenous developments (e.g., deindustrialization, the tendency to generate inflation) and by shifts in the international economy, particularly the liberalization of capital movements and the opening of trade, as well as more aggressive strategies by both employers and the state. These shifts changed some of the basic macroeconomic relations of the Fordist model. Far from being the rigid variable to which all other variables (prices, money, profits, government expenditures) had to adjust, wages became the variable that needed to adjust, generally downward, in response to shocks to other variables in the system. The liberalization of industrial relations this book has examined has to be understood against this background.

10.2 The Post-Kaleckian Analysis of Growth Models

In this section we complement the previous analysis with an examination of post-Kaleckian views on capitalism. The Post-Kaleckian and Regulation School traditions overlap to a large extent – for example, Robert Boyer has contributed to both streams of research (see Bowles and Boyer 1995). However, post-Kaleckianism brings a stronger emphasis on distributive shifts and their consequences for capitalist growth.

The emphasis on politics and distribution was a trademark of the Polish economist Michal Kalecki.[4] In his most famous essay (1943), Kalecki made full employment contingent not only on economic considerations but also and more importantly on political ones. Kalecki's economic analysis of full employment was essentially the same as Keynes' (although he developed it independently). Like Keynes, he emphasized the need for an adequate level of effective demand. Unlike Keynes, however, he thought that full employment would reduce capital's *structural power*, that is, its ability to shape collective decisions and policies without explicit coercive intervention (Culpepper 2015), and would therefore be fiercely opposed by capitalists. Kalecki's analytical perspective saw capitalists as motivated not so much or primarily by profit

---

[4] Nuti (2004) identifies the emphasis on distribution as the key point differentiating Kalecki from Keynes. See also Sawyer (1985).

maximization as by the maximization of workplace control. Anticipating the so-called "efficiency wage" models of the labor market (e.g., Shapiro and Stiglitz 1984), but with a distinct disciplinary twist, Kalecki famously argued that full employment would remove the "fear of the sack" from the capitalist's tool bag and thus would make it more difficult for bosses to motivate and control workers. According to Kalecki, the class of *rentiers* would also oppose a full employment regime, since they would fear the inflationary consequences of full employment and would be concerned about the real value of financial assets under a full employment regime.

For Kalecki, capitalist growth was "wage-led." "Wage-led" means that real wages are first and foremost the most important determinant of aggregate demand (in most countries), while their role as production costs to be minimized is of secondary concern, and is even a source of possible coordination failure in capitalist economies, in the sense that while individual firms may benefit from lower relative wages, all firms are likely to suffer from generalized wage decline. According to Kalecki, an effective way to ensure full employment, in addition to deficit spending by government as suggested by Keynes, was redistribution of income from the rich to the poor (Kalecki 1944). He acknowledged, however, that such redistribution was likely to meet with stiff capitalist opposition.

Building on Kalecki, the post-Kaleckian literature has produced more general models of the impact of distribution on growth, in which wage-led growth is a special case. In particular, Bhaduri and Marglin (1990) have shown that under plausible conditions growth may be stimulated not by wages but by profits. There are therefore two ideal-typical growth models: wage-led and profit-led. Much of the post-Kaleckian literature is devoted to understanding the conditions in which either model is likely to prevail and to estimating econometrically which type of growth model prevails in different countries and time periods.

A marginal (one percent) real wage increase, keeping labor productivity constant, is equivalent to a marginal increase in the wage share, which is thus considered exogenous in these models. The real wage increase affects the various components of aggregate demand – consumption, investment, government expenditure and net exports (exports minus imports) – differently depending on the structural characteristics of the economy. If the ultimate impact is positive, the growth model is said to be wage-led; if vice versa, it is profit-led.

Saving propensities (and conversely consumption propensities) vary positively (negatively) with income. High-income individuals and households save more and consume less as a proportion of their incomes than low-income individuals and households. Another way of expressing the same idea is to say that higher-income individuals and households use more of their income to acquire financial assets (including cash) than to acquire goods and services; i.e., they save more and consume less. There is a lot of econometric evidence suggesting that the propensity to consume out of profit income is lower than the propensity to consume out of wage income (see Hartwig 2014 and the references in Stockhammer 2015a). For example, in Germany in 2007, the top quartile had an average saving rate of 15.8 percent, the second quartile of 9 percent, the third of 8 percent and the bottom quartile of 4.1 percent (Stein 2009, as cited in Stockhammer 2015a: 943). A lower propensity to consume out of profits means that a decrease in the wage share, and a corresponding increase in the profit share, will depress aggregate consumption, and if this is a large component of aggregate demand – which is likely to be the case in large countries – it will depress GDP as a whole.

If the impact of a marginal wage increase on consumption is likely to be unambiguously positive (at least until the impact of wealth effects on consumption is considered; see below), the same cannot be said for investment. On one hand, investments are likely to be sensitive to expected profits (particularly to the difference between the expected profit rate from the investment and the expected rate of return from alternative uses of capital); on the other hand, investments may depend positively on demand growth. The latter mechanism is known as the "accelerator" of investment: if demand expands, firms are encouraged to expand their capacity too. If investments are highly sensitive to profitability and not so sensitive to demand, then the investment function will be profit-led; vice versa, if the accelerator effect prevails, investment will be wage-led.

Post-Kaleckian macroeconomics does not have much to say about the role of government expenditures in growth regimes (while it has a fair amount to say about the role of government policies, as discussed below). In fact, government expenditures are considered exogenous in all the literature consulted for this chapter. However, it seems important to note that government expenditures may reinforce or counterbalance the impact of a shift in the distribution of income. For example, redistributive taxes and transfers should contribute to reinforcing a wage-led demand regime by transferring income from categories with high saving propensity to categories with high consumption propensity. This is in addition to the well-known ability of net government expenditures to make up for temporary shortfalls in demand, as suggested by Keynesian theory.

In a closed economy, with limited exposure to international trade and imperfect mobility of capital, a wage-led model is likely to thrive. The expansive effect of real wage increases on domestic consumption is not weakened by imports. Furthermore, in an international economic regime that limits capital mobility, such as the Bretton Woods one, capital has few (legal) alternatives to investing domestically even when the expected profit rate is low. As argued in the previous section, limited internationalization and capital controls were important enabling conditions for the Fordist/wage-led model (Boyer 2004). However, the background conditions became less propitious when the economy opened up.

All other things being equal (including, first and foremost, foreign prices), a real wage increase controlling for labor productivity will lead to a deterioration of the real exchange rate, and thus to a decline of net exports (assuming plausibly that nominal exchange rates do not adjust promptly in the opposite direction). Imports will become cheaper and exports more expensive. These developments are likely to be of small importance as long as the degree of openness remains limited. However, when openness passes a certain threshold (likely to vary by country) and particularly when exports are highly sensitive to relative price differences, as captured by the real exchange rate, international openness may lead to a shift in the growth model from wage-led to a particular type of profit-led: export-led (see Baccaro and Pontusson forthcoming). In a highly open economy, wage moderation, which would be growth-depressing in a wage-led growth model, may become growth-enhancing through its effect on net exports. It needs to be observed that what matters for net exports is not the wage increase per se, but the impact of the wage increase on export prices (see Storm and Naastepad 2015). If the wage increase is accommodated by lower profit margins (controlling for labor productivity), there is no reason to expect a negative impact on exports, at least in the short run. However, in the long run, there could be smaller incentives for firms to engage in exports at all.

Distinguishing between the effects on domestic demand (consumption + investment) and on total demand (consumption + investment + net exports) leads to three ideal-typical scenarios: (1) wage-led domestic demand and wage-led total demand; (2) wage-led domestic demand and profit-led total demand; (3) profit-led domestic demand and profit-led total demand. The combination of profit-led domestic demand and wage-led total demand is impossible (Lavoie and Stockhammer 2012). The first combination is the realization of a Fordist/wage-led regime in an open economy. In this growth model, a wage impulse will probably have a negative impact on net exports, but the effect is small enough not to reverse the total demand regime because the degree of openness is limited, or because exports and imports are not very sensitive to the real exchange rate, or both. It bears highlighting that in a Fordist model wages and profits grow in tandem and a "historical compromise" between labor and capital becomes possible and a rational strategy for both parties (Przeworski and Wallerstein 1982). It is also important to emphasize, however, that such win–win compromise is not a general feature of capitalism but a special feature of this particular mode of regulation.

The configuration of profit-led domestic demand and profit-led total demand corresponds to the model of "trickle-down economics." In this model, real wage increases relative to productivity lead to smaller growth through their negative impact on investment and net exports. The short-run increase in consumption that would result from lower savings is more than counteracted by the decline in investment and the deterioration of the current account balance. To visualize this regime of domestic demand, one could think of an economy in which wage labor is a small component of GDP and most consumption is out of profits, while capital accumulation and/or net exports are highly dependent on profits and large components of aggregate demand. The Chinese economy after market liberalization comes to mind (Boyer 2015).

The most insidious combination is that between wage-led domestic demand and profit-led total demand, because it may lead policy makers to policy choices that depress domestic demand for the sake of boosting net exports. Here is what Bhaduri and Marglin (1990: 338) have to say about this combination:

A dominant trade effect tends to make the stagnationist [i.e., wage-led] logic increasingly irrelevant in a world characterized by high trade interdependence. The left social-democratic emphasis on wage-led expansion derived from the stagnationist logic may be given up in the pursuit of export surplus by following restrictive macroeconomic policies to keep down real wages (and inflation) for greater international price competitiveness. Further, so long as successful export performance maintains a high enough level of employment to overcompensate a relatively low real wage rate, *cooperation between labor and capital may continue to be feasible*...The only problem with this strategy is that it is impossible for all countries to achieve a trade surplus simultaneously. *And yet, the lure of this impossibility has contributed substantially to the disintegration of the traditional social democratic ideology without any coherent alternative taking its place* [emphasis ours].

One innovative feature of post-Kaleckian macroeconomics is its conceptualization of the relationship between wage growth, labor rigidities and labor productivity (Storm and Naastepad 2012a, 2012b). First, wage growth may lead to greater labor productivity by expanding aggregate demand and thus allowing economies of scale. This is referred to as the Kaldor/Verdoorn effect. Second, in a wage-led investment regime, wage increases lead to new investments through the "accelerator"; new investments, in turn, may improve productivity by embodying the latest technical change.[5] Third, real wage increases set in motion a process of factor substitution whereby the factor that has become relatively more expensive (labor) is replaced by the other one (capital) until the relative returns are equalized. Capital deepening (increased capital stock per unit of labor) in turn increases the productivity of the remaining labor. This is referred to as the Marx/Hicks effect. It should be noted that factor substitution per se tends to generate technological unemployment. In fact, the employment performance of a wage-led model depends on the outcome of a race between labor productivity and aggregate demand. Employment will increase only if the latter grows faster than the former. Finally, protective labor institutions such as stringent employment protection regulation may positively impact labor productivity by augmenting the motivation and commitment of the work force, as emphasized inter alia by the literature on "gift exchange" (Akerlof 1982).

These views of productivity are very different from those of mainstream economists. They generally advocate labor market deregulation to allow a more efficient allocation of factors of production. Here, instead, labor market regulation (as opposed to deregulation), and real wage increases (as opposed to wage moderation) are seen as conducive to productivity growth. However, even

---

[5] Regulationists also hypothesize that real wages increase improves labor productivity thanks to the scale effect (see Boyer 2004; 2015).

for heterodox economists, a real wage increase may reduce productivity if the investment regime is strongly profit-led by decreasing incentives to invest and thus diminishing the potential for realized technical change (Lavoie and Stockhammer 2012).

Public policy may either support or contradict the underlying features of the growth model. For policy to enhance growth, it has to be consistent with the underlying growth model; that is, there have to be wage-oriented policies in a wage-led model and profit-oriented policies in a profit-led model. When the distributional orientation of public policy is in contrast to the growth model (profit-oriented policies in a wage-led model or vice versa), the result is economic stagnation, at least for some time. In the long run, sustained application of particular policies may lead to a shift in growth model, as we discuss in the next section.[6]

What are the implications of the post-Kaleckian analysis for industrial relations? The easiest way to see them is by relaxing the assumption, which has guided the discussion so far, that the wage share is exogenous. This assumption is consistent with the post-Kaleckian literature but is clearly a simplification. In reality, the wage share is a function of politics and specifically (in line with Kalecki's own thinking) of workplace politics (Kalecki 1943). The trends this book has focused upon, the decline of trade unions and multiemployer collective bargaining, as well as public policies aimed to liberalize the labor market and reduce labor protections, have shifted the functional distribution of income away from wages and toward profits. These phenomena could have been beneficial for capitalist growth if the underlying growth model had been profit-led. In wage-led growth, however, their immediate impact has been to hinder the ability of wages to grow in line with productivity increases. Over the medium run, this has limited the growth potential of the economy

There is ample evidence suggesting that the wage share, after peaking between the 1970s and 1980s, has declined in most if not all advanced countries, as well as in many developing countries for which data are available (ILO 2008, OECD 2008). The mainstream explanation for this decline is that it is technologically determined, and particularly that it is linked to the decline of the relative price of capital goods as a result of the ICT revolution (Karabarbounis and Neiman 2014). In contrast to this version of technological determinism, post-Kaleckian economists (Stockhammer 2013) and sociologists (Kristal 2010) have argued that the functional distribution of income is the result of a

---

[6] An underresearched area is whether there are threshold effects and endogenous transitions from one growth model to the other. For example, will increasing the wage share always lead to positive growth in a wage-led model, or will the growth model remain wage-led only for certain values of parameters, after which a further wage share increase will precipitate a shift to profit-led growth and vice versa? It seems plausible to hypothesize that the returns to pro-labor distributional policies are nonlinear and that the growth increase associated with a unit increase in the wage share is lower and perhaps even negative at higher levels of the wage share.

bargaining process between capital and labor and that the causes of the generalized decline of the wage share need to be found in factors that have altered the balance of power between labor and capital (see also Hein and Mundt 2012). In a multicountry econometric analysis, Stockhammer (2014) has found that capital-augmenting technological change has limited capacity to explain movements in the wage share, and that the key explanatory variables are the increase in international capital flows and trade liberalization. Consistent with the bargaining model of the wage share, he has also found that union density and the size of the public sector are positively associated with the private sector's adjusted wage share ("adjusted" means that a wage income is imputed to the self-employed). Other factors affecting the overall wage share are compositional: industries characterized by a lower sectoral wage share (such as finance) expand, while manufacturing and the public sector (a not-for-profit sector with a wage share of 100 percent, by definition) shrink (Hein and Mundt 2012).

The results of Kristal's time-series cross-sectional analysis of the determinants of the wage share bring out the role of class politics and the shifting balance of power between labor and capital even more explicitly:

Labor's share of national income increased in the 1960s and 1970s due to unions organizing new members, the surge in strike activity, and the consolidation of the welfare state. These factors all increased labor's compensation faster than the economy's income. Labor's share declined since the early 1980s with the decline in unionization rates and levels of strike activity, stagnation in government civilian spending, and bargaining decentralization. (Kristal 2010: 758)

In addition, there is convergent econometric evidence suggesting that most advanced countries are wage-led, particularly the five countries this book has focused upon. The only exceptions to the common pattern of wage-led growth are a few small open economies such as Belgium, Austria, Ireland and Denmark (see Onaran and Obst 2015 and the literature cited therein, and Onaran and Galanis 2014). Putting together these stylized facts – the weakening of trade unions and multiemployer collective bargaining has caused a generalized decline in the wage share; in most advanced countries and particularly in France, Germany, Italy and Sweden, a marginal increase in the wage share boosts growth and a marginal increase in the profit share does the opposite – one understands why the liberalization of industrial relations has had far-reaching implications for the trajectory of capitalism: it has contributed to undermining the viability of the Fordist growth model, the most efficient and equitable capitalist variant so far, and has generated a tendency toward stagnation.

The Fordist model was for all purposes a well-functioning wage-led model in which real wage increases controlling for productivity led to both higher wages and higher profits and spurred growth and productivity in the economy as a whole. Collective bargaining played a crucial role by indexing real wages to productivity growth, thus ensuring that aggregate demand would grow in lockstep with aggregate supply. The Fordist model began to unravel when facilitating international economic conditions no longer held: increased trade exposure reinserted wage competition into the game; capital mobility increased the sensitivity of investment to profitability, since the domestic profit rate had to match the international rate of return on alternative uses of capital. While it is not possible to apportion variance as in traditional regression analysis, the discussion so far suggests that the liberalization of industrial relations and of other labor market institutions contributed to undermining the viability of Fordism by weakening the channels that transferred productivity increases into aggregate demand.

There is also robust evidence suggesting that industrial relations institutions once contributed to reducing inequality in the personal distribution of wage income, that is, between highly paid workers and low-paid ones (Rueda and Pontusson 2000, Wallerstein 1999), and that the equality-enhancing effect of these institutions has declined over time (Baccaro 2011a, Becher and Pontusson 2011). A distributional shift favoring rich wage earners over poor ones is likely to reduce aggregate consumption and increase aggregate saving through different propensities to consume and save. Thus, the liberalization of industrial relations may have contributed to undermining Fordist growth not just by shifting the functional distribution of income away from wages and toward profits, but also by increasing the unequal distribution of wage income.

10.3 The Instability of Post-Fordist Growth

As a result of the crisis of Fordism, capitalism seems to have entered a new phase that in many respects resembles interwar capitalism. As in the interwar period, the production possibilities of the economy are thwarted by the absence of well-established and, importantly, stable institutional mechanisms ensuring the transmission of productivity increases into adequate aggregate demand – which is the role that productivity-indexed wage bargaining used to play in the Fordist model.

Before proceeding further, it is helpful to point out the similarity between the analysis developed so far and current thinking about "secular stagnation" in macroeconomics. Larry Summers has recently attracted a lot of attention by arguing that advanced economies find it increasingly difficult to achieve adequate growth rates without relying on some form of artificial stimulation of demand such as asset bubbles, and that in doing so they put financial stability at risk. He argues that the main cause is a substantial decline in the "equilibrium" or "natural" real rate of interest, which he regards as currently negative. He lists several reasons that the natural interest rate is negative, all having to do with either insufficient demand for investment or excessive supply of savings. First, new high-tech ventures require less capital than old manufacturing ventures. To see this, one only needs to compare the capital requirements of, say, Whatsapp with those of GM. Second, growing life expectancy without a corresponding increase in working age implies that savings have to rise to finance retirement. Third, the decline in the relative price of capital goods and consumer durables means that for equal amounts of physical investment less capital is required. Fourth, changes in the income distribution have increased the average propensity to save (Summers 2014; see also von Weizsaecker 2013). This point is one that heterodox macroeconomists have been making for some time.

With negative interest rates, monetary policy becomes unable to pull the economy out of the doldrums. Unconventional measures are thus needed, according to Summers (2014). His favorite solution is to stimulate the economy through expansionary fiscal policy, in particular investment in infrastructure. Strangely, although inequality is in the list of causes, Summers' recipe does not include redistribution from income categories with high saving propensity to income categories with low saving propensity, nor strengthening trade unions and collective bargaining to increase wages and limit profits and rents. Nonetheless, the similarities to the heterodox analysis of capitalism are undeniable: for Summers, too, at the root of the problem of secular stagnation there is an excess of savings that generates a permanent shortfall of demand and encourages financial speculation. "We are seeing very powerfully a kind of inverse Say's Law. Say's Law was the proposition that supply creates its own demand. Here, we are observing that lack of demand creates its own lack of supply" (Summers 2014, 71).

The key problem for post-Fordist capitalist economies is to find a way to replace the lost demand at a time in which the labor market has returned to a competitive regime and wages are no longer the "independent" variable to which others adjust, but the "adjustment" variable. Two ideal types have been identified: "export-led" growth and "debt-led" growth (Stockhammer 2015a). Both attempt to solve the problem of missing demand without generalized wage growth. As vociferously argued by "indignants" around the world, real wage growth has accrued mostly to the top 1 percent in the past 35 years, while the median wage has stagnated (for international evidence see ILO 2015; for US evidence see Mishel, Gould and Bivens 2015). Both growth models seek to "steal" demand from somewhere else: from foreign trade partners in the case of export-led growth; by altering the trade-off between current and future consumption in the case of debt-led growth.

Debt-led growth implies a highly financialized economy. Financialization has been defined by Hein and Mundt (2012: 1) as "the increasing role of financial motives, financial markets, financial actors and financial institutions in the operation of the domestic and international economies.'" Krippner (2005) has suggested a useful way to identify financialization. It does not stand out if one looks at the employment share or the value-added share of finance as a sector, but becomes clearly visible if one asks where and how profits are generated. Profits are increasingly generated in the financial sector and by financial activities of nonfinancial firms. Financialization includes growing pressures to cut costs, including personnel costs, in order to maximize profits, and corporate practices aimed at boosting share prices, such as dividend distribution and share buybacks, which reduce the availability of internal funds for investment at given levels of profits (Hein and Mundt 2012).

With financialization, nonfinancial firms become adept at dabbing in finance; commercial banks start engaging in investment banking and proprietary trading; middle class individuals start managing their asset portfolios and paying attention to stock indices. Financialization also involves a transformation of identities, with wage earners increasingly perceiving themselves as holders of real (homes) and financial (pension-fund) assets rather than as producers (Lapavitsas 2011). Importantly, with financialization, consumption comes to depend on wealth effects and not only on current income. This happens if the consumption decisions of households are shaped by the value of the assets they hold (generally their homes and/or pension funds). Since asset values are linked to stock prices, which in turn are a function of profits, household consumption, too, and not just investment, becomes responsive to profits (Boyer 2000).

The category of debt-led growth seems most appropriate for the US economy in the decade preceding the crisis of 2007–2008, but the underlying logic is applicable to the UK and other economies as well. The story has been told multiple times (here we rely on Stiglitz 2009). Households pledge their appreciating home assets as collateral for accessing loans, with which they finance consumption (Mian and Sufi 2011). This allows households to increase consumption even in the absence of real wage growth. With the diffusion of the "originate-and-sell" model of mortgage finance, the actor that generates the mortgage is no longer the one that assumes the risk inherent in it. The mortgages are sold to financial intermediators – generally investment banks – which repackage them and sell them to retail customers. These practices lower credit standards and facilitate access to debt by households with risky profiles. Financial innovation generates products such as "asset-based securities" and the derivatives built on them, which give the impression that risk has been reduced through diversification but which in reality compound and spread risk. The end result is an economy that "rides an asset bubble," that is, grows at higher speed than its potential for some time, but generates at the same time high levels of debt exposure and financial speculation. When the bubble eventually explodes, banks stop lending to each other and to the real economy; a "balance sheet" recession ensues as households hurriedly deleverage, that is, drastically increase their savings to lower their debt exposure (Koo 2011).

A debt-led economy needs to attract international financial capital to cover its endemic current account deficit as a result of "excessive" consumption. Without international savers willing to lend to countries with current account deficits, the governments of these countries would be forced to shrink their economies to bring imports and exports back in line. Thus, debt-led economies tend to be characterized by large and very liquid international financial hubs such as Wall Street and the City of London, which issue securities that international investors want to hold in their portfolios. Debt-led growth would not be possible if there were not countries with structural current account surpluses, that is, export-led economies, willing to finance the current account deficits of the other countries (Iversen and Soskice 2012).

Export-led growth is an evolution of the Fordist model. In the early phases of trade liberalization, export-oriented firms sought to compensate for rapidly saturating internal markets by expanding into foreign markets. This allowed them to prolong the Fordist logic of scale-induced productivity increase for some time. The big difference, however, is that with the transition to export-led growth, the role played by wages in equilibrating the system is progressively reversed. Real wage increases are no longer the main driver of growth, as in the Fordist model; rather, nominal wage moderation becomes crucial to increase external competitiveness and net exports. In turn, the competitiveness-enhancing potential of wage moderation depends on the extent to which nominal wage dynamics affects relative prices and the real exchange rate. The more exports are sensitive to price differences, the more an export-led model turns the old Fordist logic on its head and represses domestic wage growth in order to spur export growth (Baccaro and Pontusson forthcoming). The German chapter has argued that the German economy may have shifted toward export-led growth and that the primary driver of liberalization in Germany was the export firms' attempt to boost international competitiveness by cutting costs.

Importantly, the export-led growth logic is affected by a fallacy of composition. If all countries adopt the same strategy of wage moderation in order to boost net exports, the beneficial effect of wage moderation evaporates. Generalized wage moderation reduces domestic and foreign demand for each country, and each country is poorer as a result. This observation is particularly relevant for the Euro area. Because the Euro area is not very open when considered as a whole, excessive focus on export-led growth may lead to a generalized depression of demand and employment (Onaran and Obst 2015).

Despite their different features, debt-led and export-led growth are both fundamentally unbalanced, because they lack an institutional mechanism that would ensure that effective demand would expand sufficiently to keep pace with the productive potential of the economy. Industrial relations are no longer central for the institutional architecture of these modes of regulation. With debt-led growth, workers participate in the economy more in their capacity as individual consumers and mini-financiers than as members of the working class. Consumption decisions become responsive to the profit motive through wealth effects. Nonetheless, debt-led growth may still be associated with respectable wage growth. In fact, Baccaro and Pontusson (forthcoming) have argued that while household debt has increased in the UK to support consumption, the UK pattern of growth in the precrisis period still contained some remnants of the old Fordist logic of wage-led growth. It seems that by stimulating consumption, household debt also improves the job prospects of low-skill workers (likely to be employed in the service sector) and thus indirectly boosts their wages.

The role of industrial relations changes in export-led growth as well. Collective bargaining specializes in wage restraint. Despite appearances, wage restraint – defined precisely as real wage growth trailing productivity growth – is a relatively recent phenomenon and not a general feature of centralized or coordinated collective bargaining systems, as argued until recently (Calmfors and Driffill 1988, Cameron 1984, Soskice 1990). Recent research in economic history does not support Barry Eichengreen's influential view that wage restraint laid the foundations for the "thirty glorious years" in Europe by stimulating capital accumulation (see Eichengreen 1997). In fact, recent research finds no evidence of wage restraint in the "thirty glorious years." Erik Bengstrom has found that there was no wage restraint in Sweden in the 1950s, 1960s and 1970s, but that wage restraint was a feature of the 1980s and 1990s and appeared to coincide with the declining power resources of Swedish unions (Bengtsson 2015a). Bengtsson's analysis for Germany arrives at a similar conclusion: wage restraint materialized in Germany in the 1990s and 2000s but was not present before (Bengtsson 2015b). Adding to these findings, the German chapter in this book has suggested that wage restraint is especially pronounced in the service sector and less so in the manufacturing sector. The most problematic aspect of German export-led growth is the emergence of an apparent trade-off between wage growth in the service sector and the price competitiveness of manufacturing exports.

The discussion so far has assumed that the causal arrow goes from the liberalization of industrial relations to the crisis of Fordist growth to the emergence of novel growth models, all sharing a fundamentally unbalanced nature. However, it is possible that the causation is reciprocal and that the search for an alternative growth model has accelerated the erosion of industrial relations institutions. The German case suggests, for example, that Germany's almost exclusive reliance on exports as a growth driver in the late 1990s and early 2000s may have persuaded the policy-making authorities to liberalize the labor market. Perhaps it would be more appropriate to talk of "coevolution" between industrial relations liberalization and growth models instead of unidirectional causation. We are unable to address the direction of causality here but this issue should be taken up by future research, including our own.

10.4 The Growth Profiles of France, Germany, Italy, Sweden and the United Kingdom

In this final section, we determine the main features of the growth profiles for the five countries this book has focused on. In particular, we examine the role that wages and debt play in financing growth and the extent to which growth is more or less reliant on household consumption or net exports. Based on Ameco data, Figure 10.1 reports growth rates of GDP at constant prices for Germany, France, Italy, Sweden and the United Kingdom between 1961 and 2015 in 10-year averages (except for the latest subperiod, which stops at 2015). The growth

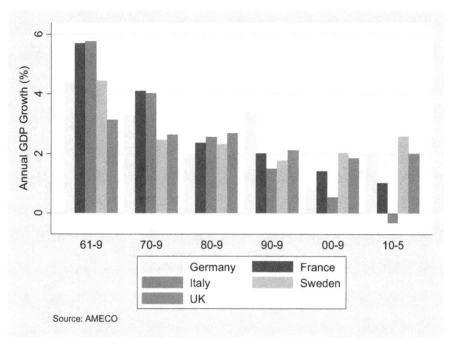

Source: AMECO

FIGURE 10.1. Growth rates at constant prices

performance of France and Italy was higher than the other countries' in the 1960s and 1970s, but afterward growth declined dramatically, particularly in Italy, where it became negative in the first six years of the 2010s. The growth rate of Germany, like that of France and Italy, declined constantly until the first half of the 1980s, and then until the mid-2000s, except for the short-lived post-unification boom. Afterward there was a turnaround: amid meagre growth rates elsewhere, Germany emerged as a strong growth performer. Sweden had lower growth rates than France and Italy until the 1970s, but afterward overcame both of these countries as well as Germany (despite the recession of the early 1990s). Considered a country in decline at the end of the 1970s, the UK also registered faster growth than the other large European countries from the second half of the 1980s on, and its growth record is on par with Sweden's. Overall, France and Italy were growth champions in the Fordist decades but then declined dramatically, especially Italy; Germany appears to have made a turnaround in the years 2000s; Sweden and the UK were strong growth performers from the 1980s on.

Also based on Ameco data, Figure 10.2 examines the sources of growth by engaging in a decomposition exercise that calculates (separately for the different decades) the growth rates of the various components of GDP (private consumption, public consumption, investment in fixed capital, inventories and

a) France and Italy

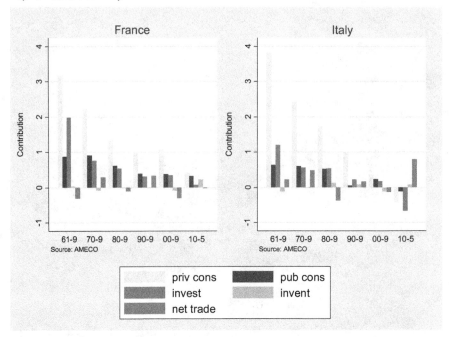

b) Germany and Sweden

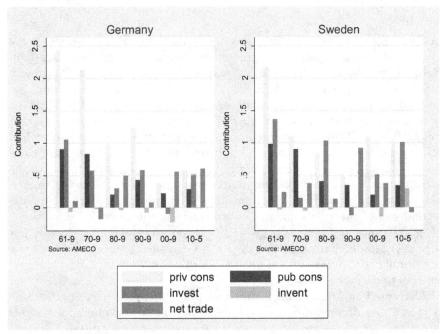

FIGURE 10.2. Contributions to GDP growth at constant prices

c) *UK*

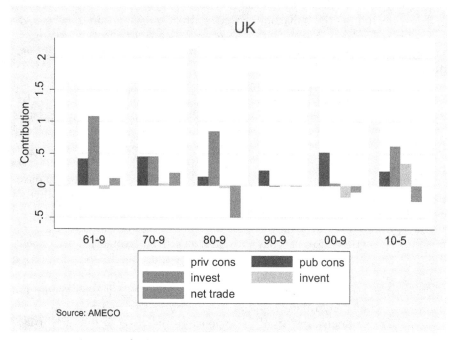

FIGURE 10.2 (*continued*)

net exports) weighted by the GDP shares of the components in question (see Baccaro and Pontusson forthcoming). In this way, we try to identify the drivers of growth in the various countries and periods. The exercise suggests that in France, Italy and the UK, growth has been predominantly pulled by private consumption. Capital accumulation also played an important role in France in the 1960s. The dismal growth performance of France and Italy from the 1980s on seems to be due primarily to the decline of the consumption component of GDP, while the more robust UK growth in the same period seems related to private consumption continuing to expand at a healthy pace. In none of these three countries does growth seem ever to have been pulled by net exports or by other components of aggregate demand. In fact, the contribution of net exports has often been negative. The one exception is Italy in the 2010s, with a positive contribution of net exports but with other components negative. The recent Italian shift is the consequence of the turn to EU-sponsored austerity, which has involved the compression of domestic demand through "internal devaluation" (Armingeon and Baccaro 2012). However, given the small size of the Italian export sector and the overappreciated real exchange rate vis-à-vis core Northern European partners such as Germany (Sinn 2014) – a consequence of the single currency – the stimulus coming from net exports has been blatantly inadequate to rekindle growth in Italy in recent years.

Germany follows the Italian and French path of consumption-driven growth until the early 1980s. Surprisingly, the growth contribution of net exports is negligible or even negative in this period. In other word, Germany has *not* always been an export-led country. In the early 1980s, the country pulled itself out of recession by relying predominantly on export-led growth. In the first half of the 1990s, the unification boom relaunched consumption-driven growth, but then from the second half of the 1990s until the crisis of 2008, an interesting phenomenon happened: as the contribution of private consumption declined, the contribution of net exports increased. These were approximately the years in which the German industrial relations system was liberalized the most. As suggested in the German chapter, liberalization may have contributed to pushing the growth model toward an export-led one. In the post-financial-crisis years, the German growth model appears to have rebalanced somewhat, with private consumption, investment and net exports contributing approximately equally to growth in 2010–15, but with record current account surpluses reaching 8 percent of GDP in 2015, it is unclear how durable this reequilibration really is.

In Sweden, too, growth was initially pulled primarily by private consumption as in other countries, although public consumption also played a role in the 1970s. As in Germany, the Swedish response to the crisis of the early 1980s was export-driven. In the early 1990s, however, while domestic demand was booming in Germany as a result of unification, Sweden relied on net exports to pull itself out of a deep crisis. In the fifteen years before the financial crisis of 2007–08, Swedish growth was pulled both by private consumption and by net exports, although the latter were less important and declined over time. In the more recent period, the Swedish growth model seems to have become more inward-oriented: the contribution of net exports has become negative and growth is driven primarily by private consumption and investment.

Figures 10.3 and 10.4 try to shed some light on how private consumption is financed. The previous discussion on debt-led growth would lead us to hypothesize that while real wages would have stagnated, levels of household debt would have soared in consumption-led economies. Based on OECD data, Figure 10.3 plots gross household debt as a percentage of net (i.e., after taxes) disposable income between 1995 and 2014 (the series are short due to data availability). UK debt levels are higher than in other countries and the accumulation of debt accelerated in the precrisis years. However, debt levels were almost as high in Sweden, and were actually higher than in the UK in the post-financial-crisis years. The levels of UK debt peaked in the second half of the 2000s and then declined a little. Although starting from lower levels, there was a clear rising trend of debt in France and Italy as well, even though the trend seems to have leveled out after the crisis. Germany is the only exception to the rule of growing debt. German household debt grew until 2000 and then declined.

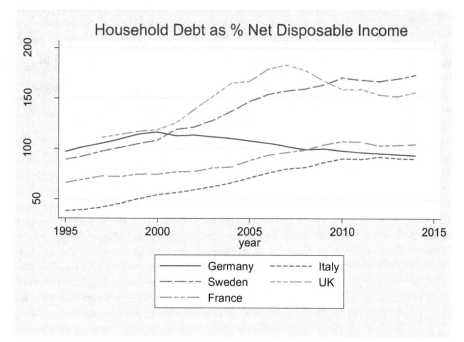

FIGURE 10.3. Household debt

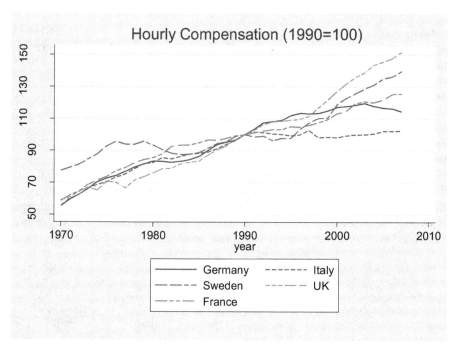

FIGURE 10.4. Real wages

Coming to real wages, Figure 10.4 is based on comparable data on hourly compensation (inclusive of employer social security contributions) from the KLEMS database deflated with consumer price indices from the OECD. The data start in 1970, permitting the examination of long trends, but are only available until 2007. The base year is 1990. The country in which real wages grew the most over 1970–2007 is paradoxically the UK, the country with the least regulated labor market. Between 1990 and 2007, average British wages grew by 51 percent in real terms. In Sweden, wages grew fast until the late 1970s; then they stagnated in the 1980s; they started growing again from the 1990s on and they increased by 40 percent between 1990 and 2007. German wages grew at approximately the same pace as in Italy, France and the United Kingdom until 1990. In the first half of the 1990s they grew faster than in other countries, but then they began to slow down; from the early 2000s on they actually slightly declined (+16 percent between 1990 and 2007). French wages grew in tandem with those in other large European countries until 1990s and then faster than German and Italian wages (26 percent), but more slowly than British and Swedish wages. In Italy, real wage growth was comparable to that in other countries until 1990. From 1990 on Italian wages stagnated. The increase was only 2.5 percent between 1990 and 2007.[7]

Considering the evidence, in all five countries, growth was primarily pulled by private consumption in the "Fordist" decades of the 1960s and 1970s, and consumption seems to have been driven primarily by real wages (although data on household debt are missing for this early period). This is consistent with these countries being wage-led economies in this period. Afterward, trajectories diverged: while growth continued to be strongly consumption-led in France, Italy and the UK, Germany and Sweden turned to export-led growth at different times: from the mid-1990s on in Germany; intermittently in the 1980s and 1990s but not in the 2000s and 2010s in Sweden. Sweden seems to be able to alternate between consumption- and export-led growth depending on economic circumstances (e.g., the need to respond to an external shock in the early 1990s) and even to combine them in interesting ways (Baccaro and Pontusson forthcoming).

As to how private consumption is financed, the data suggest that the dichotomy of wage- and debt-driven consumption is possibly overdrawn: in the countries in which private consumption grew the most, the UK and Sweden, both real wages and household debt increased. The Italian slow growth record seems to be attributable to insufficient real wage growth. Although debt levels

---

[7] Unreported data on productivity from the OECD suggest that productivity (measured as GDP at constant prices per hour worked) grew faster in France, Germany and Italy than in Sweden and the UK until 1990, but the opposite happened afterward. In particular, between 1990 and 2014, productivity grew by only 17 percent in Italy. In the same period the productivity growth of the other countries was 40 (France), 43 (Germany), 53 (Sweden) and 48 percent (UK). That productivity would grow faster in the countries where demand increased more seems to confirm the presence of the Kaldor–Verdoorn effect discussed above.

rose in Italy, the increase was probably insufficient to kindle domestic demand. The Italian case clearly illustrates that it is perfectly possible for an economy not to find any viable alternative to Fordist growth, and simply to enter into a period of protracted stagnation. In France, real wages grew faster than in Germany, let alone Italy, yet growth remained subdued. It may be argued that the French economic authorities should have stimulated domestic demand more than they did (although they stimulated it more than the Italian ones), but in doing so they were thwarted by the current account constraint, as witnessed by the negligible if not negative contribution of net exports. French growth may have been hindered by the inflexibility of the nominal exchange rate, that is, by the inability to devalue in the Euro era. The same argument applies to Italy. In Germany, real wages started to plateau at approximately the same time as exports surged, suggesting a relationship between the two trends, that is, that Germany became more export-led because it repressed wages and domestic consumption (as argued, for example, by Flassbeck and Lapavitsas 2015).

It bears mentioning that the two best growth performers of the post-1990s era, Sweden and the UK, were both outside the Euro. There is little doubt that membership in the Euro zone has contributed to depressing growth in France and Italy. The economic architecture of the Euro area is heavily tilted toward profit-oriented policies (Stockhammer 2015b). With its emphasis on monetary conservatism and rule-based fiscal policy, with free factor mobility taking precedence over any type of market-correcting policy and recently with its embrace of austerity and structural reform, including labor market liberalization and collective bargaining decentralization, as a solution to the economic crisis (Armingeon and Baccaro 2012), the economic architecture of the Euro zone is ill-suited to consumption-led economies such as France and Italy (Stockhammer 2015b). Above all, the Euro saddles these economies, as well as those of the other Mediterranean economies, with a real exchange rate that is too high for their needs (Scharpf 2011). By the same token, the Euro has served the German economy well (at least the German manufacturing sector) by providing it with a real exchange rate that is lower than a German exchange rate would be. It has been argued that the recent German export boom is a result of its membership in the Euro area (Thorckecke and Kato 2012). However, even for Germany, it is unclear how durable a growth model based on external demand and repression of internal consumption really is.

We conclude by reiterating the central message of this chapter: The liberalization of industrial relations contributed to make the Fordist model of wage-led growth – in which growth is pulled by domestic consumption financed by real wage increases – no longer viable. The growth profiles that have emerged from the crisis of Fordism are different but all unstable. What is more, they contribute to the accumulation of global imbalances. Growth that relies on the artificial stimulation of consumption through easier access to credit encourages financial speculation and leads to asset bubbles. Vice versa, export-led growth is often based on compressing domestic demand in order to gain external demand.

This strategy is only feasible if other countries do not adopt it. If they do, the end result is a deflationary spiral.

The ideal-typical industrial relations system of the preliberalization period, the Fordist industrial relations system, played a fundamental role in the institutional hierarchy of postwar capitalism by stabilizing the transformation of productivity gains into aggregate demand. This system no longer exists. It rested upon a particular balance of class forces, a balance that has fundamentally shifted against labor and in favor of capital in the period since the end of the 1970s. The dismantling of Fordist industrial relations systems through liberalization, a process that has been the focus of this book, has taken different forms in different countries, but everywhere has increased economic instability. The future of capitalism depends crucially on its ability to recreate institutions that reconnect aggregate demand and aggregate supply, enabling demand to expand in parallel with the productive capacities of the economy. It remains to be seen whether a new form of internationalism that coordinates demand expansion across countries will be able to rekindle capitalist growth (Lavoie and Stockhammer 2013), or whether reembedding capitalism – which is probably the only way to make it viable in the long run – will require a fundamental rethinking of the current globalization regime and a return to national economic sovereignty (Streeck 2014).

Bibliography

AAVV. 2002. *Non basta dire no*. Milan: Mondadori.

Acemoglu, Daron and James A. Robinson. 2006. *Economic Origins of Dictatorship and Democracy*. New York: Cambridge University Press.

Achur, James. 2011. Trade Union Membership 2010. URN 11/P77Congress: 1–43 (http://www.bis.gov.uk/assets/biscore/employment-matters/docs/t/11-p77-trade-union-membership-2010.pdf).

Adam, Hermann. 1972. *Die Konzertierte Aktion in der Bundesrepublik*. Cologne: Bund-Verlag.

Advisory Conciliation and Arbitration Service. 2008. *Annual Report and Accounts: 2007–2008*. London, UK: Advisory Conciliation and Arbitration Service.

Ahlberg, Kerstin and Niklas Bruun. 2005. "Sweden: Transition through Collective Bargaining." *Bulletin of Comparative Labour Relations* (56): 117–43.

Akerlof, George A. 1982. "Labor Contracts as Partial Gift Exchange." *Quarterly Journal of Economics* 97(4): 543–69.

Alesina, Alberto and Silvia Ardagna. 1998. "Tales of Fiscal Adjustments." *Economic Policy* 27(October): 489–545.

Alesina, Alberto and Roberto Perotti. 1997a. "The Welfare State and Competitiveness." *American Economic Review* 87(5): 921–39.

Alesina, Alberto and Roberto Perotti. 1997b. "Fiscal Adjustment in OECD Countries: Composition and Macroeconomic Effects." *International Monetary Fund Staff Papers* 44(2): 210–48.

Alexopoulos, Michelle and Jon Cohen. 2003. "Centralised Wage Bargaining and Structural Change in Sweden." *European Review of Economic History* 7(3): 331–66.

Altieri, Giovanna, C. Bellina and Mimmo Carrieri. 1984. *La vertenza sul costo del lavoro e le relazioni industrali*. Milan: Franco Angeli.

Amin, Ash, ed. 1994. *Post-Fordism: A Reader*. Oxford/Cambridge, MA: Blackwell.

Amoore, Louise. 2002. *Globalisation Contested: An International Political Economy of Work*. Manchester: Manchester University Press.

Amossé, Thomas. 2006. "Le dialogue social en entreprise." *Première Synthèses Informations* (39.1): 1–8.

Amossé, Thomas, Catherine Bloch-London and Loup Wolff, eds. 2008. Les relations sociales en entreprise: Un portrait à partir des enquêtes relations professionnelles et négociations d'entreprise. Paris: Éditions la Découverte.

Amossé, Thomas and Maria-Teresa Pignoni. 2006. "La transformation du paysage syndical depuis 1945." *Données Sociales – La Société Française*: 405–12.

Anderson, Perry and Patrick Camiller. 1994. *Mapping the West European Left*. London/New York: Verso.

Andersson, Jenny. 2015. "Explaining Neoliberalism in Sweden: The Rise of the Welfare Industrial Complex." *Paper presented at the 22nd International Conference of Europeanists*, July 10, 2015, Paris.

Andolfatto, Dominique. 2004. *Les syndicats en France*. Paris: La Documentation Française.

Antonczyk, Dirk, Bernd Fitzenberger and Katrin Sommerfeld. 2010. "Rising Wage Inequality, the Decline of Collective Bargaining, and the Gender Wage Gap." *Labour Economics* 17(5): 835–47.

Anxo, Dominique and Harald Niklasson. 2006. "The Swedish Model in Turbulent Times: Decline or Renaissance?" *International Labour Review* 145(4): 339–71.

Aprile, Rocco. 1996. "La riforma del sistema pensionistico. Le critiche che non si merita." *L'Assistenza Sociale* 50(4): 163–87.

Aprile, Rocco, Stefano Fassina and Daniele Pace. 1996. "Pensione contributiva e pensione retributiva: Un'ipotesi di riforma." In *Pensioni e risanamento della finanza pubblica*, edited by F. P. S. Kostoris. Bologna: Il Mulino.

Armingeon, Klaus and Lucio Baccaro. 2012. "Political Economy of the Sovereign Debt Crisis: The Limits of Internal Devaluation." *Industrial Law Journal* 41(3): 254–75.

Armstrong, Philip, Andrew Glyn and John Harrison. 1991. *Capitalism since 1945*. Oxford: Blackwell.

Artus, Ingrid. 2001. *Krise des Deutschen Tarifsystems: Die Erosion des Flächentarifvertrags in Ost und West*. Wiesbaden: Westdeutscher Verlag.

Askenazy, Philippe. 2013. "Working Time Regulation in France from 1996 to 2012." *Cambridge Journal of Economics* 37(2): 323–47.

Askenazy, Philippe and Susan Emanuel. 2015. *The Blind Decades: Employment and Growth in France, 1974–2014*. Oakland, CA: University of California Press.

Assemblée Nationale. 2015. *Projet de Loi relative au dialogue social et à l'emploi. Number 577*. Paris: Assemblée Nationale.

Avdagic, Sabina, Martin Rhodes and Jelle Visser, eds. 2011. *Social Pacts in Europe: Emergence, Evolution and Institutionalization*. Oxford: Oxford University Press.

Baccaro, Lucio. 1999. "The Organizational Consequences of Democracy." Ph.D. thesis, *Sloan School of Management and Department of Political Science*, MIT, Cambridge, MA.

Baccaro, Lucio. 2003. "What Is Alive and What Is Dead in the Theory of Corporatism." *British Journal of Industrial Relations* 41(4): 683–706.

Baccaro, Lucio. 2011a. "Labor, Globalization, and Inequality: Are Trade Unions Still Redistributive?" *Research in the Sociology of Work* 22: 213–85.

Baccaro, Lucio. 2011b. "Corporatism Meets Neoliberalism: The Irish and Italian Cases in Comparative Perspective." Pp. 375–401 in *Research Handbook of Comparative*

Employment Relations, edited by M. Barry and A. Wilkinson. Cheltenham, UK: Edward Elgar.

Baccaro, Lucio. 2014a. "Discursive Democracy and the Construction of Interests: Lessons from Italian Pension Reform." *In Political Representation in the Global Age*, edited by P. Hall, W. Jacoby, J. Levy and S. Meunier. New York: Cambridge University Press.

Baccaro, Lucio. 2014b. "Similar Structures, Different Outcomes: Corporatism's Surprising Resilience and Transformation." *Review of Keynesian Economics* 2(2): 207–33.

Baccaro, Lucio and Chiara Benassi. 2014. "Throwing Out the Ballast: Growth Models and the Liberalization of German Industrial Relations." *Unpublished manuscript*, University of Geneva.

Baccaro, L.ucio and Jonas Pontusson. 2015. "Rethinking Comparative Political Economy: Growth Models and Distributive Dynamics." Paper presented at the 22nd International Conference of Europeanists, Paris, France.

Baccaro, Lucio and Jonas Pontusson. Forthcoming. "Rethinking Comparative Political Economy: The Growth Model Perspective." Politics & Society.

Baccaro, Lucio and Valeria Pulignano. 2011. "Employment Relations in Italy." Pp. 138–68 in *International and Comparative Employment Relations, 5th edition*, edited by G. Bamber, R. Lansbury and N. Wailes. Crows Nest, Australia: Allen & Unwin.

Baccaro, Lucio and Marco Simoni. 2004. "The Referendum on Article 18 and Labour Market Flexibility." In *Italian Politics*, edited by S. Fabbrini and V. Della Sala. New York and Oxford: Berghahn Books.

Baccaro, Lucio and Marco Simoni. 2007. "Centralized Wage Bargaining and the 'Celtic Tiger' Phenomenon." *Industrial Relations* 46(3): 426–55.

Baccaro, Lucio and Marco Simoni. 2008. "Policy Concertation in Europe: Understanding Government Choice." *Comparative Political Studies* 41(10): 1323–48.

Bach, Stephen and Alexandra Stroleny. 2012. "Social Dialogue and the Public Services in the Aftermath of the Economic Crisis." Vol. *VP/2011/001*, September 2012. London, UK: European Commission.

Bagnasco, Arnaldo. 1977. *Tre Italie*. Bologna: Il Mulino.

Bahnmüller, Reinhard, Reinhard Bispinck and Anni Weiler. 1999. "Tarifpolitik und Lohnbildung in Deutschland: Am Beispiel Ausgewählter Wirtschaftszweige." WSI-Diskussionspapier.

Bailey, Rachel. 1994. "Annual Review Article 1993: British Public Sector Industrial Relations." *British Journal of Industrial Relations* 32(1): 113–36.

Bain, George Sayers and Robert Price. 1983. "Union Growth: Dimensions, Determinants, and Density." in *Industrial Relations in Britain*, edited by G. S. Bain. Oxford, UK: Basil Blackwell.

Barca, Fabrizio and Marco Magnani. 1989. *L'industria tra capitale e lavoro: Piccole e grandi imprese dall'autunno caldo alla ristrutturazione*. Bologna: Il Mulino.

Batstone, Eric. 1988. *The Reform of Workplace Industrial Relations: Theory, Myth, and Evidence*. Oxford and New York: Clarendon Press.

Baumol, William. 1967. "Macroeconomics of Unbalanced Growth." *American Economic Review* 53(3): 415–26.

Beaumont, P. B. 1992. *Public Sector Industrial Relations*. London and New York: Routledge.

Becher, Michael and Jonas Pontusson. 2011. "Whose Interests Do Unions Represent? Unionization by Income in Western Europe." *Research in the Sociology of Work* 23: 181–211.

Benassi, C. and L. Dorigatti. 2015. "Straight to the Core: The Ig Metall Campaign towards Agency Workers ". *British Journal of Industrial Relations* 53(3): 533–55.

Bengtsson, Erik. 2013. "Essays on Trade Unions and Functional Income Distribution." Doctoral dissertation, Department of Economy and Society, University of Gothenburg, Gothenburg, Sweden.

Bengtsson, Erik. 2015a. "Wage Restraint in Scandinavia: During the Postwar Period or the Neoliberal Age?". *European Review of Economic History.* 19(4): 359–81.

Bengtsson, Erik. 2015b. "Wage Restraint and Wage Militancy: Belgium, Germany and the Netherlands, 1950–2010." Unpublished manuscript, Economic History Unit, University of Gothenburg.

Berger, Suzanne and Ronald Philip Dore, eds. 1996. *National Diversity and Global Capitalism.* Ithaca, NY: Cornell University Press.

Bergholm, Tapio and Andreas Bieler. 2013. "Globalization and the Erosion of the Nordic Model: A Swedish–Finnish Comparison." *European Journal of Industrial Relations* 19(1): 55–70.

Béroud, Sophie and Karel Yon. 2012. "Face à la crise, la mobilisation sociale et ses limites. Une analyse des contradictions syndicales." *Modern and Contemporary France* 20(2): 169–83.

Bhaduri, Amit and Stephen A. Marglin. 1990. "Unemployment and the Real Wage: The Economic Basis for Contesting Political Ideologies." *Cambridge Journal of Economics* 14: 375–93.

Biagi, Marco, Maurizio Sacconi, Carlo Dell'Aringa, Natale Forlani, Paolo Reboani and Paolo Sestito. 2002. "White Paper on the Labour Market in Italy, the Quality of European Industrial Relations and Changing Industrial Relations." Bulletin of Comparative Labour Relations Series (August).

Bispinck, R. 1997. "The Chequered History of the Alliance for Jobs." Pp. 63–78 in *Social Pacts in Europe*, edited by G. Fajertag and P. Pochet. Brussels: European Trade Union Institute.

Bispinck, R. and T. Schulten. 2000. "Alliance for Jobs – Is Germany Following the Path of "Competitive Corporatism"?" Pp. 187–218 in *Social Pacts in Europe: New Dynamics*, edited by G. Fajertag and P. Pochet. Brussels: ETUI.

Bissuel, Bertrand. 2016. "Temps de travail, licenciement, prud'hommes: Ce qui contient le project de loi d'el Khomri." *Le Monde*, February 26.

Blair, Tony. 1997. "We Won't Look Back to the 1970s." *Times*, March 31.

Blanchard, Olivier. 2006. "European Unemployment: The Evolution of Facts and Ideas." *Economic Policy* 21(45): 5–59.

Blanchard, Olivier and Justin Wolfers. 2000. "The Role of Shocks and Institutions in the Rise of European Unemployment· The Aggregate Evidence." *Economic Journal* 110(462): 1–33.

Blanchflower, David and Alex Bryson. 2009. "Trade Union Decline and the Economics of the Workplace." Pp. 48–73 in *The Evolution of the Modern Workplace*, edited by W. Brown, A. Bryson, J. Forth and K. Whitfield. New York: Cambridge University Press

Block, Fred L. 1987. *Revising State Theory: Essays in Politics and Postindustrialism.* Philadelphia: Temple University Press.

Blyth, Mark. 2013. *Austerity: The History of a Dangerous Idea.* Oxford and New York: Oxford University Press.

Blyth, Mark M. 1997. "Review: 'Any More Bright Ideas?' The Ideational Turn of Comparative Political Economy." *Comparative Politics* 29(2): 229–50.

BMAS. 2013. "Verzeichnis der für Allgemeinverbindlich Erklärten Tarifverträge Stand: 1. April 2013."

Bodin, Raymond-Pierre. 1987. *Les lois Auroux dans les P.M.E.* Paris, France: Ministère des affaires sociales et de l'emploi, Service des études et de la statistique, Division conditions de travail et relations professionnelles.

Boeri, Tito and Vincenzo Galasso. 2007. *Contro i Giovani. Come l'Italia sta tradendo le nuove generazioni.* Milan: Mondadori.

Bonefeld, Werner. 2012. "Freedom and the Strong State: On German Ordoliberalism." *New Political Economy* 17(5): 633–56. doi: 10.1080/13563467.2012.656082.

Bordogna, Lorenzo. 1997. "Un decennio di contrattazione aziendale nell'industria." In *Relazioni industriali e contrattazione aziendale. Continuita' e riforma nell'esperienza Italiana recente,* edited by L. Bellardi and L. Bordogna. Milan: Angeli.

Bordogna, Lorenzo. 1999. "Il fattore dimensionale nelle relazioni industriali e nella contrattazione collettiva in azienda." In *La "questione dimensionale" nell'industria Italiana,* edited by F. Trau'. Bologna: Il Mulino.

Bosch, G., T. Haipeter, E. Latniak and S. Lehndorff. 2007. "Demontage oder Revitalisierung?" *KZfSS: Kölner Zeitschrift für Soziologie und Sozialpsychologie* 59(2): 318–39.

Bosch, G. and C. Weinkopf. 2008. *Low-Wage Work in Germany.* New York: Russell Sage Foundation Publications.

Boswell, Jonathan and James Peters. 1997. *Capitalism in Contention: Business Leaders and Political Economy in Modern Britain.* New York: Cambridge University Press.

Bowles, Samuel and Robert Boyer. 1995. "Wages, Aggregate Demand, and Employment in an Open Economy: An Empirical Investigation." Pp. 143–71 in *Macroeconomic Policy after the Conservative Era. Studies in Investment, Saving and Finance,* edited by G. Epstein and H. Gintis. Cambridge, UK: Cambridge University Press.

Boyer, Robert. 1990. *The Regulation School: A Critical Introduction.* Translated by C. Charney. New York: Columbia University Press.

Boyer, Robert. 2000. "Is a Finance-Led Growth Regime a Viable Alternative to Fordism? A Preliminary Analysis." *Economy and Society* 29(1): 111–45.

Boyer, Robert and Yves Saillard, eds. 2002. *Regulation Theory: The State of the Art.* London and New York: Routledge.

Boyer, Robert. 2004. *Théorie de la régulation: Les fondamentaux.* Paris: La découverte.

Boyer, Robert. 2011. "Are There Laws of Motion of Capitalism?" *Socio-Economic Review* 9(1): 59–81. doi: 10.1093/ser/mwq026.

Boyer, Robert. 2015. *Economie politique des capitalismes.* Paris: La Découverte.

Brochard, Delphine. 2008. "Logiques de gestion du travail, environment conventionnel et concurrentiel: Des politiques de rémunérations sous influences." Pp. 376–98 in *Les relations sociales en entreprise: Un portrait à partir des enquêtes relations professionnelles et négociations d'entreprise,* edited by T. Amossé, C. Bloch-London and L. Wolff. Paris, France: Éditions La Découverte.

Broughton, Andrea. 2012. "Employment Council Discusses Opposition to Regulation on Collective Action." *EIROnline*: 1–2.

Brown, William. 2011. "International Review: Industrial Relations Under New Labour, 1997–2010: A Post Mortem." *Journal of Industrial Relations* 53(3): 402–13.

Brown, William, Alex Bryson and John Forth. 2009. "Competition and the Retreat from Collective Bargaining." Pp. 22–47 in *The Evolution of the Modern Workplace,* edited by W. Brown, A. Bryson, J. Forth and K. Whitfield. New York: Cambridge University Press.

Brown, William, Simon Deakin, Maria Hudson, Cliff Pratten and Paul Ryan. 1999. "The Individualisation of Employment Contracts in Britain." *DTI Employment Relations Research Series Working Paper 4.* London, UK: Department of Trade and Industry.

Brown, William, Simon Deakin, David Nash and Sarah Oxenbridge. 2000. "The Employment Contract: From Collective Procedures to Individual Rights." *British Journal of Industrial Relations* 38(4): 611–29.

Brown, William, Simon Deakin and Paul Ryan. 1997. "The Effects of British Industrial Relations Legislation 1979–97." *National Institute Economic Review* 161(1): 69–83.

Brown, William and Paul Edwards. 2009. "Researching the Changing Workplace." Pp. 1–21 in *The Evolution of the Modern Workplace,* edited by W. Brown, A. Bryson, J. Forth and K. Whitfield. New York: Cambridge University Press.

Brown, William Arthur and Eric Batstone. 1981. *The Changing Contours of British Industrial Relations: A Survey of Manufacturing Industry.* Oxford, UK: B. Blackwell.

Bruno, M. and Jeffrey Sachs. 1985. *Economics of Worldwide Stagflation.* Cambridge, MA: Harvard University Press.

Calmfors, Lars and John Driffill. 1988. "Bargaining Structure, Corporatism and Macroeconomic Performance." *Economic Policy* 3(6): 13–61.

Cameron, David. 1984. "Social Democracy, Corporatism, Labour Quiescence, and the Representation of Economic Interests in Advanced Capitalism." Pp. 143–78 in *Order and Conflict in Contemporary Capitalism: Studies in the Political Economy of Western European Nations,* edited by J.H. Goldthorpe. Oxford, UK: Clarendon Press.

Campbell, John L. 2004. *Institutional Change and Globalization.* Princeton, N.J.: Princeton University Press.

Carlin, Wendy and David Soskice. 2006. *Macroeconomics: Imperfections, Institutions, and Policies.* New York: Oxford University Press.

Carrieri, Mimmo. 1997. *Seconda repubblica: Senza sindacati?* Rome: Ediesse.

Carrieri, Mimmo and Carlo Donolo. 1986. *Il mestiere politico del sindacato.* Rome: Editori Riuniti.

Carter, Bob and Peter Fairbrother. 1999. "The Transformation of British Public-Sector Industrial Relations: From 'Model Employer' to Marketized Relations." *Historical Studies in Industrial Relations* (7): 119–46. doi: 10.3828/hsir.1999.7.6.

Castel, Nicolas, Noélie Delahaie and Héloise Petit. 2013. "L'articulation des négociations de branche et d'entreprise dans la détermination des salaires." *Travail et Emploi* (134): 21–40.

Castellino, Onorato. 1996. "La riforma delle pensioni: Forse non sarà l'ultima." Pp. 179–96 in *Politica in Italia. I fatti dell'anno e le interpretazioni. Edizione 1996*, edited by M. Caciagli and D. Kertzer. Bologna: Il Mulino.

Cazzola, Giuliano. 1995. *Le nuove pensioni degli italiani*. Bologna: Il Mulino.

Cella, Gian Primo. 1989. "Criteria of Regulation in Italian Industrial Relations: A Case of Weak Institutions." Pp. 167–86 in *State, Market and Social Regulation: New Perspectives on Italy*, edited by P. Lange and M. Regini. New York: Cambridge University Press.

Cella, Gian Primo and Tiziano Treu. 1989. "La contrattazione collettiva." In *Relazioni industriali. Manuale per l'analisi dell'esperienza italiana*, edited by G. P. Cella and T. Treu. Bologna Il Mulino.

Cella, Gian Primo and Tiziano Treu. 2009. *Relazioni industriali e contrattazione collettiva*. Milan: Il Mulino.

CERISS. 1980. *Salari contrattuali e piattaforme rivendicative dei metalmeccanici*. Milan: Franco Angeli.

Charlwood, Andy and John Forth. 2009. "Employee Representation." Pp. 74–96 in *The Evolution of the Modern Workplace*, edited by W. Brown, A. Bryson, J. Forth and K. Whitfield. New York: Cambridge University Press.

CNEL. 2007. *Lineamenti della contrattazione aziendale nel periodo 1998–2006*. Rome: CNEL.

Coates, David, ed. 2005. *Varieties of Capitalism, Varieties of Approaches*. New York: Palgrave Macmillan.

Coffineau, Michel. 1993. *Les lois Auroux, dix ans après*. Paris, France: La Documentation Française.

Collidà, Ada Becchi and Serafino Negrelli. 1986. *La transizione nell'industria e nelle relazioni industriali. L'auto e il caso Fiat*. Milan: Franco Angeli.

Combault, Philippe. 2006. "La couverture conventionnelle a fortement progressé entre 1997 Et 2004." *Première Synthèses Informations* (46.2): 1–4.

Confederation of British Industry. 2010. "*Making Britain the Place to Work: An Employment Agenda for the New Government.*" London, UK: Confederation of British Industry.

Conservative Party. 2015. "*The Conservative Party Manifesto 2015: Strong Leadership, a Clear Economic Plan, a Brighter, More Secure Future.*" Pp. 1–84. London, UK.

Contrepois, Sylvie and Steve Jefferys. 2006. "French Government Pay Interventions and Incomes Policies, 1945–1981." *Historical Studies in Industrial Relations* (21): 1–33.

Couton, Philippe. 2004. "A Labor of Laws: Courts and the Mobilization of French Workers." *Politics and Society* 32(3): 327–65. doi: 10.1177/0032329204267294.

Cronin, James E., George Ross and James Shoch. 2011. *What's Left of the Left: Democrats and Social Democrats in Challenging Times*. Durham: Duke University Press.

Crouch, Colin. 2001. "A Third Way in Industrial Relations?" In *New Labour: The Progressive Future?* edited by S. White. Basingstoke, UK: Palgrave.

Culpepper, Pepper. 2015. "Structural Power and Political Science in the Post-crisis Era." *Business and Politics*. 17(3): 391–409.

Culpepper, Pepper D. 2001. "Employers, Public Policy, and the Politics of Decentralized Cooperation in Germany and France." Pp. 275–306 in *Varieties of Capitalism: The Institutional Foundations of Comparative Advantage*, edited by P. Hall and D. Soskice. New York: Oxford University Press.

Culpepper, Pepper D. 2006. "Capitalism, Coordination, and Economic Change: The French Political Economy since 1985." Pp. 29–49 in *Changing France: The Politics That Markets Make*, edited by P.D. Culpepper, P. Hall and B. Palier. New York: Palgrave Macmillan.

Culpepper, Pepper D. 2008. "The Politics of Common Knowledge: Ideas and Institutional Change in Wage Bargaining." *International Organization* 62(1): 1–33.

Dardot, Pierre and Christian Laval. 2009. *La nouvelle raison du monde: Essai sur la société néolibérale*. Paris: La Découverte.

Davies, Paul and Mark Freedland. 1993. *Labour Legislation and Public Policy: A Contemporary History*. Oxford, UK: Clarendon Press.

Davies, Paul and Mark Freedland. 2007. *Towards a Flexible Labour Market: Labour Legislation and Regulation since the 1990s*. Oxford, UK and New York: Oxford University Press.

Degryse, Christophe, Maria Jepsen and Philippe Pochet. 2013. *The Euro Crisis and Its Impact on National and European Social Policies*. Brussels: ETUI.

Department for Business, Innovation and Skills. 2015. "Press Release: New Legislation to Make Strike Laws Fair for Working People." London, UK.

Department of Employment. 1992. People, Jobs, Opportunity Congress.

Department of Trade and Industry. 1998. *Fairness at Work*. cm 3968Congress: 1–37.

Di Maggio, Paul J. and Walter W. Powell. 1991. *The New Institutionalism in Organizational Analysis*. Chicago: University of Chicago Press.

Doellgast, Virginia and Ian Greer. 2007. "Vertical Disintegration and the Disorganization of German Industrial Relations." *British Journal of Industrial Relations* 45(1): 55–76.

Doeringer, Peter and Michael Piore. 1971. *Internal Labor Markets and Manpower Analysis*. Lexington, MA: Heath.

Dörre, Klaus. 2012. "Diskriminierende Prekarität. Ein Neuer Typus Unsicherer Arbeits- und Lebensformen." *Der Bürger im Staat. Armut.* 4(2012): 223–30.

Dribbusch, H. and P. Birke. 2012. *Trade Unions in Germany. Organisation, Environment, Challenges*. Berlin.

Duclos, Laurent, Guy Groux and Olivier Mériaux, eds. 2009. *Les nouvelles dimensions du politique: Relations professionnelles et régulations sociales*, Vol. 19. Paris, France: Maison des Sciences de l'"Homme Réseau Européen Droit et Société.

Dufour, Christian and Adelheid Hege. 2008. "Comités d'entreprise et syndicats, quelles relations?" *La Revue de L'IRES* (59): 3–40.

Dumka, Ivan. 2014. *Coordinated Wage-Setting and the Social Partnership under Emu*. University of Victoria.

Dunn, Stephen and David Metcalf. 1994. *Trade Union Law since 1978: Ideology, Intent, Impact*. Working paper. London, UK: Centre for Economic Performance, London School of Economics.

Dustmann, Christian, Johannes Ludsteck and Uta Schönberg. 2009. "Revisiting the German Wage Structure." *Quarterly Journal of Economics* 124(2): 843–81.

EC. 1997. *European Economy*. No. 67. Brussels: European Commission.

Edvinsson, Rodney. 2010. "A Tendency for the Rate of Profit to Fall? From Primitive to Flexible Accumulation in Sweden, 1800–2005." *Review of Radical Political Economics* 42(4): 465–84.

Eichengreen, Barry. 1997. "Institutions and Economic Growth: Europe after World War II." Pp. 38–72 in *Economic Growth in Europe since 1945*, edited by N. Crafts and G. Toniolo. Cambridge, UK: Cambridge University Press.

Eichhorst, Werner and Paul Marx. 2010. *Whatever Works: Dualisation and the Service Economy in Bismarckian Welfare States*. IZA 5305. Bonn: Institute for the Study of Labor.

EIRR. 1995. "Joint Employer/Union Declaration." European Industrial Relations Review (255).

Elliott, Larry. 2010. "Budget Will Cost 1.3m Jobs – Treasury." *Guardian*, June 29.

Elvander, Nils. 2002. "The New Swedish Regime for Collective Bargaining and Conflict Resolution: A Comparative Perspective." *European Journal of Industrial Relations* 8(2): 197–216.

Elvander, Nils and Bertil Holmlund. 1997. *The Swedish Bargaining System in the Melting Pot: Institutions, Norms and Outcomes in the 1990s*. Stockholm: Arbetslivsinstitutet.

Emmenegger, Patrick. 2014. *The Power to Dismiss: Trade Unions and the Regulation of Job Security in Western Europe*. Oxford, UK: Oxford University Press.

Emmenegger, Patrick. 2015. "The Politics of Job Security Regulations in Western Europe: From Drift to Layering." *Politics and Society* 43(1): 89–118. doi: 10.1177/0032329214555099.

Estevez-Abe, Margarita, Torben Iversen and David Soskice. 2001 "Social Protection and the Formation of Skills: A Reinterpretation of the Welfare State." Pp. 145–83 in *Varieties of Capitalism: The Institutional Foundations of Comparative Advantage*, edited by P. Hall and D. Soskice. New York and Oxford, UK: Oxford University Press.

Faustini, Gino. 1986. "Il dibattito sul costo del lavoro." In *Le relazioni sindacali in Italia. Rapporto 1984–85*, edited by CESOS. Rome: Edizioni Lavoro.

Ferner, Anthony and Richard Hyman. 1992. *Industrial Relations in the New Europe*. Oxford, UK and Cambridge, MA: Blackwell Business.

Fernie, Sue and David Metcalf. 2005. *Trade Unions: Resurgence or Demise?* New York: Routledge.

Ferri, Piero. 1982. "Il patto anti-inflazione." Pp. 303–24 in *Le relazioni industriali in Italia. Rapporto 1981*, edited by CESOS. Rome: CESOS.

Ferri, Piero. 1984. "L'accordo del 22 Gennaio: Implicazioni e aspetti economici." Pp. 367–84 in *Le relazioni sindacali in Italia. Rapporto 1982–83*, edited by CESOS. Rome: Edizioni Lavoro.

Flanagan, Robert J., David W. Soskice and Lloyd Ulman. 1983. *Unionism, Economic Stabilization, and Incomes Policies: European Experience*. Washington, DC: Brookings Institution.

Flanders, Allan D. 1974. "The Tradition of Voluntarism." *British Journal of Industrial Relations* 12(3): 352–70.

Flassbeck, Heiner and Costas Lapavitsas. 2015. *Against the Troika: Crisis and Austerity in the Eurozone*. London: Verso.

Foucault, Michel. 2004. *Naissance de la biopolitique*, Seuil: Paris.

Freeman, Richard B. and James L. Medoff. 1984. *What Do Unions Do?* New York: Basic Books.

Frege, Carola M. and John E. Kelly. 2004. *Varieties of Unionism: Strategies for Union Revitalization in a Globalizing Economy*. Oxford and New York: Oxford University Press.

French, Steve. 2000. "The Impact of Unification on German Industrial Relations." *German Politics* 9(2): 195–216.

Freyssinet, Jacques. 2010. *Négocier l'emploi: 50 ans de négociation interprofessionnelles sur l'emploi et la formation*. Paris, France: Éditions Liaisons. Wolters Kluwer France.

Gallie, Duncan. 1985. "Les lois Auroux: The Reform of French Industrial Relations?" in *Economic Policy and Policy-Making under the Mitterrand Presidency*, edited by H. Machin and V. Wright. London, UK: Frances Pinter.

Gamble, Andrew. 1988. *The Free Economy and the Strong State: The Politics of Thatcherism*. Durham: Duke University Press.

Garibaldi, Pietro, Lia Pacelli and Andrea Borgarello. 2004. "Employment Protection Legislation and the Size of Firms." *Giornale degli Economisti e Annali di Economia* 33(1): 33–68.

Garilli, Alessandro. 2012. "L'art. 8 della legge N. 148/2011 nel sistema delle relazioni sindacali." Working Paper C.S.D.L.E. "Massimo D'Antona" – 139.

Garrett, Geoffrey. 1998. *Partisan Politics in the Global Economy*. New York: Cambridge University Press.

Geishecker, Ingo. 2002. *Outsourcing and the Demand for Low-Skill Labour in German Manufacturing: New Evidence*. DIW-Diskussionspapiere.

Ginsborg, Paul. 1990. *A History of Contemporary Italy*. London, UK: Penguin Books.

Glyn, Andrew. 2006. *Capitalism Unleashed: Finance, Globalization, and Welfare*. Oxford, UK: Oxford University Press.

Golden, M., M. Wallerstein and P. Lange. 1999. "Postwar Trade-Union Organization and Industrial Relations in Twelve Countries." 194–230 in *Continuity and Change in Contemporary Capitalism*, edited by H. Kitschelt, P. Lange, G. Marks and J. D. Stephens. Cambridge, UK and New York: Cambridge University Press.

Golden, Miriam. 1988. *Labor Divided: Austerity and Working-Class Politics in Contemporary Italy*. Ithaca, NY: Cornell University Press.

Golden, Miriam A. 1997. *Heroic Defeats: The Politics of Job Loss*. Cambridge, UK: Cambridge University Press.

Goldthorpe, John H. 1974. "Industrial Relations in Great Britain: A Critique of Reformism." *Politics and Society* 4: 419–52.

Goldthorpe, John H. 1984. "The End of Convergence: Corporatist and Dualist Tendencies in Modern Western Societies." Pp. 315–43 in *Order and Conflict in Contemporary Capitalism*, edited by J.H. Goldthorpe. Oxford, UK: Clarendon Press.

Gospel, Howard F. and Stephen Wood. 2003. *Representing Workers: Trade Union Recognition and Membership in Britain*. London, UK and New York: Routledge.

Gourevitch, Peter, Andrew Martin, George Ross, Christopher Allen, Stephen Bornstein and Andrei Markovits. 1984. *Unions and Economic Crisis: Britain, West Germany, and Sweden*. London, UK and Boston: Allen & Unwin.

Granqvist, Lena and Håkan Regnér. 2008. "Decentralized Wage Formation in Sweden." *British Journal of Industrial Relations* 46(3): 500–520.

Greer, I. 2008. "Organised Industrial Relations in the Information Economy: The German Automotive Sector as a Test Case." *New Technology, Work and Employment* 23(3): 181–96.

Grimshaw, Damian and Jill Rubery. 2012. "The End of the UK's Liberal Collectivist Social Model? The Implications of the Coalition Government's Policyduring the Austerity Crisis." *Cambridge Journal of Economics* 36(1): 105–26. doi: 10.1093/cje/ber033.

Gumbrell-McCormick, Rebecca and Richard Hyman. 2013. *Trade Unions in Western Europe: Hard Times, Hard Choices*. Oxford, UK: Oxford University Press.

Habermas, Juergen. 1975. *Legitimation Crisis*. Boston: Beacon Press.

Hacker, Jacob S. and Paul Pierson. 2002. "Business Power and Social Policy: Employers and the Formation of the American Welfare State." *Politics and Society* 30(2): 277–325. doi: 10.1177/0032329202030002004.

Hacker, Jacob S. and Paul Pierson. 2004. "Varieties of Capitalist Interests and Capitalist Power: A Response to Swenson." *Studies in American Political Development* 18(2): 186–95. doi: doi:10.1017/S0898588X04000100.

Haipeter, Thomas. 2009. "Kontrollierte Dezentralisierung? Abweichende Tarifvereinbarungen in Der Metall-Und Elektroindustrie." *Industrielle Beziehungen/The German Journal of Industrial Relations* 16(3): 232–53.

Hall, Mark. 2004. "Government Revises Draft Information and Consultation Regulations." EIROnline: 1–3.

Hall, Mark. 2012. "Government Announces Employment Law Reforms." EIROnline: 1–2.

Hall, Peter A. 1986. *Governing the Economy: The Politics of State Intervention in Britain and France*. Cambridge, UK and Oxford, UK: Polity Press, in association with Blackwell.

Hall, Peter A. 2007. "The Evolution of Varieties of Capitalism." Pp. 39–87 in *Beyond Varieties of Capitalism: Conflict, Contradiction, and Complementaritiesin the European Economy*, edited by B. Hancké, M. Rhodes and M. Thatcher. Oxford, UK and New York: Oxford University Press.

Hall, Peter A. and David Soskice. 2001a. "An Introduction to Varieties of Capitalism." Pp. 1–68 in Varieties of Capitalism. *The Institutional Foundations of Comparative Advantage*, edited by P.A. Hall and D. Soskice. Oxford, UK: Oxford University Press.

Hall, Peter A. and David W. Soskice, eds. 2001b. *Varieties of Capitalism: The Institutional Foundations of Comparative Advantage*. New York: Oxford University Press.

Hall, Peter A. and Rosemary C.R. Taylor. 1996. "Political Science and the Three New Institutionalisms." *Political Studies* 44(5): 936–57.

Hall, Peter A. and Kathleen Thelen. 2009. "Institutional Change in Varieties of Capitalism." *Socio-Economic Review* 7(1): 7–34. doi: 10.1093/ser/mwn020.

Hartwig, Jochen. 2014. "Testing the Bhaduri–Marglin Model with OECD Panel Data." *International Review of Applied Economics* 28(4): 419–35.

Harvey, David. 1989. *The Condition of Postmodernity: An Enquiry into the Origins of Cultural Change*. Oxford, UK and Cambridge, MA: Blackwell.

Harvey, David. 2005. *A Brief History of Neoliberalism*. New York: Oxford University Press.

Hassel, Anke. 1999. "The Erosion of the German System of Industrial Relations." *British Journal of Industrial Relations* 37(3): 483–505.

Hassel, Anke. 2001. "The Problem of Political Exchange in Complex Governance Systems: The Case of Germany's Alliance for Jobs." *European Journal of Industrial Relations* 7(3): 307–26.

Hassel, Anke. 2014. "The Paradox of Liberalization – Understanding Dualism and the Recovery of the German Political Economy." *British Journal of Industrial Relations* 52(1): 57–81.

Hassel, Anke and Britta Rehder. 2001. "Institutional Change in the German Wage Bargaining System: The Role of Big Companies." MPIfG working paper.

Hassel, Anke and Christof Schiller. 2010. *Der Fall Hartz IV: Wie Es zur Agenda 2010 Kam und Wie Es Weitergeht*. Frankfurt and New York: Campus Verlag.

Hassel, Anke and Thorsten Schulten. 1998. "Globalization and the Future of Central Collective Bargaining: The Example of the German Metal Industry." *Economy and Society* 27 (4): 486–522.

Hay, Colin. 1996. "Narrating Crisis: The Discursive Construction of the 'Winter of Discontent.'" *Sociology* 30(2): 253–77.

Hayden, Anders. 2006. "France's 35-Hour Week: Attack on Business? Win–Win Reform? Or Betrayal of Disadvantaged Workers?". *Politics and Society* 34(4):503–42.

Hayek, Friedrich von. 1939. "The Economic Conditions of Interstate Federalism." *New Commonwealth Quarterly* 5(2): 131–49.

Heery, Edmund. 2002. "Partnership versus Organising: Alternative Futures for British Trade Unionism." *Industrial Relations Journal* 33(1): 20–35.

Hein, Eckhard and Matthias Mundt. 2012. "Financialisation and the Requirements and Potentials for Wage-Led Recovery – A Review Focusing on the G20." ILO Conditions of Work and Employment Series No. 37.

Henriksson, Johannes and Mats Kullander. 2011. "Sweden: EIRO Annual Review 2009." EIROnline: 1–6.

Herrigel, Gary. 1997. "The Limits of German Manufacturing Flexibility." Pp. 177–205 in *Negotiating the New Germany. Can Social Partnership Survive*, edited by L. Turner. Ithaca, NY and London, UK: Cornell University Press.

Heyes, Jason and Paul Lewis. 2014. "Employment Protection under Fire: Labour Market Deregulation and Employment in the European Union." *Economic and Industrial Democracy* 35(4): 587–607.

Hinrichs, Karl and Helmut Wiesenthal. 1986. "Bestandsrationalität versus Kollektivinteresse: Gewerkschaftliche Handlungsprobleme im Arbeitszeitkonflikt 1984." *Soziale Welt*: 280–96.

Holst, Hajo, Oliver Nachtwey and Klaus Dörre. 2010. "The Strategic Use of Temporary Agency Work – Functional Change of a Non-standard Form of Employment." *International Journal of Action Research* 6(1): 108–38.

Höpner, Martin. 2001. "Corporate Governance in Transition: Ten Empirical Findings on Shareholder Value and Industrial Relations in Germany." *Discussion Paper 01/5*, Max-Planck-Institut für Gesellschaftsforschung, Cologne.

Höpner, Martin, Alexander Petring, Daniel Seikel and Benjamin Werner. 2014. "Liberalization Policy: An Empirical Analysis of Economic and Social Interventions in Western Democracies." *WSI Discussion Paper*. Dusseldorf, Germany: Hans Böckler Stiftung.

Howell, Chris. 1992. *Regulating Labor: The State and Industrial Relations Reform in Postwar France*. Princeton, NJ: Princeton University Press.

Howell, Chris. 1998. "Virtual Trade Unionism in France: A Commentary on the Question of Unions, Public Opinion, and the State." Pp. 205–12 in *A Century of Organized Labor in France: A Union Movement for the Twenty-First Century?* edited by H. Chapman, M. Kesselman and M. Schain. New York: St. Martin's Press.

Howell, Chris. 2004. "Is There a Third Way for Industrial Relations?" *British Journal of Industrial Relations* 42(1): 1–22.

Howell, Chris. 2005. *Trade Unions and the State: The Construction of Industrial Relations Institutions in Britain, 1890–2000*. Princeton, NJ: Princeton University Press.

Howell, Chris. 2009. "The Transformation of French Industrial Relations: Labor Representation and the State in a Post-dirigiste Era." *Politics and Society* 37(2): 229–56.

Howell, Chris. 2015. "Review Symposium: On Kathleen Thelen, Varieties of Liberalization and the New Politics of Social Solidarity." *Socio-Economic Review* 13(2): 399–409.

Hyman, Richard. 1989. *The Political Economy of Industrial Relations: Theory and Practice in a Cold Climate*. Basingstoke, UK: Macmillan.

Hyman, Richard. 2001. *Understanding European Trade Unionism: Between Market, Class and Society*. London: SAGE.

Ibsen, Christian Lyhne, Søren Kaj Andersen, Jesper Due and Jørgen Steen Madsen. 2011. "Bargaining in the Crisis – A Comparison of the 2010 Collective Bargaining Round in the Danish and Swedish Manufacturing Sectors." *Transfer: European Review of Labour and Research* 17(3): 323–39.

Ibsen, Christian Lyhne. 2012. "The 'Real' End of Solidarity?" Paper presented at the Society for the Advancement of Socio-Economics, June 28–30, 2012, Boston.

Ibsen, Christian Lyhne. 2015. "Three Approaches to Coordinated Bargaining: A Case for Power-Based Explanations." *European Journal of Industrial Relations* 21(1): 39–56.

Ichino, Pietro. 1996. *Il lavoro e il mercato. Per un diritto del lavoro maggiorenne*. Milan: Mondadori.

Ichino, Pietro. 2011. *Inchiesta sul lavoro*. Milan: Mondadori.

ICTWSS. 2011, "Database on Institutional Characteristics of Trade Unions, Wage Setting, State Intervention and Social Pacts in 34 Countries between1960 and 2007." Retrieved May 26, 2013, http://www.uva-aias.net/208.

ILO. 2008. *World of Work Report*. Geneva: ILO.

ILO. 2015. *Global Wage Report 2014/15*. Geneva: ILO.

ILO. Various years. "Laborsta." in http://laborsta.ilo.org/ (free access).

IRES. 2005. *Les mutations de l'emploi en france*. Paris, France: La Découverte.

ISTAT. 2001. *Rapporto annuale 2001*. Rome: ISTAT.

ISTAT. 2002. *La flessibilità del mercato del lavoro nel periodo 1995–96*. Rome: ISTAT.

Iversen, Torben. 1996. "Power, Flexibility, and the Breakdown of Centralized Bargaining: Denmark and Sweden in Comparative Perspective." *Comparative Politics* 28(3): 399–436.

Iversen, Torben, Jonas Pontusson and David Soskice, eds. 2000. *Unions, Employers, and Central Banks: Macroeconomic Coordination and Institutional Change in Social Market Economies*. Cambridge, UK: Cambridge University Press.

Iversen, Torben and David Soskice. 2001. "An Asset Theory of Social Policy Preferences." *American Political Science Review* 95(4): 875–93.

Iversen, Torben and David Soskice. 2012. "Modern Capitalism and the Advanced
Nation State: Understanding the Causes of the Crisis." In *Coping with Crisis: Gov-
ernment Responses to the Great Recession*, edited by N. Bermeo and J. Pontusson.
New York: Russell Sage.

Iversen, Torben and Anne Wren. 1998. "Equality, Employment, and Budgetary
Restraint, the Trilemma of the Service Economy." *World Politics* (50): 507–46.

Jacobi, Lena and Jochen Kluve. 2006. "Before and after the Hartz Reforms: The Performance of Active Labour Market Policy in Germany."

Jacobsson, Göran. 2012a. "Medlingsinstitutet Krockar Med Facket." In *Arbetet*. Stockholm, Sweden.

Jacobsson, Göran. 2012b. "Här Ökar Medlemstalen." In *Arbetet*. Stockholm, Sweden.

Jacoby, Wade. 2000. *Imitation and Politics: Redesigning Modern Germany*. Ithaca, NY:
Cornell University Press.

Jacod, Olivier and Rim Ben Dhaou. 2008. "Les élections aux comités d'entreprise de
1989 à 2004: Une étude de l'évolution des implantations et des audiences syndicales." *Document d'Études*. Paris, France: Ministére du Travail, des Relations
Sociales et de la Santé.

Jefferys, Steve. 2003. *Liberté, Égalité, and Fraternité at Work: Changing French Employment Relations and Management*. Houndmills, Basingstoke, Hampshire and New
York: Palgrave Macmillan.

Jefferys, Steve. 2011. "How Dark Are the Clouds over Sweden?" Pp. 287–98 in *Precarious Employment in Perspective: Old and New Challenges to Working Conditions
in Sweden*, edited by A. Thörnqvist and Å.-K. Engstrand. Brussels: Peter Lang.

Jenkins, Alan. 2000. *Employment Relations in France: Evolution and Innovation*. New
York and London, UK: Kluwer Academic/Plenum Publishers.

Jessop, Bob. 1990a. "Regulation Theories in Retrospect and Prospect." *Economy and
Society* 19(2): 153–216.

Jessop, Bob. 1990b. *State Theory: Putting Capitalist States in Their Place*. Cambridge,
UK: Polity Press.

Jessop, Bob. 2002. *The Future of the Capitalist State*. Cambridge, UK and Malden, MA:
Polity; distributed in the USA by Blackwell.

Jobert, Annette and Jean Saglio. 2005. *La mise en oeuvre des dispositions de la loi du 4
mai 2004 permettant aux entreprises de déroger aux accords de branche*. Congress.

Johansson, Joakim. 2005. "Undermining Corporatism." in *Power and Institutions in
Industrial Relations Regime*, edited by P. Öberg and T. Svensson. Stockholm, Sweden: Arbetslivsinstitutet.

Jürgens, U. 2004. "An Elusive Model – Diversified Quality Production and the Transformation of the German Automobile Industry." *Competition and Change* 8(4):411–
23.

Jürgens, U., T. Malsch and K. Dohse. 1993. *Breaking from Taylorism: Changing Forms
of Work in the Automobile Industry*. New York: Cambridge University Press.

Jürgens, U. and M. Krzywdzinski. 2006. "Globalisierungsdruck und
Beschäftigungssicherung – Standortsicherungsvereinbarungen in der Deutschen
Automobilindustrie zwischen 1993 und 2006." *WZB Discussion Papers SP III*.

Jürgens, Ulrich. 1997. "Germany: Implementing Lean Production." In *After Lean Production: Evolving Employment Practices in the World Auto Industry*, Vols. 117–36,

edited by T. A. Kochan, R. D. Lansbury and J. P. MacDuffie. Ithaca, NY: Cornell University Press.

Kalecki, Michal. 1943. "Political Aspects of Full Employment." *Political Quarterly* 14(4): 322–31.

Kalecki, Michal. 1944. "Three Ways to Full Employment." Pp. 39–58 in *The Economics of Full Employment*, edited by Oxford University Institute of Statistics. Oxford: Blackwell.

Karabarbounis, Loukas and Brent Neiman. 2014. "The Global Decline of the Labor Share." *Quarterly Journal of Economics* 129(1): 61–103.

Karlson, Nils and Henrik Lindberg. 2010. "The Decentralization of Wage Bargaining: A Comparative Case Study." Paper presented at the European Congress of the International Industrial Relations Association, June 2010, Copenhagen, Denmark.

Katz, Harry Charles. 1993. "The Decentralization of Collective Bargaining: A Literature Review and Comparative Analysis." *Industrial and Labor Relations Review* 47(October):3–22.

Katz, Harry Charles and Owen Darbishire. 2000. *Converging Divergences: Worldwide Changes in Employment Systems*. Ithaca, NY: Cornell University Press.

Katzenstein, Peter J., ed. 1978. *Between Power and Plenty: Foreign Economic Policies of Advanced Industrial States*. Madison, WI: University of Wisconsin Press.

Kelly, John E. 1998. *Rethinking Industrial Relations: Mobilization, Collectivism, and Long Waves*. London and New York: Routledge.

Kelly, John E. and Paul Willman. 2004. *Union Organization and Activity*. London and New York: Routledge.

Kenworthy, Lane. 2000. "Quantitative Indicators of Corporatism: A Survey and Assessment." Discussion Paper 00/4. *Max-Planck Institut für Gesellschaftsforschung*.

Kersley, Barbara, Carmen Alpin, John Forth, Alex Bryson, Helen Bewley, Gill Dix and Sarah Oxenbridge. 2005. "Inside the Workplace: First Findings from the 2004 Workplace Employment Relations Survey (Wers 2004)." London, UK: Department of Trade and Industry.

Kessler, Sidney and F. J. Bayliss. 1998. *Contemporary British Industrial Relations*. Basingstoke, Hampshire: Macmillan Business.

Keynes, John Maynard. 2007 [1936]. *The General Theory of Employment, Interest, and Money*. London: Palgrave.

Kinderman, D. 2005. "Pressure from Without, Subversion from Within: The Two-Pronged German Employer Offensive." *Comparative European Politics* 3(4): 432–63.

Kinderman, Daniel. 2014. "Challenging Varieties of Capitalism's Account of Business Interests: The New Social Market Initiative and German Employers' Quest for Liberalization, 2000–2014." Unpublished manuscript, University of Delaware.

Kinkel, Steffen and Gunter Lay. 2003. "Fertigungstiefe–Ballast oder Kapital? Stand und Effekte von Out- und Insourcing im Verarbeitenden Gewerbe Deutschlands." *Mitteilungen aus der Produktionsinnovationserhebung 30(August 2003)*. Karlsruhe: Fraunhofer-Institut für Systemtechnik und Innovationsforschung [ISI].

Kjellberg, Anders. 2009. "The Swedish Model of Industrial Relations: Self-Regulation and Combined Centralization–Decentralization." Pp. 155–98 in *Trade Unionism since 1945: Towards a Global History*, edited by C. Phelan. Oxford: Peter Lang.

Kjellberg, Anders. 2011a. "Trade Unions and Collective Agreements in a Changing World." Pp. 47–100 in *Precarious Employment in Perspective: Old and New*

Challenges to Working Conditions in Sweden, edited by A. Thörnqvist and Å.-K. Engstrand. Brussels: Peter Lang.

Kjellberg, Anders. 2011b. "The Decline in Swedish Union Density since 2007." *Nordic Journal of Working Life Studies* 1(1): 67–93.

Kjellberg, Anders. 2012. "Local Wage Setting in Sweden." Unpublished working paper, Lund University, Lund, Sweden.

Kjellberg, Anders. 2015. "Kollektivavtalens Täckningsgrad Samt Organisationgraden Hos Arbetsgivarförbund Och Fackförbund." *Studies in Social Policy, Industrial Relations, Working Life and Mobility Research Reports*. Lund, Sweden: Lund University.

Koo, Richard C. 2011. "The World in Balance Sheet Recession: Causes, Cure, and Politics." *Real-World Economics Review* (58): 19–37.

Korpi, Walter. 1983. *The Democratic Class Struggle*. London, UK and Boston: Routledge & Kegan Paul.

Korpi, Walter. 2006a. "Power Resources and Employer-Centered Approaches in Explanations of Welfare States and Varieties of Capitalism: Protagonists, Consenters and Antagonists." Paper presented at the ESPAnet Conference, Bremen, September 21–23, 2006.

Korpi, Walter. 2006b. "Power Resources and Employer-Centered Approaches in Explanations of Welfare States and Varieties of Capitalism: Protagonists, Consenters, and Antagonists." *World Politics* 58(2): 167–206.

Kotz, David M., Terrence McDonough and Michael Reich. 1994. *Social Structures of Accumulation: The Political Economy of Growth and Crisis*. Cambridge, UK and New York: Cambridge University Press.

Krippner, Greta R. 2005. "The Financialization of the American Economy." *Socio-Economic Review* 3(2): 173–208. doi: 10.1093/SER/mwi008.

Kristal, Tali. 2010. "Good Times, Bad Times: Postwar Labor's Share of National Income in Capitalist Democracies." *American Sociological Review* 75(5): 729–63.

Kullander, Mats and Malin Björklund. 2011. "'Gender Equality Fund' Sparks Tensions among Unions." EIROnline: 1–2.

Kullander, Mats and Oskar Eklund. 2010. "Largest Employer Organisation in Industry Leaves Industrial Agreement." EIROnline: 1–2.

Kullander, Mats and Elinor Häggebrink. 2009. "New Procedure for Collective Bargaining in Services Sector." EIROnline: 1–2.

Kullander, Mats and Linda Talme. 2014. "Trend towards Collective Agreements with No Fixed Pay Increase." EurWORK: 1–3.

Labour Research Department. 1994. "Pay in the Privatized Utilities." LRD Bargaining Report (136).

Labour Research Department. 1999. "Public Sector Workforce." LRD Fact Service 60(2).

Lallement, Michel. 2006. "New Patterns of Industrial Relations and Political Action since the 1980s." Pp. 50–79 in *Changing France: The Politics That Markets Make*, edited by P. D. Culpepper, P. Hall and B. Palier. New York: Palgrave Macmillan.

Lallement, Michel and Olivier Mériaux. 2003. "Status and Contracts in Industrial Relations. 'La Refondation Sociale,' a New Bottle for an Old (French) Wine?" *Industrielle Beziehungen* 10(3): 418–37.

Lama, Luciano. 1978. *Il potere del sindacato*. Rome: Editori Riuniti.

Lange, Peter, George Ross, Maurizio Vannicelli and Harvard University Center for European Studies. 1982. *Unions, Change, and Crisis: French and Italian Union Strategy and the Political Economy, 1945–1980.* London, UK and New York: Allen and Unwin.

Lange, Peter and Maurizio Vannicelli. 1982. "Strategy under Stress: The Italian Union Movement and the Italian Crisis in Developmental Perspective." Pp. 95–206 in *Unions, Change, and Crisis,* edited by P. Lange, G. Ross and M. Vannicelli. Boston: Allen and Unwin.

Lange, Peter, Michael Wallerstein and Miriam Golden. 1995. "The End of Corporatism? Wage Setting in the Nordic and Germanic Countries." Pp. 76–100 in *The Workers of Nations,* edited by S.M. Jacobi. New York: Oxford University Press.

Lapavitsas, Costas. 2011. "Theorizing Financialization." *Work, Employment and Society* 25(4): 611–26.

Lapidus, John. 2015. "An Odd Couple: Individual Wage Setting and the Largest Swedish Trade Union." *Labor History* 56(1): 1–21.

Lash, Scott and John Urry. 1987. *The End of Organized Capitalism.* Madison, WI: University of Wisconsin Press.

Lavoie, Marc. 2009. *Introduction to Post-Keynesian Economics.* London, UK: Palgrave.

Lavoie, Marc and Engelbert Stockhammer. 2012. "Wage-Led Growth: Concept, Theories and Policies." ILO Conditions of Work and Employment Series No. 41.

Lavoie, Marc and Engelbert Stockhammer. 2013. *Wage-Led Growth.* London: Palgrave.

Layard, Richard, Stephen Nickell and Richard Jackman. 2005. *Unemployment: Macroeconomic Performance and the Labour Market.* Oxford, UK and New York: Oxford University Press.

Le Barbanchon, Thomas and Franck Malherbet. 2013. "An Anatomy of the French Labour Market." Employment Working Paper Number 142 Congress: 1–34.

Lehndorff, Steffen. 2001. *Weniger Ist Mehr.* VSA-Verlag.

Levy, Jonah D. 1999. *Tocqueville's Revenge: State, Society, and Economy in Contemporary France.* Cambridge, MA: Harvard University Press.

Levy, Jonah D. 2006. *The State after Statism: New State Activities in the Age of Liberalization.* Cambridge, MA: Harvard University Press.

Liaisons Sociales. 1971. Liaisons Sociales: Législation Sociale (3785).

Lindbeck, Assar and David Snower. 1986. "Wage Setting, Unemployment, and Insider–Outsider Relations." *American Economic Review* 76(2): 235–39.

Lindberg, Henrik. 2011. "Industrial Action in Sweden: A New Pattern?" *Ratio Working Paper.* Stockholm, Sweden: Ratio Institute.

Locke, Richard M. 1992. "The Decline of the National Union in Italy: Lessons for Comparative Industrial Relations." *Industrial and Labor Relations Review* 45(January): 229–49.

Locke, Richard M. 1995. *Remaking the Italian Economy.* Ithaca, NY: Cornell University Press.

Locke, Richard M., Thomas Kochan and Michael Piore, eds. 1995. *Employment Relations in a Changing World Economy.* Cambridge, MA: MIT Press.

Locke, Richard M. and Kathleen Ann Thelen. 1995. "Apples and Oranges Revisited: Contextualized Comparisons and the Study of Comparative Labor Politics." *Politics and Society* 23(3): 337–68.

Ludwig, Udo and Hans-Ulrich Brautzsch. 2008. "Has the International Fragmentation
of German Exports Passed Its Peak?". *Intereconomics* 43(3): 176–80.

Lyon-Caen, Gérard. 1980. "Critique de la négociation collective." *Après-Demain* (221).

Machin, Stephen. 2000. "Union Decline in Britain." *British Journal of Industrial Relations* 38(4): 631–45.

Mahon, Rianne. 1999. "'Yesterday's Modern Times Are No Longer Modern': Swedish
Unions Confront the Double Shift." Pp. 75–124 in *The Brave New World of Euro-
pean Labor: European Trade Unions at the Millennium,* edited by A. Martin and
G. Ross. New York: Berghahn Books.

Malmberg, Jonas and Niklas Bruun. 2006. "Ten Years within the EU: Labour Law in
Sweden and Finland Following EU Accession." Pp. 59–96 in *Swedish Studies in
European Law,* Vol. 1, edited by N. Wahl and P. Cramér. Oxford, UK: Hart.

Marginson, Paul. 2015. "Coordinated Bargaining in Europe: From Incremental Cor-
rosion to Frontal Assault?" *European Journal of Industrial Relations* 21(2): 97–
114.

Marginson, Paul and Christian Welz. 2014. *Changes to Wage-Setting Mechanisms in
the Context of the Crisis and the Eu's New Economic Governance Regime.* Dublin:
Eurofound.

Marsh, David. 1992. *The New Politics of British Trade Unionism: Union Power and the
Thatcher Legacy.* Ithaca, NY: ILR Press.

Martin, Andrew and George Ross. 1999. *The Brave New World of European Labor:
European Trade Unions at the Millennium.* New York: Berghahn Books.

Martin, Andrew and George Ross, eds. 2004. *Euros and Europeans: Monetary Integration and the European Model of Society.* New York: Cambridge University Press.

Martin, Cathie Jo and Duane Swank. 2008. "The Political Origins of Coordinated Capitalism: Business Organizations, Party Systems, and State Structure in the Age of
Innocence." *American Political Science Review* 102(2): 181–98.

Martin, Nuria Ramos. 2011. "Sector-Level Bargaining and Possbilities for Deviations
at Company Level: France." Dublin: Eurofound.

Marx, Karl. 1970[1859]. *A Contribution to the Critique of Political Economy.* New
York: International Publishers.

Marx, Karl and Friedrich Engels. 2002. *The Communist Manifesto.* London, UK and
New York: Penguin Books.

Mascini, M. 2000. *Profitti e salari.* Bologna: Il Mulino.

McCarthy, W. E. J. 1992. "Legal Intervention in Industrial Relations: Gains and Losses."
In *Legal Intervention in Industrial Relations: Gains and Losses,* edited by W. E. J.
McCarthy. Oxford, UK and Cambridge, MA: Blackwell.

Melander, Ingrid. 2015. "France Unveils 'Jobs Act' to Boost Hiring at Small Firms."
Reuters, June 9.

Menz, Georg. 2005. "Old Bottles – New Wine: The New Dynamics of Industrial Relations." *German Politics* 14(2): 196–207.

Mériaux, Olivier. 2000. "Éléments d'un régime post-Fordiste de la négociation collective
en France." *Relations Industrielles/Industrial Relations* 55(4): 606–37.

Mery, Bernard. 1973. "La pratique de l'indexation dans les conventions collectives."
Droit Social (6).

Mian, Atif and Amir Sufi. 2011. "House Prices, Home Equity-Based Borrowing, and the
US Household Leverage Crisis." *American Economic Review* 101(5): 2132–56.

Militello, Giacinto. 1984. "Tutto cominciò quando ...." *Rassegna sindacale* 8(Feb. 24).

Millward, Neil, Mark Stevens, David Smart and W. R. Hawes. 1992. *Workplace Industrial Relations in Transition: The ED/ESRC/PSI/ACAS Surveys*. Aldershot: Dartmouth.

Millward, Neil, Alex Bryson and John Forth. 2000. *All Change at Work? British Employment Relations 1980–1998*, Portrayed by the Workplace Industrial Relations Survey Series. New York: Routledge.

Milner, Simon. 1995. "The Coverage of Collective Pay-Setting Institutions in Britain, 1895–1990." *British Journal of Industrial Relations* 33(1): 69–91.

Ministère de l'Emploi, du Travail et de la Cohésion Sociale. 2004. La négociation collective en 2003: La tendance, les dosssiers, les chiffres. Congress: 1–580 (http://www.travail-solidarite.gouv.fr/IMG/pdf/NC_2003.pdf).

Ministère de l'Emploi, du Travail et de la Cohésion Sociale. 2006. La négociation collective en 2005. Congress: 1–52 (http://www.travail-solidarite.gouv.fr/IMG/pdf/NC2005_P2_-_La_Nego.pdf).

Ministère du Travail, de l'Emploi et de la Santé. 2011. La négociation collective en 2010. Congress.

Ministère du Travail, de L'Emploi, de la Formation Professionelle, et du Dialogue Social. 2013. Rapport sur l'application des dispositions de la loi N. 2008–789 du 20 août 2008 relative a la démocratie sociale et de la loi N. 2010–1215 du octobre 2010 les complétant. Congress: 1–151.

Mishel, Lawrence, Elise Gould and Josh Bivens. 2015. "Wage Stagnation in Nine Charts." *Briefing Paper*, Economic Policy Institute.

Mitchell, Neil J. 1987. "Changing Pressure-Group Politics: The Case of the Trades Union Congress, 1976–84." *British Journal of Political Science* 17(4): 509–17.

Modigliani, Franco, Mario Baldassari and Fabio Castiglionesi. 1996. *Il miracolo possibile*. Bari: Laterza.

Moreau, Marie-Ange. 2004. "National Report: France." *The Evolving Structure of Collective Bargaining in Europe 1990–2004*. European Commission and University of Florence.

Murhem, Sofia. 2003. "Turning to Europe: A New Swedish Industrial Relations Regime in the 1990s." *Uppsala Studies in Economic History* (68): 1–53.

Murhem, Sofia. 2013. "Security and Change: The Swedish Model and Employment Protection 1995–2010." *Economic and Industrial Democracy* 34(4): 621–36.

Naboulet, Antoine. 2011a. "Que recouvre la négociation collective d'entreprise en France? Un panorama des acteurs, des textes et des thématiques entre 2005 et 2008." *Document d'études*. Paris: Ministère du Travail, de l'Emploi et de la Santé.

Naboulet, Antoine. 2011b. "Les obligations et incitations portant sur la négociation collective." *La note d'analyse*. Paris: Centre d'Analyse Stratégique.

Napoleoni, Claudio. 1982. "Per una politica programmata di rientro dall'inflazione." In *Inflazione, scala mobile e politica economica. Atti del convegno IRES-CGIL*, edited by IRES-CGIL. Rome: ESI.

National Mediation Office. 2011. The Swedish National Mediation Office Annual Report 2010. Congress: 1–8 (http://www.mi.se/files/PDF-er/ar_foreign/eng_smftn_feb2011.pdf).

National Mediation Office. 2014. Avtalsrörelsen och Lönebildningen År 2013. Congress: 1–312.

National Mediation Office. 2016. Summary of the Annual Report for 2015. Congress: 1–3.

Negrelli, Serafino. 1991. *La società dentro l'impresa. L'evoluzione dal modello norma-tivo al modello partecipativo nelle relazioni industriali delle imprese italiane.* Milan: Franco Angeli.

Neilson, David. 2012. "Remaking the Connections: Marxism and the French Regulation School." *Review of Radical Political Economics* 44(2): 160–77.

Nickell, Stephen. 1997. "Unemployment and Labor Market Rigidities: Europe vs North America." *Journal of Economic Perspectives* 11(3): 55–74.

Nickell, Stephen, Nunziata Luca and Ochel Wolfgang. 2005. "Unemployment in the OECD since the 1960s. What Do We Know?" *Economic Journal* 115(500): 1–27.

Niedenhoff, Horst-Udo. 1981. *Die Betriebsraäte von 1981 bis 1984: Eine Analyse der Betriebsratswahlen.* Institutsverlag. Cologne: Institutsverlag.

Noblecourt, Michel. 2012. "Les novations de la 'Grande conférence sociale.'" *Le Monde,* June 6.

Nuti, Mario. 2004. "Kalecki and Keynes Revisited." Pp. 3–9 in *Kalecki's Economics Today,* edited by Zdzislaw L. Sadowski and A. Szeworski. London: Routledge.

Nyström, Birgitta. 2004. "Nation Report: Sweden." *The Evolving Structure of Collective Bargaining in Europe 1990–2004.* European Commission and University of Florence.

Öberg, Tommy. 2013. "Dags Att Göra Avtal Till Lag?" *Arbetet,* October 18.

Öberg, Tommy. 2014. "Akademiker Säger Sifferlösa Avtal." *Arbetet,* March 14.

OECD. 1994. *The OECD Jobs Study. Facts, Analysis, Strategies.* Paris: OECD.

OECD. 2008. *Growing Unequal? Income Distribution and Poverty in OECD Countries.* Paris: OECD.

OECD. 2011. "Divided We Stand: Why Inequality Keeps Rising." Paris: OECD.

OECD. various years. "OECD.Stat (Annual Labour Force Statistics)." http://stats.oecd .org/Index.aspx.

Offe, Claus. 1985. *Disorganized Capitalism: Contemporary Transformations of Work and Politics.* Cambridge, MA: MIT Press.

Oliver, Rebecca. 2008. "Diverging Developments in Wage Inequality: Which Institutions Matter?" *Comparative Political Studies* 41(12): 1551–82.

Oliver, Rebecca J. 2011. "Powerful Remnants? The Politics of Egalitarian Bargaining Institutions in Italy and Sweden." *Socio-Economic Review* 9(3): 533–66.

Onaran, Ozlem and Thomas Obst. 2015. "Wage-Led Growth in the EU15 Member States: The Effects of Income Distribution on Growth, Investment, Trade Balance, and Inflation." Greenwich Papers in Political Economy, University of Greenwich, #GPERC28.

Onaran, Özlem and Giorgos Galanis. 2014. "Income Distribution and Growth: A Global Model." *Environment and Planning* A 46(10): 2489–513.

Osterman, P. 1994. "Internal Labor Markets: Theory and Change." Pp. 303–39 in *Labor Economics and Industrial Relations: Markets and Institutions,* edited by C. Kerr and P. D. Staudohar. Cambridge, MA and London, UK: Harvard University Press.

Ouest France. 2015, "Dialogue social. Vers une instance unique de répresentation du personnel?" http://www.ouest-france.fr/dialogue-social-vers-une-instance-unique-de-representation-du-personnel-3116554.

Palier, Bruno and Kathleen Thelen. 2010. "Institutionalizing Dualism: Complementarities and Change in France and Germany." *Politics and Society* 38(1): 119–48.

Paster, Thomas. 2012. *The Role of Business in the Development of the Welfare State and Labor Markets in Germany: Containing Social Reforms.* London and New York: Routledge.

Patriarca, Stefano. 1986. *La nuova scala mobile.* Rome: Ediesse.

Pernot, Jean-Marie. 2005. *Syndicats: Lendemains de crise?* Paris: Éditions Gallimard.

Pernot, Jean-Marie and Maria Theresa Pignoni. 2008. "Les salariés et les organisations syndicales de 1992 à 2004: Une longue saison de désamour." Pp. 140–62 in *Les relations sociales en entreprise: Un portrait à partir des enquêtes relations professionnelles et négociations d'entreprise*, edited by T. Amossé, C. Bloch-London and L. Wolff. Paris: Éditions la Découverte.

Peters, John. 2011. "The Rise of Finance and the Decline of Organised Labour in the Advanced Capitalist Countries." *New Political Economy* 16(1): 73–99.

Pierson, Paul. 2004. *Politics in Time: History, Institutions, and Social Analysis.* Princeton, NJ: Princeton University Press.

Pignoni, Maria Theresa and Élise Tenret. 2007. "Présence syndicale." *Première Synthèses Informations* (14.2): 1–8.

Pignoni, Maria Theresa and Émilie Raynaud. 2013. "Les relations professionnelles au début des années 2010." *Dares analyses* (026): 1–16.

Piketty, Thomas. 2013. *Le capital au Xxie siècle.* Paris: Seuil.

Piore, Michael and Charles Sabel. 1984. *The Second Industrial Divide: Possibilities for Prosperity.* New York: Basic Books.

Piore, Michael and Sean Safford. 2006. "Changing Regimes of Workplace Governance, Shifting Axes of Social Mobilization, and the Challenge to Industrial Relations Theory." *Industrial Relations* 45(3): 299–325.

Pizzorno, Alessandro, Ida Regalia, Marino Regini and Emilio Reyneri. 1978. *Lotte operaie e sindacato in Italia: 1968–1972.* Bologna: Il Mulino.

Polanyi, Karl. 1944. *The Great Transformation.* New York, Toronto,: Farrar & Rinehart.

Pontusson, Jonas. 1992. *The Limits of Social Democracy: Investment Politics in Sweden.* Ithaca, NY: Cornell University Press.

Pontusson, Jonas. 2005. "Varieties and Commonalities of Capitalism." Pp. 163–88 in *Varieties of Capitalism, Varieties of Approaches*, edited by D. Coates. New York: Palgrave Macmillan.

Pontusson, Jonas. 2011. "Once Again a Model: Nordic Social Democracy in a Globalized World." Pp. 89–115 in *What's Left of the Left: Democrats and Social Democrats in Challenging Times*, edited by J. Cronin, G. Ross and J. Shoch. Durham, NC: Duke University Press.

Pontusson, Jonas. 2013. "Unionization, Inequality and Redistribution." *British Journal of Industrial Relations* 51(4): 797–825.

Pontusson, Jonas and Peter Swenson. 1996. "Labor Markets, Production Strategies, and Wage Bargaining Institutions: The Swedish Employer Offensive in Comparative Perspective." *Comparative Political Studies* 29(2): 223–50.

Przeworski, Adam and Michael Wallerstein. 1982. "The Structure of Class Conflict in Democratic Societies." *American Political Science Review* 76: 215–38.

Purcell, John. 1993. "The End of Institutional Industrial Relations?". *Political Quarterly* 64(1): 6–23.

Raess, Damien. 2006. "Globalization and Why the 'Time Is Ripe' for the Transformation of German Industrial Relations." *Review of International Political Economy* 13(3): 449–79.

Regalia, I. and M. Regini. 1998. "Italy: The Dual Character of Industrial Relations." Pp. 459–503 in *Changing Industrial Relations in Europe*, edited by A. Ferner and R. Hyman. Malden, MA: Blackwell Publishers.

Regan, Aidan. 2011. "The Rise and Fall of Irish Social Partnership: Euro-Irish Trade Unionism in Crisis?". Unpublished manuscript, University College Dublin.

Regini, Marino and Charles F. Sabel. 1989. *Strategie di riaggiustamento industriale.* Bologna: Il Mulino.

Rehder, B. 2003. *Betriebliche Bündnisse für Arbeit in Deutschland: Mitbestimmung und Flächentarif im Wandel*, Vol. 48. Frankfurt am Main: Campus Verlag.

Rehfeldt, Udo. 2011. "France: Eiro Annual Review – 2009." *EIROnline*:1–6.

Reynaud, Jean-Daniel. 1975. *Les syndicats en France*, Vol. 1. Paris, France: Éditions du Seuil.

Rhodes, Martin. 1998. "Globalization and the Welfare State. The Emergence of Competitive Corporatism." *Revue Suisse de Science Politique* 4(1): 99–107.

Rhodes, Martin. 2001. "The Political Economy of Social Pacts: 'Competitive Corporatism' and European Welfare Reform." Pp. 165–94 in *The New Politics of the Welfare State*, edited by P. Pierson. New York: Oxford University Press.

Ritter, Gerhard A. 2007. *Der Preis der Deutschen Einheit: Die Wiedervereinigung und die Krise des Sozialstaats.* Munich: Beck.

Robin, Benoît. 2008. "New Rules for Union Representativeness and Working Time." *EIROnline*: 1–3.

Roche, William. 2011. "The Breakdown of Social Partnership." *Administration* 59(1): 23–37.

Roche, William K. 2007. "Social Partnership in Ireland and New Social Pacts." *Industrial Relations* 46(3): 395–425.

Romagnoli, Umberto and Tiziano Treu. 1981. *I sindacati in Italia dal '45 ad oggi: Storia di una strategia.* Bologna: Il Mulino.

Romiti, Cesare. 1988. *Questi anni alla Fiat.* Milan: Rizzoli.

Rönnmar, Mia. 2010. "Labour Policy on Fixed-Term Employment Contracts in Sweden." Pp. 55–68 in *Regulation of Fixed-Term Employment Contracts: A Comparative Overview*, edited by R. Blanpain, H. Nakakubo and T. Araki. Netherlands: Kluwer Law International.

Ross, George. 1982. "The Perils of Politics: French Unions and the Crisis of the 1970s." In *Unions, Change and Crisis: French and Italian Union Strategy and the Political Economy, 1945–1980*, edited by P. Lange, G. Ross and M. Vannicelli. New York: Allen and Unwin.

Rossi, Fulvio and Paolo Sestito. 2000. "Contrattazione aziendale, struttura negoziale e determinazione del salario." *Rivista di Politica Economica* 90(10–11): 129–83.

Roth, Siegfried. 1997. "Germany: Labor's Perspective on Lean Production." Pp. 117–36 in *After Lean Production: Evolving Employment Practices in the World Auto Industry*, edited by T. A. Kochan, R. D. Lansbury and J. P. MacDuffie. Ithaca, NY: Cornell University Press.

Rothstein, B. 1992. "Labour-Market Institutions and Working-Class Strength." Pp. 33–56 in *Structuring Politics: Historical Institutionalism in Comparative Analysis*, Cambridge Studies in Comparative Politics, edited by S. Steinmo, K. A. Thelen and F. H. Longstreth. Cambridge, UK; New York.

Rouilleault, Henri, ed. 2001. *Réduction du temps de travail: Les enseignements de l'observation*. Paris: La Documentation Française.

Royal Commission on Trade Unions and Employers' Associations. 1968. "Royal Commission on Trade Unions and Employers' Associations, 1965–1968: Report." London, UK.

Rubery, Jill. 2011. "Reconstruction Amid Deconstruction: Or Why We Need More of the Social in European Social Models." *Work, Employment and Society* 25(4): 658–74.

Rueda, David and Jonas Pontusson. 2000. "Wage Inequality and Varieties of Capitalism." *World Politics* 52(April): 350–83.

Ryner, J. Magnus. 2002. *Capitalist Restructuring, Globalisation, and the Third Way: Lessons from the Swedish Model*. New York: Routledge.

Sacchi, Stefano. 2012. "Policy without Politics? Domestic Agendas, Market Pressures and 'Informal but Tough' Economic Conditionality in the Italian Labour Market Reform." Unpublished Manuscript, University of Milan.

Saint-Paul, Gilles. 2002. "The Political Economy of Employment Protection." *Journal of Political Economy* 110(3): 672–704.

Salvati, Michele. 1984. *Economia e politica in Italia dal dopoguerra ad oggi*. Milan: Garzanti.

Salvati, Michele. 2000. *Occasioni mancate. Economia e politica in Italia dagli anni '60 ad oggi*. Bari: Laterza.

Sanz, Sofia. 2011. "Intersectoral Agreement on Representativeness Heals Rift." *EIRO*. http://www.eurofound.europa.eu/eiro/2011/08/articles/it1108029i.htm.

Sawyer, Malcolm C. 1985. "The Economics of Michał Kalecki." *Eastern European Economics* 23(3/4): v–319.

Scharpf, Fritz Wilhelm. 1987. *Sozialdemokratische Krisenpolitik in Europa*, Vol. 7. Frankfurt am Main: Campus.

Scharpf, Fritz W. 1997a. "Employment and the Welfare State: A Continental Dilemma.". MPIfG working paper.

Scharpf, Fritz Wilhelm. 1997b. *Games Real Actors Play: Actor-Centered Institutionalism in Policy Research*. Boulder, CO: Westview Press.

Scharpf, Fritz W. 2010. "The Asymmetry of European Integration, or Why the EU Cannot Be a 'Social Market Economy.'" *Socio-economic Review* 8(2): 211–50.

Scharpf, Fritz. 2011. "Monetary Union, Fiscal Crisis and the Preemption of Democracy." Max-Planck-Institute Cologne Working Paper.

Scharpf, Fritz W. 2013. "Monetary Union, Fiscal Crisis and the Disabling of Democratic Accountability." In *Politics in the Age of Austerity*, edited by A. Schaäfer and W. Streeck. Cambridge, UK: Polity.

Schattschneider, Elmer Eric. 1960. *The Semi-sovereign People*. Boston: Wadswoth.

Schivardi, Fabiano and Roberto Torrini. 2004. "Firm Size Distribution and Employment Protection Legislation in Italy." Temi di discussione, Bank of Italy, no. 504.

Schmitter, Philippe C. 1974. "Still the Century of Corporatism?" *The Review of Politics* 36(1): 85–131.

Schnyder, Gerhard and Gregory Jackson. 2013. "Germany and Sweden in the Crisis: Re-coordination or Resilient Liberalism?" Pp. 313–73 in *Resilient Liberalism in Europe's Political Economy*, edited by M. Thatcher and V. Schmidt. New York: Cambridge University Press.

Schulten, T. 2001. "Solidarische Lohnpolitik in Europa. Ansätze Und Perspektiven Einer Europäisierung Gewerkschaftlicher Lohnpolitik." WSI Diskussionspapier Nr. 92. Düsseldorf.

Schulten, T. 2004. "Foundations and Perspectives of Trade Union Wage Policy in Europe." WSI-Diskussionspapiere 92. Düsseldorf.

Seifert, Hartmut and Heiko Massa-Wirth. 2005. "Pacts for Employment and Competitiveness in Germany." *Industrial Relations Journal* 36(3): 217–40.

Seifert, Roger V. 1992. *Industrial Relations in the NHS*. London: Chapman & Hall.

Shapiro, Carl and Joseph E. Stiglitz. 1984. "Equilibrium Unemployment as a Worker Discipline Device." *American Economic Review* 74(3): 433–44.

Sheldon, P. and L. Thornthwaite. 1999. "Swedish Engineering Employers: The Search for Industrial Peace in the Absence of Centralised Collective Bargaining." *Industrial Relations Journal* 30(5): 514–32.

Shonfield, Andrew. 1965. *Modern Capitalism: The Changing Balance of Public and Private Power*. New York: Oxford University Press.

Shorter, Edward and Charles Tilly. 1974. *Strikes in France, 1830–1968*. London, UK and New York: Cambridge University Press.

Siebert, Horst. 1997. "Labor Market Rigidities: At the Root of Unemployment in Europe." *Journal of Economic Perspectives* 11(3): 37–54.

Silvia, Stephen J. 1997. "German Unification and Emerging Divisions within German Employers' Associations: Cause or Catalyst?". *Comparative Politics* 29(2): 187–208.

Silvia, Stephen J. 2010. "Mitgliederentwicklung und Organisationsstaerke der Arbeitgeberverbaende, Wirtschaftsverbaende und Industrie- und Handelskammern." Pp. 169–82 in Handbuch Arbeitgeber- und Wirtschaftsverbände in Deutschland, edited by W. Schroeder and B. Weßels. Wiesbaden: VS Verlag.

Silvia, Stephen J and Wolfgang Schroeder. 2007. "Why Are German Employers Associations Declining? Arguments and Evidence." *Comparative Political Studies* 40(12): 1433–59.

Simoni, Marco. 2012. *Senza alibi: Perché il capitalismo italiano non cresce più*. Padua: Marsilio.

Singer, Daniel. 1988. *Is Socialism Doomed? The Meaning of Mitterrand*. New York: Oxford University Press.

Sinn, Gerlinde and Hans-Werner Sinn. 1994. *Jumpstart: The Economic Unification of Germany*. Cambridge, MA: MIT Press.

Sinn, Hans-Werner. 2006. "The Pathological Export Boom and the Bazaar Effect: How to Solve the German Puzzle." *World Economy* 29(9): 1157–75.

Sinn, Hans-Werner. 2014. *The Euro Trap: On Bursting Bubbles, Budgets, and Belief*. Oxford University Press: Oxford.

Smith, Paul. 2009. "New Labour and the Commonsense of Neoliberalism: Trade Unionism, Collective Bargaining, and Workers' Rights." *Industrial Relations Journal* 40(4): 337–55.

Sorge, Arndt and Wolfgang Streeck. 1987. *Industrial Relations and Technical Change: The Case for an Extended Perspective*, Vol. 81. Berlin: Wissenschaftszentrum Berlin für Sozialforschung.

Soskice, David. 1990. "Wage Determination: The Changing Role of Institutions in Advanced Industrialized Countries." *Oxford Review of Economic Policy* 6(4): 36–61.

Soskice, David. 1999. "Divergent Production Regimes: Coordinated and Uncoordinated Market Economies in the 1980s and 1990s." Pp. 101–34 in *Continuity and Change in Contemporary Capitalism*, edited by H. Kitschelt, P. Lange, G. Marks and J. D. Stephens. Cambridge, UK and New York: Cambridge University Press.

Spermann, Alexander. 2013. "Sector Surcharges for Temporary Agency Workers in Germany: A Way out of the Low-Wage Sector?" *IZA Policy Paper* 67. Bonn: Institute for the Study of Labor.

Stein, Ulrike. 2009. "Zur Entwicklung der Sparquoten der Privaten Haushalte – Eine Auswertung von Haushaltsdaten des SOEP." SOEP Papers on Multidisciplinary Panel Data Research at DIW Berlin (249).

Steinmo, Sven, Kathleen Thelen and Frank Longstreth, eds. 1992. *Structuring Politics: Historical Institutionalism in Comparative Analysis*. New York: Cambridge University Press.

Steinmo, Sven. 2010. *The Evolution of Modern States: Sweden, Japan, and the United States*. Cambridge, UK and New York: Cambridge University Press.

Stephens, John D. 1979. *The Transition from Capitalism to Socialism*. London: Macmillan.

Stiglitz, Joseph. 2009. *Freefall: Free Markets and the Sinking of the Global Economy*. London: Penguin

Stockhammer, Engelbert. 2013. "Why Have Wage Shares Fallen? An Analysis of the Determinants of Functional Income Distribution." In *Wage-Led Growth*, edited by M. Lavoie and E. Stockhammer. London: Palgrave.

Stockhammer, Engelbert. 2015a. "Rising Inequality as a Cause of the Present Crisis." *Cambridge Journal of Economics* 39(3): 935–58.

Stockhammer, Engelbert. 2015b. "Neoliberal Growth Models, Monetary Union and the Euro Crisis. A Post-Keynesian Perspective." *New Political Economy* 21(4): 365–79.

Stockhammer, Engelbert, Eckhard Hein and Lucas Grafl. 2011. "Globalization and the Effects of Changes in Functional Income Distribution on Aggregate Demand in Germany." *International Review of Applied Economics* 25(1): 1–23.

Stockhammer, Engelbert and Ozlem Onaran. 2013. "Wage-Led Growth: Theory, Evidence, Policy." *Review of Keynesian Economics* 1(1): 61–78.

Stokke, Torgeir and Christer Thörnqvist. 2001. "Strikes and Collective Bargaining in the Nordic Countries." *European Journal of Industrial Relations* 7(3): 245–67.

Storm, Servaas and C.W.M. Naastepad. 2012a. *Macroeconomics Beyond the NAIRU*. Cambridge, MA: Harvard University Press.

Storm, Servaas and C.W.M. Naastepad. 2012b. "Wage-Led or Profit-Led Supply: Wages, Productivity and Investment." ILO Conditions of Work and Employment Series No. 36.

Storm, Servaas and C. W. M. Naastepad. 2015. "Crisis and Recovery in the German Economy: The Real Lessons." *Structural Change and Economic Dynamics* 32: 11–24.

Strange, Susan. 1986. *Casino Capitalism*. Oxford, UK and New York: Blackwell.

Streeck, W. 1992. *Social Institutions and Economic Performance: Studies of Industrial Relations in Advanced Capitalist Economies*. London: Sage Publications.

Streeck, Wolfgang. 1984. "Neo-Corporatist Industrial Relations and the Economic Crisis in West Germany." Pp. 291–314 in *Order and Conflict in Contemporary Capitalism*, edited by J. Goldthorpe. Oxford: Clarendon.

Streeck, Wolfgang. 1991. "On the Institutional Preconditions of Diversified Quality Production." Pp. 21–61 in *Beyond Keynesianism: The Socio-Economics of Production and Full Employment*, edited by E. Matzner and W. Streeck. Aldershot: Elgar.

Streeck, Wolfgang. 1997a. "Beneficial Constraints: On the Economic Limits of Rational Voluntarism." Pp. 197–219 in *Contemporary Capitalism: The Embeddedness of Institutions*, edited by R. Boyer and R. J. Hollingsworth. Cambridge, UK and New York: Cambridge University Press.

Streeck, Wolfgang. 1997b. "German Capitalism: Does It Exist? Can It Survive?" *New Political Economy* 2(2): 237–56.

Streeck, Wolfgang. 2001. "Tarifautonomie und Politik: Von der Konzertierten Aktion zum Bündnis für Arbeit." Die deutschen Arbeitsbeziehungen am Anfang des 21: 76–102.

Streeck, Wolfgang. 2003. "No Longer the Century of Corporatism. Das Ende des 'Bündnisses für Arbeit.'" MPIfG Working Paper 03/4.

Streeck, Wolfgang. 2007. "Globalization: Nothing New under the Sun?" *Socio-Economic Review* 5(3): 537–47.

Streeck, Wolfgang. 2009. *Re-forming Capitalism: Institutional Change in the German Political Economy*. Oxford, UK and New York: Oxford University Press.

Streeck, Wolfgang. 2011. "Taking Capitalism Seriously: Towards an Institutionalist Approach to Contemporary Political Economy." *Socio-Economic Review* 9(1): 137–67. doi: 10.1093/ser/mwq028.

Streeck, Wolfgang. 2014. *Buying Time: The Delayed Crisis of Democratic Capitalism*. London, UK and New York: Verso.

Streeck, Wolfgang and Anke Hassel. 2004. "The Crumbling Pillars of Social Partnership." In *Germany. Beyond the Stable State*, edited by H. Kitschelt and W. Streeck. Special Issue of *West European Politics* 26(4): 101–24.

Streeck, Wolfgang and Armin Schaäfer. 2013. *Politics in the Age of Austerity*. Cambridge, UK: Polity.

Streeck, Wolfgang and Philippe C. Schmitter. 1991. "From National Corporatism to Transnational Pluralism: Organized Interests in the Single European Market." *Politics and Society* 19: 133–64.

Streeck, Wolfgang and Kathleen Ann Thelen, eds. 2005. *Beyond Continuity: Institutional Change in Advanced Political Economies*. New York: Oxford University Press.

Streeck, Wolfgang and Kozo Yamamura, eds. 2001. *The Origins of Nonliberal Capitalism: Germany and Japan in Comparison*. Ithaca, NY: Cornell University Press.

Summers, Lawrence H. 2014. "U.S. Economic Prospects: Secular Stagnation, Hysteresis, and the Zero Lower Bound." *Business Economics* 4(2): 65–73.

Svenskt Näringsliv. 2006. "New Dispute Regulations on the Labour Market." Theme Sheets. Svenskt Näringsliv, Stockholm, Sweden.

Svenskt Näringsliv. 2012. "*Fakta Om Löner Och Arbetstider 2012.*" Vol. Stockholm: Svenskt Näringsliv.

Swenson, Peter. 1989. *Fair Shares: Unions, Pay, and Politics in Sweden and West Germany.* Ithaca, NY: Cornell University Press.

Swenson, Peter. 1991. "Bringing Capital Back In, or Social Democracy Reconsidered: Employer Power, Cross-Class Alliances, and Centralization of Industrial Relations in Denmark and Sweden." *World Politics* 43(4): 513–44.

Swenson, Peter. 2002. *Capitalists against Markets: The Making of Labor Markets and Welfare States in the United States and Sweden.* Oxford, UK and New York: Oxford University Press.

Swenson, Peter. 2004a. "Varieties of Capitalist Interests: Power, Institutions, and the Regulatory Welfare State in the United States and Sweden." *Studies in American Political Development* 18(1): 1–29.

Swenson, Peter A. 2004b. "Yes, and Comparative Analysis Too: Rejoinder to Hacker and Pierson." *Studies in American Political Development* 18(2): 196–200.

Tarantelli, Ezio. 1986a. *Economia politica del lavoro.* Turin: UTET.

Tarantelli, Ezio. 1986b. "The Regulation of Inflation and Unemployment." *Industrial Relations* 25(1): 1–15.

Terry, Michael. 1983. "Shop Steward Development and Managerial Strategies." In *Industrial Relations in Britain*, edited by G. S. Bain. Oxford, UK: Blackwell.

Testorf, Christian. 2011. "Welcher Bruch? Lohnpolitik Zwischen den Krisen: Gewerkschaftliche Tarifpolitik von 1966 bis 1974." Pp. 293–316 in "*Nach dem Strukturbruch" Kontinuität und Wandel von Arebitsbeziehungen und Arbeitswelt(en) seit den 1970er Jahren*, edited by K. Andresen, U. Bitzegeio and J. Mittag. Bonn: Dietz.

Thelen, Kathleen. 1991. *Union of Parts: Labor Politics in Postwar Germany.* Ithaca, NY: Cornell University Press.

Thelen, Kathleen. 2000. "Why German Employers Cannot Bring Themselves to Dismantle the German Model?" Pp. 138–69 in *Unions, Employers, and Central Banks*, edited by T. Iversen, J. Pontusson and D. Soskice. New York: Cambridge University Press.

Thelen, Kathleen. 2001. ""Varieties of Labour Politics in the Developed Democracies"." Pp. 71–103 in *Varieties of Capitalism: The Institutional Foundations of Comparative Advantage*, edited by P. A. Hall and D. Soskice. Oxford, UK: Oxford University Press

Thelen, Kathleen. 2004. *How Institutions Evolve: The Political Economy of Skills in Germany, Britain, the United States, and Japan.* New York: Cambridge University Press.

Thelen, Kathleen. 2009. "Institutional Change in Advanced Political Economies." *British Journal of Industrial Relations* 47(3): 471–98.

Thelen, Kathleen. 2012. "Varieties of Capitalism: Trajectories of Liberalization and the New Politics of Social Solidarity." *Annual Review of Political Science* 15(1): 137–59. doi:10.1146/annurev-polisci-070110–122959.

Thelen, Kathleen Ann. 2014. *Varieties of Liberalization and the New Politics of Social Solidarity.* Cambridge, UK and New York: Cambridge University Press.

Thoemmes, Jens. 2009. "Négociation et régulation intermédiaire: Le cas du mandatement syndical." *Revue Française de Sociologie* 50(4): 817–41.

Thorckecke, Willem and Atsuyuki Kato. 2012. "The Effect of Exchange Rate Changes on Germany's Exports." RIETI Discussion Paper Series 12(E-081).

Thörnqvist, Christer. 1999. "The Decentralization of Industrial Relations: The Swedish Case in Comparative Perspective." *European Journal of Industrial Relations* 5(1): 71–87.

Thörnqvist, Christer. 2007. "Changing Industrial Relations in the Swedish Public Sector." *International Journal of Public Sector Management* 20(1): 16–33.

Tissandier, Hélène. 2011. "Negotiated Redundancies and French Law." EIROnline: 1–3.

Trade Union Congress. 1995. *Your Voice at Work: TUC Proposals for Rights to Representation at Work.* London, UK: Trade Union Congress.

Traxler, Franz. 1995. "Farewell to Labour Market Associations? Organized versus Disorganized Decentralization as a Map for Industrial Relations." Pp. 3–19 in *Organized Industrial Relations in Europe: What Future?* edited by C. Crouch and F. Traxler. Aldershot, UK: Avebury.

Traxler, Franz. 2004. "The Metamorphoses of Corporatism: From Classical to Lean Patterns." *European Journal of Political Research* 43(4): 571–98.

Trentin, Bruno. 1994. *Il coraggio dell'utopia: La sinistra e il sindacato dopo il Taylorismo.* Milan: Rizzoli.

Treu, Tiziano. 1984. *Il patto contro l'inflazione.* Rome: Edizioni Lavoro.

Treu, Tiziano. 2001. *Politiche del lavoro.* Bologna: Il Mulino.

Trigilia, Carlo. 1986. *Grandi partiti e piccole imprese.* Bologna: Il Mulino.

Truman, David B. 1962. *The Governmental Process. Political Interests and Public Opinion.* New York: Alfred A. Knopf.

Trumbull, Gunnar. 2002. "Policy Activism in a Globalized Economy: France's 35-Hour Workweek." *French Politics, Culture and Society* 20: 1–21.

Turlan, Frédéric. 2012. "CFTC Fights to Maintain Its Representativeness." EIROnline: 1–2.

Turlan, Frédéric and Gilbert Cette. 2013. "Landmark Agreement Paces the Way for Labour Market Reform." EIROnline.

Turner, Lowell 1991. *Democracy at Work: Changing World Markets and the Future of Labor Unions.* Ithaca, NY: Cornell University Press.

Turner, Lowell. 1998. *Fighting for Partnership: Labor and Politics in Unified Germany.* Ithaca, NY: Cornell University Press.

Turone, Sergio. 1992. *Storia del sindacato in Italia.* Bari: Laterza.

Ulman, Lloyd, Barry Eichengreen and William Dickens, eds. 1993. *Labor and an Integrated Europe.* Washington, DC: The Brookings Institution.

Undy, Roger, Patricia Fosh, Huw Morris, Paul Smith and Roderick Martin. 1996. *Managing the Unions: The Impact of Legislation on Trade Unions' Behaviour.* New York: Oxford University Press.

Upchurch, Martin. 2000. "The Crisis of Labour Relations in Germany." *Capital and Class* 24(1): 65–93.

Urban, Hans Jürgen 2010. "Wohlfahrtsstaat und Gewerkschaftsmacht im Finanzmarkt-Kapitalismus: Der Fall Deutschland." *WSI Mitteilungen* 9: 443–50.

Vacca, Giuseppe. 1987. *Tra Compromesso E Solidarietà.* Rome: Editori Riuniti.

Vaciago, Giacomo. 1993. "Exchange Rate Stability and Market Expectations: The Crisis of the EMS." *Review of Economic Conditions in Italy* 1(January–April): 11–29.

Vail, Mark. 2004. "The Myth of the Frozen Welfare State and the Dynamics of Contemporary French and German Social-Protection Reform." *French Politics* 2(2): 151–83.

Van Rie, Tim, Ive Marx and Jeroen Horemans. 2011. "Ghent Revisited: Unemployment Insurance and Union Membership in Belgium and the Nordic Countries." *European Journal of Industrial Relations* 17(2): 125–39.

van Wanrooy, Brigid, Helen Bewley, Alex Bryson, John Forth, Stephanie Freeth, Lucy Stokes and Stephen Wood. 2013. *Employment Relations in the Shadow of the Recession: Findings from the 2011 Workplace Employment Relations Study.* Basingstoke, UK: Palgrave Macmillan.

Venn, Danielle. 2009. "Legislation, Collective Bargaining and Enforcement: Updating the Oecd Employment Protection Indicators." OECD Social, Employment and Migration Working Paper 89. OECD.

Verdun, Amy. 2013. "The Building of Economic Governance in the European Union." *Transfer: European Review of Labour and Research* 19(1): 23–35.

Visser, Jelle. 2013. "Data Base on Institutional Characteristics of Trade Unions, Wage Setting, State Intervention and Social Pacts, 1960–2011 (ICTWSS), Version 4: Codebook." Unpublished document, Amsterdam Institute for Advanced Labour Studies (AIAS), University of Amsterdam.

Vitols, K. 2008. *Zwischen Stabilitaet und Wandel: Die Sozialpartnerschaft in Deutschland und die Atypische Beschaeftigungsform Zeitarbeit.* Hamburg: Verlag Dr. Kova.

von Weizsaecker, Carl Christian. 2013. "Public Debt and Price Stability." *German Economic Review* 15(1): 42–61.

Wainwright, Martin and Richard Nelsson. 2002. "Long Decline of a Once Mighty Union." *Guardian*, January 15.

Wallerstein, Michael. 1999. "Wage-Setting Institutions and Pay Inequality in Advanced Industrial Societies." *American Journal of Political Science* 43(3): 649–80.

Wallerstein, Michael, Miriam Golden and Peter Lange. 1997. "Unions, Employers' Associations, and Wage-Setting Institutions in Northern and Central Europe, 1950–1992." *Industrial and Labor Relations Review* 50(3): 379–401.

Wallin, Gunhild. 2016. "The Swedish Agreement Model's Big Test." Nordic Labour Journal: 247–74.

Wedderburn, Lord. 1991. *Employment Rights in Britain and Europe: Selected Papers in Labour Law.* London, UK: Lawrence and Wishart.

Weinkopf, C. 2009. "Germany: Precarious Employment and the Rise of Mini-jobs." Vol. GWD/CPD Working Paper Series. Canada.

Williams, Steve and Peter Scott. 2010. "Shooting the Past? The Modernisation of Conservative Party Employment Relations Policy under David Cameron." *Industrial Relations Journal* 41(1): 4–18.

Williams, Steve and Peter Scott, eds. 2016. *Employment Relations under Coalition Government: The UK Experience, 2010–15.* New York: Routledge.

Williamson, John. 1989. "What Washington Means by Policy Reform." Pp. 5–20 in *Latin American Readjustment: How Much Has Happened,* edited by J. Williamson. Washington, DC: Institute for International Economics.

Wolff, Loup. 2008a. "Des instances représentatives de personnel qui, malgré les évolutions de tissu productif, se maintiennent." Pp. 85–101 in *Les relations sociales en entreprise: Un portrait à partir des enquêtes relations professionnelles et négociations d'entreprise*, edited by T. Amossé, C. Bloch-London and L. Wolff. Paris: Éditions la Découverte.

Wolff, Loup. 2008b. "Le paradoxe du syndicalisme français." *Première Synthèses Informations* (16.1): 1–7.

Woll, Cornelia. 2006. "National Business Associations under Stress: Lessons from the French Case." *West European Politics* 29(3): 489–512.

Wood, Stewart. 2001. "Business, Government, and Patterns of Labor Market Policy in Britain and the Federal Republic of Germany." Pp. 247–74 in *Varieties of Capitalism: The Institutional Foundations of Comparative Advantage*, edited by P. A. Hall and D. W. Soskice. New York: Oxford University Press.

Woolfson, C., C. Thörnqvist and J. Sommers. 2010. "The Swedish Model and the Future of Labour Standards after Laval." *Industrial Relations Journal* 41(4): 333–50.

Zysman, John. 1983. *Governments, Markets, and Growth: Financial Systems and the Politics of Industrial Change*. Ithaca, NY: Cornell University Press.

Index

Sweden (*cont.*)
  expansion of employer discretion, 166–8
  foreign direct investment (FDI), 148
  Ghent-style system of unemployment
    insurance, 145–6
  growth profile, 214–22
  impacts of EU membership, 148–9, 159
  impacts of international competition, 148–9
  impacts of the economic crisis in 2008, 158,
    168
  income inequality, 170
  indicators of liberalization, 168–71
  Industrial Agreement (1997), 154–8, 160,
    162
  institutions of the Swedish model, 145–6
  labor law, 146
  legislative challenges to self-regulation,
    146–7
  liberalization index, 16, 49
  LO blue collar union confederation, 144–5,
    151, 154, 156–7, 169
  National Mediation Office (NMO), 154–6
  possible resistance to liberalization, 143–4
  postwar corporatist bargaining model, 143
  quantitative analysis of industrial relations
    change, 26
  reengineering coordination for a neoliberal
    era, 152–60
  Rehn–Meidner bargaining model, 14, 144–5
  restricted employer discretion in the 1970s,
    147
  right to strike, 146, 158–9
  SAF employer federation, 144–5, 149–50
  Saltzjöbaden era of industrial relations,
    144–7
  signs of extensive, transformational
    liberalization, 143–4
  SN (Confederation of Swedish Enterprise),
    149–50, 156–7
  Stabilization Drive (1990–93), 152, 153,
    154, 156
  state role in liberalization of industrial
    relations, 152
  state support for the Swedish model, 145
  survival of collective regulation, 143
  wage drift effects, 147
  See also country cases comparison

Tarantelli, Ezio, 127
Thatcher, Margaret, 54, 63
Thatcherism, 56–63, 67
Thibault, Bernard, 70

trade liberalization
  destabilizing effect on the Fordist model,
    202
trade unions
  indicators of liberalization, 1
trade unions and employers
  comparison of five country cases, 176–81
trajectory of change
  drivers of, 11
  quantitative analysis, 46–50
Trentin, Bruno, 129
trickle-down economics, 206

union density rates, 27–31
United Kingdom
  achieving supply-side hyperflexibility, 55–6
  adoption of the EU Social Charter, 65
  alternative forms of consultation, 70
  architecture of contemporary industrial
    relations, 67–71
  austerity measures, 66
  bargaining power of 1970s trade unions,
    51–3
  changes in employer discretion, 70
  changes in employment rights, 61
  changes in industrial relations after 1979,
    53–6
  collective laissez faire situation, 51–2
  Conservative industrial relations legislation
    after 1979, 53–63
  Conservative-Liberal Democrat coalition
    (2010–15), 51, 66
  Conservative onslaught on collective
    regulation, 56–63
  decollectivization of industrial relations,
    56–63, 71–2
  decollectivization under Conservative
    governments, 51
  diminished role of trade unions, 58
  dismantling of collective bargaining
    institutions, 60
  Donovan Commission report (1968), 51–2,
    54
  downfall of the Heath government (1974),
    54
  employment tribunal system, 65
  end of tripartism, 62–3
  erosion and dismantling of institutions, 51
  expansion of employer discretion, 71–2
  Fordist influences, 51–2
  from industry-level to firm-level bargaining,
    51–2